# THE INSTITUTE FOR POLISH-JEWISH STUDIES

The Institute for Polish–Jewish Studies in Oxford and its sister organization, the American Association for Polish–Jewish Studies, which publish *Polin*, are learned societies that were established in 1984, following the International Conference on Polish–Jewish Studies, held in Oxford. The Institute is an associate institute of the Oxford Centre for Hebrew and Jewish Studies, and the American Association is linked with the Department of Near Eastern and Judaic Studies at Brandeis University.

Both the Institute and the American Association aim to promote understanding of the Polish Jewish past. They have no building or library of their own and no paid staff; they achieve their aims by encouraging scholarly research and facilitating its publication, and by creating forums for people with a scholarly interest in Polish Jewish topics, both past and present.

To this end the Institute and the American Association help organize lectures and international conferences. Venues for these activities have included Brandeis University in Waltham, Massachusetts, the Hebrew University in Jerusalem, the Institute for the Study of Human Sciences in Vienna, King's College in London, the Jagiellonian University in Kraków, the Oxford Centre for Hebrew and Jewish Studies, the University of Łódź, University College London, and the Polish Cultural Institute and the Polish embassy in London. They have encouraged academic exchanges between Israel, Poland, the United States, and western Europe. In particular they seek to help train a new generation of scholars, in Poland and elsewhere, to study the culture and history of the Jews in Poland.

Each year since 1986 the Institute has published a volume of scholarly papers in the series *Polin: Studies in Polish Jewry* under the general editorship of Professor Antony Polonsky of Brandeis University. Since 1994 the series has been published on its behalf by the Littman Library of Jewish Civilization, and since 1998 the publication has been linked with the American Association as well. In March 2000 the entire series was honoured with a National Jewish Book Award from the Jewish Book Council in the United States. More than twenty other works on Polish Jewish topics have also been published with the Institute's assistance.

Further information on the Institute for Polish–Jewish Studies can be found on its website, <www.polishjewishstudies.co.uk>. For the website of the American Association for Polish–Jewish Studies, see <www.aapjstudies.org>.

# THE LITTMAN LIBRARY OF
# JEWISH CIVILIZATION

*Dedicated to the memory of*
LOUIS THOMAS SIDNEY LITTMAN
*who founded the Littman Library for the love of God
and as an act of charity in memory of his father*
JOSEPH AARON LITTMAN
*and to the memory of*
ROBERT JOSEPH LITTMAN
*who continued what his father Louis had begun*

יהא זכרם ברוך

'Get wisdom, get understanding:
Forsake her not and she shall preserve thee'

PROV. 4: 5

*The Littman Library of Jewish Civilization is a registered UK charity
Registered charity no. 1000784*

# POLIN
## STUDIES IN POLISH JEWRY

VOLUME SEVEN

*Jewish Life in
Nazi-Occupied Warsaw*

Edited by
ANTONY POLONSKY

*Published for*
The Institute for Polish–Jewish Studies

The Littman Library of Jewish Civilization
in association with Liverpool University Press

The Littman Library of Jewish Civilization
in association with Liverpool University Press
4 Cambridge Street, Liverpool L69 7ZU, UK

www.liverpooluniversitypress.co.uk/littman

Managing Editor: Connie Webber

Distributed in North America by
Oxford University Press Inc., 198 Madison Avenue,
New York, NY 10016, USA

First published in hardback 1992 by Basil Blackwell Ltd
First published in paperback 2008

© Institute for Polish–Jewish Studies 1992

All rights reserved.
No part of this publication may be reproduced,
stored in a retrieval system, or transmitted, in any form or by
any means, without the prior permission in writing of
The Littman Library of Jewish Civilization

The paperback edition of this book is sold subject to the condition
that it shall not, by way of trade or otherwise, be lent, re-sold,
hired out or otherwise circulated without the publisher's prior consent
in any form of binding or cover other than that in which it is published
and without a similar condition including this condition
being imposed on the subsequent purchaser

Catalogue records for this book are available from the
British Library and the Library of Congress

ISSN 0268 1056
ISBN 978-1-904113-80-5

Publishing coordinator: Janet Moth
Cover design: Pete Russell, Faringdon, Oxon.

Printed in Great Britain by
CPI Group (UK) Ltd., Croydon, CR0 4YY

*To*
ESTER LAUFER SARNER

———

The Institute for Polish–Jewish Studies and
the American Foundation for Polish–Jewish Studies, which sponsors
*Polin*, have benefited from the support of the following:

Harvey Sarner, the Polonia Aid Fund and Trust,
Mrs Irene Pipes, Mrs Genia Shrut,
the M. B. Grabowski Fund,
the American Jewish Committee; the Polish American Congress,
the Anti-Defamation League of B'nai B'rith,
*Commentary* magazine, *Present Tense* magazine,
Gadsby & Hannah, Paisner & Co., Edmund Gibbs &Co.,
and the American Foundation for Polish–Jewish Studies

# Editors and Advisers

### EDITORS

Monika Adamczyk-Garbowska, *Lublin*
Israel Bartal, *Jerusalem*
Antony Polonsky (Chair), *Waltham, Mass.*
Michael Steinlauf, *Philadelphia*
Jerzy Tomaszewski, *Warsaw*

### EDITORIAL BOARD

Chimen Abramsky, *London*
David Assaf, *Tel Aviv*
Władysław T. Bartoszewski, *Warsaw*
Glenn Dynner, *Bronxville, NY*
David Engel, *New York*
David Fishman, *New York*
ChaeRan Freeze, *Waltham, Mass.*
Józef Gierowski, *Kraków*
Jacob Goldberg, *Jerusalem*
Yisrael Gutman, *Jerusalem*
Jerzy Kłoczowski, *Lublin*
Ezra Mendelsohn, *Jerusalem*
Joanna Michlic, *Stockton, NY*

Elchanan Reiner, *Tel Aviv*
Jehuda Reinharz, *Waltham, Mass.*
Moshe Rosman, *Tel Aviv*
Szymon Rudnicki, *Warsaw*
Henryk Samsonowicz, *Warsaw*
Robert Shapiro, *New York*
Adam Teller, *Haifa*
Daniel Tollet, *Paris*
Piotr S. Wandycz, *New Haven, Conn.*
Jonathan Webber, *Birmingham, UK*
Joshua Zimmerman, *New York*
Steven Zipperstein, *Stanford, Calif.*

### ADVISORY BOARD

Władysław Bartoszewski, *Warsaw*
Jan Błoński, *Kraków*
Abraham Brumberg, *Washington*
Andrzej Chojnowski, *Warsaw*
Tadeusz Chrzanowski, *Kraków*
Andrzej Ciechanowiecki, *London*
Norman Davies, *London*
Victor Erlich, *New Haven, Conn.*
Frank Golczewski, *Hamburg*
Olga Goldberg, *Jerusalem*
Feliks Gross, *New York*
Czesław Hernas, *Wrocław*
Jerzy Jedlicki, *Warsaw*
Andrzej Kamiński, *London*

Hillel Levine, *Boston*
Lucjan Lewitter, *Cambridge, Mass.*
Stanisław Litak, *Lublin*
Heinz-Dietrich Löwe, *Heidelberg*
Emanuel Meltzer, *Tel Aviv*
Shlomo Netzer, *Tel Aviv*
Zbigniew Pełczyński, *Oxford*
Alexander Schenker, *New Haven, Conn.*
David Sorkin, *Madison, Wis.*
Edward Stankiewicz, *New Haven, Conn.*
Norman Stone, *Ankara*
Shmuel Werses, *Jerusalem*
Jacek Woźniakowski, *Lublin*
Piotr Wróbel, *Toronto*

# CONTENTS

STATEMENT FROM THE EDITORS · · · 1

ARTICLES
**Zenon Nowak** A Brief History of the Jews in Royal Prussia Before 1772 · · · 3
**Ritchie Robertson** From the Ghetto to Modern Culture: The Autobiographies of Salomon Maimon and Jakob Fromer · · · 12
**Adam Gałkowski** Jan Czyński and the Question of Equality of Rights for all Religious Faiths in Poland · · · 31
**Joanna Rostropowicz Clark** Adam Mickiewicz's 'Forty and Four' or the Dangers of Playing with Kabbalahs · · · 57
**Shaul Stampfer** Gender Differentiation and Education of the Jewish Woman in Nineteenth-Century Eastern Europe · · · 63
**Mark W. Kiel** *Vox Populi, Vox Dei*: The Centrality of Peretz in Jewish Folkloristics · · · 88
**Tomasz Wiśniewski** The Linas-Hatsedek Charitable Fraternity in Białystok, 1885–1939 · · · 121
**Czesław Brzoza** The Jewish Press in Kraków (1918–1939) · · · 133
**Szymon Rudnicki** Ritual Slaughter as a Political Issue · · · 147
**Ariel Joseph Kochavi** Britain and the Jewish Exodus from Poland Following the Second World War · · · 161
**Jósef Wróbel** Henryk Grynberg Calls Poland to Account · · · 176

LIFE IN NAZI-OCCUPIED WARSAW
**Jan Marek Groński** Three Ghetto Sketches · · · 192
**Marek Rudnicki** My Recollections of the Deportation of Janusz Korczak · · · 219
**Jerzy Lewiński** The Death of Adam Czerniaków and Janusz Korczak's Last Journey · · · 224
**Anna Clarke** Sister Wanda · · · 253

## NOTES

**Aharon Weiss** The Activities of the Democratic Societies and Democratic Party in Defending Jewish Rights in Poland on the Eve of Hitler's Invasion — 260

**Dora Katzenelson** Documents Dealing with the History of Jews in Galicia in Lwow Archives — 268

## REVIEW ARTICLES

**Zygmunt Bauman** The Literary Afterlife of Polish Jewry — 273

**Laura Quercioli** Jewish Themes in 'The Beautiful Mrs Seidenmann' by Andrzej Szczypiorski — 300

**Aleksander Zyga** About the 'Jews-in-Poland' Exhibition in Kraków June–October 1989 — 313

CONTRIBUTORS — 334
NOTES FOR CONTRIBUTORS — 338

# POLIN

We did not know, but our fathers told us how the exiles of Israel came to the land of Polin (Poland).

When Israel saw how its sufferings were constantly renewed, oppressions increased, persecutions multiplied, and how the evil authorities piled decree on decree and followed expulsion with expulsion, so that there was no way to escape the enemies of Israel, they went out on the road and sought an answer from the paths of the wide world: which is the correct road to traverse to find rest for the soul? Then a piece of paper fell from heaven, and on it the words:

*Go to Polaniya* (Poland).

So they came to the land of Polin and they gave a mountain of gold to the king, and he received them with great honour. And God had mercy on them, so that they found favour from the king and the nobles. And the king gave them permission to reside in all the lands of his kingdom, to trade over its length and breadth, and to serve God according to the precepts of their religion. And the king protected them against every foe and enemy.

And Israel lived in Polin in tranquillity for a long time. They devoted themselves to trade and handicrafts. And God sent a blessing on them so that they were blessed in the land, and their name was exalted among the peoples. And they traded with the surrounding countries and they also struck coins with inscriptions in the holy language and the language of the country. These are the coins which have on them a lion rampant towards the right. And on the coins are the words 'Mieszko, King of Poland' or 'Mieszko, Król of Poland'. The Poles call their king 'Król'.

And those who seek for names say: 'This is why it is called Polin. For thus spoke Israel when they came to the land, "Here rest for the night [Po lin]." And this means that we shall rest here until we are all gathered into the Land of Israel.'

Since this is the tradition, we accept it as such.

S. Y. AGNON, 1916

# POLIN
*Studies in Polish Jewry*

VOLUME 1 *Poles and Jews: Renewing the Dialogue* (1986)

VOLUME 2 *Jews and the Emerging Polish State* (1987)

VOLUME 3 *The Jews of Warsaw* (1988)

VOLUME 4 *Poles and Jews: Perceptions and Misperceptions* (1989)

VOLUME 5 *New Research, New Views* (1990)

VOLUME 6 *Jews in Łódź, 1820–1939* (1991)

VOLUME 7 *Jewish Life in Nazi-Occupied Warsaw* (1992)

*From Shtetl to Socialism* (1993): selected articles from volumes 1–7

VOLUME 8 *Jews in Independent Poland, 1918–1939* (1994)

VOLUME 9 *Jews, Poles, Socialists: The Failure of an Ideal* (1996)

VOLUME 10 *Jews in Early Modern Poland* (1997)

VOLUME 11 *Aspects and Experiences of Religion* (1998)

VOLUME 12 *Galicia: Jews, Poles, and Ukrainians, 1772–1918* (1999)

*Index to Volumes 1–12* (2000)

VOLUME 13 *The Holocaust and its Aftermath* (2000)

VOLUME 14 *Jews in the Polish Borderlands* (2001)

VOLUME 15 *Jewish Religious Life, 1500–1900* (2002)

VOLUME 16 *Jewish Popular Culture and its Afterlife* (2003)

VOLUME 17 *The Shtetl: Myth and Reality* (2004)

VOLUME 18 *Jewish Women in Eastern Europe* (2005)

VOLUME 19 *Polish–Jewish Relations in North America* (2006)

VOLUME 20 *Making Holocaust Memory* (2008)

VOLUME 21 *1968: Forty Years After* (2009)

VOLUME 22 *Early Modern Poland: Borders and Boundaries* (2010)

VOLUME 23 *Jews in Kraków* (2011)

# STATEMENT FROM THE EDITORS

This issue of *POLIN* appears in the year of the fiftieth anniversary of the Warsaw ghetto uprising. With the passage of time, the momentous decision of the small number of ill-armed young men and women to take up arms against the might of the Third Reich takes on an ever greater significance. It was a demonstration of the Jewish will to resist the inhuman policies of the Nazis, to demonstrate that Jews could fight and die with honour and it was an example not only to the remnants of European Jewry still suffering under German policies of genocide but to the whole world. To commemorate this anniversary, we have included a special section in this volume. So much has been written on occupied Warsaw and yet so much still remains to be explained. We have attempted in our special section to include memoir and other material which will shed significant new light on the Jewish experience under Nazis in Warsaw.

This volume of *POLIN* also has a new home. Antony Polonsky has accepted the position of Professor of East European Jewish History in the Near Eastern and Judaic Studies Department of Brandeis University, Waltham, Massachusetts. He will be taking *POLIN* with him. This will undoubtedly provide a much firmer institutional basis for the journal and will enable us to carry on our work without the pressure of constant financial crises. We hope, too, in the new conditions, to extend our coverage of those lands which were formerly part of the Polish-Lithuanian commonwealth and which are now, after a long period of repression, starting out on the path of national independence and democratic change, above all Ukraine, Belarus and Lithuania.

The last year has seen the death of a number of individuals closely linked with *POLIN*. Isaac Bashevis Singer, one of the towering giants of Yiddish literature, who was a Patron of the American Institute for Polish-Jewish Studies, which supports *POLIN*, has gone to his eternal rest. So too have Professor Stefan Kieniewicz, a member of the editorial board of *POLIN* and the doyen of nineteenth century Polish historiography and

Adolf Rudnicki, one of the leading post-war Polish-Jewish writers. We salute their memory and achievements. As the older generation passes from the scene, the obligation of the middle and younger generation to take up the burden of preserving the fast-fading memory of the lost world of Polish Jewry becomes more imperative.

This volume contains a section with review essays, but does not include a book review section. We hope to re-establish this section in volume VIII, which will also include a section dealing with the history of the Jews in interwar Poland. Like every journal, we are dependent for our life and character on our readers and contributors. We should like to express our gratitude to them for their continued support and to appeal again to them for their suggestions and input. We are convinced that the move to Brandeis is the start of an even more flourishing period for *POLIN*.

ARTICLES

# A BRIEF HISTORY OF THE JEWS IN ROYAL PRUSSIA BEFORE 1772
## Zenon Nowak

The province of Royal Prussia owed its absorption into the Kingdom of Poland to an uprising of the people of Pomorze (Pomerania) against the Order of the Teutonic Knights in 1454, followed by the Thirteen Years War, which ended with the Peace of Toruń (Thorn) in 1466. Its territory comprised those western areas of the Teutonic state (Danzig, Pomorze, Chełm region, Powiśle with Malbork (Marienburg) and Elbląg, and Warmia) which were the last to be united with the Polish Commonwealth. Certain socio-economic and legal peculiarities, traces of its long history under a foreign rule, distinguished it from the other provinces. The socio-political forms of life in Royal Prussia developed under different historical conditions from those in the rest of the country and were to last, despite their continual change and assimilation to other Polish provinces, until the first partition of Poland – in Danzig and Toruń even till the second partition. The three main towns of Danzig, Toruń and Elbląg were also the political centres, moulding the economic life of the Prussian province.

Royal Prussia also differed from other Polish lands through its attitude towards the Jews, who were not tolerated, or rather, to be more precise, had no right to settle there. This practice went back to Teutonic rule, when Jews were not allowed to cross the border of the Crusader state at all. As a knightly order, based on Crusader principles, the Teutonic Knights had conquered Prussia to extend Christian rule. Thus they would not tolerate the presence of other religions within their country.[1] It should be noted, however, that the Teutonic Knights did not forbid Jews to live in their possessions in the German Reich, for example, in Mergentheim, which from 1525 became the residence of the Grand Master.[2] In their attitude towards Jews they were no different from other liege lords. In the New Margraviate purchased by the Order in 1402, not only did they not expel the Jews but, on the contrary, the New Margraviate *wójts* defended 'their Jews', as they put it, in a dispute between them and merchants from other countries.³ A description of a Jewish settlement in Prussia in the fourteenth century does indeed exist, but it is questionable. According to this account, during the Black Death a baptised Jew by the name of Rumbold was supposed to have poisoned wells, causing the death of many people in Elbląg, Malbork, Königsberg and other towns. In punishment, the Jews of Elbląg were burned at the stake.⁴ It would, however, seem impossible for a permanent Jewish settlement in the Teutonic state to have left no trace in the scrupulous financial records kept by the Teutonic Order. The Teutonic Knights did, of course, attach importance to the conversion of Jews to Christianity, but it appears that, in their activity in this field, they did not differ much from other Christian monarchs. Baptised Jews were under the Order's care, and helped with the Grand Master's finances. Despite this protection, their life in Prussian towns was not easy, as the case of Kasper of Malbork in 1436 indicates. He complained to the Grand Master that he was pointed to as a Jew, although he had been baptised in Kraków in 1415 or 1416.⁵

It should not be forgotten also that Prussia was influenced economically and culturally by the Hanse, whose towns did not tolerate Jews.⁶ Important Prussian towns like Danzig, Toruń and Elbląg, like other Hanseatic Baltic towns such as Lübeck, under the rule of merchants and artisans, refused entry to Jews, to keep out competition.

In the first half of the fifteenth century, Jewish merchants tried to trade on a larger scale with the Prussian towns, especially after the signing of the treaties of Mełno in 1422 and Brześć in 1435, guaranteeing free trade between the Polish monarchy and the Teutonic state. But fear of competition led the Prussian towns to carry a vote at a meeting of the Teutonic state estates on 6 December 1435, declaring that 'according to old tradition no Jew has the right to come to Prussia with the intention of carrying on trade'.⁷ It cannot have been very effective as the resolution had to be passed again two years later.⁸ Jewish merchants were allowed to enter the boundaries of the Teutonic state only if they had a safe-conduct issued by the Grand Master, or by the commander of the border district in the name of the Grand Master – a safe-conduct which they had to surrender on leaving the state. These safe-conducts raised a considerable income, especially when the Order experienced financial problems. Certainly in 1446 the commander of Toruń counted on this income from the Jews of nearby Nieszawa, which had been under Polish rule since 1422.⁹ By the end of their rule, the policy of the Teutonic Knights in this sphere conflicted with the interests of the big towns. Toruń reluctantly let Jewish merchants in. But it is difficult to estimate the scale of Jewish business on the basis of this one piece of information.

It should be added that the Grand Masters readily accepted the services of Jewish doctors from Poland. Again, educated Jews were commonly sent as envoys to the Teutonic Knights by the *starostas* of the lands bordering on the Teutonic state, such as Mikołaj Szarlejski, *starosta* of Bydgoszcz, and Jan Kretkowski, general *starosta* of Kujawy.[10]

We must stress that the anti-Jewish spirit of the resolutions passed by these estate meetings was the result of economic pressure. This is clearly shown after Prussia surrendered to the Polish Commonwealth in 1454. The big towns had numerous privileges, guaranteeing their trade monopoly, granted by King Kazimierz Jagiellończyk. Danzig, as the largest Prussian centre, was guaranteed by its privilege of 1454, confirmed in the following year, that '*none from Nuremberg, Lombardy, no Englishman, Dutchman, Fleming, Jew, or any other outsider from any other country*' may live or trade in the town without the prior consent of the town council.[11] Here the Jewish merchant is placed on the same footing as any other merchant from outside Royal Prussia.

Despite all these prohibitions, Jewish immigration into Royal Prussia continued to grow, especially after the sixteenth century, as can be deduced from the resolutions passed by the Dietines of Royal Prussia. A Dietine meeting on 29 May 1530 in Grudziądz voted to expel Jewish merchants from Prussia.[12] Judging by the number of anti-Jewish resolutions passed by Dietines up till the end of the century, they can have had very little effect.[13] They were issued as much against Scottish as against Jewish pedlars in 1551 and primarily against Jewish craftsmen – tailors, furriers and clothmakers – in 1581.[14] Voivodes openly defended Jews, as when the voivode of Malbork supported Chaim of Poznań's claim to be allowed into Toruń with his goods.[15] In the sixteenth century, the two largest towns, Danzig and Toruń, became major business centres for Jewish merchants, despite the heavy obstacles put in their way.[16] The third main town of Royal Prussia, Elbląg, was of lesser interest to them.[17] Jewish merchants were allowed to stay in Prussian towns only during fairs, when in possession of safe-conducts granted by the town authorities. They usually tried to evade this prohibition and remain longer in town and were often allowed to do so. By the end of the sixteenth century, they even had a synagogue in the Danzig suburbs, in an inn on the right bank of the river Mołtawa, where they held regular services.[18] The synagogue came to an end in 1605.

With the increasing number of Jewish merchants in Danzig, the town multiplied its restrictions in an effort to force them out completely from the fairs. The third *Ordynek* in particular, consisting of craftsmen and petty traders, tried to force such laws through.[19] In their complaint in 1616 about Jewish competition and dishonesty, their practices and, in general, their hostility towards Christians, they demanded a limit of one month maximum stay in Danzig for Jewish merchants. Under such pressure, the Council agreed to some restrictions but not to total expulsion of the Jews. Even these concessions were not enough for the third *Ordynek* and, finally, the Council ordered Jews to leave town within one month. The Jewish merchants of Kraków, Poznań, Lublin and Lwów, appealed to King Zygmunt III, who told the Danzig Council that it had acted '*contra iuria publica regni nostri et consuetudinem antiquam*' and ordered it to allow Jews into the town fairs again.[20] Jews returned to the Dominican fair in 1620, as the result of a compromise in which they were still only allowed to stay in town for 16 days, i.e. 8 days before and 8 days after the feast of St Dominic.

We are indebted to Jan Małecki, who has written on the role of Jewish merchants in trade between Danzig and Polish towns up to the mid-seventeenth century, for drawing our attention to the considerable activity of Jews compared to Christian Poles in this field.[21] Sources on this question are scarce, so I would like to refer to a list of safe-conducts issued to Jews by the mayor of Danzig for participation in the fair of 1641, which has survived in the Danzig State Archives.[22] It is an exceptional source, giving us a good picture of Jewish involvement in Danzig trade. During that year a total 670 safe-conducts were issued to Jews. They were valid for seven days, though merchants tried to extend them, some of them several times over; such as Samuel Amsterdamczyk from Sandomierz, and Balcer Amsterdamczyk from Lublin. The geographical range of the safe-conducts issued points to a broad spread of Jewish merchants from almost every province of the Commonwealth, the majority of them from towns in the eastern borderlands, including Kobryń, Stryja and Lwów. However, most Jews arriving in Danzig came from Poznań (211 safe-conducts), Lublin (48), Sandomierz (38), Kraków (24), Piła (16), Włocławek (14), and Kalisz (10). Jewish merchants from Poznań also conducted a lively trade with Toruń.[23] In Prussia they bought a wide range of goods, especially raw materials and, to a somewhat smaller extent, less common manufactured articles. In Toruń, Jewish merchants sold caps.[24] They also played a considerable part in timber and grain trading. Jews appeared in Danzig as brokers and stockbrokers.

Jewish trade penetrated not only into the main towns, but also into the smaller towns and villages of Royal Prussia, although on this we have less information. It does appear that a fairly large group of Jews must have settled in Prussia, as the Dietines of the end of the seventeenth century dredge up Prussia's intolerant anti-Jewish laws and refuse permission to build synagogues.[25] On the other hand, the 1664 Dietine called for severe punishment of the unruly mob for rioting and murdering Jews – in other Polish provinces, of course; and the instructions given to the deputies to the Warsaw Diet in 1670 caused an outcry against over-severe sentences passed on Jews where confiscation of property and expulsion from the province where the crime took place would have been enough.

The eighteenth century saw changes in the status of Jews in the main Prussian towns, changes which should be seen as a consequence of serious economic difficulties. An increase in the number of Jewish merchants was considered an important element, which would contribute to the strength of economic life. Jews were therefore permitted to stay on long after the fairs and a blind eye was turned to their residence. In Toruń, probably within the New Town, Jews had a synagogue and obtained a site for a cemetery.[26] But they lived in constant anxiety, with an ever present risk of expulsion. If expelled, they came back to the same spot a few years later. They were all chased out of Toruń in 1766 except for 6 merchants.[27] The same thing happened to Jewish families in Danzig in 1719.[28] Eight years later they returned and even managed to form a synagogue. In the 1740s the Jewish community numbered as many as 32 families, mostly from the Commonwealth's eastern territories. In 1745 the Jews were again forced to move out, except for Joel Lewin, a diamond cutter from Amsterdam, who was allowed to stay only because of his much-needed trade.[29] An exception was also made for a Jewish cook. No doubt the historian of the Danzig Jews, Samuel Echt, is right in maintaining that economic reasons dictated the expulsion of the Jewish population.[30] In restricting residence permits only to Jews thought indispensable, the town was influenced by purely selfish motives. Nevertheless the Danzig Council found it possible to defend Jews against attack from the raftmen, issuing a special order in 1740.[31] It should be stressed here that the Toruń and the Danzig town councils were quite favourable towards the Jews and tried to evade the existing legal statutes so as to allow them to stay. But this attitude was confined to the patriciate, i.e. the wealthiest merchants. Small businessmen and craftsmen remained uncompromising against Jews, seeing them above all as competitors.

Hostility towards the Jews, as demonstrated by these social groups under the guise of religious fanaticism, was really a symptom of economic struggle. The craftsmen and petty merchants of the big towns were the main sufferers in this contest. A typical example is the campaign carried on for years between the furriers' guild from Toruń and the Poznań Jews, who imported caps to sell at the fairs.[32] The Toruń craftsmen would not accept the voivode's orders and even resorted to violence in order to prevent Jewish merchants bringing their caps to the fair. They insisted that they held the monopoly on the guild products, relying on their old privileges dating back to the Middle Ages. Thus we should not be surprised that it was the third *Ordynek*, constituting craftsmen and petty merchants, which insisted on tightening the rules. This body put pressure on the less extreme town council to reduce the duration of Jewish residence permits, even during fairs. So safe-conducts issued to Jews were valid for a shorter period of time and became more expensive. They finished up as an important part of the town's income. In Danzig and Toruń the safe-conducts were issued by the veto-office, while power over Jews within the town walls was exercised by the major-burgrave, who exercised it in the name of the monarch. The Toruń burgrave was called the 'Messiah' by the Jews. Burgraves received money (*Schutzgeld*) for this 'protection' which – as is attested by complaints in Toruń – were collected 'often with an inhuman ruthlessness'.[33] According to the regulations of the Great Poland Synod, the functions of the elders (sometimes called judges) of the Toruń fair were to be exercised by the members of the Leszno and Inowrocław communities.[34] The Jews' status in Danzig and Toruń did not, of course, enable them to play any role in the political and economic life of those towns.

Jews had far better opportunities to settle in clerical, noble and royal estates. Our information is the greatest and most detailed for the Jewish population of Stare Szkoty, Chełm, Chmielnik and Wrzeszcz near Danzig, which belonged to the Włocławek bishops and the monastery of Pelplin.[35] These enclaves, stretching out on hills south-east of the town, took root in the sixteenth century and grew into bustling craft and trade centres. The main cause of this development was large-scale immigration as the Jews were turned away from Danzig. The town tried to stop this happening, destroying Stare Szkoty three times in the sixteenth century, but under the bishop's protection this was where the Jews established their first community in Royal Prussia. On the other hand, the bishop's grace was also proved fickle and in 1710 the community was driven out, to be permitted to return in the early 1720s. It was then that two communities were founded, one in Stare Szkoty and Chmielnik, the other in Chełm and a small settlement at Winnica (Weinberg). The Stare Szkoty community had two synagogues, the 'big' and the 'upper', and in 1757 numbered 47 families. From 1724 a *Hevra Kadisha* functioned at the 'upper' synagogue, on whose initiative a hospital was erected. Communities in Stare Szkoty, Chełm, and also in Wrzeszcz, where a separate community soon developed, provided shelter for Jewish merchants going to the Danzig fair. Of the three communities, which united in 1787, Stare Szkoty was the richest and the most populous. A large part of its income was used to pay for its protection, yet it still could afford to invite a learned rabbi, Elchan (1752–1780) from Fordon, son of the rabbi of Bonn. First precise data for calculating the population of the communities around Danzig comes from the year 1772.[36] Together they numbered 1257 inhabitants (240 families) of whom 584 lived in Stare Szkoty, 402 in Chełm and 271 in Wrzeszcz.[37] This is quite a big number if we remember the legal position of the Jews in Royal Prussia, and that it constituted almost 41 per cent of the total Jewish population in that province.

From the Prussian tax register compiled during 1772–3, after the first partition of the Polish Commonwealth, we learn that a total of 3,962 Jews lived within Royal Prussia (excluding Danzig and Toruń), of whom 2,048 lived in Pomorze Gdańskie (Danzig Pomerania) (including towns close to Danzig), 882 in the Chełm region, 132 in Powiśle, i.e. the province of Malbork, and 2 in Warmia.[38] Jews made up less than 1 per cent of the total population, which for Poland was a very low proportion. The fact that they were basically living outside towns should be stressed.[39] Nobles who allowed Jews to settle in their domains acted like the bishops of Włocławek and the monastery of Pelplin, albeit on a smaller scale.[40] Jews also settled in the royal estates under the protection of the *starostas*. There were synagogues in four villages altogether in Gdańskie Pomorze: in Kilincz (Tczew district), Bukowiec (Świecie district), Kułmaga (Nowe district)) and in Nowa Tuchola (Tuchola district).[41] In the village of Kilincz, belonging to a member of a very rich family, Władysław Bystram, 232 inhabitants out of 313 were Jews. Similar situations existed in other regions of Royal Prussia, e.g. the district of Chełm, where there were synagogues in three villages: Fitowo, Kuriady and Pokrzywno.[42] In Fitowo near the town of New Lubawsk, 176 Jews easily outnumbered a mere 34 Christians. Jews settling in those villages engaged in crafts, but innkeepers and *arendars* could also be found among them.[43]

After the first partition of Poland, the legal position of Jews living on the territory of former Royal Prussia did not, in principle, change. The Prussian king, Frederick II (the Great), treated the Jewish population as instruments of his policy. He tried to use Jews from the settlements near Danzig in his plans to weaken Danzig's economic position. He did the same with Toruń, through creating new Jewish trade centres near these towns.[44] Again, he made no attempt to allow Jews to engage in trade in villages and poor Jews, with less than 100 thalers and no permanent place of residence, were to be driven out of the country on his orders. Only Jews with a fortune valued over 1,000 thalers were to remain.[45]

In concluding this article, I would like to point to the fact that my research, which is after all very rudimentary, allows only a superficial survey of Jewish history in Royal Prussia from the fifteenth to eighteenth centuries. Although not as rich as in other parts of Poland, because of the mediaeval but still prevalent rule *de non tolerandis Iudaeis*, it calls for closer attention by historians. The importance of Prussia's main towns, especially Danzig, to Polish history both in economic and general terms, and the part played in it by Jewish merchants – a quite considerable part – is surely sufficient reason. Sources for trade relations between Jews and these trading centres are fairly rich, but scattered, and thus need wide-ranging investigation. Let me mention here just one of these sources – a very important authority, but not one used so far and one which could become a mine of information for the topic under discussion, namely the Municipal Court Records. The town courts often dealt with cases during fairs, and these cases often involved Jewish merchants.

## NOTES

1 See K. Forstreuter, *Die ersten Juden in Ostpreussen*, Altpreussischen Forschung, 14, Königsberg, 1937, p. 42 and n: also S. Grunau, *Preussische Chronik*, ed. M. Perlbach, I, Leipzig 1876, pp. 474 and 600.
2 (Ed.) Zvi Avneri *Germania Judaica*, II, 2, p. 1238 and n, Tübingen, 1968, p. 538.
3 *Regesta historico-diplomatica Ordinis S. Mariae Theutenicorum 1198-1525* (quoted further as *Regesta*), part 1: 2, rev. E. Joachim, ed. W. Hubatsch, Göttingen, 1949, no. 9020. See also K. Forstreuter, *Die ersten Juden*, p. 45.
4 (Ed.) C. P. Woelky, *Codex diplomaticus Warmiensis*, III Braunsberg/Leipzig, 1874, p. 634, no. 633. See also *Germanica Judaica*, II, 1, p. 200.
5 A. Kolberg, 'Ein preussisches Formelbuch des 15. Jahrhunderts', *Zeitschrift für die Geschichte und Altertumskunde Ermlands*, 9 (Braunsberg), 1888, p. 299.
6 See R. Sprandel, *Das mittelalterliche Zahlungssystem nach hansischen-nordischen Quellen des 13.-15. Jahrhunderts*, Monographien zur Geschichte des Mittelalters, 10, Stuttgart, 1975, pp. 60 and n.; also E. Baasch, 'Die Juden und der Handel in Lübeck', *Vierteljahrschrift für Sozial- und Wirtschaftsgeschichte*, 16, (1922), pp. 370: The Lübeck chronicler Reiner Kocka wrote in 1499, that 'tho Lübeck syn kene Juden, man bedarf erer ock nicht'.
7 M. Toeppen (ed.), *Akten der Standetage Preussens unter der Herrschaft des Deutschen Ordens* (quoted further as *AST*), I, Leipzig, 1874, p. 701.
8 *Ibid.*, II, Leipzig, 1880, p. 54; M. Aschkewitz, *Zur Geschichte der Juden in Westpreussen*, Wissenschaftliche Beiträge zur Geschichte und Landeskunde Ost- und Mitteleuropas, 81, Marburg/Lahn, 1967, p. 2.
9 *Regesta*, I, 1, no. 9060.
10 *Ibid*, I, 1, nos. 12688, 12708, 12724.
11 *AST*, IV, Leipzig, 1884, pp. 5, 59; see also P. Simson, *Geschichte der Stadt Danzig*, I, Danzig, 1913, pp. 107, 200, 352.
12 K. Górski (ed.), *Inwentarz aktów sejmikowych Prus Królewskich 1600-1764* (An inventory of the Royal Prussian Dietines' Acts 1600-1764 *Tow. Nauk. w Toruniu, Fontes*); quoted further as *Inwentarz*, 34, Toruń, 1950, p. 261, no. 2337.
13 *Ibid.*, p. 262.
14 *Ibid.*, p. 262, no. 2338.
15 See L. Koczy, *Studia nad dziejami gospodarczymi Żydów poznańskich przed poł. XVII w.*, Kronika miasta Poznania, Year 12, no. 4, Poznań, 1934, pp. 345 and n.
16 J. Małecki, *Związki handlowe miast polskich z Gdańskiem w XVI i pierwszej połowie XVII w.*, Wrocław/Warsaw/Kraków, 1968, *passim*.
17 J. Małecki, 'Związki handlowe miast polskich z Elblągiem w XVI w. i pierwszej połowie XVII w.', *Rocznik Elbląski* (Elbląg Annual), 5, (1972), pp. 129 ff.
18 S. Echt, *Die Geschichte der Juden in Danzig*, Leer/Ostfriesland 1972, p. 15.
19 Ibid., pp. 15 and n., 27 and n.
20 G. Lengnich, *Geschichte der Preussischen Lände Konigl.-Polnische Anteils*, V, Danzig, 1727, pp. 116 and n.
21 Małecki, *Związki handlowe miast polskich z Gdańskiem*, *passim*.
22 AP, Danzig, MS 300, 1/234; see also Małecki, *Związki handlowe miast polskich z Gdańskiem*, pp. 53–54.
23 Koczy, *Studia*, p. 356.
24 AP, Toruń, Kat. II, sygn. II, 2, pp. 54, 56, 71, 133, 149, 157, 175, 221.
25 *Inwentarz*, p. 262, no. 2347.
26 AP, Toruń, Kat. II, sygn. II, 8 and 9.
27 A. Semrau, 'Thorn in den Jahren 1770–1793', *Mitteilungen des Coppernicus - Vereins*,

8, Thorn (1893), p. 39. See also S. L. Geret, *Das jetztlebende Thorn im merkwürdingen Jahr 1793*, Frankfurt/Leipzig, 1793, p. 114.
28 AP, Danzig, sygn. 300, 93/39. See also Echt, *Geschichte der Juden in Danzig*, p. 30.
29 Ibid., sygn. 300, 58/78.
30 Echt, *Geschichte der Juden in Danzig*, p. 31.
31 Ibid., p. 34.
32 AP, Toruń, Kat. II, sygn. II, 17, pp. 149-51; II, 20, pp. 14 and n., 19 and n., 22 and n.; *Akten-Inventar der Synagogen-Gemeinde Thorn* (quoted further as *Akten-Inventar*), Mitteilungen des Gesamtarchivs der deutschen Juden, ed. E. Taubler, Year 2, Leipzig, 1910, pp. 7-8.
33 Semrau, *Thorn 1770-1793*, p. 38.
34 *Akten-Inventar*, p. 5, no. 1; see also L. Lewin, *Die Synode der Grosspolnischen Judenschaft*, Schriften der Gesellschaft zur Forderung der Wissenschaft des Judentums, Frankfurt/Main, 1926, pp. 42, 49/50.
35 Echt, *Geschichte der Juden in Danzig*, p. 14, has given this question the broadest treatment.
36 Ibid., p. 21.
37 Ibid., p. 21; see also M. Aschkewitz, 'Die Juden in Westpreussen am Ende der polnischen Herrschaft 1772', *Zeitschrift für Ostforschung*, Marburg/Lahn, 6 (1957), p. 568.
38 Ibid., esp. p. 568.
39 Ibid., *passim*.
40 For Danzig Pomorze, refer to the work of G. Dabinus, *Die ländliche Bevölkerung Pommerellens im Jahre 1772 mit Einschluss des Danziger Landgebietes im Jahre 1793*, Wissenschaftliche Beiträge zur Geschichte und Landeskunde Ost- und Mitteleuropas, 6, Marburg/Lahn, 1953.
41 Ibid., pp. 115, 119, 125, 132.
42 S. Cackowski, *Nauczyciele wiejscy województwa chełmińskiego w pruskim katastrze podatkowym z 1772/1773. Przyczynek do historii szkolnictwa*, Acta Universitatis Nicolai Copernici, Historia, 20, Nauki Hum.-Społ., fasc. 158, Toruń, 1985, p. 149.
43 For example there were 4 butchers, 3 glaziers, 2 tailors and 1 inn-keeper in Kuriady, and 2 tailors, 2 glaziers, 9 butchers, 2 dyers and 1 barber-surgeon in Titów. I would like to thank Prof. Stefan Cackowski for passing me these data.
44 M. Bar, *Westpreussen unter Friedrich der Grossen, I*, Publikationen aus dem K. Preussischen Staatsarchiven, 23, Leipzig, 1909, p. 429, and fn. 3; Semrau, *Thorn 1770-1793*, p. 14.
45 Bar, *Westpreussen*, pp. 429-30.

# FROM THE GHETTO TO MODERN CULTURE: THE AUTOBIOGRAPHIES OF SALOMON MAIMON AND JAKOB FROMER

Ritchie Robertson

An autobiography cannot be a complete account of a person's life. It is an interpretation of one's life as a meaningful narrative, and so it concentrates on those events and periods which are recognized in retrospect as being of crucial importance. In Western autobiography the meaning of the subject's life has most often been spiritual. A life is interpreted as a narrative of spiritual development, and its central event is most often a spiritual crisis, leading to conversion and a new life. The greatest example of the spiritual crisis-autobiography is St Augustine's *Confessions*. The author of such an autobiography has to make sense of the apparent discontinuity in his life. He has to explain how he got from there to here, how his unregenerate past self became his present regenerate self. And for this he must disclose a hidden purpose in his life, a teleology which only gradually becomes manifest.[1]

The Jewish autobiographies I want to discuss are also narratives of development, but the development is outward as well as inward: it is geographical as well as intellectual. 'There' is the Eastern European ghetto; 'here' is the civilization of the modern secular West; and between the two lie long and arduous struggles. The teleology which gives meaning to their narratives is not a hidden design; it comes from the authors' stubborn, unyielding efforts to educate themselves in the ways of Western Europe and to gain acceptance there. Their lives do not centre on a spiritual crisis: these are not narratives of conversion, but rather of de-conversion. The authors of these texts recount a prolonged rebellion against the traditional Judaism in which they were brought up, and reveal that they never succeeded in casting off its influence.

One of these autobiographies is deservedly famous. It was referred to by George Eliot as 'that wonderful bit of autobiography, the life of the Polish Jew, Salomon Maimon'[2]; and she borrowed from it the name Lapidoth for one of the characters in *Daniel Deronda*. Maimon's *Lebensgeschichte* was first published in Berlin in two parts, which appeared in 1792 and 1793, with an introduction by the novelist and psychologist Karl Philipp Moritz. There have been several more recent editions, and also an English translation. The best edition, however – the only one which is both unabridged and annotated – was published at Munich in 1911 and edited by Jakob Fromer, another Polish Jew who, like Maimon, had laboriously gained access to Western culture. And Fromer wrote his autobiography, published at Berlin in 1906 as *Vom Ghetto zur modernen Kultur* ('From the Ghetto to Modern Culture') and reissued with revisions in 1911 as *Ghetto-Dämmerung* ('The Twilight of the Ghetto').[3]

Before examining these autobiographical texts, I will present a very brief sketch of the two men's lives. Maimon was born in 1754 in Lithuania. Much of his early life was spent in or near Nieśwież in what is now Byelorussia. He underwent a Talmudic education, in which he distinguished himself, and was married at eleven, becoming a father at fourteen. He left his wife, worked as a private tutor, and eventually set off to Berlin in pursuit of the Enlightenment. Refused entry by the Jewish community, who rightly suspected him of being a free-thinker, he begged his way through Poland and was eventually enabled by benefactors to return to Germany. This time he was taken up by Moses Mendelssohn and enabled to study philosophy. After quarrels with his benefactors and further wanderings, he settled in Berlin and began to publish philosophical works, beginning with a critique of Kant, *Versuch über die Transcendentalphilosophie* ('Essay on Transcendental Philosophy', 1790). He sent the manuscript to Kant, who said that 'a glance at its contents enabled me to appreciate its excellence at once and to recognize that none of my opponents have understood me and my essential meaning so well as Maimon'.[4] Thereafter Maimon published further philosophical works, including a Hebrew commentary on Maimonides' *Guide to the Perplexed*; it was in honour of Maimonides that he had changed his name from Shlomo ben Yehoshua to Salomon Maimon. He was supported by an aristocratic patron, Graf Kalckreuth. His hardships and his dissipated way of life had undermined his health, however, and he died in 1800.

Information about Jakob Fromer's life is harder to come by, and so I will go into slightly more detail about him. He was born on 2 February 1865 at Bałuty, a suburb of Łódź; his father was an unworldly Talmudic scholar, and his mother supported the family. Fromer was likewise married in his early teens, when he had already acquired the reputation of a heretic. Eventually he left Łódź for Berlin, but, like Maimon, was refused permission to stay: this was 1884, when the large numbers of Polish and Russian Jews seeking refuge from poverty and pogroms were already provoking an anti-immigrant backlash. Fromer was brought back to his home-town in handcuffs, but his friends enabled him to escape across the

Austrian border. After a year of vagrancy and begging, he set up as a private tutor in Galicia and struggled to educate himself in Western knowledge. At long last, after many hardships and disappointments, he obtained a doctorate in Semitic languages from the University of Breslau; after appealing personally to the Emperor Wilhelm II, he was granted German citizenship in 1899, and, probably thanks to the literary scholar Ludwig Geiger, became librarian to the Jewish community in Berlin. His alienation from Judaism, however, led him to publish, in a well-known Berlin periodical, *Die Zukunft*, on 18 June 1904, an essay entitled 'Das Wesen des Judentums' ('The Essence of Judaism') which demanded that Jews should either return to the ghetto or assimilate so entirely as to lose their Jewish identity. Only that, he claimed, could put an end to antisemitism. For writing this essay (a book-length version of which was published the following year) he was dismissed from his post as librarian and ostracized. It was in this crisis that he wrote his autobiography, which ends with an account of his dismissal and the failure of his appeal. Its publication, however, brought him friends and patrons, and he was enabled to devote himself to studying and editing the Talmud and preparing a concordance. As a prolegomenon to his edition, Fromer wrote *Der Organismus des Judentums* ('The Organism of Judaism'), a highly polemical book which was denounced by many scholars, though it was also among the books that Kafka read in 1912 in order to learn about his Jewish heritage.[5] The concordance never appeared, but Fromer did publish a study of the Talmud and a volume of selections from it in his own translation. In his later years he wrote pamphlets about Messianism. One of these, a cranky production called *Messianismus und Völkerbund*, advocates the establishment of messianic societies in every country which would provide an ideology with popular appeal for the League of Nations and thus assist its essentially messianic work of unifying mankind. Fromer died at Bratislava in March 1938.[6]

It is now recognized that autobiographies are highly complex literary structures, and that the boundaries between autobiography and fiction are difficult to determine. Autobiographers, like novelists, have to negotiate problems of tone, verisimilitude, and narrative structure. In these two works, the problem of tone – of finding an appropriate voice in which to address the reader – is particularly difficult. Maimon and Fromer are addressing Western readers, including non-Jews. Indeed, it is especially important for them to have their work read by non-Jews and thus to have confirmation of their acceptance within European civilization. One of their main purposes, however, is to inform Western readers about the culture of the Eastern Jews, a culture which must strike Westerners as almost unimaginably alien. Accordingly Fromer begins his introduction to Maimon's autobiography with the words: 'Anyone who wants to experience an ethnological sensation has no need to roam in distant continents. A day's journey from Berlin is sufficient. One need only cross the Russian border to find a breed of humanity almost unknown to the civilized world and full of enigmas and marvels' (M 7). Maimon and Fromer must prove their Western credentials by stressing the alien character of Eastern Jewish culture, as Fromer does here. At the same time, they must show themselves to be trustworthy reporters by displaying an intimate knowledge of it.

Maimon gains the reader's credence by establishing a detached and factual tone at the beginning of his introductory chapter: 'The inhabitants of Poland may properly be divided into the following six classes or estates: upper nobility, inferior nobility, semi-nobility, townspeople, peasants and Jews' (M 67). This is the style of a statistical account, a form of writing which grew out of travel literature and was favoured by the Enlightenment as a means of geographical and ethnographic description. Many statistical accounts of Eastern Europe, in particular, were produced, which systematically catalogue the various ethnic groups along with the geographical features and agricultural and mineral products. Such a descriptive method suggests that the peoples described can also be possessed, as objects of knowledge and often also as subjects of political domination. It reassures the Western reader by placing other peoples at a safe distance and depriving them of their mysteriousness.[7]

The tone in which Maimon addressed the readers is often humorous. Describing his family, he gives a drily ironic account of how his grandfather kept an inn. The first chapter title, 'My grandfather's domestic economy', sets up a comic tension between the learned word 'ökonomie' and the absurd incompetence with which Maimon's grandfather conducted his business: for example, he thought it wasteful to burn candles, and so used lighted strips of wool instead, which often set fire to the house and caused far greater expense than candles would have; instead of windows, the store-room had mere openings in the wall, through which thieves would often climb and drink their fill of the brandy; and so on. 'In short,' Maimon concludes, 'he was the poorest rich man in the world' (M 81). The comedy continues for much of the book, with chapter headings like 'People fight over me, I get two women at once, and am at last kidnapped' (M 126). Another comic technique Maimon favours is mock-heroic allusion, as when his family, expelled from their home, wander about 'like the Israelites in the desert of Arabia' (M 105). The comedy invites the reader to take Maimon's side against an environment which is by turns foolish and oppressive; but it also renders milder Maimon's criticism of Jewish backwardness, folly, and superstition. The more Maimon tells us about his family and their acquaintances, the less remote these people seem. His improvident grandfather, his kindly father, and his tyrannical mother-in-law become recognizable players in the human comedy. Mothers-in-law, apparently, are the same the world over.

Moreover, Maimon willingly makes himself the object of comedy, as when he tries to practise as a doctor and dogmatically tells his patients what symptoms they *must* have to fit his diagnoses.

If Maimon's humour represents one form of collusion with the reader, another method is to display one's intimacy with Western culture. This establishes the writer as the beneficiary of a Western education, which may indeed be superior to the reader's, and accentuates his distance from the ghetto. Both Maimon and Fromer use many Latin tags, especially when describing Jewish behaviour that they consider particularly absurd. Thus Maimon says that his grandfather could have been wealthy, '*si mens non laeva fuisset*'(M 73). Coming from Book 2 of the *Aeneid*, where the fall of Troy is recounted, this quotation again has a mock-heroic effect. Elsewhere Maimon uses a Latin tag to round off his satirical account of *pilpul*. First he cites absurd-seeming problems such as these: 'How many white hairs can a red heifer have and still remain a red heifer? Did the High priest put on his shirt before his trousers, or the other way round? If the *yabam* (a man whose brother has died childless and who is obliged by law to marry his widow) falls off the roof and sticks in the mud, is he relieved from his duties or not?' And then the Latin phrase puts all this in an unclassical limbo of absurdity: '*Ohe iam satis est*!'(M 93). The explanation of Hebrew and Yiddish terms like *yabam* in the text also serves to make the ghetto more remote. Maimon likes using French and Latin phrases in an incongruous context, as when he describes somebody as 'a Jewish beggar *ex professo*' (M 220) or mentions a passage from the Psalms 'in which King David shows himself *en maître* in cursing' (M 268). References to Rousseau, Sterne, Mandeville, Hogarth, and Samuel 'Hudibras' Butler enhance Maimon's self-presentation as a witty and cultivated European.

Classical allusion is employed more seriously when Maimon particularly wants the reader's sympathy. The low point of his narrative is his arrival at Berlin, after a dangerous journey by land and sea, only to be refused admission by the Jewish authorities. 'The final goal of all my hopes and desires,' says Maimon, 'was suddenly removed just as I was so close to it. I found myself in the situation of Tantalus, and was completely at a loss' (M 219). Fromer uses the same reference at the point where he is denied permission to proceed to a doctorate because he lacks a school-leaving certificate: 'Here I lie, a Tantalus, I see the good things for which I am languishing, so close at hand, and yet I must perish!' (F 143).

The author's relationship with the reader helps to enhance the verisimilitude of his text. Like the novelist, the autobiographer has to present unfamiliar scenes, people, and institutions in such a way as to compel the reader's belief. Maimon does this, as we have seen, by stressing the universally human traits of the characters he presents, and at the same time by cultivating a tone of factual description. In the nineteenth century these devices were widely adopted by the authors of ghetto fiction. This genre of writing aims to describe the traditional Jews of Eastern Europe for the benefit of Western readers, just as Maimon did, and it combines fictional narrative with ethnographic description. Hebrew and Yiddish words are explained in brackets or footnotes, as they are by Maimon. Certain Jewish institutions are repeatedly described, usually with explicit disapproval. These include the practice of early marriage, which Maimon had experienced; the brutality of the *heder*, where young children were kept in a squalid room and often savagely beaten, as Maimon recounts (M 98); the absurd over-ingenuity of Talmudic argument, Maimon's version of which has already been quoted; and the supposed charlatanry of Hasidic spiritual leaders, denounced by Maimon in the section which describes his visit to a Hasidic court.[8]

All these *topoi* recur throughout ghetto fiction, especially in the masterpiece of the genre, Karl Emil Franzos's novel *Der Pojaz* (1905). It would have been wellnigh impossible for Fromer, writing just after the publication of *Der Pojaz*, to avoid shaping his recollections in accordance with this other fictional model. If one compares Franzos's description of a *heder* in *Der Pojaz* with Fromer's in his autobiography, one sees that the two correspond down to the most inessential details. In both we find a dark, stuffy room; children sitting on the floor; the *melamed* administering punishment, in one case with a metal ruler, in the other with a strap; and his wife cooking on a stove in the corner. The punishment is described grandiosely as 'Exekution' by both writers (F 10). The suggestions of hell and its torments, implicit but easily detectable in Franzos, are made explicit in Fromer (F 11).[9] Another literary model seems to be present when Fromer describes his Talmud studies: the upbringing of Jehuda ben Halevy in Heine's *Hebräische Melodien*. Fromer distinguishes, just as Heine does, between the arid legal discussions of the *Halakha* and the charming stories of the *Agada*. Both Fromer and Heine cite, as an example of a halakhic problem, the case of the egg laid on the Sabbath (F 15).[10] Finally, Fromer uses fiction quite openly in the episode concerning his visit to a Hasidic centre. He describes a debate about the Talmud and a negotiation about a marriage, both of which he claims to have overheard in the streets. This is obviously a fictional device for presenting typical aspects of Jewish life as vividly as possible. The upshot is that the incidents recounted by Fromer have a special kind of plausibility: the verisimilitude of things that readers are accustomed to find in fiction.

Maimon's conception of verisimilitude is based on a narrowly rationalistic model of human behaviour. This limits what he can describe, and, perhaps, what he can understand. Although he came from an intensely religious, theocratic culture, he displays no feeling for religion. He describes the Jewish religion in functional terms, as the means of preserving the unity of the Jewish nation in the Diaspora, and gives a very cynical account of the rabbinate: 'The Jewish nation, leaving aside accidental modifications, is an everlasting aristocracy in the guise of a theocracy. The scholars who compose the nobility of this nation succeeded many centuries ago in gaining such respect, as the legislative body, from the common people, that they were able to do anything they wanted with them' (M 321–2). Talmudic and Kabbalistic scholarship is dismissed as obscurantism. Intense piety is dismissed as superstition or enthusiasm, and illustrated by tales of extravagant fasting practised by extreme *Hasidim*.

The two autobiographies differ markedly in narrative form. Maimon's is simpler. He recounts a sequence of dramatic incidents, in a manner that recalls the picaresque novel and reminds us that he was familiar with *Don Quixote* (mentioned on p. 170). His principal model, however, was undoubtedly the autobiographical novel by his friend Moritz, *Anton Reiser*, which appeared in instalments from 1785 to 1790. The hero of *Anton Reiser* is likewise brought up in an oppressively religious atmosphere – that of a small Pietist sect; he acquires an education amid terrible hardship, humiliation, and loneliness; and he hero-worships Goethe, as Maimon does Mendelssohn, though Moritz ends his autobiography well before his meeting with Goethe. The obvious difference between Moritz and Maimon is that the former is a fascinating explorer of psychological states, whereas Maimon does not not dwell on his emotions, and hence comes across as a much more robust and resilient character. Maimon very rarely draws attention to the activity of writing or moves from the narrated past into the present of narration: the major exception is a paragraph in which he sums up his teens as a time of poverty, wretchedness and wasted energy, 'in describing which, the pen falls from my hand, and I try to smother the painful recollection of it' (M 139). The narrative is often episodic, especially as it is frequently interrupted by ethnographic description. The longest excursus is an account of the philosophy of Maimonides (transferred, in Fromer's edition, from the beginning of Book 2 to an appendix). This strains the unity of the book almost to breaking point, but its inclusion is justified by the parallel it creates between Maimonides and Maimon's other intellectual hero, Mendelssohn. Mendelssohn appears in person and hence more vividly, but Maimonides is represented at much greater length by the summary of his philosophy.

For the most part, the narrative and the ethnographic portions of Maimon's autobiography are held together by a clear teleology: Maimon's struggle for Enlightenment. He ends Book 1 by stating that the fanaticism he encountered during his stay in Posen (Poznań) aroused his desire to 'travel to Berlin and, by means of Enlightenment, annihilate the remaining superstition that still adhered to me' (M 233). The superstition with which he had to contend is illustrated by the ethnographic descriptions, while the narrative sections project the search for Enlightenment back on to his childhood, by showing him to have had an innate curiosity and imagination which his environment does not understand and cannot satisfy. His principle, he tells us, was to 'think about everything for himself' (M 173). 'Thinking for oneself' is a repeated phrase (M 230, 265). This ideal comes from Kant, who declared in his essay 'What is Enlightenment?': '*Sapere aude!* have the courage to use your own intellect! is the watchword of Enlightenment.'[11] The centre of Enlightenment, for a Polish Jew, is Berlin which represents the goal both of Maimon's physical travels and of his intellectual development. When he is at last admitted to Berlin, for him the centre of Enlightenment, he suffers some disappointments. One day he goes into a dairy and finds the shopkeeper tearing up an old book to wrap butter in: Maimon discovers the book to be Christian Wolff's *Metaphysics*, and is astonished 'that anyone in such an enlightened city as Berlin could handle such important works so barbarously' (M 246).

The journey to the Enlightenment is not only geographical and intellectual, but also social. Maimon is expected to adopt civilized manners and discard the intonation and gesticulation associated with Polish Jews. On his arrival in Berlin his appearance struck some people as bizarre. One of Mendelssohn's friends, the philosopher Markus Herz, apparently reacted to Maimon as follows:

> At first this friend regarded me as a *talking animal* and was pleased by me just as one is pleased by a dog or by a starling that has learnt to utter a few words. His imagination was more stimulated by the *strange mixture* of *animal qualities* in my countenance, my choice of words and my entire outward behaviour with rationality in my ideas, than his intellect by the *content* of such conversation (M 250; Maimon's emphasis).

This makes Maimon sound like the exotic visitors from the South Seas who were received in Europe in the late eighteenth century: Auturu, who was brought from Tahiti to Paris by Bougainville, or Omai, whom Cook brought to London from his second voyage to Polynesia.[12] Maimon never, in fact, lost the characteristics that marked him out as a semi-assimilated Polish Jew. When he became excited in arguments, for example, he would adopt the sing-song usual in Talmudic disputation. 'Enlightenment' is not only an intellectual but a social ideal, implying a command of civilized manners and languages; Maimon indicates as much when he remarks that the French language 'was at that time considered the summit of Enlightenment' (M 269).[13]

Fromer is more unabashed about the fact that access to Western society requires mastery of numerous trivial skills. In a diary entry dated 1891, he reflects:

> I am now private tutor in one of the most respected Jewish-German families in Oświęcim. I also give lessons for 15 florins a month in

German, French, Latin, mathematics and fine art. I can also walk straight, speak High German, wear gloves, and no longer close my eyes in shame when I say to a lady 'I kiss your hand' or even do it. In company, too, I know perfectly how to bow, how to hold one's knife and one's fork. At this rate I shall soon feel the need to learn how to dance (F 137).

It is this aspect of assimilation, the acquisition of 'civilized' manners, that Kafka was to caricature some ten years later in his *Ein Bericht für eine Akademie* ('A Report for an Academy'), where an ape claims to have succeeded in becoming a human being and displays his social talents on the stage.

Fromer's autobiography is more obviously fictionalized than Maimon's. His favourite manner of beginning a chapter is to take the reader into a scene already in progess: for example, Chapter 4 starts with Fromer dozing over the Talmud which he is supposed to be studying with his father-in-law. Usually the imperfect tense is used, but Chapter 5 opens in the present tense with an external view of Fromer walking along the highway; in the third paragraph, we enter Fromer's mind, and in the fourth we return to past-tense narrative. Chapter 3 is more complicated: it begins, without reference to Fromer's own point of view, by describing the family's room as though from the viewpoint of an outsider, then moving into the consciousness of Fromer's mother and reporting her thoughts. To make matters more elaborate, an inward present-tense evocation of her thoughts alternates with a detached past-tense summary. And the narrator even interrupts the evocation of her thoughts to interpose German translations of the Yiddish words she uses (pp. 78–9). This is not yet stream of consciousness narration, but a rather artificial instance of free indirect speech, the varieties of which in nineteenth-century fiction have been well described by Roy Pascal.[14] Later the illusion of immediacy is maintained by very fictitious-looking letters and diary entries. Hence Fromer's autobiography is more inward than Maimon's, even if the devices by which he suggests inwardness are somewhat clumsily handled. Its structure lets him relive the despair and frustration of his youth. Unlike Maimon, who has consigned his early experience to the almost unimaginable geographical and cultural remoteness of his Polish past, Fromer conveys that his youthful experience still haunts him.

Just as the past is still present to Fromer, so the goal of Enlightenment has become suspect. Fromer scarcely uses the word Enlightenment ('Aufklärung') without irony. At an early stage he describes himself as 'an enlightened man' (F 50), but even before that he has developed doubts about reason and concluded that it is flimsy and unreliable (F 49). Later he refers to himself ironically as 'the enlightened man, with experience of the world, who had already read so many novels!' (F 90). When he is about to be expelled from Berlin by an anti-semitic policeman, he calls himself 'an enlightened Bakhur' (F 10). The Enlightenment is further trivialized when Fromer tells us that it suddenly spread through Łódź like an epidemic, so that people read heretical letters even in the *bays-medresh* (F 104). Thus the Enlightenment has been reduced to the most trivial secular knowledge, and such knowledge is also shown to be often extremely arid, as when Fromer tries to learn German by painfully memorizing the German and Latin names of the verb-tenses (F 100). From Fromer's disillusioned perspective, there seems to be no positive ideal for the assimilationist to struggle towards. He never suggests that secular learning is valuable in itself, and although he ends up in Berlin as a librarian in charge of Talmudic literature, he declares that he finds the Talmud repellent. He is not reacting against disillusionment with the West by taking a renewed interest in his own heritage. Rather he is in the ironic position of owing a foothold in Western society only to the specialized knowledge that marks him out irremediably as an Eastern Jew.

Both writers describe visits to the courts of miracle-working Hasidic rabbis or *tsaddikim*. To Maimon, the seeker after Enlightenment, this is the very heart of darkness, or rather of superstition. Maimon's narrative is of great historical importance: it provides almost the only glimpse of the early days of Hasidism by somebody who was not in sympathy with the movement.[15] He visited the court of Dov Ber, the *Magid* of Mezhirech, and decided that the great man was a charlatan. The *Magid* displayed his powers by addressing all the guests assembled at his table, most of them unknown to him, by their names and towns of origin. He then asked each to recite a verse of the Bible and delivered a discourse in which all these verses were combined into a connected whole. Soon, however, Maimon perceived that the subject-matter of Hasidic discourses was extremely limited, while the knowledge displayed by *tsaddikim* probably resulted from their good intelligence service: 'By means of correspondences, spies, and a certain degree of insight into human nature with which, thanks to the art of reading physiognomy and skilful questioning, they succeeded in drawing out indirectly the secrets of the heart, they acquired among these simple people a reputation for prophetic inspiration.' (M 204) As this passage implies, Maimon regards Hasidism as primarily a political conspiracy. He speaks of it as a 'secret society' (M 185) and compares it to the order of Illuminati, a society with egalitarian aims that flourished in Bavaria until its exposure in the mid-1780s (M 363).[16] He is wholly unimpressed by Hasidism as a religious movement.

Fromer, on the other hand, portrays himself as susceptible, though reluctantly, to the spell of Hasidism. In order to cure him of heretical inclinations, his mother sends the young Fromer to his uncle, the *tsaddik* of Szochlin (perhaps a fictitious name). His experiences there confirm the doubts about reason expressed at the end of the previous chapter. His youthful scepticism crumbles, first on seeing the faith displayed by a Germanized Jew whom he meets on the way, then when he finds himself amid a community of believers, and finally when faced with the Rabbi's authority. The Rabbi not only subjects Fromer to emotional pressure but confutes his Spinozistic scepticism with powerful arguments. There is no way of knowing how accurately this chapter reports Fromer's early experiences. It is structured as a gradual penetration through the outer circles of Hasidism (its effect on a Germanized Jew) to the centre of its authority. Along the way Fromer emphasises the absurd and superstitious aspects of Hasidism. Another traveller met *en route* tells an obviously ridiculous story about an alleged miracle. At Szochlin itself the Rabbi ceremonially exorcises a *dibbuk* or unclean spirit. And yet the pressure of communal belief is too much for the young Fromer: 'At that time I was a single, tiny intellect among thousands of stronger intellects who crowded upon me, swallowed me up and swept me away. My mental apparatus had almost ceased to function. I was guided only by the emotional impressions which assailed me so powerfully'(F 66).

In its substance, Fromer's account of Hasidism is not very different from Maimon's. Fromer likewise judges Hasidism by rational standards and condemns it as superstitious. Unlike Maimon, however, Fromer no longer trusts in the power of reason to overcome superstition. He knows that a superstition becomes irresistible when a whole community believes in it. Instead of Maimon's robust rationalism, Fromer has only the ineffectual conviction of being the only sane man among lunatics. Fromer does not concede that Hasidism has any positive qualities. He acknowledges its power while giving an entirely negative account of it. This distinguishes Fromer from Martin Buber, who as a boy also encountered Hasidism – admittedly as more of an outsider – and sensed the charismatic authority wielded by the *Tsaddik*. Buber, however, represents this authority as legitimate and Hasidism as a genuine and profound religious movement answering the deepest human needs.[17]

Both Maimon and Fromer acknowledge that the allure of the Gentile world is erotic as well as intellectual. Maimon, whose sexual interests were aroused at the age of eleven by the sight of a pretty girl bathing in the river, and appeased by an early marriage, recounts an occasion when Prince Radziwiłł, his daughter, and their retinue came to the village where Maimon's family lived, in order to attend a hunt. The young princess entered the room in the inn where the child Maimon was sitting behind the stove; Maimon could not help admiring her beauty, whereupon his father whispered to him: 'Little fool! In the next world the princess will heat the stove for us' (M 90). Maimon tells us that he was greatly perplexed by this: he welcomed the prospect, but felt sorry for the sumptuously-dressed princess who would have to perform such a menial and incongruous task. Since Maimon does not often pause to analyse complex emotions, this passage is all the more significant. It pinpoints the contrast between the drabness of Maimon's Jewish surroundings and the erotic allure of the Gentile world outside.

Sex is more prominent in the early pages of Fromer's narrative. Yiddish popular fiction, he tells us, generally recounts the struggles of a *Bakhur* who eventually acquires a doctorate and marries a Baroness. After reading one such novel, at the age of twelve, Fromer is tormented by sexual fantasies inspired by the beautiful heroine. Thus the Gentile world becomes sexually alluring. (It is characteristic that in his introduction to Maimon's *Lebensgeschichte* Fromer makes much of the episode of the Princess Radziwiłł, whom he calls a 'young, blooming fairy' (M 181).) At Szochlin, Fromer's uncle the Rabbi seems able to read his inmost thoughts, so that Fromer feels like Adam after the fall (p. 68). This implies that it is not just his intellectual heresies but also his sexual fantasies which the Rabbi perceives.

In the Szochlin episode it becomes clear that sex is the locus of authority and of resistance. The Rabbi believes that his daughter will bear the Messiah, and therefore strictly monitors her intercourse with her husband, permitting it only at auspicious times. But there is also, at the Rabbi's court, a young woman possessed by a *dibbuk*, which apparently entered her body at the same moment when she was sinning by kissing a young man. Fromer watches her being dragged through the town by a crowd, and observes how she blasphemes, insults the Rabbi, and boxes his ears. These two young women complement each other so neatly that Fromer's narrative seems even more like fiction. The one is allowed to practise legitimate sexuality only under the severest restriction. In the other, illegitimate sexuality breaks loose, and the most sacred rules of the community are violated. The female body, normally kept under strict control, is exhibited before the crowd. The pretext for this is possession by the spirit of a male apostate. Just as one young woman is supposed to bear the Messiah, a divine being which will assume human shape, the other carries in her body the Messiah's antithesis, a human being transformed into a demonic spirit. In the one case, sex is legitimated by a religious aim; in the other, a sexual misdemeanour unleashes indiscipline, heresy, and blasphemy. Thus Fromer's narrative implies that traditional Judaism is a tyranny of the intellect which can be dethroned, not by the intellectual counter-forces of the Enlightenment, but by a revolt of the body.

Authority constitutes a problem for both authors. Not only do they reject the authority of the *Magid* of Mezhirech and the Rabbi of Szochlin; by rebelling against their environment they reject the authority of their parents. The ideal of 'thinking for oneself' implies, indeed, the rejection of all authority as such. Their rebellion, however, makes it difficult for Maimon and Fromer to find models for mature behaviour. Hence self-control and discipline remain unresolved problems throughout their autobiographies and, in Maimon's case, throughout his life. The adult Maimon was a heavy drinker who led a very disorderly existence. He himself tells how Mendelssohn rebuked him for not living according to any plan (M 273) and admits that his studies were unsystematic (M 287). His friend and biographer Sabattia Joseph Wolff describes his quick temper, his untidy room (made worse by his pet dog Belline, which was not house-trained), his habit of wearing muddy boots and an overcoat all the time, and how, when not working, he spent most of his time in cafés and restaurants.[18]

It may be that, as Sander Gilman has suggested, Maimon's lack of self-control resulted from the allure of the Gentile world. In his account of his childhood, Maimon describes the antics of the local nobleman, Prince Radziwiłł. These included urinating in church; vandalizing synagogues; performing a blood-letting operation on a barber, and doing the man a severe injury; and on one occasion holding a luxurious banquet in the squalor of the inn kept by Maimon's grandfather. Gilman argues that Prince Radziwiłł provided Maimon with one pattern of behaviour, 'the pattern of the acceptable, powerful Christian'.[19] Since Radziwiłł enjoyed supreme freedom and used it to outrage others, he was the obvious model for a young man set on breaking with his community. Maimon on several occasions went out of his way to affront the orthodox. For example, in the wall of the synagogue at Poznań there was a stag's horn which, it was believed, would cause the instant death of anyone who touched it; Maimon touched it and made himself highly unpopular by remaining alive (M 233). On another occasion, a Rabbi showed Maimon a *shofar* and asked him: 'Do you know what that is?' to which Maimon boldly replied: 'Yes! It is the horn of a goat' (M 295). Gilman's suggestion is also supported by the extent to which Maimon's account of Radziwiłł reads like self-projection. Radziwiłł's desecration of synagogues matches Maimon's rebellion against traditional Judaism, while the blood-letting trick recalls the ineptitude Maimon was later to display as a doctor.

In the absence of actual models of behaviour, literary ones might suffice. Fromer, like many Eastern Jews of his time, greatly admired Schiller.[20] In his youth he appears to have been shocked to discover that Don Carlos is in love with his mother. In fact Don Carlos is in love with his stepmother, and there is no question of incest, but the suspicion of forbidden sexuality no doubt formed part of the play's allure. The play also attracted Fromer because of its other hero, the Marquis Posa, and his appeal to King Philip of Spain: 'Geben Sie Gedankenfreiheit!' ('Grant freedom of thought) which Fromer quotes from Yiddish as 'O Melech, gib die Machschowes frei!' (M 32). An intellectual rebel could readily identify with Posa. Much later in the book, just after he has made a successful personal appeal to the Emperor to grant him Prussian citizenship, Fromer quotes from a letter to a friend in which he cites another famous line: 'So forder ich mein

Jahrhundert in die Schranken' ('I call my century into the lists'). In writing to the Emperor, Fromer evidently identifies himself with Posa confronting King Philip. His letter to Wilhelm II is an extremely interesting document. It includes the following statement:

> I have now lived in Prussia for six years. During this period I have had the opportunity of becoming acquainted with this country's culture and of comparing it with the cultures that I know at first or second hand. I have become convinced that Prussia with its rigid discipline, its inflexible sense of law and order, and its extremely high level of education, is completely unsurpassed. This realization has increased my yearning desire to become the citizen of a state that I admire and love so infinitely, to which I would so gladly devote my feeble energies for the whole of my life (M 150).

Although Fromer may have said this to ingratiate himself, these sentiments are quite consistent with the intense admiration he expresses elsewhere for the achievements of German culture. He mentions not only Kant, Goethe, and Schiller, but the scientists Helmholtz and Virchow, the politician Bismarck, and the general Moltke (F 153). Moreover, many Jews born outside Prussian territory and in search of complete assimilation identified with Prussia, even when Austria was the obvious choice: Karl Emil Franzos and Fritz Mauthner are the best-known examples. Mauthner, indeed, so worshipped Bismarck that he added to his autobiography the invocation: ' Sancte Bismarck, magister Germaniae, ora pro nobis'.[21] Thus if Berlin was for Maimon the city of Mendelssohn, for Fromer it was the city of Bismarck. On a more personal level, the letter to Wilhelm II expresses Fromer's own desire for discipline and order. In youth he was warned that by leaving his community he might become a wastrel. Precisely because his studies required great determination, he responded to setbacks with depression and paralysis of the will. The letter dated April 1893 describes such a state (F 140–1). Hence the need for an externally imposed discipline. It is appropriate that after acquiring his doctorate Fromer became a librarian and was concerned with ordering, cataloguing and editing. He even includes in his autobiography a diatribe against Jewish scholars for their undisciplined and unsystematic writings, and an outline of his proposed concordance to the Talmud, including a schematic list of the subjects to be treated, which is presumably intended to display his own sense of order.

Despite his professed love of system, the latter part of Fromer's autobiography is extraordinarily scrappy. The letter to Wilhelm II is followed by numerous diary entries criticizing Jewish scholarship and complaining of the ignorance and obstructiveness of the library administrators. He then prints the full text of 'Das Wesen des Judentums', an abridged version of which appeared in *Die Zukunft* and led to his dismissal. There follow extracts from correspondence concerning his dismissal and other letters from eminent scholars refusing support for his concordance. The book ends with an account of the failure of his appeal and a Timon-like expression of loathing for mankind. Much of this material is excised from *Ghetto-Dämmerung*, the revised edition of his autobiography, whose title pays homage to Wagner and Nietzsche. *Ghetto-Dämmerung* ends, however, with references to the controversy aroused by the publication of *Der Organismus des Judentums*, and with the resolve to go on fighting. Ironically, both books exhibit the very fragmentariness and lack of structure that Fromer criticizes so severely as a typical vice of Jewish writers.

The essay 'Das Wesen des Judentums' is, however, connected with Fromer's account of his early life. It argues that Judaism aims at the supremacy of ethics and is hostile to aesthetics and logic, except when the latter serve ethical purposes. Judaism has therefore always been in conflict with human nature, which includes the desire for beauty and truth, and the backslidings recorded throughout the Old Testament are the expressions of these natural desires. By aesthetic needs, however, Fromer turns out to mean the desire for 'sensual pleasures' (F 210) in defiance of the restrictions placed on 'the flesh' (F 211); while the paradoxical charge of hostility to logic turns out to be polemic against the irrational rituals prescribed by the Talmud. Clearly Fromer is generalizing from his own experiences. While claiming to analyse Judaism as a whole, he is really attacking the sensual and intellectual restrictions imposed by his early environment.

The unnatural character of the Jews is the reason, in Fromer's opinion, why they always arouse anti-semitism. Referring to the recent Kishinev pogrom, he points out its similarity to pogroms in antiquity and the Middle Ages. Even if they do not suffer violence, Jews can never be accepted in Western society. The only way to gain acceptance is to cease to be Jews. The Jews must accept that Western culture, especially German culture, is superior to anything they can nowadays offer; they must discard the trivial logic-chopping inculcated by a Talmudic education, and learn simplicity and clarity. In a diary entry dated 1900 Fromer declares: 'We must shake off our compulsion to chop logic, to pick holes and make idle jests about everything. We must learn to think simply, to feel naïvely, to respect and love the beautiful for the sake of beauty, the true for the sake of truth'(F 154). The essay 'Das Wesen des Judentums' concludes with the advice: 'Disappear, with your Oriental physiognomies, your character at odds with your surroundings, your "mission", and, above all, your exclusively ethical outlook'(F 234).

Fromer's advocacy of total assimilation was extreme but not unique. Seven years earlier, the assimilated Jew Walther Rathenau, also writing in *Die Zukunft*, had condemned the Prussian Jews as an alien presence, 'an

Asiatic horde on the sands of the Mark', and urged them to discard their racial characteristics and become 'Jews who are German by nature and upbringing'.²² Both Fromer and Rathenau are demanding the impossible. They demand that Jews shall cease to be alien by becoming Germans, even if several generations are required. But the criteria by which they condemn Jews as alien are derived from the new racist discourse, which credits the German with inalienable qualities such as profundity, responsibility, creativity, and a holistic view of the world. Such qualities cannot be acquired; they can only be inherited. Any attempt to emulate them can always be dismissed as inauthentic, just as in Wagner's *Das Judentum in der Musik* ('Judaism in Music', 1850) westernized Jews are condemned as mere imitators of Western civilization. Jews are denounced for what they are, not for anything they do. Racism presents the Jewish question as a scientific, not a moral matter, and affects a scientifically neutral attitude.²³ Both Rathenau and Fromer betray their acceptance of *völkisch* discourse by their use of organic imagery. To Rathenau the German Jews are 'not a living limb of the people, but an alien organism in its body'.²⁴ Fromer denounces anti-semites by calling them 'the boils on the body of the host people, produced by the unassimilable foreign body' (F 254). Both imply that the Jews are bacteria, endangering the health of the body they inhabit, and that the assimilation of the Jews is prohibited by the laws of nature.²⁵

Given this insistence on complete assimilation, how does Fromer present Maimon in his introduction to the latter's autobiography? Naturally he depicts Maimon's assimilation as a failure, claiming that his cast of mind remained Talmudic. His philosophical works, despite their profundity, are unstructured, clumsily written, full of hair-splitting arguments, and almost impossible to follow (F 31). He remained a 'barbarian' (F 32), although a sincere and honest one; and he received the same kind of admiration that Polish Jews bestow on their *tsaddikim*. This is indeed a back-handed compliment. Fromer deplores the fact that Maimon did not adopt a practical profession: evidently the only way in which Maimon could have escaped from his Eastern-Jewish heritage would have been to abandon the life of the intellect altogether. His representation of Maimon and Maimon's environment as barbaric elicited an apposite comment from Franz Rosenzweig, in a private letter:

> It is nonsense to describe the condition of the Jews at that time as 'barbaric' ('decline' etc.). We are talking about a self-sufficient culture. Only the individual (Maimon) who abandons it, becomes a barbarian. Seen from outside, without linguistic or factual knowledge, such a culture can only be understood as barbarism; but the present-day German system *also* seems barbaric to Westerners, though it is just different.²⁶

Moreover, Fromer undermines Maimon's entire project of assimilation by disparaging the Enlightenment. He asserts that Frederick the Great had assembled an 'intellectual aristocracy' of philosophers and writers who were just as devoted to useless learning as the Talmud scholars from whom Maimon had escaped. Thus Maimon 'found here essentially the same situation that he had left' (p. 28). If Maimon was accepted, therefore, it was in a Berlin that was already Judaized, and thus it was not real acceptance. This shows that Fromer's own attitude to German culture has come full circle. Originally he set out from Łódź in search of the Enlightenment. Now he has concluded that the Enlightenment was not truly German. Assimilation to German culture has become impossible because in the meantime German culture has been redefined: the international humanism of the Enlightenment has been replaced by racist chauvinism. It is in accepting the Germans' changing definition of what is 'German' that Fromer surrenders most pathetically to his host culture.

Fromer makes a revealing comment on the incident in the *Lebensgeschichte* when Maimon, after a reverse in Amsterdam, contemplates suicide but cannot quite bring himself to jump into the water. 'Thus,' says Fromer, 'he stands for a while, bending over the water: in his head the civilized man, in his legs the ghetto Jew' (M 23). This implies that the ghetto Jew is not fully human but does instead possess an animal-like will to live which becomes weakened by civilization. And it recalls a passage in Fromer's own memoirs when he reflects that despite all his efforts to acquire a Western education he is still basically a ghetto student: 'I am and remain the *Bakhur* without a future. Yes, the *Bakhur*. A modern person in my place would have the courage to put an end to his wretched existence. But I whine and complain and cling to life with the cowardice of the Polish Jew' (F 143). These passages encapsulate Fromer's understanding of the Jewish problem. The intellectual who has left the ghetto is neither one thing nor the other. He cannot be accepted in Western society, but he cannot return to the community of the ghetto. Caught between the two, he has not even the strength of character to commit suicide. Even when all allowances have been made for Fromer's bitterness and eccentricity, the comparison between him and Maimon casts a harsh light on the 'German-Jewish symbiosis'. It suggests that in the intervening hundred years the transition from the traditional community to Western society had become, if anything, more difficult, and that Jews were tempted to respond to the difficulties by turning their frustration against themselves and their fellow-Jews.

NOTES

1 On spiritual autobiography, see M. H. Abrams, *Natural Supernaturalism: Tradition and Revolt in Romantic Literature* (New York, 1971), ch.2. On traditions of Jewish

autobiography, see Natalie Zemon Davis, 'Fame and secrecy: Leon Modena's *Life as an early modern autobiography*', in *The Autobiography of a Seventeenth-Century Venetian Rabbi: Leon Modena's 'Life of Judah'*, ed. Mark R. Cohen *et al.* (Princeton, 1988), pp. 50–70; Alan Mintz, 'Guenzburg, Lilienblum, and the shape of Haskalah autobiography', *Association for Jewish Studies Review*, 4 (1979), 71–110.

2 George Eliot, *Daniel Deronda* (Harmondsworth, 1967), p. 436.

3 *Salomon Maimon's Lebensgeschichte von ihm selbst geschrieben und herausgegeben von K.P. Moritz* (Berlin, 1792–3); *Salomon Maimon's Lebensgeschichte, mit einer Einleitung und mit Anmerkungen herausgegeben von Dr. Jakob Fromer* (Munich, 1911), quoted as M and page number; Salomon Maimon, *An Autobiography*, tr. J. Clark Murray (Paisley and London, 1888). Jakob Fromer, *Vom Ghetto zur modernen Kultur: eine Lebensgeschichte* (Charlottenburg, 1906), quoted as F and page number; *Ghetto-Dämmerung: Eine Lebensgeschichte* (Berlin, 1911). All translations are my own.

4 Quoted in Samuel Hugo Bergman, *The Philosophy of Salomon Maimon*, tr. Noah J. Jacobs (Jerusalem, 1967), p. 5.

5 See Franz Kafka, *Tagebücher 1910–1923* (Frankfurt, 1951), p. 242.

6 Besides his autobiography, Fromer's principal works are *Das Wesen des Judentums* (Berlin, 1905); *Der Organismus des Judentums* (Charlottenburg, 1909); *Der Talmud: Geschichte, Wesen and Zukunft* (Berlin, 1920). I have seen his pamphlet *Messianismus und Völkerbund* (n.p. [Berlin], 1930), but not *Die messianische Weltordnung: Idee und Plan einer Weltorganisation* (Potsdam, 1925). The dates of Fromer's birth and death are given in Renate Heuer (ed.), *Bibliographia Judaica: Verzeichnis jüdischer Autoren deutscher Sprache*, vol.1 (Frankfurt and New York, 1982), p. 109. Of those reference books that mention him, the one with the longest entry by far is the anti-semitic compilation *Sigilla Veri: Lexikon der Juden, -Genossen und -Gegner aller Zeiten und Zonen, insbesondere Deutschlands, der Lehren, Gebräuche, Kunstgriffe und Statistiken der Juden sowie ihrer Gaunersprache, Trugnamen, Geheimbünde usw.*, ed. E. Ekkehard, 2nd edn. (n.p., 1929), vol.2, pp. 586–9. While much of this consists of excerpts from his autobiography, there is also some gossipy information about the controversies he was embroiled in. I am grateful to the staff of the Wiener Library, London, for helping me in my inquiries about Fromer.

7 On systematic ethnography, Mohammed Rassem and Justin Stagl (eds.) *Statistik und Staatsbeschreibung in der Neuzeit* (Paderborn, 1980); on statistical accounts of the Eastern Jews, see Wolfgang Häusler, *Das galizische Judentum in der Habsburgermonarchie im Lichte der zeitgenössischen Publizistik und Reiseliteratur von 1772–1848* (Vienna, 1979).

8 The only survey of ghetto fiction to date is J. W. H. Stoffers, *Juden und Ghetto in der deutschen Literatur bis zum Ausgang des Weltkrieges* (Graz, 1939). See also Ritchie Robertson, 'Roth's *Hiob* and the traditions of ghetto fiction', in Helen Chambers (ed.) *Co-existent Contradictions: Joseph Roth in Retrospect* (Riverside, CA., 1991) pp. 185–200.

9 Karl Emil Franzos, *Der Pojaz* (Königstein/Ts., 1979), pp. 36–7. Cf. Günther A. Höfler, *Psychoanalyse und Entwicklungsroman: Karl Emil Franzos, 'Der Pojaz'* (Munich, 1987), p. 91.

10 Heinrich Heine, *Sämtliche Schriften*, ed. Karl Briegleb (6 vols., Munich, 1968–76), vi.133, lines 128–30.

11 'Beantwortung der Frage: Was ist Aufklärung?' in Immanuel Kant, *Was ist Aufklärung? Aufsätze zur Geschichte und Philosophie* (Göttingen, 1975), p. 55.

12 See Urs Bitterli, *Cultures in Conflict* (Cambridge, 1989), pp. 167–8.

13 On this aspect of Jewish assimilation, see Peter Freimark, 'Language behaviour and assimilation: the situation of the Jews in northern Germany in the first half of the nineteenth century', *Leo Baeck Institute Year Book*, 24 (1979), 157–77. With reference

to the Enlightenment, see Martin L. Davies, 'The theme of communication in *Anton Reiser*: a reflection of the feasibility of the Enlightenment', *Oxford German Studies*, 12 (1981), 18–38.

14 Roy Pascal, *The Dual Voice* (Manchester, 1977).
15 See Simon Dubnow, *Geschichte des Chassidismus*, tr. A. Steinberg (2 vols., Berlin, 1931), i. 139–44.
16 See J.M. Roberts, *The Mythology of the Secret Societies* (London, 1972), ch.5.
17 See 'Mein Weg zum Chassidismus', in Martin Buber, *Werke* (3 vols., Munich, 1963), iii. 959–73.
18 Sabattia Joseph Wolff, *Maimoniana oder Rhapsodien zur Charakteristik Salomon Maimon's* (Berlin, 1813).
19 Sander L. Gilman, *Jewish Self-Hatred: Anti-Semitism and the Hidden Language of the Jews* (Baltimore, 1986), p. 129. This book contains the most important study of Maimon's *Lebensgeschichte* to date.
20 See Franzos, 'Schiller in Barnow', in his *Aus Halb-Asien: Kulturbilder aus Galizien, der Bukowina, Südrussland und Rumänien* (2 vols., Leipzig, 1876), i. 69–90; Steven E. Aschheim, *Brothers and Strangers: The East European Jew in German and German Jewish Consciousness, 1800–1923* (Madison, Wis., 1982), pp. 29–30.
21 On Franzos, see Fred Sommer, *'Halb-Asien': German Nationalism and the Eastern European Works of Karl Emil Franzos* (Stuttgart, 1984); on Mauthner, Joachim Kühn, *Gescheiterte Sprachkritik: Fritz Mauthners Leben und Werk* (Berlin, 1975), esp. p. 258.
22 'Höre, Israel!' in Walter Rathenau, *Schriften*, ed. Arnold Harttung *et al.* (Berlin, 1965), pp. 89–93 (quotations from pp. 89 and 91); originally published in *Die Zukunft* on 6 March 1897. For another statement of extreme assimilationism, see Karl Kraus, *Die Fackel*, no.23 (November 1989), p. 7.
23 See *Rembrandt als Erzieher. Von einem Deutschen* (Leipzig, 1890); Fritz Stern, *The Politics of Cultural Despair: A Study in the Rise of the Germanic Ideology* (Berkeley, 1961).
24 Rathenau, 'Höre, Israel!', p. 89.
25 On this imagery, see Alex Bein, 'The Jewish parasite: notes on the semantics of the Jewish problem, with special reference to Germany', *Leo Baeck Institute Year Book*, 9 (1964), 3–40.
26 Letter of 9 July 1916 in Franz Rosenzweig, *Briefe* (Berlin, 1935), pp. 97–9.

# JAN CZYŃSKI AND THE QUESTION OF EQUALITY OF RIGHTS FOR ALL RELIGIOUS FAITHS IN POLAND

Adam Gałkowski

Jan Czyński (1801–1867), political activist and campaigner for social causes, journalist, essayist, novelist, dramatist and lawyer by training, is one of the most interesting and most controversial figures of the Polish 'Great Emigration'.[1] He came from a wealthy Warsaw Frankist family. His father was a captain in the National Army during the Kościuszko Insurrection (1794). After graduating from Warsaw University's Department of Law and Administration (1822), he became an advocate in the Civil Tribunal court in Lublin (1822–1830). He took an active and leading part in the November Rising in the Lublin region (where, among other activities, he was the organizer of the National Guard and publisher of the *Kurier Lubelski*) and in Warsaw. As a vice-president of the Society of Patriots (*Towarzystwo Patriotów*), and excellent speaker and essayist, he quickly gained the reputation of being a radical and a democrat.

Following the collapse of the Rising he emigrated to France. Initially linked with Joachim Lelewel's *Komitet Narodowy Polski* (Polish National Committee – KNP) and later with the *Towarzystwo Demokratyczne Polskie* (Polish Democratic Society – TDP – 1834–1835), he gradually withdrew from an active role in émigré political life. For virtually the whole of 1835 he published, together with Szymon Konarski, the journal *Północ* (midnight) However at the turn of the year he finally broke with the Society (TDP), as a consequence of deep-rooted differences with the Polish Democrats. Certainly, Czyński's political, scholarly and literary aspirations were now extending ever more frequently beyond the confines of émigré life.

For the next eight years he was absorbed by his interests – political, social, academic and literary – which bore fruit in his two 'Cossack novels' (1836–1837), his publication of *Russie pittoresque* (1837–1838) and his Fourierist essays. These interests were no doubt furthered by the fact that Czyński managed to adapt fairly easily to French surroundings, and his political and literary activity brought him the recognition and friendship of well-known French, Belgian and German liberals, democrats and socialists.

He returned to émigré affairs in 1843 – this time as a spokesman for the interests of the Polish middle-class (His *Echo Miast Polskich* – Echo of Polish Towns – was one of the most interesting and original Polish periodicals of the 19th century). At the same time he intensified his efforts in the struggle for the emancipation of the Jewish community, and collaborated for twenty years with the Journal *Archives Israëlites*. His political views underwent a thorough transformation – from a position of irreconcilable enmity towards the circle of Prince Adam Czartoryski, which he maintained until the mid-1830s, he eventually came around to cooperating with them (1843). After the collapse of the 1848/9 revolutions in Europe, he once again turned his back on political activity (this time in favour of literary and theatrical interests) only to take it up again in 1861 in connection with the developing situation in Poland. He spent the last year of his life in London, where he created the Union of Polish Workers (*Zjednoczenie Pracowników Polskich*). From 1864 onwards he wrote regularly to the *Gazeta Narodowa* in Lwów, which printed some 280 of his contributions in its columns. During the years 1865–1867, he also took part in the sessions of the First International organized to discuss the Polish question.

Czyński was an original and controversial figure. He fell out with the 'emigration' over his social and political outlook (his programme for the emancipation of the middle-classes and the Jews and his attempts to adapt the theories of French socialists to Polish conditions), and he had little respect either for national figures (amongst others, he critized Adam Mickiewicz and Joachim Lelewel). He is remembered as the most famous of the Polish 'Fourierists' of the 1830's and 1840's and one of the most famous populansers and commentators on these theories on French soil. As a 'defender' of the Jews, the man of letters and dramatist enjoyed more authority among outsiders than he did among his own people – witness the numerous translations of his works into other languages, and his membership of the Paris Historical and the French Literary Association.

Religion was fundamental to Jan Czyński's general outlook and philosophy. Indeed it was the nub of several disagreements, polemics and mutual recriminations with such people as Mickiewicz and Towiański. His religious outlook was the object of often bitter criticism, and provided a field for innovatory concepts in general (Fourierism) as well as for projects for the internal administration of a future, free Poland in particular.

Both contemporaries and those who have come after him, have accused Czyński of anti-clericalism – and they certainly had grounds for doing so. How else should one describe someone who campaigned with all his strength and resources against ultra-montanism, bigotry, the clergy and the 'official' church? A man who, in the columns of *Północ* denounced

Father Hieronim Kajsiewicz and his group of friends; who, in his 'Cossack' novels ('The Cossack' and 'Stenko the Rebel') called the Roman Catholic priesthood in the pre-partition Republic the servants and agents of Rome, acting against the interests of their own country? In this connection Czyński even came to the conclusion that complete emancipation from Rome (along the lines of the Orthodox faith) and the creation of a national church would be to Poland's advantage.[2] He also argued, from the standpoint of a rationalist and a follower of the laws of nature, against the Church's excessively one-sided view of mankind. 'The thought of bringing contentment only to the spirit in beings which consist of both a body and a spirit is not enough', he contended in *Północ* in 1843.[3] 'Man is what he is – a moral and physical being. No-one can change this two-sided creature of nature; neither laws, nor upbringing, nor persuasion, nor force. Accordingly, the teaching of Christ, who did not view mankind as God created it, as it is, but rather regarded people as he would have liked them to be, is radically false.' Moreover, 'spirit and body are indivisible in Man', mankind should aim to maintain 'peace and harmony' between the two extremes of its existence (this was one of the tenets of the Fourierists!). Christianity, in Czyński's opinion, was 'love, sacrifice and brotherhood' – and so it was essential to combat the intolerance of the Catholic Church which violated the 'cardinal laws of nature'.

Going beyond the moral side of this issue (which is of secondary importance here and has the flavour of provocation), we should appreciate that Czyński understood the laws of nature in a very broad sense. He was concerned above all about freedom and equality of rights for all religious faiths, and about tolerance. Catholic Poland should be a liberal Poland, wrote Czynski in 1848, once again harking back to the religious mosaic on the territory of the former Republic.[4]

A leading element in the broad problem of the emancipation of the under-privileged classes in feudal society was the Jewish question in Poland. At least this was how Jewish writers or those of Jewish origin (J. Czyński, S. Hernisz, L. Lubliner) perceived it. At any rate, apart from other characteristics, it also possessed the specific feature on Polish soil that it was one of the last phases in the process of social emancipation.

'The label of conversion clung so firmly to Czyński, to his person, to his political and literary activity, that it could not be detached. From under the red cap of the Polish Jacobin, the skull-cap became increasingly visible' – one contributor wrote in *Myśl Narodowa* in 1933,[5] providing in this way evidence of the longevity of a certain chauvinist tendency in Polish political thought; a tendency which, to be sure, became more marked during the two inter-war decades, but which had its equivalent in attitudes of dislike, or even hostility, towards Jews, in the first half of the nineteenth century.

Czyński, it is true, was a Catholic, but he too was the victim of such attitudes, since from his schooldays he suffered humiliation because of his

Jewish origins.[6] Even if such incidents only occurred sporadically, they left a sufficiently clear stigma to remain the sources of complexes and, perhaps, also, of a particular kind of sensitivity. This fact weighed, it seems, in no small degree, on his devotion to the matter of emancipating Jews in Poland. As a campaigner and essayist, Czyński left a very rich output in this field. In historiograpy, indeed, the label, 'Jewish essayist' has become attached to him.[7] At times this had a ring of contempt,[8] and on occasions, much provoked, Czyński gave evidence of his faith.[9] His ideological beliefs as a democrat and a freemason were, he claimed, more important motives for interesting himself in the Jewish question than his Frankist descent.

We should remind ourselves also perhaps of the material side of this affair – how this defender of Jewish interests in Poland had (for over twenty years) an assured salary thanks to a position on the Northern Railways Board in Paris. The largest shareholder in the firm was James Rothschild, the famous banker, who had soon directed his closest attention to the Polish emigrant. It remains true, however, that Czyński served the cause of Polish Jewry with as much dedication before, as after, meeting the Rothschild family.

The first recorded views of Jan Czyński on the subject date from the period of the November Rising, and are linked with the attempt to foster that Rising. On 14 December 1830 he spoke publicly to the Jews of Lublin, appealing for their support in the Poles' cause. 'The young people declared their willingness to sacrifice their strength and their health on the altar of the homeland. Tears appeared in the eyes of the Jews gathered there. After this', recalled Czyński later,[10] 'I went along to the local unit commander, accompanied by a group of Jewish volunteers, and by the joyful cheers of the crowd which followed on behind us. It was the most beautiful day of my life.' References to the part played by Polish Jews in the Rising appear also in the *Kurier Lubelski* which Czyński edited and published.[11] In December 1830, moreover, he presented a memorandum on the Jewish question to the Warsaw Society of Patriots (*Towarzystwo Patriotów*), but this was rejected by the majority.[12]

## JOACHIM LELEWEL AND THE POLISH NATIONAL COMMITTEE'S APPEAL TO JEWS

Emigration to the west in no way weakened Jan Czyński's interest in the Jewish question. As was soon to become clear, the move resulted in his participation in several important initiatives. The first of these was the appeal of the Polish National Committee to the Jews (the Polish language version bears the date 3 November 1831).[13] It is true that Jan Czyński's signature is missing from the bottom of the document, but there is no doubt that he played a part in its drafting.[14] In any case the authorship of the document has aroused many doubts, while confirming at the same time the existence of serious divergences on this question between leading democrat campaigners within the Emigration. Furthermore, although we cannot define precisely the influence Czyński had on the final shape of the appeal, there remains no doubt that it was he who years later provoked discussion on the origins of the document and on the position of Joachim Lelewel.[15] But this comes later. At this time, during the years 1832–33, Czyński's relations with Lelewel were still extremely cordial. The senior scholar even praised his younger colleague from the National Committee on his brochure on the Jews.[16] Czyński's letter to *Archives Israelites* in 1843 passed without an echo in emigration, as did the work of Leon Hollaenderski on the Jews in Poland. Only the publication in 1861 of the letters between the two men, a few months after Lelewel's death, aroused a reaction.

The origin of the dispute was the course of a meeting in a Paris hotel on the rue Cordier at the end of 1832. On that occasion Bartłomiej Beniowski is supposed to have spoken first in support of the emancipation of Jews in Poland. In response, Lelewel, the president of the KNP reportedly burst out in anger, ' . . . I hate Jews, they are leeches on our country, spies, traitors; let them go to Jerusalem, I have no trust in converts until the sixth generation – they are an accursed race.'[17] In the opinion of Lubliner, also an advocate of the idea of the emancipation of Polish Jews, and present at the meeting, the assertion that Lelewel has spoken these words was a falsehood deriving from 'the personal hatred of Mr Czyński'. As regards Hollaenderski's publication, however, 'and the accusations against Lelewel manifested in it, all the sweet-scented praises which poured forth in support of Mr Czyński, did not come from Mr Hollaenderski's pen – but from the conceited vanity of Czyński himself'. In the process Lubliner refutes Hollaenderski's argument about the alleged Jewish origins of Lelewel who, he claimed, 'although of Catholic grandparents, was, as a philosopher and a republican, always a supporter of the emancipation of Polish Jews'. Lelewel's defender also expresses sorrow that 'old quarrels' in Polish-Jewish relations have been drawn out into the light of day. And this, at a moment which, by any measure, was most unsuitable, when in Poland 'the union, or rather fusion of Polish Catholics and Polish Jews was taking place in a miraculous fashion.'[18] The view that Lelewel's signature under the Polish National Committee's appeal to the Jews had been secured by trickery or deceit (by Beniowski), has naturally had an influence on historiography.[19] Contemporaries however were outraged and embarrassed rather that a shadow should have been thrown across the great scholar's reputation. Jan Nepomucen Janowski also spoke out on the matter, admitting that after so many years he could not with complete certainty remember who had, and who had not, been at the meeting at the Rue Cordiers. Nevertheless he was inclined to agree with Czyński on the point that Lelewel during this period 'had not expressed himself in support of the Jews.'[20]

Czyński however, in response to Lubliner, confessed that the sharpness of his response, and that from an Orthodox Jew, had surprised him greatly.[21] As regards the reproach that he was reviving 'old quarrels', he confessed that he had been aiming at something else entirely. It had been intended as 'his closing statement', the summation of thirty years of dedicated work in this field. Indeed the letters published under the collective title *Israel en Pologne* were intended as a kind of testament. Returning to the subject of the dispute, he considered that one should not mistake the achievements made in one discipline with the mistakes committed in another. Lubliner was wrong – argued Czyński – when he maintained that Lelewel took part in the 1832 meeting called to express support for the Jews. It had been completely the other way around. He had outraged Beniowski with his 'prejudiced comments' about Orthodox Jews. For his part Beniowski confirmed this version, although he admitted that after so many years, argument about the issue 'could neither help, nor harm' Lelewel.[22]

What happened in reality is difficult to determine in view of the fundamental difference of views held by those who participated in the meeting. Many years had passed. Time had wiped the details from their memories. What remains an indisputable fact however, is the KNP's appeal itself which was an important gesture by émigré democrats towards inhabitants of the Jewish faith in Poland; this – despite the idealization it contains of Polish-Jewish relations, and its vagueness on the question of equality of rights. In 1861 polemics on the subject were indeed unnecessary – but that is another matter.

THE COMMITTEE FOR THE EMANCIPATION OF JEWS

The Appeal of the KNP was a collective deed and an expression of compromise. For Czyński the episode was an interesting experience and it proved helpful to him in thinking out his own, independent ideas. An opportunity to set his ideas out occurred only a few months later. Bartłomiej Beniowski, one of those Jews who, in Czyński's words, ' . . . in order to achieve a great deal of good for his fellow Jews made a pretence of converting to Christianity', launched the idea (most probably at the end of February or the beginning of March 1833) of creating a 'society the aim of which would be to free Jews from the yoke of Polish opinion'.[23] The idea met with Lelewel's approval,[24] and also gradually received increasing support from known figures in French political life, who accepted an invitation to the inaugural meeting of the society.[25] The venerable Lafayette was named honorary president.

The project, which had been Beniowski's idea, became the creature of others, both in the organizational sense and as regards its aims. Most energy in this direction was shown by Jan Czyński who found out about the Society from Lelewel. In his letter to Lelewel of 7 March 1833, he emphasized its importance and expressed hope in the victory of truth and justice over prejudice, while not concealing his fears that success in the matter might be some way off.[26]

Czyński took over responsibility for organizational matters.[27] His brochure on Polish Jews, published in November 1833, was a direct answer to the information and propaganda needs of the Committee.[28] In fact, however, it saw the light of day only after the Committee had ceased its activity. From the end of April the Committee had faced a crisis of a political character. The French authorities strongly opposed any secret societies of a republican or a revolutionary nature. Because of this Adolf Crémieux put forward the proposal (at the suggestion of Baron Rothschild) that the Committee be reorganized in order, on the one hand, to assuage the fears of the Government, and on the other, to save the Committee. Czyński and other democrats, however, were against this suggestion.[29]

A further factor which hampered the normal working of the Lafayette Committee was the apperance of divisions and quarrels among the Polish emigration over the Jewish question. Czyński had already broken with Tadeusz Krępowiecki, Stanisław Worcell, Kazimierz Puławski, and J.N. Janowski. Ignacy R. Pluzański in turn, as a member of the Polish Democratic Society, criticised the aim of emancipating the Jews, as this would, in his opinion, automatically place other minority and social questions at a disadvantage.[30]

The Committee ceased to function in the autumn of 1833,[31] although officially its existence only ceased after Lafayette's death in May 1834. This occurrence – as researchers have pointed out with some justification[32] – was partly due to the radicalism of its most active member, Jan Czyński, and partly due to the effect of existing political conditions in Europe (the strengthening of reactionary tendencies).

'THE JEWISH QUESTION AS A EUROPEAN ISSUE'

Czyński wrote this brochure during a three-month period of exile in Brussels (August-October 1841). Szymon Konarski, helping him at that time to copy it, thought it very important.[33] After his return to the French capital, Czyński began at once to prepare an expanded, Polish language version.[34] There was a problem over money though. It concerned a sum of 200 francs which the author had hoped to receive (thanks to the mediation and sponsorship of Antoni Ostrowski) from General Lafayette.[35] These efforts in all likelihood came to nothing, since we have no evidence that the Polish version of the work was completed, and still less is known about proposed translations into English and German.[36]

In spite of this 'La Question des Juifs polonaises' was not only well received by French and Jewish opinion, it became something of a success for the author. Evidence of its positive reception is the opening of the columns of French periodicals such as *Reformateur Tribune, Constitutionel,* or *Courier Français* to Czyński.[37] This period was a turning point in the efforts of the essayist and campaigner to break out of the rut of émigré life. Adolf Crémieux, later a deputy and chairman of the Consistory, published a special letter to the French people in *Le National*. In it he cited the attitude of Polish Catholics as an example, adding that ' ... from this moment the name of Mr Czyński will be recorded in the memory of the Jewish nation'.[38] Adam Gurowski also praised the author's brochures and particularly his way of writing the absolute truth: ' ... in order to remedy evil', as he wrote in one issue of his journal *Przyszłość*, 'we must first get to know it'.[39] At the same time he expressed the view that Poland ' ... would be reborn – only by the participation of all its people, without consideration to creed or custom'. A letter, which was apparently 'very complimentary', arrived from the Polish Democratic Society (TDP). Antoni Ostrowski observed also that Czyński's brochure was ' ... the first publication whose subject matter drew the attention of the enlightened philanthropists of France and as it presents the question of Polish Jews from a sound point of view, it would create a positive impression in this country'[41] Lelewel's opinion was, as we have already seen, positive, although rather off-hand.

Czyński's, aim as he stated in the introduction, was to speak for the Jews, who ' ... are reproached generally for not having taken part in the last Rising' as well as demonstrating a lack of commitment to Poland. 'We hope to help our compatriots and to fulfil a duty to humanity in making clear the real reasons why the Jews unfortunately displayed an indifference to our cause in this disastrous war', and also to show that Poles had every reason to believe that they would find in their midst a 'powerful ally'.[42]

In an attempt to justify this last contention, Czyński referred to their common past; he pointed out what had united and what had divided the two peoples. He then referred to the beginning of Jewish settlement on Polish territory, where they had found the only safe haven in Europe (p.5). This harmony, however, as a result of Catholic religious intolerance led eventually to the situation at the eve of the partitions, whereby many of the religious minorities living in the Republic quite naturally gravitated towards the neighbouring states, contributing to the weakening of Poland's position in Europe and to the violation of her national sovereignty. There existed the need for radical reforms. Major obstacles however, were, ' ... the priests and the gentry class' (p.9). Their domination had not been shaken either by the Constitution of the Third of May, or by the Napoleonic period (p.10). Subsequently the Constitution of the Congress Kingdom had given the Roman Catholic Church 'particular protection' (p.11). As evidence of this tendency, Czyński cited the order of the vice-regent of the Congress Kingdom, General Józef Zajączek, expelling more than a thousand Jewish families from the centre of Warsaw. All of these Jews, irrespective of how prosperous they were, were forced to abandon the places in which they left their means of livelihood (p.12) Czyński also referred to the discrimination against the Jewish population in the taxation policy of the finance minister, Ksawery Drucki-Lubecki.[43] So that this picture should not be too one-sided, Czyński drew attention also to the importance of the political ideas of the Enlightenment whose 'truth and justice have undermined privilege and prejudice' (p.15) He referred at the same time to examples of Jews who had displayed great patriotism during in 1794 Kościuszko Rising (Berek Joselewicz) and to the social advances made by others (Abraham Stern, member of the Society of Friends of Learning in Warsaw).

On balance though, in the opinion of the writer, retrograde tendencies now predominated – and ones which were harmful to Poland. In any case, neither the gentry nor the clergy, with their unwillingness to find an answer to the burgeoning minority problems (both religious and secular) on Polish soil, had very much influence on the policies of the partitioning powers. One example was the behaviour of Grand Duke Konstanty, on whose orders Jews in the Congress Kingdom had to submit to 'unparallelled' persecution (p.17) and who, following a *ukase* of Tsar Nicholas I in 1827, deported more than thirty thousand Jewish children to the depths of Russia, with the intention of conscripting them to the army.[44] It is understandable then, that – as the author further asserts in his brochure – 'the indignation of the Jews with the Russian system' coincided with the outbreak of 29 November 1830. What was it all worth, though, when the insurgents' Sejm did not issue 'the slightest protest against the persecutions the Jews had had to endure under Tsarist rule?' (p.19); and the Minister of War, General Franciszek Morawski, opposed the recruitment of Jews to the army?[45] A similar reluctance on the part of the authorities showed – we read further (p.19) – in almost all their subsequent acts. A. Ostrowski also refers to this in a letter to Czyński supporting the idea of the Committee (pp.20–2). The author of the brochure also seized the opportunity to dispose of the belief that the Jewish population harboured an aversion to cultivating the soil. How were Jews to farm, when almost all of the land in Poland was in the hands of the gentry? (p.23).

Czyński perceived a differentiation in the Jewish community; he writes of the residents of large towns desiring to be transformed from 'Jews' into 'Poles of the Mosaic faith', and of a more numerous category 'groaning under the yoke of prejudice and under the influence of fanatical rabbis' (p.25). 'That is why', confirms the writer, 'while the first category wanted to become soldiers of the Polish army, the second category considered creating a Jewish legion.' Neither of these standpoints, however, does he condemn. He admits though, that as long as Poland was not independent, there was little hope for an improvement in the position of Jews. These two issues were linked by a common fate and a common enemy. The question of Polish Jews is therefore a European question, because the situation of 'three million people cannot be a matter of indifference to any friend of humanity' (p. 27).[46]

The strength of Czyński's publication lies in the sense of balancing accounts, of providing information and of demasking; the weaker side is his programme for the future, which is restricted to a general proposal for a Polish-Jewish alliance. This was caused, though, not because the author lacked ideas as to how those relations should develop, but because of assumptions contained in the brochure. For he did have ideas. And they were perfectly lucid: 'The number of Orthodox Jews is in Poland quite high,' Czyński wrote to Ostrowski on 29 December 1833, 'and to extend political rights to all of them, given the present backwardness of the peasants, would give the Jews an advantage over the peasantry. In looking for a way around this, not only do we not need to ruin the Jewish community, we should stimulate and enliven it. These Orthodox Jews, who would like to become Poles, should be regarded as our brothers and every freedom should be given to them. The rest, whose thoughts are preoccupied with the Messiah and Jerusalem, should be permitted to dream of their saviour and their homeland. We will not return to Poland ... unless we have a weapon in our hands, we will not regain our homeland ... unless we spill blood in battle; we will not fight battles in the Napoleonic style – we must mobilize the masses. In this time of struggle, the task of saving Poland deserves the highest sacrifice. Jews therefore must be compelled to make a splendid contribution ... '

We see from this, that as early as 1833, Czyński had a clear idea of how the Jewish question in Poland should be resolved. In return for Jewish support for the independence struggle and their loyalty towards the reborn state, the Jews would be guaranteed respect for their separate national, cultural and religious traditions. This liberal vision of minority group relations resulted from the author's democratic convictions and, more or less consciously, harkened back to the traditions of tolerance of the old Republic. It was certainly a challenge to negative stereotypes. On the other hand, it also had a more practical side – involving a new ally for Poland: the increasingly wealthy and politically influential Jews of western Europe.[47]

The Jewish question was on a number of occasions for Czyński an important point of departure; it was an important measure of his relations with his surroundings. This was understandable since it occupied a singular, privileged position in his hierarchy of interests: 'la cause juive est ma vie ... ' he is reputed to have said.⁴⁸ In the case of his contacts with Antoni Ostrowski, this subject was a plane on which they drew closer, in spite of growing differences of opinion between them. The general-wojewode, as a founder of Tomaszów Mazowiecki, understood the need for a growth in towns in Poland, and equally saw the need to regulate the Jewish question on new principles. He appreciated the propaganda value of the brochure *La Question des Juifs polonaises*, and supported the Lafayette Committee. We can understand therefore why he asked Czyński to read his treatise 'Pomysły o potrzebie reformy' (Ideas on the Need for Reforms), before it was completed in March 1834.⁴⁹ Czyński expressed approval of the treatise and promised to review it in the French press.⁵⁰

The work of Czyński and Ostrowski met with strong disapproval in the columns of the journal *Nowa Polska*, whose authors were in fact in favour of extending the principle of equal rights to Jews, but only after they had assimilated.⁵¹ These polemicists did not take seriously the political benefits arising from the more liberal proposals for settling the Jewish question in Poland and they also ignored the historical arguments to which Czyński had attached considerable weight.⁵²

## HOTEL LAMBERT

For some years Czyński ignored the Jewish question to which he returned in 1843. This 'new campaign'⁵³ for Polish Jews was linked closely to the new policy of the Tsarist authorities towards the Jewish population. This was a policy which, taken generally, imposed greater obligations towards the state, while maintaining legal discrimination against the Jews. It was a policy, furthermore, which resulted in a growing emigration to the west of Polish Jews from the Russian partition area. This provoked Czyński to write extensively on the subject *Archives Israelites* and *Echo Miast Polskich*.⁵⁴

Indeed, from the mid-1840s onwards, the Jewish problem (treated throughout as part of a wider programme of social and political reform in Poland) became one of the most important areas of collaboration between Czyński and the Conversative camp of the Polish emigration. Prince Adam Jerzy Czartoryski and his collaborators did not at first appreciate the importance of the question for the national cause.⁵⁵ Certain signs that attitudes were changing began to appear after 1840, but one can speak of a more decisive break with former policy only from 1846 onwards. What were the reasons for this reorientation?

Leon Hollaenderski writes about the 'great influence' that Jan Czyński's wife, Anastazja, had on Prince Adam's attitude towards refugees of Jewish origin.⁵⁶ Abraham Duker attributes the Hotel Lambert's new course with regard to the Jewish problem to the campaign conducted by Czyński.⁵⁷

Artur Eisenbach, for his part, explains it against the background of the general political situation in Europe (and in the Polish lands) which developed from 1846. He emphasizes the importance of the declaration by the Kraków National Government on 23 February 1846, *Do braci Izraelitów* 'To our Jewish Brothers', and considers Czyński's role to have been only of moderate importance.[58] This latter view seems to me to be nearer to the truth.

Jan Czyński's statements in support of all the residents of Polish towns, beginning particularly in 1843, were carefully listened to by activists within the Convervative camp. Generally speaking, they did not exert any significant influence on the Conservatives' policy. There are, however, certain exceptions. In 1844, a few days before the anniversary celebrations of the outbreak of the November Rising, the publisher of *Echo Miast Polskich* addressed a letter to Prince Czartoryski in which he called for the prince to join in a planned public meeting for Orthodox Jews, in the name of the centuries old tradition of religious tolerance in Poland, as well as the common fate of the two communities under the partitions.[59] He did not ask a great deal. 'A few words from you about the Jews,' he explained, 'would not only serve to break down the prejudices on both sides, but would also gain powerful new support and sympathy for the Polish cause.'

At the Paris meeting on 29 November 1844, commemorating the 1830 uprising, the Prince expressed his hope for cooperation between Poles and Jews.[60] It was a largely symbolic gesture, but was accepted by Czyński with joy and optimism for the future as 'an important political event'.[61] From this moment on, whenever the subject of Jews and their part in the Polish struggle for independence came up, Czyński had more trust in the Hotel Lambert group, than in the Democrats. More and more frequently he acted as intermediary in the contacts between Conservative representatives and well-known Jewish politicians, and he sent Adam Czartoryski his new publications as they appeared.[62]

## PHILANTHROPIC WORK

Charity work and the backing of young (chiefly Jewish) arrivals from Poland by wealthy and influential people became, to some extent for Czyński, a symbolic measure of Polish-Jewish unity. Around the year 1843 he began to direct requests for help to the Rothschilds – mainly on behalf on young people wishing to study or work. These requests met with a positive reception, showing that he had to some extent succeeded in convincing French Jews that 'the fate of their co-religionists on the banks of the Vistula is closely linked with the fate of our nation'.[63] On the other hand, though, Czyński tried not to abuse this aid, since he felt it would be better to make use of it 'only in the most important cases'.[64]

We know only as much about the scope of these activities as Czyński himself wrote down – and there is no means of verifying it. On one occasion he mentions eight hundred 'Jewish brothers';[65] on another occasion – around a thousand 'fellow-countrymen of various beliefs'.[66] One way or another, if we are to believe these figures, the number who received help from the emigrants in the years 1840–1860 was considerable.

What kind of help was offered and who benefited from it? In general it was aimed at easing the adaptation of younger emigrants to their new surroundings. Each case was different. For example, there was the son of a rabbi; young, educated, with a command of four languages (apart from Polish); 'He assured me', explained Czyński, 'that we would try to perfect his speech, which should be his first lesson'.[67] He had no means of support and no work. Another emigrant, wishing in 1848 to return home in order to 'serve the Polish cause', asked for help, using Lubliner as an intermediary. Czyński promised to obtain a free rail ticket and recommended him to the Rothschilds, but – as he warned – 'there is now such a multitude of applicants, that Kerstenberg will doubtless not receive more than 5 francs'.[68]

One of the most important items on the list of Jan Czyński's charitable gestures towards his needy compatriots was that of arranging railway journeys. From the moment in 1845 that he began work in the accounts department,[69] he attempted, as we see clearly from the surviving correspondence, to help all those who applied. Usually this help involved free or reduced rail travel – but only within the Rothschild network.[70] On another occasion he intervened to recover some items lost during a journey.[71]

The great majority of these cases never came to light, so there is all the more reason for us to dwell on one particular case which – while not wholly typical – seems to have certain characteristics in common with those of other arrivals from Poland. This is that of Leon Hollaenderski.[72] Hollaenderski, who was later to become a writer, came from the Suwałki region. After graduating from the University of Königsberg in 1833, he returned to Poland and worked in an office in Suwałki. Soon he had built up a thriving lithographic works and bookshop. He quickly aroused the (justified) suspicions of the authorities, that he was disseminating illegal books and pamphlets – and he was forced to flee. In 1843 he arrived in Paris, where he met, among others, Czyński, who took him under his wing and exercised a huge influence on him and on his career as a writer.[73]

This philanthropic work would clearly not have been possible were it not for a chain of wealthy and well-disposed people. (Czyński was only a link in this chain.) The names which occur most frequently in the correspondence are those of the Rothschilds, Adolf Crémieux, Antoni Ostrowski, and Adam Czartoryski. It was easier to secure *ad hoc* offers of help, but more difficult to get it secured on a more permanent basis. The majority of cases, though, were settled positively.

The motives of the benefactors and sponsors were varied. Some did it for patriotic and humanitarian reasons; others attempted to use it as a means to secure allies, friends and popularity. On occasions misunderstandings arose, there was manipulation and accusations flew.[74] These were isolated incidents, though, and they could not damage the generally positive reputation of Jan Czyński's philanthropic efforts – efforts which did much to serve the ideal of the 'unity of faiths' and the emancipation of the Jewish community in Poland.

## FROM THE 'UNITY OF FAITHS' TO THE INDEPENDENCE OF POLAND

The view that a Polish-Jewish alliance would aid in the achievement both of Polish independence and of Jewish emancipation was not a new concept of Czyński's; it was to be the very core of his work in the period 1861–1865. This work led chiefly to cooperation with *Archives Israelites* and, within the Polish Alliance of all Religious Faiths, to a campaign in support of the January Rising and to mediation between the National Government, the émigré community and Jewish circles in Western Europe.[75]

The Polish Alliance of all Religious Faiths (*Alliance Polonaise de toutes les Croyances Religieuses* – referred to in historical source material as the Polish Fellowship, the National Fellowship, or the Polish Alliance) was created in Paris at the beginning of August 1862.[76] According to its statute, its chief aim was to 'unite all religious faiths on Polish soil' and bring help and welfare to the needy 'irrespective of creed' – with the proviso (almost certainly intended for the French authorities) that this charitable work would not take on a political character.[77]

The Alliance was the brainchild of Jan Czyński and there is no doubt that it came into being as a direct result of the political situation in Poland, since in 1862 a Tsarist decree (*ukase*) came into force guaranteeing equality of rights for Jews. It also seems natural that the experienced émigré activist should have wished to crown his efforts over several years – at a time when his ideas were being realised – by creating an influential institution and one which effectively supported the Polish cause; an institution which supported the Polish cause; and an institution created and led by Czyński himself.

'We took the name,' reads the proclamation of the Alliance's steering committee, 'from the historical events which happened in Warsaw and also to indicate the aim of our activities.[78] This aim is to lead the intellect to follow those emotions and to acknowledge the truth, which became apparent in a moment of holy fervour – that differences in faith or creed do not make people different – they do not convert or absolve anybody from common duties with regard to their homeland ... Our task is to unite all faiths, not to defer to this or that faith'. In explaining the name of the association by reference to the 'historic events in Warsaw' – most surely a reference to the patriotic demonstrations of 1861, in which Jews also took part – there is also an echo of the names of other international associations of similar character: *Alliance Religieuse Universelle, Alliance Chrétienne Universelle* and *Alliance Israelite Universelle*. The latter, brought into existence in Paris in 1860, appears to be in many respects the closest to the Polish Alliance.

In disseminating publicity and information, special emphasis was placed upon the publication of materials in several languages – Polish, Russian, French, German and Hebrew – depending upon circumstances. It was also anticipated that a network of correspondents would be organized in various towns and contact established with the overseas press, with international organizations and with the freemasons. Managing the operations of the Alliance with the help of such varying media required now the full potential, talents, and commitment of its members.

The Polish Alliance was inspired by Czyński. His idea fell upon fertile ground, though, since, in its earliest days it received the support of almost thirty people who became its founding group.[79] One could say that its success was two-fold, since not only did an organization come into being which backed the ideals to which Czyński had devoted more than thiry years of his life, but, from the very beginning the composition of the Alliance's membership revealed a mosaic of different religious faiths, social backgrounds, vocations and political orientations. Apart from Catholic priests (F. Różański), rabbis also joined (E.A. Anstuc, I. Ulman); alongside lawyers (A. Franck, N. Leven) we find literary figures (J.M. Rabbinowicz, W. H. de Rochetin), military men (R. Różański and A. Waskiewicz) and doctors (B. Levi). Along with Poles we find Jews, Frenchmen, a Czech and somewhat later, Englishmen. We notice also that a number of these names are familiar from Czyński's earlier periods of public activity (e.g. de Rochetin).

As time passed and the reputation of the Alliance grew, new members were drawn in. In April 1863 there were 53 of them, at the beginning of 1866 – 150.[80] Among them were known, influential figures, but also lesser-known names. One thing linked all of them: a lengthy acquaintance, and often friendship, with Jan Czyński. In this category may be included A. Crémieux, Ignacy Handvogel, Albert Cohn, Mikołaj Akielewicz, Bartłomiej Beniowski, Stanisław Bratkowski, Leon Hollaenderski and Leon Zienkowicz. The British members were a separate issue, but they doubtless exercised a positive influence on British public opinion towards the Polish question in the period 1863–1866. At the head of the Alliance was an elected Council. It included in its ranks a president, a vice-president, a treasurer and secretaries. The first president, probably until March 1864, was Czyński.[84]

The Polish Alliance did not have its own newspaper or journal. But a bulletin was produced (anonymously – although Czyński was probably responsible for writing and editing most of the material) and individual documents and notices were issued. The journals *Polska* and *La Pologne* were in fact – though not formally – vehicles for propagating the aims and theories of the group's programme.[82]

*Polska* was published (1 March 1863–15 January 1864) in Brussels, although some of the editors were based in Paris. In all eleven issues appeared. It was edited initially by Andrzej Gawroński, Feliks Różański and Lubliner; from May-June of 1863 Czyński edited it. It made public the aims ot the Rising. The journal's editors appealed to their compatriots for unity, to the Slavic peoples and to 'free-thinking' Germans for solidarity in the struggle against Russian despotism.[83]

There is no doubt that *Polska* served the national cause well during the January Rising, met with a lively interest from the foreign press and had an invigorating influence on the Polish Alliance.[84] Nevertheless, printed in Polish, it could not entirely satisfy the publicity needs, nor Czyński's political and journalistic ambitions. For this reason, some three months before the journal ceased to appear, its editor brought out a new title – the French language *La Pologne* (18 May 1863 – 10 April 1864). Edited by Czynski, Andrzej Gawroński and Kazimierz Urbanowski – officially in Brussels and Paris, but mainly in fact from the latter – twenty-six issues appeared.

If one remembers that it was an émigré enterprise, then one is struck by the scale of the undertaking. The authors of the paper happily used material from the French, British, Belgian, Galician and Poznań press. They informed their readership about the situation in Poland, presented the opinions of others on the situation, revealed provocative acts of the Russians, and carried on debates with Herzen, Garibaldi, and especially with Proudhon. One notices the authors' friendly stance vis-à-vis the Ottoman states and the comment that Poland 'is a natural ally of Turkey, and religious differences cannot be serious grounds for enmity in the 19th century'. These words fit well with the expressions of support which the Council of the Polish Alliance extended in 1863 to Sultan Abdul-Azir in recognition of what it described as his intelligent and tolerant religious policy – one which contrasted markedly with the 'barbaric' policy of the Russians.[85] Czyński's daily did much to spread throughout Europe the conviction that the Polish insurgent leadership was tolerant in religious matters. His novel about Casimir the Great and his work on Copernicus also referred to the traditions of tolerance.[86]

*La Pologne* was, above all, Jan Czyński's work, but his old friend K. Urbanowski, H. de Rochetin and Henri Carle also made a considerable contribution. The paper did not, of course, meet with the unanimous approval of the emigration. An anonymous reviewer in *Głos Wolny*, for example, wrote sneeringly of the squandering of capital on an 'expensive diplomatic endeavour'. The call for unity and equality of rights for all religious and social classes, was, he claimed, based on a 'misunderstanding'. If, after all, there were amongst us 'stragglers, relics of the past' who persecuted Jews, peasants, the middle classes, then they should be called to account individually, and the problem not generalised 'when the whole of Poland thinks and feels differently'.[87]

The new daily met with the approval of Władysław Czartoryski and his circle, who even tried to defend it from the wrath of the French Government.[88] In the end, though, this help was ineffective, since in April 1864 *La Pologne* ceased its short life without having received the right of circulation in France.[89]

One means of securing allies for the Polish cause during the years 1863–1864 was Czyński's mediation between the National Government and the Polish emigration and Jewish circles in Western Europe. His knowledge of matters at home and trustworthiness both in Jewish eyes and to the collaborators of W. Czartoryski, made Czyński very suitable for this role. 'Today the *Alliance Israelite* under the new leadership of Adolph Crémieux, former minister and government member, and a man who has given me numerous proofs of his friendly disposition towards the Polish cause, may take a more positive turn and our Association, which the minister charged with the matter, is working to this end,' he reported to Count Władysław.[90]

We do not know what role (if he took part in it at all) the president of the Polish Alliance played in the attempts to establish contact between the National Government and the *Alliance Israélite Universelle*. Certainly, though, in September Władysław Czartoryski received a letter (dated 26 August 1863) from Poland and invited Czyński for talks. Czyński indeed, for his part, assured Czartoryski that he would do all in his power to see that 'the wishes of the National Government had their desired effect.'[91] It could have had to do with conveying by hand a document from the National Government to the *Alliance Israelite Universelle*, or even, and this seems more likely, of arranging a meeting between Czartoryski and Crémieux. For we know that in October of that year he arranged such a meeting, and even attempted to exercise some influence on its course, suggesting to the Duke that French and British Jews should be persuaded to go 'to their respective parliaments' to ask for help for their brothers by the Vistula, and Crémieux to bear Poland in mind during his meeting with the Turkish sultan. Although Czyński did not take part in that meeting, he must have been familiar with what was discussed, since he apparently wrote up the minutes at the request of his influential French friend.[92] Of similar, although less important, roles, we may mention here his mediation between Count Władysław and the French – for example, with a certain Bru and one Mejer.⁹³

The Polish Alliance was active until the middle of 1866. (A historian of the movement links its demise – no doubt correctly – with the creation of the *Zjednoczenie Emigracji Polskiej* (Union of Polish Emigration).⁹⁴ It was not in reality an apolitical association, as the authors of its statute declared in 1862, but then anything Polish in France during this period could scarcely fail to have been political. The Alliance had in its name 'all faiths', although in practice the organization concentrated chiefly on Jewish problems. This should not be taken, though, as evidence of discrimination against other creeds, since the watchword of religious tolerance was emphasised on every suitable occasion. The particular emphasis on the Jewish question however, resulted both from its international ramifications and from its special significance for the Polish cause. Just as the birth of the Polish Alliance was undoubtedly linked with the international interest in the Polish situation, so its collapse originated in the passing of the situation which had aroused that interest. A full assessment of the effects of the four years of the Association's activities is not easy. Of one thing though there is no doubt; the Association distributed complex and sensitive political information concerning the principles of tolerance and unity of religious beliefs and achieved a great deal in improving the image of Poles as a people who respected faiths other than Roman Catholicism. This publicity, at times portraying Poland in over-optimistic terms in this regard, effectively rebutted the image of Poland put out by the governments of the partitioning states, and Russia in particular. Suspending its activities in 1866, the campaigners of the Polish Alliance did not by any means claim that all the aims of the organization's statute had been satisfactorily achieved. Even further, they were aware, as never before, of the existence of serious obstacles on the road to 'real fellowship', and compared their perseverance to the seventeenth-century Polish Brethren.⁹⁵ They acted as they did, though, because of the circumstances which had arisen. In 1865 Czyński was no longer on the Council of the Polish Alliance. He had not withdrawn from involvement in its work, though. On 1 March 1865 he took part in a large meeting organized in London to commemorate the second anniversary of the January Rising.⁹⁶ As a delegate of the Fellowship, he brought with him an address in which the authors repudiated the growing accusations in England of Polish religious intolerance.

Our analysis of the rich legacy of this political campaigner and essayist enable us to formulate the following conclusions: the religious question (in this particular case – the question of equal rights for religious groups) occupied a very important place in Czyński's social and political thought, in his writing and campaigning. The fact that the issue became dominated by the Jewish question creates the impression that this was the only issue

Czyński felt was important. This is a mistaken impression, though, since there is no doubt that it was for him only a part of the wider problem of the emancipation of all faiths which were in a minority on Polish soil in relation to the Roman Catholic Church. Even further, it was part of the problem of the emancipation of all social, national and religious minorities that were discrimated against in any way whatsoever. The political and social importance of the Jewish question in Poland and also Czyński's personal involvement, mutually complementing one another, justified fully the treating of this question in the wider sense – also as a kind of symbol of all kinds of oppression. There is one further matter. As a supporter of the assimilation (voluntary assimilation, that is) of religious and national minorities in Poland; as propagator of the concepts of 'Poles of the Jewish faith' or 'Poles of the Evangelical faith' (i.e. Polish Germans), Czyński had his mind continually on a national programme which would lead to the rebirth of the Polish state (within the pre-partition boundaries, but with a more modern political and social order). He offered the minorities then a liberalism in return for collaboration and loyalty, dignity and civic rights as the price for dedication and sacrifice equal to that of Poles themselves. He proposed a clear and logical pact of benefit to Poles and to the minorities, since it would also be of benefit to their common homeland – the reborn Republic.

Assessing the many-sided achievements of Czyński in the field of the emancipation of religious minorities in Poland, from the perspective of intervening decades – decades marked at times with the stamp of a dramatic and irreversible deterioration in inter-ethnic relations – it might seem that his fine idea was perhaps more of an ideal Utopia than a realistic programme. Its author encountered various obstacles and stereotypes, the strength of which he did not, perhaps, appreciate. Should he then, because of this, share the fate of so many other forgotten political campaigners, writers and advocates of once original ideas? My article will, I hope, dispel all doubts on this question and make clear the relevance of Czyński's ideals, not only for his own period.

## NOTES

1 See among others: K. Świerczewska, 'Jan Czyński – działacz polityczny, literat i publicysta czasów Wielkiej Emigracji 1801–1867'. *Prace Polonistyczne*, 1950, pp. 111–36; J. Frejlich, 'Czyński, Jan' in *Polski Słownik Biograficzny* (henceforth PSB), vol. IV (Kraków, 1938), pp. 375–8. M. Mieses, *Polacy Chrześcijanie pochodzenia żydowskiego*, vol. I (Lwów, 1939), pp. 82–92; L. & A. Ciolkosz, *Zarys dziejów socjalizmu polskiego*, vol. I (London, 1966), pp. 199–222; M. Tyrowicz, *Towarzystwo Demokratyczne Polskie 1832–1863. Przywódcy i kadry członkowskie. Przewodnik biobibliograficzny* (Warsaw, 1964); R. Gerber, *Studenci Uniwersytetu Warszawskiego 1808–1831* (Wrocław, 1977); *Bibliografia literatury polskiej*, vol. VII: Romantyzm (Warsaw, 1968), pp. 249–52; J. W. Borejsza, 'Czyński, Jan' in *Słownik biograficzny działaczy*

*polskiego ruchu robotniczego*, vol. I (Warsaw, 1978), pp. 374–5; (also 2nd edition, Warsaw 1985, vol. I, pp. 491–492). *Dictionnaire biographique du mouvement ouvrier Français*, vol. I: 1789–1864 (Paris, 1964), pp. 478–88. M. Vishnitsel, 'Chinskii Yan' in *Yevrieyskaya entsiklopiediya*, vol. XV (St. Petersburg, 1913): A. P., 'Czyński, Jan' in *The Jewish Encyclopedia*, vol. III (New York, 1925); *Encyclopaedia Judaica*, vol. IV (Berlin, 1930); *La Grande Encyclopedie. Inventaire raisonnée des Sciences, des lettres et des Arts*, vol. XIII (Paris, after 1885); Z. Markiewicz, T. Sivert, *Melpomena polska na paryskim bruku. Teatralia polskie we Francji w XIX w.* (Warsaw, 1973), pp. 73–146; A. Gałkowski, *Jan Czyński (1801–67). Życie i myśl polityczno-społeczna*, Ph.D. thesis (Warsaw, 1988), (typescript in the Library of the Institute of History, Polish Academy of Sciences (PAN)); A. Gałkowski 'Problematyka czerkieska w publicystyce Jana Czyńskiego' *Studia z Dziejów ZSSR i Europy Środkowej*, vol. XXII (1986), pp. 47–64.

2 *Północ* (Paris), no. 14, 1835, pp. 53–5.

3 Op. cit., pp. 5–7, 64.

4 J. Czyński, *La Pologne catholique, la Pologne libérale* (Paris, 1848).

5 P. Maczewski, 'Czyński i Lubliner'. *Myśl Narodowa*, 1933, p. 233.

6 *Echo Miast Polskich*, no. 6 (Paris, 1844), p. 64. (henceforth EMP); A. Eisenbach, 'Jana Czyńskiego polemiki z Janem Nepoucenem Janowskim' *Przegląd Historyczny*, no. 1 (1979), p. 91.

7 J. K. Urban, *Udział Żydów w walce o niepodległość Polski* (1938), p. 175; S. Pigoń, *Zręby nowej Polski, w publicystyce Wielkiej Emigracji* (Warsaw, 1938), p. 22.

8 P. Maczewski, op. cit.; J. Jędrzejewicz, *Zwycięstwo pokonanych* (Warsaw, 1974), p. 245.

9 As he wrote, for example, in one of his letters to H. Kajsiewicz in 1864: 'I was christened in the Church of Our Lady in Praga (a district of Warsaw); in a church where the traces of blood shed by Suvorov were preserved to that day. Thereafter I learned to speak my first words ... Accustomed from my childhood to raise my spirit to the eternal Father, I never retired for the night, never rose from my bed, without humbly offering my thoughts and prayers to the Almighty' (Arch. Congregationis Resurrectionis, Roma. No. 46021). It is not out of place here to recall that some others even posed the question of whether Czyński was a reconvert. (S. Pigoń, *Zręby*, p. 15). Others treated the above version as almost certainly true. (J. Jędrzejewicz, *Zwycięstwo*, pp. 435–77).

10 J. Czyński, *Israel en Pologne* (Paris, 1861), pp. 33–4; *Question des Juifs polonaises envisagée comme une question européenne par J. Czyński* (Paris, 1833), p. 22; L. Hollaenderski, *Les Israelites de Pologne* (Paris, 1846), pp. 134–5; J. Schall, 'Żydzi w powstaniu listopadowym' in *Żydzi Bojownicy o niepodległość Polski* (Lwów, 1939), p. 48 (by mistake as J. Czyński); J. Ziołek, 'Warunki wewnętrzne prowadzenia wojny' in *'Powstanie listopadowe 1830–1831. Geneza, uwarunkowania, bilans, porównania* edited by Jerzy Skowroński and Maria Zmigrodzka, (Wrocław 1983), p. 71.

11 *Kurier Lubelski*, no. 10 (1831), p. 16.

12 A. Eisenbach, *Wielka Emigracja wobec kwesti żydowskiej 1832–1849* (Warsaw, 1976), pp. 93–4.

13 *Całoroczne trudy Komitetu Narodowego Polskiego* (Paris, 1831–1833), pp. 243–9.

14 L. Hollaenderski, op. cit., pp. 114–16; K. Świerczewska, op. cit., p. 122; A. Eisenbach, op. cit., p. 112.

15 In letters to *Archives Israelite* in 1843. Hollaenderski referred to them (op. cit., p. 116) and the author published them separately as a brochure (*Israel en Pologne*, Paris 1861).

16 J. Lelewel, *Listy emigracyjne* (collected by H. Wieckowska), vol. I (Kraków, 1848), p. 234.

17 L. Lubliner, 'Jan Czyński obrońca Żydów' *Przegląd Rzeczy Polskich* (Paris), 20 December 1861, pp. 7-11; This and the following quotations come from this source. See also L. Lubliner, *Jan Czyński obmówca sp Joachima Lelewela w prawdziwym świetle wystawiony* (Brussels, 1862).

18 Lubliner considered that 'since the most recent events in the Polish Kingdom, which took place during February and April of 1861, Jews need neither advocates, nor patrons to help them win their political rights; Czyński, Hollaenderski, Beniowski, Lubliner have already completed their mission leading in the minds of Polish Christians to the granting of civic equally to Jews'. (*Przegląd Rzeczy Polskich*, 20 December 1861, p. 11).

19 H. Graetz, *Geschichte der Juden*, vol. XI (Leipzig, 1900), p. 407; S. Pigoń, *Zręby nowej Polski*, p. 14.

20 Lelewel – as Janowski contends in a letter to Czyński 'Odpowiedź panu Lublinerowi' (*Przegląd Rzeczy Polskich* 27 January 1862, pp. 19-25) – who 'in the course of the November Rising was against the enfranchisement of peasants and desired only progress towards the renting out of government estates, was also against the emancipation of the Jews and did not make a secret of it even after his arrival in France. At the meeting of which we are speaking, he said – and I remember the words: Jews can be granted civic and legal rights perhaps in the third generation. By these words he greatly angered Beniowski and others. I admit therefore, that basically you are right; only repeat, that I would prefer not to hear about this dispute ... ' It seems likely that Janowski showed this letter to the addressee before it was published (Library of the Jagiellonian University, Kraków; henceforth BJ -manuscript 3687 III, pp. 243-4). Concerning Lelewel's views on the Jewish question see also A.-M. Kempiński, 'Joachim Lelewel face à Bruxelles de 1833 à 1861. Actes du colloque organisé les 17 et 18 avril 1986' (*Textes réunis par Teresa Wysokinska et Stéphane Pirard*), (Bruxelles, 1987), pp. 155-76.

21 J. Czyński, 'Odpowiedź panu Lublinerowi' *Przegląd Rzeczy Polskich* 27 January 1862, pp. 19-25.

22 B. Beniowski to J. Czyński, 25 January 1862, op. cit., pp. 19-22.

23 J. Czyński to A. Ostrowski, 16 March 1833. AGAD (Archiwum Akt Dawnych w Warszawie – the Warsaw Archive of Pre-Modern Records), The Ostrowski Collection, manuscript 390, k. 186. Concerning the political circumstances in which the Committee came into being see: A.G. Duker, 'The Lafayette Committee for Jewish Emancipation' in *Essays on Jewish Life and Thought* (1959), pp. 169-82; A. Eisenbach, *Wielka Emigracja*, pp. 127-9; Eisenbach, *Emancypacja Żydów na ziemiach polskich 1785-1870 na tle europejskim* (Warsaw, 1988), pp. 302-4.

24 Beniowski's project ' ... is very much to my liking,' wrote the scholar from his exile at La Grange to the voivode, Antoni Ostrowski, on 5 March 1833, 'and so I am writing to you, so that you may turn your mind to it, before the proposal is put forward to him. Beniowski wished to create in Paris a Committee for the Emancipation of Jews composed of Poles and Frenchmen, exclusively Christians, and he is a Christian himself. But those who become involved might be found in Brody, in Berdyczów, in Brześć, in Livorno, or London. It is a scientific-philanthropic issue. Czyński is seen as the Polish secretary ... ' J. Lelewel, *Listy emigracyjne*, vol V, p. 29.

25 The Society was called The Philanthropic Society for the Acceleration of Jewish Emancipation throughout the World, and, in its later version, the Lafayette Committee (A. Duker, *The Lafayette Committee*, pp. 170-1). Among the French members Czyński mentions Le Mercier, Crémieux, Odillon-Barrot, Maugin. Among the Poles – Lelewel and Ostrowski, and he hoped that Antoni Hluśniewicz and Roman Soltyka would also take part. (AGAD, Ostrowski Papers, manuscript 390, k. 187). See also Czyński's letter to Lelewel of 17 March 1833. (A. Duker, op.

cit., appendix 2); A. Eisenbach, *Wielka Emigracja*, pp. 133–4; Eisenbach, *Emancypacja Żydów*, pp. 302–4.
26 A. Duker, op. cit., appendix 1.
27 Ibid., appendix 2.
28 J. Czyński, *Question des Juifs polonais envisagée comme une question européenne* (Paris, 1833). The following works subsequently appeared; Antoni Ostrowski, *Pomysły o potrzebie reformy towarzyskiej w ogólności, a mianowicie co do Izraelitów w Polsce* (Paris, 29 November 1834), and Włodzimierz Gadon, *Zbiór ustaw i obrzędów wymagających najrychlejszej reformy Izraelitów osiadłych w prowincjach do Polski należących* (Paris, 1835).
29 'At the last meeting of the Society, with regard to the Jewish question, Adolphe Crémieux, having come to an agreement with Rothschild, put forward the idea that we choose a president who does not have such a strong political character as Laffaied (sic). He maintained that it would be possible to accomplish more in May, as long as opinion was still weak, or if the Society did not have a political character. It was decided therefore to invite several more people of varying political hues such as Tracy, Chateaubriand, many scholars, etc ... this would have been at odds with our original aim and I would have quit the Society in protest and would have revealed in what manner our original idea became distorted out of recognition. I imagine that this will not be necessary.' J. Czyński to J. Lelewel, 23 April 1833, in A. Duker, *The Lafayette Committee*, appendix 4.
30 'Lelewel and other born saviours of freedom, who did nothing for Catholics, Protestants, and for non-Jews in general,' as he wrote on 7 April 1833 to J. N. Janowski (BJ, manuscript 3685, vol. 6, k. 261–2, 'now wish to practise their art on the Jews ... Amusing ... undertaking'.
31 Czyński lays the responsibility for this at the door of the French Government, *Question des Juifs*, p. 20.
32 L. Hollaenderski, *Les Israelites de Pologne*, p. 136; A. Duker, *The Lafayette Committee*, p. 173; A. Eisenbach, *Wielka Emigracja*, p. 144.
33 Sz. Konarski, *Dziennik z lat 1831–1834* (edited by B. Lopuszański and A. Smirnow), (Wrocław, 1973).
34 'I intend to publish my work on the Jews in Polish ... The Polish pamphlet must deal with the subject more broadly, especially taking into account political economy. I will add a number of facts which I did not wish to reveal to foreigners, for example about the hanging of innocent people, etc. I must write something about converted Jews, and the contempt displayed when they are discussed, something about the Frankists...' J. Czyński to A. Ostrowski, 28 December 1833, AGAD, Ostrowski Collection, Manuscript 390, k. 703.
35 Ibid.
36 J. Czyński to A. Ostrowski, 22 February 1834. Ibid., manuscript 391, k. 133.
37 L. Hollaenderski, op. cit., p. 136; B. Boleslawita (J.I. Kraszewski) *Rachunki*, vol. II, Chapter 2 (Poznań, 1868), p. 381; S. Mstislawskaya, 'Yevrei w polskom vostanii 1831 g.' in *Yevreyskaya Starina* (1910), p. 246; K. Swierczewska, *Jan Czyński*, pp. 130–1.
38 L. Hollaenderski, op. cit. It should be added that this politician helped to have Czyński freed from the prison of Ste-Pélagie in January 1834 (AGAD, Ostrowski Collection, manuscript 391, k. 35–6) and also welcomed the Polish emigrant for talks on several occasions. (Ibid., manuscript 390, k. 261–2; A. Eisenbach, *Wielka Emigracja*, p. 166.
39 *Przyszłość*, no.1 (Paris, 1834), pp. 31–2.
40 AGAD, Ostrowski Collection, manuscript 390, k. 670.
41 A. Ostrowski, *Pomysły*, p. 7.

42 Compare J. Czyński, *Cesarzewicz Konstanty . . . czyli Jakubini polscy* (Warsaw, 1956), p. 239.
43 Cf. M. Mochnacki, *Powstanie narodu polskiego w roku 1830 i 1831* (edited with a foreword by Stefan Kieniewicz, vol. I, Warsaw 1984. pp. 93–4.)
44 This concerns the speech of F. Morawski in the *Sejm* on 16 May 1831 and the debate which followed. Czyński was convinced that it was precisely for this reason that 'bankers throughout the world have refused us loans'. (Letter of 16 March 1833, AGAD, Ostrowski Collection, manuscript 390, k. 185). This view was repeated by Maurycy Mochnacki (*Powstanie narodu*, vol. I, pp. 91–7). See also S. Pigoń, *Zręby nowej Polski*, p. 16; A. Eisenbach, *Wielka Emigracja*, pp. 94–5.
45 Czyński drew the statistics of Polish Jews – as did other authors during this period – from the work of Stanisław Plater, *Geografia wschodniej części Europy* (Breslau, 1825). Émigré writers however attempted to 'correct' these figures, with the result that they are in this case somewhat exaggerated. See A. Eisenbach, *Z dziejów ludności żydowskiej w Polsce w XVIII i XIX wieku* (Warsaw, 1983), p. 15; ibid., *Wielka Emigracja*, p. 20.
46 Letter of 28 December 1833, AGAD, Ostrowski Collection, Manuscript 390, k. 701–4.
47 'I am strongly persuaded of the value of reconciling Poles and Jews,' admitted Czyński elsewhere in the letter quoted above (k. 702), 'and of rooting out ridiculous prejudices. The stronger should reach out a hand, the oppressors should above all cease to oppress. The most painful aspect is contempt. Contempt must be rapidly eliminated. No reform will succeed if Catholics continue to impose their prejudices on to Jews. Prejudice will be eroded by education, and as people come together and communicate with each other. There is no need to shave beards, to change one's garb, to suppress the Talmud . . . ' See also A. Eisenbach, *Emancypacja Żydów*, pp. 344–6.
48 L. Hollaenderski, 'Jan Czyński'. *Archives Israélites* (1867), p. 168.
49 AGAD, Ostrowski Collection, man. 390, k. 701.
50 Ibid., man. 390, k.701; man. 391, k. 528, 562; man. 398., k. 13–14.
51 *Północ* (1835). no. 5, p. 18; *Nowa Polska*, (Paris, 1835), p. 345; *Północ*, no. 9, pp. 33–5; *Nowa Polska*, pp. 357–8, 362–6; AFAD, Ostrowski Collection, man. 392, k. 375; A. Duker, 'The Polish Democratic Society and the Jewish Problem 1832–46' *Jewish Social Studies*, vol. XIX (1957), no. 3/4. pp. 103–4.
52 J. Czyński, *Le roi des paysans*. This historical novel set in the times of Casimir the Great (one of the Polish rulers most respected by Czyński) in its German version appeared, not without reason, under the title, *Der Bauern-König und die Jüdin* (Frankfurt am Main, 1845). There were several important Jewish subplots in this novel. See also J. Czyński, *Cesarzewicz Konstanty*, p. 155, 426; J. Czyński to J. N. Janowski (letter undated), BJ, man. 3685, vol. 1, k. 451–4.
53 A. Duker, *The Polish Democratic Society*, p. 107.
54 In the course of 1843–44 alone, Czyński published over a dozen articles in the *Archives Israélites*. The Jewish question is raised too in almost every issue of *Echo Miast Polskich*; 'Let our readers not think', we read on page 34 of this journal, 'that we are blind adorers, flatterers of Polish Jewry, that we commend their squalour, their negative features. No. But we do not attribute to blood, tribe or creed something that is the fault of bad social organization, bad laws, and bad upbringing . . . We are convinced that positive treatment by Catholics, brotherly love, light, feeling, will draw the Jews to us as warm-hearted brothers, as useful inhabitants of this country. The Tsar raised an axe over the head of those to whom Poland gave shelter. May the Poland that is to be reborn not be an unworthy successor of the Poland of Casimir the Great.'

55 This is, of necessity, a very broad generalization. For more on this subject see: A. Duker, 'Prince Czartoryski. The Émigré on the Jewish problem', in *The Joshua Bloch Memorial Volume* (New York, 1960); A. Eisenbach, 'Hotel Lambert wobec sprawy żydowskiej w przededniu Wiosny Ludów' *Przegląd Historyczny* no.3 (1976), pp. 369–98; ibid., *Wielka Emigracja*, p. 239.
56 L. Hollaenderski, op. cit., p. 137.
57 A. Duker, Prince Czartoryski, p. 160.
58 A. Eisenbach, Hotel Lambert, p. 374; see also S. Mstislawskaya, *Jevrey*, p. 247.
59 J. Czyński to A. Czartoryski, 23 November 1844, B.Cz. (The Czartoryski Library in Kraków), man. IV 5653, k. 153–5; A. Eisenbach, *Wielka Emigracja*, p. 260.
60 A. Czartoryski, *Mowy Księcia. Od roku 1839–1847* (Paris, 1847), pp. 55, 64.
61 EMP, no. 23 (1845), p. 24.
62 J. Czyński to Błotnicki, 3 October 1848, B.Cz., man.Ew 5423 IV, k. 1339–1141; J. Czyński to A. Czartoryski, 12 January 1848, B.Cz. man. 1148; A. Duker. 'Leon Hollaenderski's Statement of Resignation', *Jewish Social Studies*, vol. XV (1953), p. 301; A. Eisenbach, *Wielka Emigracja*, p. 455.
63 J. Czyński to H. Błotnicki, 14 May (1845) and undated (1846?), B.Cz, man. Ew. 1548. Czyński's opinion regarding the generosity of Jewish bankers towards emigrants was shared by Hollaenderski too. Rothschild, in his opinion, 'never refused help to a Polish emigrant, particularly to Christians, as long as they came with a recommendation, and he helped some former officers with considerable sums. Each year he sent a certain sum to the Fund for the Society of Polish Ladies, and this summer he provided Princess Czartoryska with a considerable amount in bread vouchers for destitute Poles. Where Rothschild and the Pereires (also Jews) are concerned, Poles have priority in being granted work on the (iron) railroad. Almost all the Poles who applied were given well-paid jobs. (It is estimated that there are more than three hundred Poles working under Rothschild)'. This letter from 1847 is in, A. Duker, Leon Hollaenderski's statement, p. 301; compare A. Muhlstein, *Baron James. The Rise of the French Romantics* (London, 1983), p. 153.
64 J. Czyński to H. Błotnicki, (1846?), B.Cz., Ew. 1548.
65 J. Czyński to N.N., 12 October 1864, BN (National Library in Warsaw), manuscript III 2674, vol. I, k. 47.
66 *Gazeta Narodowa*, no. 165 (Lwów, 1864). Compare no. 94.
67 J. Czyński to H. Błotnicki, 27 November 1844, B.Cz., Ew. 1548.
68 J. Czyński to 'Mr Jakubowski', 10 April 1848, BPP (Polish Library in Paris), Emigrants' Collections, ref. 444, vol. 27, k. 445.
69 More precisely in the Department of 'Accounts, Transfers and Control'. By a decision of the Administrative Board of the Northern Railway Company on 8 December 1845, he was granted an annual wage of 1,500 francs (National Archives, Paris. 48 AQ 54, p. 37); I. Cahen (J. Czyński), *Archives Israélites* (1867), p. 169.
70 J. Czyński to H. Błotnicki (?) 12 May 1849, B.Cz., Ew. 1548; BPP, Emigrants' Collections, ref. 444, vol. 27, k. 445.
71 Czaplicki (?) from Brussels to A. Czartoryski, 14 June 1848, B.Cz. Ew. 1548; J. Czyński to H. Błotnicki, 5 August 1853, B.Cz. 5546 III, k. 367.
72 More precisely, Leon Löb Ben David Hollaenderski (1808–1878). Other examples included: Aleksander Mogielnicki who 'wanted to study' (AGAD, Ostrowski Collection, ref. 390, k.609; ref. 391, k. 166, 225–226); Świerczewski – employed in P. Boduin's printing works (ibid., ref. 391, k. 295); the archivist Kwapiszewski, freshly arrived in Paris (Ibid, ref. 392, k. 376); the Grabiański family (J. Czyński to H. Błotnicki, 14 March 1845; A. Czyńska to A. Czartoryski, 17 April 1845 – B.Cz., Ew. 1548); Romuald Jankowski, who wanted to travel in 1854 to Turkey (B.Cz., 5633 IV, k. 243–4).

73 'This house became a meeting place for all these unfortunates, who had fled the Russian tyranny. More than one', he recalled in his book *Les Israélites en Pologne* (p. 137). Hollaenderski's estate in Poland was eventually confiscated, which was inevitable in the circumstances. The new emigrant became as a result completely penniless. Undoubtedly using Czyński's influence, and in a similar manner to the latter, Hollaenderski joined the Compagnie de Chemin de Fer du Nord for the next few decades, where he received a salary of 1,500 francs (from 8 December 1845), raised in 1864 to 1,600 francs. (National Archives, Paris, 48 AQ 54, p. 37; 48 AQ 86, p. 219. Compare also A. Eisenbach, *Wielka Emigracja*, pp. 175–8.)

74 As in the case of Tobiasz Gerber, studying with French monks with the help of Czyński and the Rothschilds. The boy fell under the influence of the Society of the Resurrection – he was baptised and reputedly complained that he was being persecuted by his 'former protector'. What the truth was we do not know. This delicate matter indeed became most probably a pretext for criticism of the Society by Czyński for making charitable acts conditional upon the subject's renunciation of the religion of his forefathers and taking baptism. (AGAD, Ostrowski Collection, ref.386, k. 281–184, 346–7; ref. 398, letter of 1844, EMP, no. 21, p. 100.)

75 The editor of the journal *Archives Israélites*, Isidor Cohen, to popularise the articles by Czyński which appeared in that Journal (I. Cohen to W. Zamoyski, 18 July 1861, Kornicka Library, manuscript ref. 2431; I. Cohen to Władysław Czartoryski, 19 July 1861, B.Cz. 1157, k.167–8). Even before the outbreak of the Uprising in Poland Czyński was one of the signatories of an open letter (dated 15 March 1862) from the Committee for the Polish Emigration to the editor of 'Archives' *(Żydzi a powstanie styczniowe, Materiały i dokumenty* edited by A. Eisenbach, D. Fajnhauz, A. Wein. Warsaw, 1963, p. 54).

76 J. M. Borejsza, *Emigracja polska po powstaniu styczniowym* (Warsaw, 1966), p. 83; A. Eisenbach, 'Zbratanie Polskie Wszystkich Wyznań Religijnych' *Kwartalnik Historyczny*, no. 1 (1979), pp. 43–66. For a revised English-language version, see *Polin* , V, pp. 193–220. The Papers of the Polish Alliance, collected by the Rapperswil Library and deposited in the National Library in Warsaw, were destroyed during the last war.

77 *Polska*, no. 1 (1863); *Bulletin*, Polish Alliance . . . , no.1 (Paris, 1863); A. Eisenbach, *Zbratanie Polskie*, p. 43.

78 'To fellow countrymen in Poland and abroad', 28 January 1866. *Głos Wolny*, no. 96 (London), pp. 389–90.

79 Amongst others: Aristide Astuc, Father Blawaczyński, Edmund Chojecki, Kasper Cieglewicz, J. Czyński, Josef Fricz, Colonel Gawroński, W. Grochowski, Stanisław Hernisz, Józef Kasparek, Karol Kostnicki, Ludwik Krowlikowski, Jan Ledochowski, Narciz Leven, Bernard Levi, L. Lubliner, Jan N. Młodecki, Georg Nevison, Father Feliks Różański, Henri de Rochetin, Isidor Ulman, Józef Wien, Włodzimierz Wolski, Wemar Marks, Konstanty Zaleski (*Polska*, no. 1 (1863); *Głos Wolny* (1866), p. 390; A. Eisenbach, *Zbratanie Polskie*, p. 47).

80 A. Eisenbach, *Zbratanie Polskie*, p. 48.

81 Ibid.

82 *Bulletin*. Polish Alliance of all religious Faiths, no.1–2 (1863); K. Estriecher, *Bibliografia polska XIXw.* , 2nd edition, vol. 1 (Kraków, 1960), p. 101. On *Polska* and *La Pologne* see S. Kalembka, 'Czasopiśmiennictwo emgracji popowstaniowych XIX w.', in *Historia prasy polskiej* edited by Jersy Lojek, vol. 1 (Warsaw, 1976), pp. 342–3; J. Borejsza, *Emigracja polska*, p. 83; A. Eisenbach, *Zbratanie Polskie*, p. 49. Cf. *La Pologne*, no. 3 (1863), p. 3.

83 *Polska*, no. 1 (1863), pp. 1–2; A. Eisenbach, *Zbratanie Polskie*, p. 50.

84 A. Eisenbach, *Zbratanie Polskie*, p. 50.

85 The article 'Pologne et Turquie', *La Pologne*, no. 2 (1863). The Board of the Alliance sent the Sultan 'a respectful expression of the most sincere sympathy, in order to make clear that a generous word which falls from the lips of a monarch is never lost and finds an echo beyond the frontiers of his empire.' (*Bulletin*, no. 2 (1863)).
86 *La Pologne*, nos. 2–18, 21–2, 24–6 (1863–64).
87 *Głos Wolny*, no. 35 (1865).
88 B.Cz., Ew. 1148, k.481–2; Ew. 1160, k.220–1.
89 *La Pologne*, no, 26 (1864), p. 4.
90 B.Cz., Ew. 1148, k. 474.
91 Ibid., k. 473; *Polska działalność dyplomatyczna 1863–1864*. A collection of documents edited by Adam Lewak, Vol. I (Warsaw, 1937), p. 353; *Dokumenty Komitetu Centralnego Narodowego i Rządu Narodowego, 1863–1864* (in the series, *Powstanie Styczniowe, Materiały i dokumenty*) (Wrocław, 1968), pp. 226–8; S. Kieniewicz, *Powstanie Styczniowe*, 2nd edition (Warsaw, 1983), p. 599.
92 B.Cz., Ew. 1148, k. 475–6.
93 Ibid., k. 477–80; Ew. 1160, k. 219.
94 A. Eisenbach, *Zbratanie Polskie*, pp. 62–5.
95 In an appeal to his compatriots he wrote: ' we know that realization of the concept of joint responsibility is not close at hand, that true fellowship will not happen tomorrow, however our duty is to continue to strive to achieve it ... freedom of conscience is a sacred thing that guarantees all other freedoms.' *Głos Wolny*, no. 96 (1866), p. 390.
96 *Głos Wolny*, nos. 62–63 (1865): *The Morning Star* (London), 2 March 1865; *Pierwsza Międzynarodówka a sprawa polska, Dokumenty i materiały*, collected by J. K. Borejsza and others under the editorship of Henryk Katz (Warsaw, 1964), pp. 289, 291.

# ADAM MICKIEWICZ'S 'FORTY AND FOUR' OR THE DANGERS OF PLAYING WITH KABBALAHS

Joanna Rostropowicz Clark

There are two ways in which Mickiewicz exists in the consciousness of us, his native readers. One is as the most accessible and therefore the best known of Polish poets – our book of common prayer, our bedtime story, our national anthem. The other way is as our great unknown, the open but seldom *read* book. The latter view was most conspicuously represented by Tadeusz Boy Żeleński who, more than half a century ago, embarked on a one-man campaign to revive the poet as poet, to dismount him from the monument 'gilded with bronze', in the phrase of Boy that has become a cliché.

The rhetoric of Boy's effort is better remembered than its substance. For several years this critic fought against the guardians of the canonized image of Mickiewicz, trying to recover the hidden and partly destroyed documents relating to those aspects of the poet's life that were considered unbecoming to the national bard, the Polish icon. These included sexual 'scandals' but also, as Boy persisted in his search, those pointing toward Mickiewicz's deeply felt, conflicted interest in Jews and Judaism. Convinced that a distorted knowledge of the man impedes the understanding of his poetry, Boy regarded Polish literary criticism as a victim of the nation's history, of the justified demand that art should symbolize survival first, and then life – as 'burdened by social categories, traditions, pieties'. Boy was attacked by his ultra-conservative opponents as a blasphemist and was condescendingly dismissed by the mainstream intellectual élite as not 'intricate' enough. He abandoned his campaign only when he realized that his quest for the unholy grail had begun to fuel the rising bonfires of anti-semitism. Most of his findings, however, were incorporated into Mieczysław Jastrun's novelistic *Mickiewicz*, published in 1948, which subtly weaves into its narrative almost all the existing information about the poet's Jewish affinities.[1]

Yet as Poland continued to suffer through threats to her survival, literary criticism — always more involved with ideology than literature itself — has gone again into the trenches, either drafted to serve the rulers or joining the resistance. Banners and monuments would have priority over detached research, quiet reading, contemplative analysis. Not surprisingly, Mickiewicz's modern biography still waits to be written, and gradually a sense of his remaining an *unknown* poet has begun to surface on the margins of scholarly discourse, perhaps most remarkably in Adam Ważyk's slim volume of essays, *Cudowny Kantorek* [The Marvellous Cabinet], published in 1979 and devoted mostly to Mickiewicz. There, after discovering an amazing interpretational gap in scholarly analyses of *Dziady, Część IV* [Forefathers' Eve, Part IV], Ważyk writes: 'This absent-mindedness, if not wilful neglect, has become a rule of today's academic knowledge, observed in commentaries and larger publications. It is hard to believe, and yet it is true.' He then recalls Boy:

> After my visits with distinguished scholars I looked into Boy. Unburdened by the duties of a historian of literature, he wrote about what interested him, and mysticism would be the last on that list. And yet, in his short introduction to Mickiewicz's collected works, he wrote something about the scene between Gustaw and the Priest which instantly reveals the nature of Mickiewicz's spiritual temperament: 'Ravaged by pain, Gustaw in the Priest's house will years later come to life. Only then, not the love of a woman but the torment of a nation will tear his heart, and he won't be nagging a poor little Byelorussian priest but will challenge, face to face, the Pope.' And that is exactly this improbable poet — the heretic in his youth and unconvincingly converted mystic-realist so magically incarnated in *Pan Tadeusz*, the unsurpassed lyricist and author of trivial fables, the tribune of socialism and the inspired prophet commanding his Legion[2] consisting of a bunch of ragged volunteers, the great humorist, the lover of fairy tales, and the schizophrenic visionary — the authentic Romantic who burst like a meteor into ten pieces but in every one of them remained himself.

As if in defense of scorned scholars, Zdzisław Kępiński in 1980 published a 400-page work, *Mickiewicz Hermetyczny*, an exquisitely researched study of yet another 'unknown' Mickiewicz — in a word, a Freemason. Although not a Lodge member for any marked length of time, the poet, as Kępiński convincingly documents, had been strongly influenced in his youth by close friends (particularly the Wereszczaka family circle) who were dedicated Masons. If any defects can be charged to Kępiński's study, it is certainly not absentmindedness. His erudition is breathtaking in all matters concerning Mickiewicz's curriculum vitae, in history, philosophy and mysticism, and in what used to be known as esoteric or hermetic science. Step by step, he develops the thesis that not only was Mickiewicz deeply influenced by the Freemasonry system, which informed the whole Romantic movement, but that he consciously incorporated its coded language into much of his poetry, most significantly in *The Forefathers' Eve, Part III*. It functions there – and Kępiński wonders if this is perhaps not true in all of Mickiewicz's major works – as the underlying structure that connects the seemingly disjointed parts, according to the Master-Builder's plan.

Take, as examples, the symbols of raven and rose which baffled critics because of the universality, and therefore vagueness, of their meaning. When interpreted in the light of their significance in Freemasonry's ideography, they become clearly specific and instrumental in the dramatic development of the spiritual motif of *Part III* – from Konrad's rebellion against God (shown to be erroneous by the symbolic appearance of the raven, the guardian of the secrets of Destiny), through Ewa's embrace of the rose, *rosa mistica* (symbol of integrity, of harmonious union between the human and the divine, of spiritual love). Thus Ewa/Poland breathes life/love into Konrad/rose. From then on Konrad would no longer think of himself as an all-powerful equal of God but as His humble Christian servant, a leader still but anonymous, a worker among workers. Like Mickiewicz in Andrzej Towiański's *Koło Boże* [God's Circle] his name will be a number – *forty and four*.

And now, with the key of the Masonic code, Kępiński offers his masterstroke – the unravelling of the famous prophetic passage at the end of Father Piotr's 'vision'. In a literal translation it reads:

> And his life – toil of toils.
> And his title – people of peoples.
> From an alien mother, his blood ancient heroes'
> And his name forty and four
> Glory! Glory! Glory!

As every Pole knows, the interpretation of the passage depends on solving – or not solving – the riddle of 'an alien mother' and 'forty and four'. Is the referent an actual person whose name is disguised by the kabbalistic formula (with an additional hint that his mother was stranger, *obca*) or is it a symbolic composite of a prophet/spirit, one of whose hypothetical incarnations could be the poet himself as well as his alter ego, Konrad? After all, almost every great prophet, including Moses and Christ, had an 'alien' mother. But so, according to rumour reinforced by this fragment of *Dziady*, did Mickiewicz.

Kępiński, like Juliusz Kleiner and the majority of the contemporary Mickiewiczologists, believes the second interpretation to be true – that Mickiewicz, deliberately created this quintessentially Romantic tension between the metaphorical and apocryphal meanings of the prophecy. He provides an astounding proof of this view, surprised that no one before had thought of it.

According to Kępiński, Mickiewicz and his tutor in mystical/hermetic matters, Józef Oleszkiewicz, while browsing through various kabbalistic writings, could not have failed to become acquainted with magic tablets representing the planets. Each tablet was a square whose sides were divided according to the numerical symbol of a respective planet, from 3 to 10, and the enclosed chequered field was marked with the letters/numbers of the Hebrew alphabet. The number representing the most powerful heavenly body, the Sun, is six. When filled in with 36 letters, the magic *Quadratus Solis* would yield such results as – the sum total of all its vertical and horizontal lines equals 666 (the number of *daemonium Solis*, signifying in the Kabbalah the apocalyptic beast); the sum of its diagonals equals 111, which, divided by two (with only a minor and kabbalistically justified cheating), produces the number 55 for the radius of the circle described on the *Quadratus Solis*. What the two young adepts of the magic arts did, Kępiński tells us, was simply to replace the Hebrew with the Polish alphabet, and the music of the spheres burst forth in a Messianic hymn of hope and glory.[3]

The numerical value of *Sol*, Sun in Latin, is $23 + 18 + 14 = 55$. (It is also the numerical value of the Polish world *matka*, mother, which Kępiński does not note). The value of the diagonal, 111, forms the word *Zbawienie*, meaning Salvation. 'Salvation ascribed by the radius of the Sun!', Kępiński comments. But the key we are looking for should solve the riddle of 'forty and four',[4] and indeed it is there. The numerical equivalents of three crucial words – *lud* [people], *duch* [spirit], and *baran* [lamb] – add up to 44. Since in Hebrew the letter 'd' (daleth) stands for four and the letter 'm' (mem) for 40, and their conjunction is pronounced *dam*, meaning 'blood', we arrive at the association with the sacrificial lamb, with the line 'his blood is ancient heroes'' and, as had always been recognized, with the name Adam Mickiewicz. Multiplying 44 by three (the envisioned saviour had *trzy oblicza* -three faces) we get the number 132, which is the numerical value of *Lud Ludów* [the people of peoples], of *odkupienie* [redemption] and – *Mickiewicz*! Four times forty-four comes to 176, the value of *Polska i Litwa* [Poland and Lithuania]. Gaping in amazement, we are ready for the triumphant scholar's closing statement, which reads as follows:

> Should it be surprising that the symbol of such a fitting and miraculous key as this 'forty and four' appears to Father Piotr in the Vision which highlights the historiosophical thought of the greatest work of the Villenian poet – the bard of the Polish nation? It dazzlingly appeared before the eyes of Adam Mickiewicz! Could the Polish, Villenian poet resist the request of Józef Oleszkiewicz,

repeated to many friends, 'Learn the properties and secrets of number'?

It is no longer possible to consider the sign 'forty and four' as either entirely *meaningless* or filled only with an incidental meaning tied to the context of the *nearest words* (emphasis added) in this part of the Vision. The symbol 'forty and four' contains and expresses the principal historiosophical ideas of Adam Mickiewicz ... crystallizing, in a sense, the very core of the ideology of the great Polish democrat.

Those of us who were taught by Boy and other modern blasphemists, Gombrowicz, Witkacy, Mrożek, to prick up our ears upon hearing such phrases as 'the bard of the Polish nation' may begin to feel slightly uneasy and stop clapping. Of course Mickiewicz is Polish and Villenian, but why is the author bothering to mention that unspecified 'incidental meaning tied to the context of the nearest words' — words none other than *z matki obcej* (of an alien mother]? We turn back to the magic instrument and stare at the keys. It is still playing. The letters in the word *Polak* (Pole) add up to 66, six and six — two sides of the square, its two arms. And so do the letters in the word *Żyd* [Jew]. Together, 66 and 66 — the two peoples of identical value, of equal spiritual importance, as in Andrzej Towiański's doctrine which Mickiewicz had come to accept as his own — enclose the square's Salvation, Redemption, Spirit and Blood. This was the vision of whose fulfilment the poet dreamed in the last month of his life when, at the age of 55, he created the Jewish Legion while supervising the Polish participation in the Crimean War.

There is really no conclusion except to wonder about the unknown poet. Unknown because all great poetry is unfathomable, or because, as Boy thought, we are blinded by 'social categories, traditions, pieties'? Perhaps the best we can do is to follow Mickiewicz's own passionately Romantic command in the last line of his youthful poem *Romantyczność*: *Miej serce i patrzaj w serce*, which in word-by-word translation means 'Have heart and look into the heart'. To another's heart, anyone's heart, as I have always understood it — to feel and identify with another's feelings. And yet, in Czesław Miłosz's translation of the poem, in his *This History of Polish Literature*, the line reads: 'Cold eye, look into your heart'.

Does it suffice to read only from one's own heart, or do we understand better if we also look into the hearts of others, no matter how unlike our own they may seem? Ważyk complained about the absentmindedness of scholars who would simply skip evidence that disturbed their line of argument, their preconception of the meaning of the text. Lay readers do that too, of course -no act of reading can be ideally open-minded. Zdzisław Kępiński's superb *Mickiewicz hermetyczny*, probably the product of a decade of rigorous work, does not leave a leaf unturned in the dense forest of Mickiewiczology, and yet, like the scientist in *Romantyczność*, he gets carried away by the need to rationalise his bias. The same bias, which prevented the authors of the most recent books⁵ about Mickiewicz in Towiański's *Koło Boże* from even uttering the word 'Jew' or 'Judaism', or (God forbid!) from quoting the poet's line (in one of his College de France lectures of the period) that some of Polish poetry (his own!) belongs to 'Israelian' literature.

The Romantic revolution, more intensely in Poland than anywhere else, was aimed against, in Mickiewicz's words, 'prejudices which dim the light' (*Przesądy światło ćmiące*), or, as the American scholar Northrop Frye phrased it, 'prisons of habit'. Rather than to claim and reclaim the poetry of Mickiewicz, we ought to let it be what it has always been – one nation of many peoples sharing their common suffering, failures and hopes. This unity in diversity is best symbolized in the poetry of *Pan Tadeusz*, a wish-fulfilling image of the nation's life which, as Juliusz Kleiner wrote, 'quite revealingly could be dominated by a Jew's tavern'.

## NOTES

1 Jastrun does not dwell on the unresolved question of the possible Jewish ancestry of Mickiewicz's mother.
2 Ważyk refers here to the Polish Legion Mickiewicz formed in Italy in 1848 – not the Jewish Legion of 1855 (against the Russians in the Crimean War), since the poet did not 'command' the latter.
3 The tables are reproduced after Z. Kępiński.
4 Kępiński devotes several pages to the symbolism of the numbers 40 and 4 in the Bible and other mythologies, as have other scholars before him, but not as thoroughly.
5 Konrad Górski, *Mickiewicz-Towiański* (Warsaw, 1986); Krzysztof Rutkowski, *Braterstwo albo śmierć* (Paris, 1988); Alina Witkowska, *Towiańczycy* (Warsaw, 1989).

## REFERENCES

Adam Mickiewicz, *Dziady, część trzecia* in *Dzieła, vol. III* (Warsaw, 1949).
Adam Ważyk, *Cudowny Kantorek* (Warsaw, 1978), p. 55.
Tadeusz Boy Żeleński, *Brązownicy i inne szkice* (Warsaw, 1957).
Zdzisław Kępiński, *Mickiewicz hermetyczny* (Warsaw, 1980), pp. 333–4.
Juliusz Kleiner, *Mickiewicz* (Warsaw, 1948), p. 525.

# GENDER DIFFERENTIATION AND EDUCATION OF THE JEWISH WOMAN IN NINETEENTH-CENTURY EASTERN EUROPE

Shaul Stampfer

An assessment of the role, function and extent of women's education in nineteenth-century East European Jewry requires a substantial effort to distinguish facts from images. Our picture of the past is affected, of course, by present-day attitudes and stereotypes but even at the time, the contemporary reality was seen in light of assumptions based on cultural postulates. There were a variety of images of the Jewish woman and her education – and they were not necessarily consistent. Therefore, pointing out the differences between the realities and the images not only adds to an understanding of women's education in Eastern Europe but also clarifies the value system of the Jewish community in the previous century. It will be necessary to consider the image of women's education as well as relevant quantitative and qualitative data in order to understand the realities of women's education, the way this education was integrated into broader gender classifications and the implications and consequences of women's education.

## THE IMAGE AND FRAMEWORKS OF WOMEN'S EDUCATION

There is a widely held misconception that, in nineteenth-century Eastern Europe, Jewish women were relatively ignorant from a Jewish point of view while many received a good general education.[1] A classic expression of this view is that of Zvi Scharfstein who wrote a number of widely used studies on the history of Jewish education and who stated in the opening to a (short) chapter on the education of girls:[2]

> The education of the Hebrew daughter – if we measure education as the degree of knowledge of Torah and books – was on a very low level

in our midst. So low as to be a disgrace for the people ... The
Hebrews held that women are just for children and the kitchen and
that he who teaches his daughter Torah taught her worthlessness ...
Only the national revival saved the Hebrew daughter from the shame
of her ignorance – ignorance from the point of view of Judaism.

A typical portrayal of sex differences in Jewish and general education is
that of D. Flinker.[3] While discussing education in Warsaw he noted that,
compared with the education of boys, the education of girls was backward.
At best, the elementary teacher would teach the girl to read Hebrew and
Yiddish and with that all the Jewish education of the Jewish daughter
came to an end. At the same time:

> In the small towns the men would study and acquired a broad and
> deep Torah education and their wives and daughters were
> uneducated and absolute boors. However, in the cities in the most
> recent generations, the girls as well were educated and cultured but
> their culture was different and alien to that of their parents and
> husbands.

It is not hard to find justification of such a situation in classical Jewish
texts. The classic prooftext is 'anyone who teaches his daughter Torah
taught her *tiflut*' (usually translated as indecency or frivolity).[4] This
statement clearly indicates that women do not need any Jewish education
at all. However, the existence of such statements does not mean that they
were accepted, and even if accepted, that they were realized. Students of
the history of Jewish education have often tended to see them as a true
reflection of reality. However, this cannot be taken for granted. It is
necessary to check the accuracy of this image by examining the education
girls actually received.

A number of frameworks existed in which girls could, and did, study,
but there was no standard pattern for women's education as there was for
boys. This variety might well be a product of the lack of interest evoked by
women's education. In many locations special *hederim*[5] operated for girls.
In Tyszowce, a girls' *heder* operated in the same house as the boys' *heder*
but in an adjoining room. The girls were taught by an old widow, Binele
the '*rebitzin*'.[6] The programme of study consisted of prayers, reading and
writing Yiddish, arithmetic and writing addresses in Russian. The text
books were the prayerbook and three Yiddish texts tekhines (women's
prayers), *Tse'ena Ureena* (on this see below),[7] and *Nachlas Tsvi* (a Yiddish
ethical and kabbalistic tract). Sewing was also taught. The young students
spent most of their time at play and were called when it was their turn for
recitation.[8] Many other girls' *hederim* were probably no different.

Other girls were tutored at home. The tutor was often a 'learned' woman who would teach both reading and writing, though at times specialists were hired to teach each skill. Inevitably, such tutoring was for short periods during the day and probably did not amount to more than an hour a day. Since it was expensive, it was limited to the well-off:

> The well-off who gave any education at all to their daughters limited it to prayer and religious matters. Even they didn't send their daughters to school but they were satisfied with a house teacher and the curriculum was limited to reading and writing in Yiddish.[9]

Girls' education was a practical one. Writing was taught by copying business letters and not authoritative religious texts. Countless Jewish girls began their studies with the deathless words 'I went to Odessa to purchase merchandise' – which reflected the utilitarian nature of their education.[10] Their education was seen as the antithesis of that of boys' which was devoted to Torah study, or in other words, cultural education. This is illustrated in the following anecdote about a little boy who wanted very much to write (and ultimately did).[11]

> In our house it was seen as unnecessary for a boy to learn how to write. My sister was sent to Avrom Note the *Shrayber* (writing teacher) but I wasn't. I was supposed to study just Gemara with the Rabbi and not to trouble my head with silly ideas like writing . . .

For some girls, the question of where to study was resolved by their being sent to a *heder* along with the boys. The mixing of the sexes apparently was not considered worthy of note or reaction[12] and the decision to send a girl to a *heder* was usually based on convenience and cost. A *heder* was less expensive than a tutor. As Khaya Weizman-Lichtenstein wrote:[13]

> In the town it wasn't customary to send girls to *heder*, rather a rebbe would come to the house for an hour and teach the girls. In this manner, they would manage to acquire very little knowledge of the Torah and few of them knew Hebrew. For my older sister Miriam my parents hired a private tutor and he taught her all of the curriculum. However, this was impossible to do for the rest of the daughters because the family was too large. Therefore I was sent to (a boys') *heder*.

After basic reading was mastered, boys went on to study classical Jewish texts, the Bible and then Talmud, while girls dropped out.

## QUANTITATIVE DATA ON WOMEN'S EDUCATION

The clearest quantitative picture of the educational realities of East European Jewry at the end of the nineteenth century is provided in a comprehensive survey of Jewish life in Tsarist Russia conducted by ICA (Jewish Colonization Association) at the time.[14] The total number of female *heder* students, whether with boys in a regular *heder* or in special girls' *hederim* was, not surprisingly, low when compared with the number of boys. In 1894, out of 13,683 *hederim*, (which were probably less than half of the *hederim* in the Tsarist empire), 191,505 male pupils were enrolled and 10,459 female pupils.[15] This figure includes girls in special *hederim* for girls as well as girls in boys' *hederim*. These statistics yield a ratio of about one to eighteen. However, this ratio is deceptive with regard to the number of girls *exposed* to education because female students studied for fewer years than males. If we can assume that girls studied at the most four years and boys an average of nine, the ratio for the first four years would be about one to eight. There was some regional variation, with the ratio of female students three times as high, for example, in the south west (which included Odessa) as in Central Poland.[16]

Despite the various opportunities for formal education for girls, it seems that many girls, and probably most, did not get a formal education, and if they did, they studied fewer years than boys. This fits the accepted picture of the education of women. However, if we look at educational achievements and not at schooling, then the stereotype becomes problematic. Women, as a group, were far from being illiterate or uneducated. An indication of the level of women's education can be seen by the distribution of Russian language literacy among the various age cohorts of the Jewish population as recorded in the 1897 census.[17]

Starting from the cohort of men and women born in the 1850s (i.e. ages

### TABLE 1: JEWISH LITERACY AND POST ELEMENTARY EDUCATION IN EUROPEAN RUSSIA IN 1897 BY AGE AND SEX

| Age Group | Literacy in Russian (%) Male/Female | | Post Elementary Education (%) Male/Female | |
|---|---|---|---|---|
| 1–9 | 6 | 5 | – | – |
| 10–19 | 41 | 30 | 1 | 2 |
| 20–29 | 51 | 28 | 2 | 2 |
| 30–39 | 47 | 17 | 2 | 1 |
| 40–49 | 40 | 9 | 1 | – |
| 50–59 | 31 | 6 | – | – |
| 60+ | 22 | 4 | – | – |

40–49), the levels of male and female Russian language literacy begin to converge. This suggests an advance in women's education. However, these data are only for literacy in Russian, while much of women's education, as noted above, was in Yiddish.

The levels of elementary ability to read Russian are surprisingly high. It is of course impossible to determine how careful the census takers were in accepting statements about literacy. When the data are broken down in Table 2 to urban and non-urban populations, the results indicate that urban populations were more literate than non-urban populations, which makes sense. Moreover, the gaps were larger between urban and non-urban females than among males. If the surprisingly high level of female literacy was simply the result of sloppy record-keeping by census takers, the sloppiness should have applied equally to town and country. Hence there is good reason to take the census data seriously.

TABLE 2: JEWISH LITERARY IN PERCENTAGES IN TWO AGE COHORTS IN EUROPEAN RUSSIA IN 1897 BY LOCATION AND SEX

|  | 10–19 male/female | | 20–29 male/female | |
|---|---|---|---|---|
| urban | 49 | 36 | 53 | 33 |
| non urban | 33 | 24 | 48 | 22 |

Unfortunately, the census material does not state in which non-Russian language individuals were literate. The questionnaire of the 1897 census did include a question on literacy in any language which theoretically should have included Yiddish. However, apparently Yiddish was not given the status of a language and the census statistics are clearly unreliable on this score. To learn about literacy in Yiddish we need to turn to other sources.

One of the most useful sources on women's literacy is a survey of the literacy of sample groups of Jewish immigrants carried out in 1913 in the USA.[18] It was conducted by a Jewish organization which was interested in dispelling the image of Jews as illiterates, but with a commitment to objectivity as well. In one sample, consisting of a group of 110 women that arrived in New York, 28 women were recorded as illiterate (25 per cent) but of these, eight of them were able to read the prayerbook leaving only 18 per cent totally illiterate. In a similar study conducted at the same time in Houston, much higher levels of illiteracy for female immigrants (40 per cent) were recorded but this second study apparently did not take into account an ability to read a prayerbook. These data cannot be taken as irrefutable evidence for the educational level of the East European Jewish woman. Migrants to America were not only younger on the whole than the general Jewish population in Eastern Europe but they were also made up of the lower status elements of Jewish society, were less educated and less traditional.[19] Hence it would be quite likely that the higher class contemporaries who stayed behind in the Tsarist empire had even higher levels of literacy.[20]

Within Eastern Europe, the differences were almost certainly not just a question of socio-economic class. There appear to have been significant differences between levels of female literacy in cities and in towns. A study of Jewish workers in Wilno, Warsaw, and Berdichev in 1913 found that in Wilno less than 1 per cent of female workers surveyed were illiterate and less than 7 per cent in Berdichev and Warsaw.[21] At the same time, Lestchinsky found that in the town Horodisht (in the region of Kiev) many of the Jewish factory girls were absolutely illiterate and that almost half of the female population was illiterate, though it is not clear how typical a small town this was.[22]

Given the low figures on school attendance by girls, it appears that most of the literate women learned how to read on their own or with the help of friends or relatives. However, women who learned how to read in this fashion were not necessarily drilled in writing and received, of course, a less systematic course of study than the women who studied in school. Women who learned informally how to read were therefore not likely to write autobiographies, so testimony about this kind of education is difficult to cite. However, the gap between the number of women who read and those who could have gone to school cannot be explained otherwise.[23]

## QUALITATIVE EVIDENCE FOR WOMEN'S EDUCATION

One can often question the accuracy of statistical data and wonder if there were overstatements or understatements of literacy in Yiddish or how representative a sample of the total population was taken. However, one can bring additional strong evidence for significant literacy among women. A long tradition exists regarding the printing of romances and popular literature directed to women.[24] To be sure, this literature was read by many men, who also found it appealing. What is significant is that addressing these books to women, irrespective of who really read them, presumes a reality in which many women could read and were in effect educated – even if they were not recognized as such. As we shall see below, the religious literature for women also played an important role in their lives and reading it was seen as significant behaviour. The Gaon of Wilno called on his female descendants to read this literature,[25] apparently instead of frivolous literature, and he took for granted their ability to read.

One could argue that his daughters may have been exceptional, but the publicity given to the Gaon's views indicate that they were regarded as role models for the general Jewish population.

The discrepancy between statistics on schooling and on literacy makes it necessary to carefully consider what the term 'women's education' means. Education usually relates to two important activities. One is the teaching of practical skills which can aid a person in earning a living or be useful in day-to-day life. The other function involves the study of the cultural tradition of a society.[26] All societies have to meet cultural and practical needs whether formally or informally. The specific determination of what is taught and how, is of course the product of traditions, needs and resources.

Among Eastern European Jewry, as in many societies, formal schooling (such as the *heder*, *bet midrash* and the *yeshiva*), the most visible aspect of education, concentrated on males and was devoted solely to the cultural tradition of the community. Occupational training for both males and females was carried out within the framework of informal education. Crafts were learned by apprentices on the job under the supervision of skilled individuals. Preparation for commerce or business was also learned on the job – though private teachers for specific skills like arithmetic were often used. As long as Jews did not enter occupations which required academic credentials or highly technical expertise, there was no need to include career preparation in the curriculum. The setting up of commercial and trade schools for Jews starting from the latter part of the nineteenth century with programs like that of ORT were important innovations in the Jewish educational systems and they drew on foreign, non-Jewish models and not on precedents within the local educational tradition.[27] The study of Torah was different because it was not practical, and obviously, it did not yield direct economic benefits.

Even *heder* did not emphasize applied knowledge. In a society which saw personal salvation, and possibly also group redemption, as the product of correct ritual behaviour, one might have anticipated that the goal of study would be to ensure that males were familiar with all the fine points of the law. This was not the case. *Halakha* (Jewish Law) was not on the curriculum of either the *heder* or the *yeshiva*. As with other practical skills, Jewish law was generally learned by example, a system possible in a context where most Jews observed law.[28] Since women were not regarded as obligated to study Torah, it was easier to justify formal study of secular topics on their part. Rabbi Elijah Rogoler, the rabbi of Kalisz, boasted in a letter written in 1840 that his younger sister (a candidate for a match) is not only beautiful but knows grammar and how to write Hebrew, Polish and German perfectly, and also has a knowledge of Russian. Her sister (also a candidate for a match) is described as beautiful as well, but no details are provided on her linguistic skills. Apparently such a knowledge of languages was desirable but not standard – even in circles where provisions were made for their study.²⁹

In reality, while males and females were provided with very different frameworks for acquiring literacy education, women were not necessarily inferior to men in Jewish knowledge. Women not only knew how to read but read often. The image of the uneducated woman of the masses coexists with that of the Jewish woman who sat down at home in her chair every Saturday afternoon and read the weekly Torah portion – in Yiddish. It is quite possible, that of all the books sold in Eastern Europe, the two best-sellers were books specifically intended for a female audience and read only by women – *Tse'ena Urena* and *tekhines*. The *Tse'ena Urena* is a Yiddish text consisting of a free retelling of aggadic material. While originally written (around 1600) for both men and women it quickly became the classic women's text. Khone Shmeruk counted 110 editions printed between 1786 and 1900, and he affirms that there were no doubt many more.³⁰ While the regular reading of *Tse'ena Urena* was seen as an act of piety, the ability to read it was clearly not seen as exceptional. The repeated reading of *Tse'ena Urena* gave a woman a good picture of the biblical narrative as seen through the eyes of rabbis. In terms of knowledge of the biblical narrative women who read *Tse'ena Urena* regularly should have known at least as much of the biblical narrative as a male who had finished the *heder* curriculum.

One could cite the custom of having *zogerkes* or prayer prompters for women in the synagogue, who told women what to say and when to cry, as evidence for female illiteracy and ignorance. This would not be accurate. An ability to peruse a Yiddish text is not the same as being able to catch the Hebrew of the prayer service, and reading in the quiet of the home is not the same as finding one's place through the din of the women's section of the synagogue.

There were of course significant differences between the ways men studied classical Hebrew texts and women studied *Tse'ena Urena*. Male study usually took place in the *Bet Midrash* (communal study hall), in the company of peers, and therefore this study was a public demonstration of religious devotion and piety. *Tse'ena Urena* was read in the home and it was family members who served as an 'audience' for the woman's study activity. Males often had additional reasons for studying in public. The many males who were not capable of independent study participated in study societies (*hevrot*) and heard regular classes and lectures on classical texts. Even more advanced individuals who could study on their own anticipated an occasional need for assistance or to consult in order to understand the difficult texts studied, and therefore preferred to study in *Bet Midrash*. Since *Tse'ena Urena* was a Yiddish text it did not present linguistic problems. Moreover, since it lacked the status and classical character of a rabbinic book, it could be and was continually updated from a linguistic point of view, as Shmeruk's work points out. This meant that the *Tse'ena Urena* was easy to understand and it could be studied in private without the necessity of anticipating a need for assistance in understanding a difficult passage. Perhaps the most significant difference between the evaluation of male study of classical Hebrew texts and female study of *Tse'ena Urena* was that only the former was regarded as true study of the Torah while the latter was merely an act of piety.

The world of prayer also exhibited differences between patterns of male and female behavior. An examination of the role of *tekhinot*[31] makes this clear. *Tekhinot* were prayers written in Yiddish and organized around the weekly routine and life cycle of the East European Jewish woman. The *tekhine* literature reflects similar religious values and activities to those of men but radically different frameworks. The *tekhinot* were read by women individually and usually not in a synagogue. They were not chanted nor said in public. They were said therefore only by literate women. Women were free to choose which *tekhin* book to use, which *tekhinot* to say and when. Many of them were presented as having been written by women for women and were adapted to new realities and needs. The covers of *tekhin* books advertised the contents as including 'nice new *tekhines*' – even when that was not the case. A value was placed on the relevance and novelty of the *tekhinot*. All of this was very different from male prayer. Men prayed out of the fixed Hebrew text of the prayerbook. The sanctity of male prayers was closely tied to their ancient origins and novelty was disguised. Men prayed according to a ritual calendar and not according to the needs they felt. The writers of male prayers were figures out of the distant past, and not individuals with whom one could easily identify. What was common to both men and women was that prayer was said from a written text and that literacy was taken for granted.

GENDER DEFINITION IN TRADITIONAL JEWISH SOCIETY[32]

The use of *Tse'ena Urena* and the *tekhine* literature by women instead of the *Humash* (Pentateuch) and *Siddur* (Hebrew prayer book) were just two elements of a much wider range of distinctive gender-defined expressions for similar functions. Jewish men and women could be seen as occupying adjacent but different cultural worlds in Eastern Europe, in which the expression of a function in one gender was the mirror image of its expression in the other gender. Men and women shared a common spoken language and a common religious/national identity. However much else was radically different. Socially, men and women had no direct relationships unless they had common family ties. In the synagogue or *bet midrash*, the holiest place in the community, the seating of men and women was separated. Men came daily to the synagogue for prayer and study, often more than once a day, while women came less often and just for prayer. Men belonged to formal associations (*hevrot*), whereas for women, social life was informal. To a large extent men and women also did not share a literary language. Men were supposed to read Hebrew and if they could, wrote Hebrew, while if women were literate, it was generally in Yiddish. While Yiddish is of course written in Hebrew letters, up until the mid-nineteenth century there was generally no mistaking of a book written in Hebrew – e.g. directed solely to men, and a book written in Yiddish and ostensibly directed to women, because different fonts or types of letters were generally used for Hebrew and Yiddish.[33] When men gave charity it was usually in the synagogue while women gave charity into the 'pushke' or home charity box.[34] Even the concepts of beauty were different. The ideal man was the retiring, pale, delicate Talmudist with sensitive hands and long white fingers, while the ideal woman was an active, even aggressive, full-bodied woman with multiple chins.[35]

To be sure, there were many exceptions to this gender division and they did not extend to every sphere of life. Both men and women generally worked and contributed to the family income, so that there was no clear distinction between the males as breadwinners and the women as homemakers, as was common in many other societies. The economic conditions did not allow for that. Of course, the women's responsibilities for the home were clear – hers was the responsibility of running the house – even if she was the main breadwinner.[36] Generally, the occupational distribution of men and women was such that there was little direct competition between them. Even in the late nineteenth century when factory work became more common, men and women still did not work side by side in factories. To be sure, many men read Yiddish material, while there were also women who could read literature published in Hebrew. However, men were expected to read Hebrew while Yiddish works were generally, if not for the women, specifically directed to the unlearned. Similarly, the number of women who could understand a Hebrew text was probably statistically insignificant.

THE EDUCATIONAL REALITIES OF JEWISH WOMEN

In light of the fact that gender differences often concealed similar functions, it is worth re-examining basic educational institutions among Jews with the intention of distinguishing between the image and the reality. From this perspective, it is clear that the differences between the educational achievements of boys and girls on the level of elementary education, were more perceived than real – just as the differences in knowledge and prayer experience between men and women were more apparent and linguistic than real. Boys spent all day in the *heder*. However, much of their day was spent in play and story-telling, while the *melamed*[37] sat down for short periods of time with individuals or groups of two and three.[38] Thus the result of a boy's full day of non-intensive study in a *heder* was not necessarily much more than those of tutored girls who may have studied an hour or two a day. Women's education was certainly less stressful, which may explain in part why female education was not usually accompanied by the violence which so often characterized heder education. It was considered right for boys to be beaten but not for girls – though there were exceptions. Esther Rosenthal-Schneiderman (b. circa 1900) recalled never being beaten by her teacher, the *rebitzin* – but got plenty of slaps and pinches from the teacher's husband, the rabbi![39]

The low pressure and often informal elementary education of women was made possible by limitation to Yiddish. Among the many virtues of the Yiddish language is that, in written Yiddish, each letter has one sound and vowels are represented by letters – with the exception of words of Hebrew origin which are limited in number. In Hebrew, letters also have one phonic meaning, but vowels are represented by dots (often smudgy) in vocalized Hebrew texts and by nothing at all in unvocalized texts – and most printed Hebrew texts were unvocalized. Since Yiddish was the spoken language, the beginning reader could anticipate words and sounds from the context, which further facilitated learning to read Yiddish. As a result, while it sometimes took well over a year of *heder* study for a little boy to learn how to read Hebrew freely, a young woman should have been able to learn to read Yiddish in a short time – perhaps only a few weeks. Moreover, as soon as she could read she could understand what she read – which was an achievement not every *heder* student reached even after years of study. In short, women had an easier time than men in reaching functional literacy. Moreover, most men did not get much further than functional literacy in Hebrew despite all their years of study. While advanced Talmudic study was the goal of male study, it must be remembered that only a minority of students went on to such study.

Women could also go on 'past' *Tse'ena Urena* to acquire additional Jewish knowledge. A wide number of aggadic texts (texts of the non legal rabbinic literature) were also available in Yiddish and even much of the Zohar (the classic kabbalistic text) was, theoretically at least, available in Yiddish. In the early nineteenth century no general works in Yiddish on Jewish law were available and certainly no adaptations of classical rabbinic texts (such as the Talmud) into Yiddish for women.[40]

There were a few books of Jewish law in Yiddish that were specifically directed to a female audience. These were limited to topics which were relevant specifically to women, such as the laws dealing with kosher food and the laws relating to the times when intercourse after menstruation was permitted. The publication of such literature had been a topic of controversy when these books were first printed, and at least one important rabbi in Eastern Europe regarded this literature with misgivings and praised women for not relying on it.[41] This was apparently too close to the men's 'territory'. At the same time, since the study of Jewish law – in any form – was not part of the standard *heder* curriculum, there was no significant difference, in fact, in the way most men and women learned Jewish law. What should be noted is that, given the amount and variety of sources available in Yiddish, a reader limited to Yiddish could still become quite familiar with most areas of Jewish knowledge.[42]

Women's life contained functional equivalents to male activities which required reading, but these activities lacked the same status. For women these activities were voluntary, whereas for men they were obligatory. However, while women recognized the value of male activities such as prayer and study, men did not place similar value on the parallel activities among women or demand that women devote their time to these activities. The image of female ignorance made it possible to regard women as inferior to men, even though the image had little truth to it. The function of limited access to knowledge as a means of social repression was not unique to women in Jewish society. Among men as well, knowledge of Talmud, which was restricted to a socio-economic élite, served as a means of proving to the ignorant masses that they deserved their inferior position in society.[43]

## ACCEPTANCE AND REJECTION OF WOMEN'S ROLES IN EDUCATION

In most cases, this system of limited formal education for most women was appropriate for the realities of traditional Jewish society in the early nineteenth century. Most women worked, either independently or helping their fathers or husbands, because their families could hardly make a living otherwise. Moreover they were also burdened by family responsibilities. With a high birthrate and without technologies to save time in housework, even most non-working housewives had few leisure moments or time to study difficult Hebrew texts. An education that trained them to devote hours every day to the study of the Talmud would have been an education designed to maximize frustration. Lack of 'school education' was part of a system that functioned to condition women to accept their role in the family and society with a minimum of conflict – just as the fact that most men were unlearned (and knew it!) was one of the ways that led them to accept communal authority. While most women apparently accepted this role and found fulfilment in the parallel culture that was theirs – and was meaningful to them,[44] that does not mean that all did. The daughter of the famous Yiddish writer Shomer wrote of her mother:[45]

> My mother in all the days of her long life bitterly resented the meagerness of her youthful education and cordially despised the three special duties [incumbent on women – candle lighting, ritual bathing and baking bread in accordance with Jewish law – S.S.] even if she did, in a manner of speaking, observe them ... According to my mother, her father spent thousands of rubles on every cause and every charity in the town but denied her a ruble with which to pay for instruction in the Russian or Hebrew she had desired so much.

In her case, economic pressure could not justify the lack of investment in her education and this may have contributed to her frustration.

That this dissatisfaction could exist in the circles of the rabbinic élite as well, we learn from a description, written by the well known Rabbi Boruch Epstein about his aunt, the wife of the Rosh Yeshiva of Volozhin, Rabbi Naftali Zvi Yehuda Berlin[46]: The events described took place around 1875.

> ... she was worried and vexed about the defiled honour of the women and their lowly status due to the fact that the Rabbis forbid teaching them Torah. One time she told me that if Eve (meaning the female sex) was cursed with ten curses, the prohibition of learning Torah, is equivalent to all the curses and is even more than all of them. There was no end to the grief. One time, while she was speaking excitably on this subject, I said to her, 'But my aunt, you women are blaming the men for this prohibition when they are not at fault. You yourselves caused this and you are guilty in the matter', and I explained my words. Our sages said (at the end of the second chapter of *Avot de Rabbi Natan*) that Torah should only be taught to a humble person. About women, our Sages decided in *Yerushalmi Shabbat*, Chapter 6, that 'they [women] are ostentatious' meaning conceited beings. If so, isn't it forbidden to teach them Torah because of their character traits, and who is to blame if not they themselves, and why do they complain? ... She said to me: 'When I have free time I will do research on the word and find out the exact meaning. In the meantime bring me *Avot de Rabbi Natan* and I will look for the words which you mentioned from them.' I went and brought ... and fell right into the trap! In *Avot de Rabbi Natan* the wording is as follows: Bet Shammai says: 'A person shall only teach to one who is clever, humble and rich' and Bet Hillel says: 'We teach to everyone because there were many sinners in Israel and they started learning the Torah and became righteous, observant men'.

As she finished reading these words, she raised her voice in anger and said, 'How did you do this evil thing, or was it because you wanted to trick me that you took the opinion of Bet Shammai as the basis for your word? Every boy who has studied even a little Talmud knows that when there is a disagreement between Bet Shammai and Bet Hillel, the law is in accordance with Bet Hillel, and Bet Hillel permits teaching Torah to everyone!!' ... As she was in good spirits at her victory over me, she was no longer angry with me, and when she saw that I had taken it somewhat to heart, she comforted me ... and began to talk about this topic in a general manner ... I remember that when she mentioned the name of Bruria, the wife of Rabbi Meir, I told her that a wrongdoing was found against her – that she mocked the words of our Sages, for 'women are light-headed.' In the end she herself was guilty of light-headedness, as is brought out in the story of Rashi on *Avoda Zara* 18b. She answered me, 'In truth, I know of this legend, but did our Sages find all men guilty because of the sin of Aher, who left the right way (*Hagiga* 15a)? Furthermore, Bruria did not mock with contempt and derision. She only thought that our Sages did not fully understand the rationale of women. According to her view, women are also strong-minded. This was the entire incident and nothing more.

There is no reason to take cases as evidence for widespread dissatisfaction among women. Indeed, there were probably as many boys who envied their sisters who were free of the *heder* as vice versa. However, they do indicate the tensions inherent in the educational system for women and the potential for change even in the most conservative circles.

CHANGING PATTERNS OF EDUCATION OF THE JEWISH WOMAN

Changes in women's education can be traced back to early in the nineteenth century. While almost no attention has been given to the fact, in two important centres of modernization in Eastern Europe – Warsaw and in Wilno – secular schools for girls were founded before secular schools for boys. In 1818, a 'modern' girls' school which taught secular topics was organized in Warsaw and almost immediately there was an initiative to open up a second school for girls. The first secular school for boys in Poland was set up only the following year by Jacob Tugenhold.[47] The first school for girls in the Pale of Settlement was founded in Wilno in 1826. It was succesful and continued to function through the 1840s. The famous Talmud Torah in Odessa was founded seven years later and the first school for boys in Wilno which included secular studies was founded only in 1841.[48] These developments were of course exceptions. However, by the

1860s, the traditional patterns of women's education began to erode and increasing numbers of women were studying in the modern schools, public and private, that were appearing, especially in the large cities.[49] However, the high cost of such an education makes it clear that the female students could have come only from families that were well off – which was not typical for the Jewish community.[50] This shift was related to many factors of which the most important were probably the influence of 'modern' values and models as well as a rise in the average age at marriage among the upper class of the Jewish community. While the first is generally well known, the second deserves some attention.[51]

Early in the nineteenth century, and long before as well, high status was demonstrated in Eastern European Jewry by marrying off the children at an early age.[52] Before reaching her teens, a girl from an élite home would become a '*baalebosta*'[53] with all of the duties that it entailed. For her parents, this meant undertaking to support an adolescent son-in-law (who often had a very healthy appetite) as well as potential grandchildren, for a number of years. For a variety of reasons, this pattern shifted in the course of the nineteenth century, as is shown by the following table:[54]

TABLE 3: AGE AT MARRIAGE IN PERCENTAGES OF ALL JEWISH WOMEN MARRYING IN THE TSARIST EMPIRE

| Age | 1867 | 1885 | 1902 |
|---|---|---|---|
| 20 and below | 60.8 | 47.0 | 23.9 |
| 21–25 | 21.2 | 37.1 | 52.5 |
| 26–30 | 8.1 | 8.0 | 13.0 |

This rise in the age of marriage created, by the late nineteenth century, a population of teen-age girls from well-off families who had to pass time until marriage. It was necessary to find legitimate ways for young women to spend this time until they got married. Study was an ideal solution because it was consonant with contemporary non-Jewish elite views that women's education was desirable. One option was tutoring for women. However, this was expensive and, moreover, was becoming outmoded. Schools were the answer – whether government-sponsored or under Jewish auspices. The number of women in these schools was constantly on the rise from the mid-nineteenth century on.[55]

To justify devoting a few years to its study entailed having a sufficiently respectable syllabus. What was to be studied? The traditional rabbinic literacy corpus in Hebrew was regarded of course as suitable only for males. Yiddish texts, intended for independent study, were too 'easy' to justify a formal education. There were a number of options. One possibility was to provide a commercial education. This fitted the ideal of the working woman who supported her scholarly husband, an ideal that coexisted with that of the rich merchant, and a reality where many women worked. However, many young women and their parents preferred a cultural education. Such an education was of course testimony to the wealth of the household. Among the standard elements adopted were the study of French and the playing of piano – both suitably esoteric and non-utilitarian – and valued by the surrounding society as well. At a time when secular studies were traditionally seen in Jewish circles as irrelevant but not evil or harmful, such an education, which was typical for the non-Jewish élite, could easily be seen as not only permissible but even desirable for Jewish women.

However, what men thought general education was about, was not always what women found. Even without social contacts with non-Jewish society, a woman who received a general education was introduced to a world, even if only a literary one, which promised not only status but a very different set of values. Women often accepted these values and made radical changes in their life-style which led to estrangement from traditional forms of Judaism. Thus by the mid-nineteenth century there was no lack of families in which boys studied Talmud and their sisters French literature. This looked incongruous in later generations which viewed secular studies as evil or leading to evil. It can not be overemphasized that only a small minority of Jewish girls grew up in such homes. None the less, this secular situation attracted attention and began to be seen as typical – even though most Jewish homes were far too poor to provide either sons or daughters with higher education.

While only a minority of women went to modern schools, the number who did was not insignificant by the end of the nineteenth century. In 1899, a survey of such schools in the Tsarist empire found 193 girls' schools and 68 schools for both boys and girls (usually in separate classes) as opposed to 383 boys' schools.[56] This yields very different ratios between males and females than the *hederim*. Of the 50,773 students enrolled in such schools, about a third were girls. When population is taken into account, one finds that the most favourable ratio of female students to the total Jewish population was in the south (one female pupil for every 109 Jews) followed by the northwest (one per 208) with the least favourable the southwest (one per 458). The vast majority of the girls' schools were private (172), while of the boys' schools only 187 were private, and the rest were government or communal schools. In Eastern Europe the cost of tuition of girls in private schools was 50 per cent higher than that of boys. The large number of private girls' schools clearly indicates widespread interest in girls' education and willingness to pay for it along with an unwillingness or lack of interest on the part of the communities or government to invest in women's education. The girls' schools, it should be noted, were not just finishing schools with lots of glitter and little content. The academic level of the teachers in the girls schools was significantly higher than the average in the boys' schools and many of the teachers were women – positive role models.

These figures do not come near to fully reflecting the hunger for knowledge among the Jewish women of the Tsarist Empire – or of their parents. A study in 1894 showed that for almost every girl who applied for admission to a private school and was accepted – another was turned down for lack of space. It was equally difficult for a girl to gain admission to a coeducational school. The highest level of refusals was for admission to communal schools which enrolled mainly males. These schools had the advantage of being inexpensive and also under Jewish administration. In addition, Jewish girls tended to remain in private schools much longer than Jewish boys did.[57]

The pressure for admission to girls' schools in the Tsarist empire probably explains the differences between the enrolment of Jewish boys and girls in government schools. Reports from 1898 dealing with public elementary schools in the Wilno and Kiev districts indicate that in Wilno more Jewish girls went to public non-Jewish schools than did Jewish boys. About 14 per cent of the female students in the Wilno schools were Jewish while the Jewish boys made up 2.7 per cent. In Kiev the male Jewish pupils outnumbered the females by five to one, but both males and females made up about 4 per cent of the pupils of their respective sexes.[58] One must be careful about drawing conclusions from these data because attendance at these schools was hindered both by administrative hurdles designed to keep out Jews, especially boys, and by a policy which demanded that Jewish children attend classes on the sabbath and on holidays and violate the Jewish sabbath laws by writing.

The situation in Galicia, in the Austro-Hungarian empire, which had a far more effective program of public schools for Jews than existed in the Tsarist empire, was quite different and illustrates the potential for change in an East European Jewish population.

Unfortunately, we do not have detailed age breakdowns of the base population which would enable us to assess the exact percentage of school-age children actually attending school. However, there are rough figures on the age breakdown of Galician Jewry in 1890.[60] There were about 230,000 children under the age of 10 in Galicia in 1890 and 180,000 in the 10 to 20 year olds. Thus school age yearly cohorts were probably roughly 20,000. Assuming elementary schools had 6–8 grades, in 1890 the number of school-age children was about 150,000 and roughly 25 per cent of school-age boys and 40 per cent of school-age girls were in these schools. A decade later (assuming no dramatic changes in the size of the cohorts) roughly 45 per cent of the boys were in these schools and 60 per cent of the

## TABLE 4: ATTENDANCE OF JEWS IN MODERN ELEMENTARY SCHOOLS IN GALICIA[86]

| Year | Government Schools | | Private Schools | | Total | |
|---|---|---|---|---|---|---|
| | Boys | Girls | Boys | Girls | Boys | Girls |
| 1880 | 10599 | 18271 | 1910 | 2620 | 12509 | 20891 |
| 1890 | 15497 | 29573 | 2555 | 2666 | 18052 | 32239 |
| 1900 | 22666 | 43855 | 10298 | 1647 | 32964 | 45502 |

girls. It is clear that the number of girls who received a modern education was increasing rapidly at the end of the nineteenth century. The masses of the Jewish population still retained traditional distinctions between what was proper for boys to study and for girls – though this was changing. However, in secondary and higher education, which was directly geared to careers and was common only among the socio-economic élite, the sexual balance was sharply reversed and boys far outnumbered girls.[61]

## THE BACKGROUND OF THE STEREOTYPE OF WOMEN'S EDUCATION

The fact that women did not study in formal institutions contributed to the stereotype of East European women as having very limited education. Studies of educational history or descriptions of educational realities tend to centre on the development and growth of schools – whatever their function. Schools are highly visible institutions and make easy topics for research and description. However, limiting the history of education to schools is justifiable only to the degree that education is concentrated in formal frameworks. For example, in studying American student societies in the eighteenth and nineteenth centuries, James McLachlan found this to be the case in the formal classroom and justifiably claimed that 'the study of the formal curriculum of the early 19th century American College cannot be carried on in isolation from an equally intense study of the students' extra curriculum. To do so produces a completely misleading – in fact, downright false – impression of the history of American higher education.'[62] The same is true for Jewish women's education in Eastern Europe.

The traditional image of the extremely low level of women's education in traditional Jewish society can be accepted only if one adopts a very narrow definition of education which limits it to schooling and assumes that a religious text written in Hebrew is significant, whereas one written in

Yiddish is not. This distinction is artificial and misleading. To be sure, precisely such an identification of education with schooling was actually held by both men and women in the past. Their attention, like that of later observers, was caught by the fact that, in sharp contrast to the situation among males, few educational institutions were available for Jewish women and those which existed were elementary, poorly documented, and not well developed. However, since only males were really expected to go to school, concentrating on schools means in effect squeezing women into male categories, rather than seeing the full educational life of women. Far more significant is the fact that large numbers of women could read and did so – despite the fact that they hardly went to school. They acquired knowledge through reading and in this respect they were more self-sufficient than men who learned by listening to lectures and sermons! This behaviour was regarded as standard and desirable and not as deviant. It was also not categorized as Torah study, since women studied in Yiddish and mastered different texts from those which men did. However, these are not grounds for characterising these women as uneducated – despite the fact that at the time that is how they were viewed by others and also how they saw themselves. To accept this assessment is to assume male-oriented values as having absolute value and to miss the far more complex manner in which women's achievements were devalued. In short, to understand the past it is not sufficient to rediscover what was known in the past. It is also necessary to point out that which people in the past were not always aware of.

## CONSEQUENCES

By the beginning of the twentieth century, women's education among East European Jewry was in a state of ferment. Significant numbers of women were exploring new educational frameworks. Traditional patterns, such as the regular reading of *Tse'ena Urena* and other religious texts, had exposed women to reading and accustomed them to turn to the printed text as a normal way to knowledge. At the same time, the traditional attitudes which had denied women access to classical Jewish literature, had allowed women to read Yiddish *belles lettres*. However, for males, reading for pleasure was a problem because, in theory at least, men were supposed to spend as much time as possible on Torah study.[63] Men had to justify not spending time in study either on practical grounds, such as the need to earn a living or on theological grounds such as involvement in other pious deeds. Reading literature does not fall into either category. However, women, who were not expected to study Torah, did not have to justify how they spent their time and hence their freedom to read for pleasure. Thus, inadvertently, the traditional Jewish patterns themselves facilitated change and developement in the lives of women. Women, even in traditional circles, were easily exposed to new bodies of literature. The *Haskala* literature and the Hebrew newspaper which served in the second half of the nineteenth century as agents of change in the intellectual world of men had their contemporary parallels in the developing Yiddish press and literature which was more directed to women – and the uneducated men.[64] Tsederbaum's influential newspaper *HaMelitz*, directed to a Hebrew-reading male public, was outsold in the 1860s by the emerging Yiddish press with its start in works directed to female readers. There is no question that there was a larger body of female readers. As Roskies points out in an article on this topic, the Yiddish popular writer Isaac Meir Dik could boast in 1860 that, after only five years of writing, 100,000 copies of his works had been sold.[65] The whole development of Yiddish literature was possible only because even in traditional Jewish society, a high proportion of the female Jewish population was literate, knowledgeable and accustomed to the written word.[66] The female immigrants to the United States and their daughters displayed an exceptional thirst for education and their educational achievements were far above those of other immigrants.[67] No single factor can explain the success of first and second generation American Jewish women in the American educational system. However, the fact that in East European Jewish society, the ideal mother read regularly and studied from books certainly did not have a negative effect. Here, as in many other cases, a careful consideration of the realities of Jewish life allows for a significant correction of stereotypical views.

## ACKNOWLEDGEMENTS

\* My thanks to Israel Bartal, Menahem Blondheim, Lisa Epstein, Michael Silber, Deborah Weissman, Zvi Wolf and Sarah Zfatman, for their constructive comments and criticisms. As usual, I am responsible for the results.

## NOTES

1 One notable exception is a very perceptible unpublished paper by Jeffrey Shandler, currently at the YIVO Institute, titled 'Towards an Assessment of the Education of Women in Ashkenaz'(1985). The author very generously shared his paper with me, and, independently, we reached similar conclusion. The scope of his paper is much broader and it is very suggestive on a number of topics which are not dealt with here. For a useful and enlightening survey of realities and developments in women's education in Central European Jewry in the enlightenment period see Mordechai

Eliav *Jewish Education in Germany in the Period of Enlightenment and Emancipation* (Jerusalem, 1960) Ch. 11 'Education of Daughters' pp. 271–9.
2 *Hadeher Bekhayei Amenu*, 2nd ed. (Tel Aviv, 1951) p. 127.
3 D. Flinker, 'Warsaw' (in *Arim ve-Imahot Be-Yisrael* pt.III ed. J.Fishman) (Jerusalem, 1948) (in Hebrew) p. 163.
4 *Talmud Babli Sota* 20a.
5 A Hebrew term for a private one-room/one-teacher school.
6 The term literally means rabbi's wife – though it may have been used for learned women in general.
7 On *Tse'ena Urena* see below.
8 Yekhiel Shtern, *Kheyder un Beys-medresh* (NY, 1950).
9 Shlomo Zaltsman, *Ayarati* (Tel Aviv, 1947), p. 45.
10 P. Sharagrodska, 'Der Shura Gruss' *Filologishe Shriften fun Yivo* I (1926) pp. 67–72.
11 Mordkhe Spektor, *Mayn lebn* (Warsaw, 19..), p. 159.
12 This may be a bit surprising to readers today, given the contemporary concern (or obsession) in certain very orthodox-Jewish circles about co-educational education even in elementary grades, but it should be emphasized that a century ago, sending a girl to a boys' *heder* was not considered as having symbolic significance or reflecting an ideological commitment. *Hederim* were not competing with a co-ed system.
13 *Betsel Koroteynu* (Tel Aviv, 1948), p. 19.
14 *Recueil de materiaux sur la situation Économique des Israelites de Russie* (Paris, Felix Alcan, 1906). This is the source for all the following data up until references to the 1897 census.
15 Ibid. p. 279.
16 Ibid. P.294–5. It would be premature to attribute this to modern attitudes in the south-west or differing approaches to women's education. This variation was very possibly due to the fact that many of these *hederim* were in small towns where patterns were more fluid and where there were no alternatives for little girls, and not necessarily to a regional interest in reform. Most modernisers sent their children to a very different kind of school – coed or otherwise – and not to a *heder*. The attempt at the end of the nineteenth century to set up a new modern type of *heder* which emphasized Hebrew and was known as the *heder metukan* was a small-scale phenomenon which would not have affected these figures. On this new type of *heder* see Yossi Goldstein 'The Heder Metukan in Russia as a Basis for the Zionist Movement' *Iyunim Bechinuch* 45 (June 1986) pp. 147–57 (in Hebrew).
17 *Obshchi Svod Po Imperii Rezultatov Razrabotki Dannix Pervoi Bceobshchi Perepisi Naselenia* I (St. Peterburg, 1905) Table XVI In this census, literacy was defined very broadly, as compared with later censuses, as has been pointed out. 'In 1897 . . . people who stated that they could read were considered literate; in 1926 people were considered literate if they were able to write their last name; by 1959, the questionnaire asked whether respondents could read and write . . . 'Ralph Clem *Research Guide to the Russian and Soviet Censuses* (Ithaca, 1986) p. 167.
18 *Jewish Immigrant/Report of a Special Committee of the National Jewish Immigration Council Appointed to Examine into the Question of Illiteracy Among Jewish Immigrants and its Causes* Senate Document 611 63rd Congress 2nd Session (Washington DC Government Printing Office, 1914).
19 See S. Kuznets, 'Immigration of Russian Jews to the United States: Background and Structure', *Perspectives in American History* 9 (1975), pp. 35–126 and Z. Halevy, 'Were the Jewish Immigrants to the United States Representative of Russian Jews', *Migration* 16:2 (1978), pp. 66–73.

20 These data are of course very revealing about the make-up of the immigrant community. If the sample was typical for the immigrants, and there is no reason to suspect that it was not, it shows that most women who came knew how to read even though most of them came from the 'lower classes' of East European Jewish society and the less traditional element.
21 S. Rabinowitsh – Margolin, 'Zur Bildungsstatistik der Jüdischen Arbeiter in Russland', *Zeitschrift fuer Demographie und Statistik der Juden* IX:11 Nov. 1913 pp. 153–61.
22 J. Lestchinsky, 'Statistics of a Town', *The Jewish Dispersion* (in Hebrew) (Jerusalem, 1961), pp. 17–38, especially 34–5.
23 Being able to read does not mean that women knew how to write. A survey of signatures on marriage contracts in Warsaw in 1845 and 1860 indicates that only a third of the Jewish men and a similar percentage of Jewish women could sign their names. S. Kowalska-Glikman, 'Ludność Żydowska Warszawy ... w Świetle Akt Stanu Cywilnego', *BZIH* 1981:2 (118), pp. 37–49.
24 For information in English on this topic see David Roskies, 'Yiddish Popular Literature and the Female Reader', *Journal of Popular Culture* (1979), pp. 852–8 and 'The Medium and Message of the Maskilic Chapbook', *Jewish Social Studies*, XLI: 3–4 (1979), pp. 275–90, and see the forthcoming study of Chava Weissler, 'For Women and For Men Who Are Like Women', in *Journal of Feminist Studies in Religion*.
25 See the letter he wrote to his family on his way to Eretz Israel. It was first printed in *Alim Litrufa* (Minsk) and often reprinted. This was by no means unique. The Hatam Sofer in Pressburg, Hungary (= Bratislava) also called on his daughters to read religious works written in Yiddish – but no more. See his will, which has been translated into English in J. Reimer, and N. Stampfer, *Ethical Wills/A Modern Jewish Treasury*, (New York, 1983), pp. 18–21.
26 This does not mean that there are not other functions to education as well. For example, schools are often expected to encourage the development of proper character or personality among their students. However in practice, these are usually secondary to one or both of the two main functions.
27 On trade education among Jews in Germany see Mordechai Eliav, *Jewish Education in Germany in the Period of Enlightenment and Emancipation* (Jerusalem, 1960), Ch. 12. On ORT in Russia see Leon Shapiro, *The History of ORT*, (New York, Schocken, 1980). On vocational training in general see Bernard Weinryb, *Jewish Vocational Education* (NY, 1948), esp. part 2.
28 The tractates of the Talmud that were most often studied were not related to everyday life and even when relevant ones were studied, the halakhic implications and the legal conclusions were often ignored. When questions of practice came up, recourse was had to written guides on occasion, but in most questions of doubt, the rabbi was asked. To be sure, convenient summaries of Jewish law such as *Khayei Adam* were very popular and many study circles studied them regularly. However, in quantitative terms, the number of circles devoted to popular halakha was far smaller than those devoted to the saying of Psalms or the study of Aggada, Mishna, Talmud or similar texts.
29 See 'A Collection of Letters of R. Elijah Rogolier' ed. Efraim Urbach, *Kobez Al Yad*, VI (XVI), Pt. II (Jerusalem, 1966), p. 549. I thank Michael Silber for the reference.
30 Khone Shmeruk 'East European Versions of Tse'ene-Rene 1786–1859', *For Max Weinreich on the Seventieth Birthday* (Hague, 1964), pp. 320–36. On *Tse'ena Urena* see also K. Turniansky, 'Translations and Adaptations of the Tse'ena Urena' in the *Dov Sadan Jubilee Volume* (Tel Aviv, 1977), pp. 165–90. In the opening of her article she

mentions that it was an 'integral part of the 'oneg shabat' (shabat joy) in every Jewish home in Western and Eastern Europen and that it was the most popular Yiddish book'. On the *tekhinot* see the important articles of Chava Weissler: 'The Traditional Piety of Ashkenazic Women' in *Jewish Spirituality from the Sixteenth-Century Revival to the Present* ed. Arthur Green (New York, 1987), pp. 245–75 and 'The Religion of Traditional Ashkenazic Women: Some Methodological Issues', *AJS Review* XII:1, (Spring, 1987), pp. 73–94.

32 This topic has not received a great deal of attention in the literature, and much of what there is has hardly gone past the descriptive. See, for example, M. Zborowski and E. Herzog, *Life is with People* (NY, 1952), Part II Chapter 4. An example of what can be done by means of careful analysis in Chava Weissler's article 'For Women And For Men Who Are Like Women' forthcoming in *Journal of Feminist Studies in Religion*.

33 See M. Weinreich, *Oisgeklibene Shriftn* (Buenos Aires, 1974), p. 66. I am grateful to Prof. Turniansky for the Reference.

34 On the social history of the *pushke* see my article 'The Pushke and its Development', (in Hebrew) *Katedra* 21 (October 1981), pp. 89–102.

35 T. Somogyi, *Die Scheinen und die Prosten* (Berlin, 1982).

36 Michael Silber has found references in literature dealing with Hungarian Jews of men who were supported by their wives and were expected to do household chores. I have not found any such cases in Eastern Europe.

37 teacher.

38 See the vivid description of Yekhiel Shtern, 'A Heder in Tyszowce', *YIVO Annual* V (1950), p. 164. The article was reprinted in *Studies in Modern Jewish Social History* ed. Joshua Fishman (NY, 1972). The citation there is on p. 36.

39 *Naftulei Drakhim* (Tel Aviv, 1970), p. 31.

40 Works such as *Lekah Tov* – a Yiddish crib of the Talmud for *heder* teachers and students, was not part of the woman's library. There was no translation into Yiddish of a comprehensive guide to Jewish law, such as the *Shulkhan Aruch*, in the pre-modern period. The creation of popular guides to Jewish law, even in Hebrew, is itself a modern innovation. *Khayei Adam*, a very popular summary of Jewish law directed to non-learned readers, appeared in 1810, while the first Yiddish translation found in the National Library in Jerusalem dates to 1865. On this book see A. Goldrat 'On the Book "Khayei Adam" and its Author', in *Sefer Margaliot*, (Jerusalem, 1973), pp. 255–78. The first Yiddish translation found in the National Library of the *Kizzur Shulkhan Aruch* (a similar summary published in Hebrew in the 1860's) appeared in 1882. In short, general guides to Jewish law became available in Yiddish in the second half of the nineteenth century. On aspects of Jewish law specifically related to Jewish women there were Yiddish publications. See Agnes Segal, 'Yiddish Works on Women's Commandments in the Sixteenth Century', in *Studies in Yiddish Literature and Folklore* (Jerusalem, 1986), pp. 37–59 and Simcha Asaf, 'A Responsum Against the Writing of Law Books in Yiddish', in his *Mekorot Umekhkarim* (Jerusalem, 1946), pp. 249–51 (in Hebrew).

41 'It was never the custom to teach women from books and I never heard of such a practice. Rather the known (e.g. relevant) laws are taught by each woman to her daughter and daughter in law and recently books of womens' law have been printed in the language of the nations (e.g. Yiddish!) and they can read them and our women are energetic in every case of doubt and ask and do not rely on their (book) knowledge in even the slightest matter.' Yechiel Michel Epstein, *Aruch Hashulchan*, Yore Death, 246:19.

42 See Yosef Yerushalmi, *From Spanish Court to Italian Ghetto* (NY, 1971), for an example of what a marrano could learn from translations into Spanish.

43 See Amos Funkenstein, and Adin Steinsaltz, *Sociology of Ignorance*, (in Hebrew, Tel Aviv 1987), and my 'Heder Study, Knowledge of Torah, and the Maintenance of Social Stratification in Traditional East European Jewish Society' in *Studies in Jewish Education* III (Jerusalem, 1988), pp. 271–89.
44 S. Zaltsman, *Ayarati* (Tel Aviv, 1947), p. 47.
45 Miriam Zunser, *Yesterday* (NY, 1978), p. 66.
46 Borukh Epstein, *Mekor Boruch*, selection trans. by Malka Bina in *Petach* II (Jerusalem, 1975), pp. 98–100.
47 Jacob Shatzky, *Jewish Educational Policies in Poland from 1806 to 1866* (NY, 1943) [Yiddish], p. 210–12. See also Sabina Levin, 'The First Elementary Schools for Children of the Mosaic Faith in Warsaw 1818–1830' in *Galed* I (1973), pp. 63–100, esp. pp. 78–9.
48 See Israel Klausner, *Vilna, Jerusalem of Lithuania/Generations from 1495–1881* (Ghetto Fighter's House, Israel), pp. 207–8 [in Hebrew].
49 This phenomenom will be discussed by Semyon Kreis in a Ph.D thesis now in progress at the Hebrew University.
50 See Kh. Kazdan, *From Kheder and Shkoles to CYSHO* (Mexico City, 1956) [Yiddish], p. 202. He also brings interesting material on calls for reform.
51 See Deborah Weissman, 'Bais Yaakov: A Historical Model for Jewish Feminists' in Elizabeth Koltun ed. *The Jewish Woman: New Perspective* (NY, 1976), pp. 139–48.
52 See Jacob Goldberg, 'Die Ehe bei den Juden Polens im 18. Jahrhundert' *Jahrbücher fuer Geschichte Osteuropas* XXXI (1983), pp. 481–515 and my study 'The Social Significance of Premature Marriages in Eastern Europe in the Nineteenth Century' (in Hebrew) *Studies on Polish Jewry/Paul Glikson Memorial Volume* (Jerusalem, 1987), pp. 65–77.
53 Homemaker.
54 Based on S. Rabinowitsh-Margolin 'Die Heiraten der Juden im europäischen Russland vom Jahr 1867 bis 1902' *Zeitschrift für Demographie und Statistik des Juden* V (1909) issues 9, 10, 11, 12.
55 The best study I know of on the topic is an unpublished paper of Naomi Shiloah written at Haifa University.
56 See the ICA report cited above, note 14, p. 318, 314.
57 Ibid., p. 324.
58 I do not have an explanation for the differences between the two cities.
59 This table is based on data provided by Jacob Thon, *Die Juden in Oesterreich* (Berlin, 1908), pp. 81–8. I am very grateful to Michael Silber for having brought this important source to my attention.
60 Ibid., Table XXIII on page 46.
61 Thon does not provide data on the sexual breakdown of students in secondary and higher education. However, Michael Silber found that in Hungary boys by far outnumbered girls in advanced education and there is no reason for the situation in Galicia to have been different. Indeed, had this been the case, Thon would have no doubt noted it. See Michael Silber, *Roots of Schism in Hungarian Jewry*, unpublished Hebrew University Ph.D thesis (in Hebrew) (Jerusalem, 1985), esp. p. 226 Table III.8.
62 James McLachlan, 'The Choice of Hercules: American Student Societies' in L. Stone ed. *The University in Society* II (Princeton NJ, 1974), p. 485.
63 Jakob Katz, *Tradition and Crisis* (Glencoe, 1961), ch. XVI 'Associations and Social Life'.
64 On *Kol Mevaser* see Khone Shmeruk, *Sifrut Yiddish* (Tel Aviv, 1978), Ch. VII and Alexander Orbach, *New Voices of Russian Jewry*, Leiden 1980, Chs. V, VII.

65 David Roskies, 'Yiddish Popular Literature and the Female Reader, *Journal of Popular Culture* (1979), pp. 852–8.
66 The world of the female readership is explored in depth by S. Niger *Bleter geshikhte fun der yiddishe literatur* (NY, 1959), in section 'Di yiddishe literatur un di lezerin' pp. 35–108.
67 Thomas Kessner, *The Golden Door*, (NY), pp. 90–1; and see his sources there.

# VOX POPULI, VOX DEI: THE CENTRALITY OF PERETZ IN JEWISH FOLKLORISTICS*
## Mark W. Kiel

>Peretz was the leader of this era . . .
>its midpoint, a centre of influences.
>Everything was reflected in him and
>refracted through him like a prism.
>                    H. D. Nomberg

>Guest after guest came ringing,
>and later took to singing,
>Like *Hasidim* for their *Rebbe*:
>Long may he live 'our *Rebbenyu*'.
>
>It was a new kind of 'Khsidish':
>Worldly free and worldly Yiddish.
>Soon followed by a folk song,
>Piously, in chorus sung.
>         Abraham Reisin, 'Warsaw'

Some time around 1895 or 1896, Y.L. Kahan, the great Jewish folklorist, overheard two Jews in a Warsaw cafe on Dzika Street discussing Peretz's interest in folklore. The conversation, as he remembered it, went as follows:

>So how come a great writer like Peretz is interested in such silly songs? What's he need it for?
>Maybe he wants to publish it in his journal?

---

* An earlier version of this paper was read at the Third International Conference on Research in Yiddish Language and Literature, October 13, 1987.

But I don't understand. How does he get these songs? How does he get to the plain folk, to all the boys and girls who sing these folk songs? After all, he isn't just anybody.
Very simple. Where he lives on Ceglana Street, there is a large courtyard. A lot of bourgeois people live there, modern types, *Hasidim*, *Misnagdim*, and almost all of them have servant girls who sing, usually at work, in the kitchen while rolling noodles, washing dishes. When Peretz hears the songs through the windows, he gets excited and wants to write them down. He calls on the girls to sing their songs to him.
Aren't they embarrassed?
What do you mean, embarrassed? He pays for it! He pays cash for each song, a half a ruble, and even a ruble. Yes, yes.
And just exactly how do you you know all this?
I certainly didn't make it up. A guy I know told it to me. He's a writer. . . at least he wants to be a writer, and he already wrote some songs and theatrical pieces which are probably not worth a thing. He often goes to see Peretz at home for advice about his scrawl. He told me so himself. He saw Peretz writing down all kinds of folk songs that girls sang for him. And he paid them too! That's what he told me, this guy I know. True, he's a cripple of a writer, but you can trust him, besides, why should he make it up?[1]

From the legendary address of 1 Ceglana, Peretz's home in Warsaw, the word went out to all types and classes of Jews, assimilated, maskilic, nationalist, middle class and socialist, even the 'man on the street': folklore – Jewish folklore, that is – had genuine value. It seemed incredible, but it was true; Peretz actually paid for folk songs![2] What was so shocking to the men overheard by Kahan, however, was not just that folk songs were a commodity, but that they were taken seriously at all. *Das lied als Wäre*, which naturally went hand in hand with packaging the goods to suit contemporary tastes, had long been a factor in European folkloristics.[3] As the new century was about to dawn, the changing times and, with them, the 'decreasing relic landscape' were no less obvious to Jews than to others.[4] But scarce goods need a market where demand is identified. Until Peretz came along, Jewish folklore suffered not only from a lack of material value, or even from a lack of interest, but, more to the point, from a lack of respect. For Peretz these were symptoms of a profound shortcoming in the emerging national consciousness, and the consequence of the people's lack of self-esteem.

Among the 'common folk,' folklore was, as it remains among all peoples, a bewildering if not embarrassing intrusion.[5] Although the study of folklore offered to rehabilitate the maligned reputation of *minhag* and *mayse* (religious customs and tales), traditional East European Orthodoxy could no more accommodate the transformation of *sancta* into a secular aesthetic than it could the earlier maskilic efforts to render folkways obsolete.[6] Modern, educated Jews, anticipating their integration into European society as part of a distinct religious community but otherwise linguistically and culturally assimilated, shunned Jewish folklore as a Yiddish mark of Cain that signified an irredeemably alien status.[7] In varying degrees, this position was common to the spokesmen of the three Jewish religious movements in Germany and their maskilic admirers in the East.[8] Certainly, there had been a degree of interest in one form or another of Jewish folklore since the *Haskala* and even earlier.[9] Jewish *Wissenschaft*, like Yiddish fiction, however, was generally ambivalent about Jewish folklore and slow to recognize it.[10] Prior to Grünwald's founding of an independent journal of Jewish folklore in 1898, the subject had received substantial scholarly attention, especially in the second half of the nineteenth century, from a coterie of Hungarian Jewish scholars writing in German, including, Leopold Dukes, Joseph Pereles, Adolph Brill, Alexander Kohut, and Leopold Löw. Yet even they, irrespective of their religious allegiances, skirted the issue by subsuming their interest in the subject under less politically charged fields, such as *Sagenkunde, Kostümenkunde, Alterthumskunde, Germanistik,* and *Sprachenkunde*. Only when camouflaged in these component subjects of Volkskunde could Jewish folklore be legitimately utilized for statistical, apologetic, antiquarian, philological, juridical, geographical, and polemical-satirical purposes. For all that, however, a Jewish folklore could not appear out in the open to serve itself, through its own organizing principles, as an independent discipline.[11]

Quite remarkably, writers whose fictional and scholarly works clearly evinced a certain nostalgia and even sympathy for their subject, rarely dared call the material by any of its identifiable names, whether ethnography, ethnology, Volkskunde or folklore.[12] The idea of the Jews as a *Volk* in the writings of Zunz and Graetz, or even in the works of the social historians Berliner and Güdemann, stopped short of supporting the notion of a Jewish folklore.[13] Moreover, whatever interest existed in Jewish folklore was directed, on the whole, toward explicating medieval historical-literary texts. This was in stark contrast to the interests of German folklorists who urged people to 'collect and preserve' and thereby 'rescue' from imminent and irretrievable loss, the still living oral traditions of their ancestors.[14]

*Wissenschaft des Judenthums* was directed towards building the kind of dignity and pride Jews could display in an enlightened *Rechtsstaat*, i.e., a historical consciousness that delimited the self-perception of Jews to something less than the 'folk' concept as developed by their volkish German contemporaries.[15] *Jüdische Wissenschaft*, in other words, though modelled on *deutsche Wissenschaft*, was not its equivalent.[16] *Volkskunde*, as a means of rescuing the traditional völkish legacy from modern social transformations was an important basis of the German romantic national awakening.[17] The fact that Wilhelm Riehl, the father of *Volkskunde als Wissenschaft* (which, in the 1860s united the component fields into a canon of academic respectability) was also one of the völkish fathers of modern antisemitism, could not have escaped the notice of thoughtful Jews. In these circumstances, advocacy of the notion of a Jewish folklore was a measure of one's readiness to declare full national parity for the Jews whatever the consequences to the still-unresolved struggle for emancipation.[18] But there was in fact little such readiness, so long as folklore was conceived romantically as the fountainhead of eternal verities and the reflection of a folk striving for political expression.

For the Jews, neither a religious nor a *Wissenschaft*-historical consciousness of Judaism could provide the self-confidence needed to assert the reality of a Jewish folklore. The mere use of folkloric material compelled such an enthusiast of Yiddish *Sprichwörter und Redensarten* as Abraham Tendlau, in 1860, to deny that he was engaged in Jewish folklore and to disclaim any separatist intentions.[19] In that decade, Szymon Dankiewicz and Feliks Cohn, two precursors of Jewish folkloristics in Poland, were forced to desist from propagating the field by outraged 'Poles of the Mosaic persuasion.'[20]

Denial bordered on self-deception in the case of Friedrich Salomon Krauss, Viennese editor of *Urquell*, a leading journal of comparative folklore. Krauss frequently published Jewish folklore in the original Yiddish and Ladino (Judezmo), a policy contrary to that of other folklore journals such as the *Globus* and *Wisła*, which published Jewish folklore only in the *Landsprache*. However, even though he referred to the material, apparently when his guard was down, as Jewish folklore, Krauss nevertheless dubiously declared upon hearing of Grünwald's journal, that folklore could no more be 'Jewish' than Catholic or Moslem.[21]

Krauss had a romantic appreciation of the national significance of folklore, but it was tempered by a cosmopolitan positivism which found in the comparative approach to folklore a vehicle for mutual understanding between nations and peoples. He represented the international approach to folklore, in contrast to the exclusivist *volkisch* perspective. By revealing the inner life of the Jews, Krauss hoped to demonstrate their humanity, and therefore, their suitability for emancipation and assimilation.[22] It was an argument intended to disarm those who claimed Jews were essentially alien. In fact, the medium Krauss provided proved more powerful than the message. Enemies of the Jews did not rely on Krauss to substantiate their racial views. Yet, ironically, the very respectability accorded Jewish folklore in his prestigious journal nurtured a nascent Jewish folklorism. When he provided a platform for Peretz's vision of a national Jewish folklore, Krauss unwittingly added Yiddish to the *Stimmen der Völker in Liedern*.[23]

Similar views were held by B.W. Segel, perhaps the most famous Jewish folklorist at the turn of the century if not the most prolific. His articles on the folklore of Galician Jewry were wide-ranging in themes and genres, from *Sprichwörter* to *Volksmärchen*. His work appeared, beginning in 1891, in Polish and German journals including, *Wisła*, *Urquell*, the Jewish *Ost und West*, and *Globus*, which was edited by Richard Andree, the anti-semitic author of the first book on Jewish folklore.[24] All of Segel's work appeared, presumably by intention, in Polish and German translations, never in Jewish journals such as the *Mitteilungen zur jüdischen Volkskunde*, which would have insisted on (unlike *Urquell*, which merely tolerated) the original Yiddish. Ironically, like Krauss, he gave great impetus to the emergence of precisely the kind of Yiddishist folklore studies he staunchly opposed all his life.[25]

Amid what was tantamount to a vast conspiracy of silence, lasting well into the twentieth century, there were nevertheless, a few lone voices that spoke of Jewish folklore. The most important of these were: the English folklorists Joseph Jacobs and Moses Gaster;[26] the French scholar Isadore Loeb and others whose work was published in the *Revue des Études Juives*;[27] Dubnow and the Historical Ethnographic Commission he helped found in St. Petersburg in 1892;[28] and a number of Polish journals, particularly *Wisła*, founded in 1889 as the 'ethnographic-geographic' journal of the Warsaw positivists.[29]

In the English and French settings, with their traditions of political liberalism, Enlightenment, and Comtean positivism, the word 'folk' and the subject of folklore or popular traditions were primarily of anthropological, rather than ideological, concern.[30] To the corpus of *Wissenschaft*, Jacobs, Gaster, and the *Revue* made methodological contributions on medieval themes and provided Jewish folkloristics with legitimating precedents.[31]

Despite having the word 'ethnographic' in its name, the Historical Ethnographic Commission emphasized the collection and transcription of historical documents, rather than folklore as such. The elements of social life that the commission recorded, with the help of many enthusiastic correspondents included folklore, but research was not, as yet, particularly focused on the field.[32] The operative program was drawn from Dubnow's earlier appeal to the Jewish intelligentsia and to the maskilic-minded yeshiva students to rescue from oblivion the sources of Russian and Polish Jewish history. Dubnow proclaimed this task a sacred duty and a national obligation.[33]

As a positivist, Dubnov regarded folklore and ethnography, like literature and philology, as historiography's ancillary disciplines.[34] Each provided data for the kind of self-knowledge Dubnov believed would form the basis of a secular Jewish identity.[35] For *Wissenschaft* scholars such as Berliner, Güdemann and Leopold Löw (who were, respectively, Orthodox, Conservative, and Reform, and who preceded Dubnow as social historians) religion remained the self-consciously defining factor of their identity.[36] For Dubnow, folklore was a component of a new secular and nationalistic Torah. Passionately 'for' the people, Dubnow and the learned members of the commission were not 'of' the people. While they won greater appreciation for the study of folklore, it was not their intention to found a movement. Still, six years before Grünwald, Dubnow publicly called for the creation of an ethnographic journal and a Jewish museum.[37]

The Warsaw based *Wisła* was liberal and enlightened, but most important, it was located at the epicentre of an emerging Jewish national movement. Moreover, unlike the French, English or Russian examples, which were strictly Jewish affairs and therefore of limited authority, *Wisła* provided recognition for Jewish folklore by the spokesmen of Polish nationalism. Though their interest in Jews and Judaism was in fact rather limited, the Warsaw positivists also provided a model for other peoples bereft, like the Poles, of a political base and state support.

Having been handed the field, proponents of a Jewish folklore had only to acquire a romantic sense of its national importance. Once Jewish nationalism became a prevailing force in Jewish life, the recognition of folklore was inevitable. In its romantic version, folklore required an artist-hero through whom to bring the idea to life. 'For the artist,' in the words of Przybyszewski, 'is the strongest embodiment of the essential inner spirit of the nation, he is the mystic King Spirit, the glory and the resurrection of the nation'.[38] Like Percy, Mickiewicz, the Grimm brothers and Pushkin, Peretz played this role of classic source for the inspiration of the folk spirit. Through Peretz, whose picture hung on the walls of Jewish institutions everywhere, even in Soviet institutions, alongside that of Marx, Jewish folklore moved from academia into the modern vocabulary and consciousness of 'the people.'[39] Through Peretz, Jewish folklore became everything its opponents feared most: a source of modern national pride and a means of preserving tradition, the folk's defining character, in a new secular key.

The founding of Jewish folkloristics as a field is deservedly credited to Rabbi Dr Max Grünwald of Hamburg for establishing the first Society of Jewish Folklore (*Gesellschaft fur jüdische Volkskunde*), the first ethnographical museum, and the first journal devoted exclusively to Jewish folklore, the *Mitteilungen zur jüdischen Volkskunde*.[40] No less than Peretz, Grünwald's interest in Jewish folklore was linked to his dreams of a national awakening. Grünwald, moreover, was a professional folklorist who, at considerable personal risk, applied the exacting standards of the discipline to create, paraphrasing Riehl, a *Jüdische Volkskunde als Wissenschaft*. But relatively isolated from the masses of Jews in Eastern Europe who were frequently but not exclusively his subject, and writing in a language the Jewish folk did not read, Grünwald could not play a decisive role in creating the kind of folklore movement which subsequently emerged in the

Yiddish. That role belonged to Peretz.⁴¹ Already the hub of a pre-eminent literary circle, Peretz was equally pivotal in creating a climate receptive towards folklore and the impetus for the active study of all its forms.⁴²

Peretz's interest in Jewish folklore crystallized in the mid 1890s, the decade that saw the first flurry of sustained Jewish folkloristic activity, just as the predominant intellectual climate in Poland changed from positivism to neo-romanticism.⁴³ Always sensitive to the surrounding cultural scene, Peretz, like many *maskilim* and Polonized Jews of varying degrees, had been deeply influenced by positivism.⁴⁴ He was personally close to Ignaz Bernstein, the great Yiddish paremiologist who, in 1888, published his classic collection of *Yiddishe sprikhverter un redensarten* in Spektor's *Hoyzfraynd* (Spektor was also a folk-saying enthusiast), and to his son-in-law, Samuel Adalberg, the equally renowned Polish paremiologist who had translated the *Sprikhverter* into Polish for *Wisła*.⁴⁵

Unlike his father-in-law, a *Hovev Tsion* whose patronage of both Polish and Jewish learning was symbolic of a Jewish agenda that sought to accommodate the temporary hospitality of Polish positivism on its own terms, Adalberg was first and foremost a Polish patriot who subscribed to the positivist program for the assimilation of the Jews into a secular, enlightened, but decidedly Polish society.⁴⁶ His interest in Jewish folklore, like that of *Wisła's* editor, Jan Karlowicz, and that of Alexander Świętochowski, its most distinguished writer, was strictly utilitarian.⁴⁷ For the Jews to be assimilated, they first had to be understood and, in their economic prowess and, ironically, in their national tenacity, they even had to be appreciated and emulated. Anti-semitism had to be combated and myths and prejudices had to be dispelled. The ethnographic facts, disappearing with progress, had to be objectively ascertained and preserved for the historical record.⁴⁸

To that end, Karlowicz, a friend of Krauss, encouraged Henryk Lew to gather about him at *Wisła* a circle of Jews and a Polish woman, Ignaca Piatokowska, to concentrate on Jewish folklore. *Wisła* sponsored their fieldwork and public lectures on a wide variety of Jewish subjects and genres, including folk theatre, proverbs, tales, life-cycle customs, superstitions and descriptions of trades. It published their findings and worked in concert with other Polish and Jewish journals, particularly *Izraelita*, the positivist tribune of Polonized Jewry, edited since 1896 by Nahum Sokolow.⁴⁹ Members of the circle later became Peretz's Polish translators and contributed to his Yiddish journals, the *Yontiv Bletlekh* and the *Yiddisher Bibliotek*. Regina Lilienthal in particular, achieved a lasting reputation as a Jewish folklorist in Polish folkloristics.⁵⁰

The receptivity of *Izraelita* towards Jewish folklore throughout the 1890s represented a significant change in its thinking. Although it was no more successful than *Wisła* in motivating its readers to collect Jewish folklore, *Izraelita* advanced from a position that imitated the German version of

Reform Judaism to a positivist, utilitarian recognition of Yiddish as a means to reach the masses and a more sympathetic understanding of Jewish folk life. Though influenced by Adalberg, Sokolow, writing in 1890, went beyond the Polish programme, in some respects adumbrating Peretz's mature vision of Jewish folklore.[51]

Against the background of a scarcely discernible, emerging Yiddish and Hebrew literary community, Sokolow, like Peretz at the time, propagated *Bildung*. Like *Wisła*, he urged a positive re-evaluation of the folk which required a re-acquaintance of the alienated intelligentsia with the people and a departure from the maskilic strategy of rebuking and ridiculing the folk into accepting reform imposed from above. Sokolow wanted to save the moral essence of the Jewish people which he thought was preserved and embedded in their traditions, and have it serve as the basis of their enlightened regeneration. At the time not yet a convinced Zionist or an advocate of Yiddish, except as a way station towards assimilation, Sokolow appealed for an organic process of change, one that would not directly assault the sensibilities of the folk. Like the attitude of Polish positivists to Polish culture, Sokolow's programme stood on the borderline of romanticism and helped pave the way for the full-fledged, unambiguous, national Jewish folkloristic program that was presented in 1901 by Henryk Lucjan Kohn in the pages of *Izraelita*.[52]

The crucial difference between Polish and Jewish positivism was, of course, that the former, from the very beginning, was the ideology of Polish nationalism, whereas the latter was not an ideology of Jewish nationalism. Jewish positivism, though it served its own ends, was, nevertheless, an instrument of Polish positivism. Just before and during the insurrection of 1863, in a much touted 'moral revolution' of fraternal Polish-Jewish relations, some Poles had become convinced of the need to provide to the Jews conditions in which assimilation would be possible. But this episode proved short-lived. The end of the insurrection was accompanied by a mutual sense of disappointment between Polish and Jewish intellectuals, which extended to mutual charges of betrayal. As the century wore on, the conditions set by the Poles were not satisfactorily met by the Jews. In fact, more was expected of the Jews than their cultural and linguistic assimilation. To be considered really Polish, the Jews had to convert to Catholicism and intermarry.[53]

With regard to the Jews, Polish liberalism did not fully return to the mood of 1863 though tolerance certainly survived in certain social circles, particularly on the political left. Generally, however, with the tide of nationalism and Catholic revivalism sweeping over Poland, the intolerance and anti-semitism that was implicit in the agenda of some Polish liberals emerged and became explicit. Świętochowski, the 'hetman of positivism,' joined the National Democrats and added his prestigious name to those who called the Jews 'unwelcome guests.' This was a position which Peretz strongly protested, though the opinion that Yiddish-speaking Jews were not to be fully considered Poles had been expressed by *Wisła* from the very beginning.[54]

Conscious of its secular European roots and its historical debt to the Enlightenment, Jewish nationalism retained an abiding loyalty to positivism, though not specifically to Polish positivism, that was reflected in its curricula and was perhaps best evident in a habit of rational scepticism.[55] While increasingly self-assertive, Jews continued to work alongside Poles on *Wisła* into the twentieth century, in time openly advocating a Jewish folkloristics.[56] Peretz never really turned his back on positivism. All his life he believed, although not consistently, in a liberal rationalism and engaged in what Polish positivists called 'practical' or 'organic work' (*praca organiczna*), 'at the foundations' (*praca u podstaw*); that is, he promoted the Jewish intelligentsia's work among the common folk, just as Świętochowski urged the gentry to take up the cause of the peasants in order to advance the national interest.[57] But with no place for the Jews in Polish national aspirations, the promise of posivitism waned; it simply became, as Mendele had predicted in another context, spiritually inadequate. Secularized but disappointed in their rationalist faith, some found consolation waiting on the left in the 'iron laws of history.' Peretz, though drawn at first in this direction, recoiled in existential doubt from what he saw as the tyranny of their certainties. For those in search of meaning, Peretz offered not a solution – indeed he despaired of one – but rather, an existential vision that legitimized the search.[58]

Other great Jewish writers and thinkers had traversed the same road from sober positivism to spiritual and ethical secular nationalism. Like Peretz, Ahad Haam, Dubnov, and Berdichevsky, each in his own way, felt a need to fill the vacuum left by religion. Among this group, Ahad Haam remained the most rooted in positivism. Notwithstanding the (carefully studied) democratic implications of his pen-name, he wanted to raise the folk from their culture, particularly the Yiddish folklore which he found repugnant, to his level of enlightenment in order to 'ennoble' them. His elitist appeal had considerable impact on the Jewish national idea.[59]

Dubnow achieved the position of East European Jewry's preeminent historian and entered the political fray with his *Folkspartay*. By means of a sociologically oriented history, Dubnow looked for models to serve the modern national movement. To that end, he rehabilitated Hasidism as a great mass social phenomenon, depicting it as a veritable folk movement which had brought ordinary people to the forefront of history. Dubnow did not dismiss what the earlier Maskilim had so roundly rejected as reactionary and obscurantist. As Peretz, Berdichevsky and others would do, he gave early Hasidism a new positive and inspiring image. While not devoid of romanticism, his work, like that of Ahad Haam, was essentially intellectual and theoretical.[60]

Berdichevsky and Peretz gave artistic expression to the revised and revived image of the *Hasidim* and of the folk in general. Peretz, however won the place of the people's tribune, although it was Berdichevsky who had shown greater faith in the people by accepting them, *amor fati*, for what they were. A more daring romantic than Peretz, Berdichevsky tapped the subterranean traditions of the folk that *Wissenschaft* and literature ignored. But his early work was premature for a new movement that was then too insecure to tolerate such individualist deviations.[61] Despite his own developing interest in folklore, Peretz had actually taken Berdichevsky to task for using unedifying street Yiddish in his literary dialogues.[62] By European and all contemporary standards, Berdichevsky's language was in fact so tame that one can hardly find his rebellion shocking. Peretz's apparent failure to appreciate the obvious folkloristic value in authentically transcribing the folk argot was, on the other hand, no drawback to his own literary success or its achievement.

Peretz himself was not exactly well received by the literary establishment. The Odessa literati found his *rebbe* posturing insufferable and his expressionist poetry and symbolist dramas incomprehensible.[63] His talent was nonetheless acknowledged, however reluctantly. But this old-fashioned group, suspicious of teeming Warsaw, spoke only for themselves. Peretz, unlike Berdichevsky, gave the people respectability and in so doing struck a popular chord. Unlike Dubnow and Ahad Haam, who gave the people something to think about, Peretz also gave them, as we shall see, something to do. Moreover, whereas Berdichevsky suffered bohemian isolation and Ahad Haam restricted his political activity to an élitist club (just as Dubnov had a small middle class following), Peretz took part in the socialist underground and was even arrested.[64] This episode, together with his literary reputation, enshrined him in the Jewish socialist and labour pantheon. His reputation survived intact even in the Soviet Union, where his tendency to romanticize folklore was criticized as reactionary.[65]

With his enormous talent and charisma, Peretz exuded great confidence and wielded wide authority. For many writers (including Berdichevsky, Bialik, Sholom Asch, Nahum Sokolow, and S. Ansky), Peretz served as a mentor and an arbiter of taste.[66] Peretz inspired the intelligentsia of the national movement with the idea that Jewish folklore could serve as a link between past and present. The quintessence of historical Jewish life, Jewish folklore, Peretz believed, maintained its validity in the modern world by continuing to inspire and shape Jewish life, while ensuring the integrity of the people's threatened identity in the future.

Taking up Sokolow's challenge, Peretz responded to the crisis of faith by fusing Jewish humanism with a romantic reinterpretation or *iberdikhtung* (as the process of poetic transformation was commonly called), of Jewish culture and history. Out of this new if imperfect synthesis of what was later, particularly in the Soviet Union, often construed as his 'contradictory' tendencies, Peretz forged a method of reinvigorating the folk with the spirit of the past.[67] He made an about-face on his maskilic attitude toward Yiddish, which as late as 1891 he still regard positivistically as merely a didactic tool for popular enlightenment.[68] It was not until he came to regard Yiddish as worthy of literary and linguistic cultivation on its own terms, just as Polish was for positivists and neo-romantics alike, that Peretz accepted folklore as an end.

Peretz's earliest interest in folklore was actually more of an ethnographic nature than a folkloristic one. In other words, Peretz was more interested in the material of folklore as it was relevant to maskilic aims than he was in the idealized sense of the folk inspired by romanticism. This is evident from his literary response to the 1890 expedition he undertook along with Sokolow and others, at the behest of Jan Bloch. Out of this anthropological fieldwork in the Tomaszow province, came Peretz's *Tristes Tropique* of the *shtetl*, the *Bilder fun a provints rayze*, published a year later.[69] It is unlikely that either Peretz or Sokolow shared Bloch's hopes that their findings would ameliorate the Jews' legal status by demonstrating so-called 'Jewish productivity'. Ethnography as a legal brief, as Moisei Berlin and Ilya Orshansky had discovered much earlier, did little, if anything, to improve the lot of the Jews.[70] For Peretz and Sokolow, Bloch provided employment and an opportunity to see the folk firsthand, a trend that had begun after 1881 with the return of the russified and polonized Jewish intellectuals 'to the people'.[71]

The rich ethnographic detail of the *Rayzebilder*, illustrating the decline of the *shtetl* and its cultural decadence, cannot then be construed as a manifestation of a specific interest in folklore. Similarly, Peretz's popular brochure on the prevention of cholera, which appeared in 1892, might have been a precursor of Jewish folk medicine and folk hygiene studies, but its ethnographic aspects were not yet a reflection of Peretz's eventual folklorism.[72] This impulse to, in Oislender's words, 'tap the factual ... statistical ground of Jewish life' surfaced again in 1902, in Peretz's series on the *shtet un shtetlekh*. Even after Peretz developed an idealized vision of folklore, he employed positivistic methods in order to take stock of his romantic flights. Editing and rewriting the reports of correspondents in the field for his series, he found that his romanticized version of Jewish life as presented in *Khsidish* was alive in the moral essence of provincial life but, as in the *Rayzebilder*, not in the obsolete and desperate circumstances of the workday world or, for that matter, in its folkloric reality.[73]

Ironically then, in his more or less straightforward ethnographic reportage, Peretz might have been (by present standards) a better folklorist than he was when he consciously assumed the role. As Peretz began to take a conscious interest in folklore, he made of it the means by which to display his romantically idealized picture of the Jews as well as the source of this image. For these purposes, Peretz could hardly resort to the kind of reliable mimetic descriptions found in the pre-Mendele writers who were intent on destroying the vestiges of *shtetl* culture or to the kind of objective reporting offered by the more benevolent positivists. For Peretz, Jewish folklore was more than the ethnographic data on Jews that *Wisła*, particularly Swiętochowski, wanted to gather. It became, in the familiar romantic metaphor, more what the folklore of the nations was for Krauss: a fountain of youth and a source of a national renaissance. Jewish folklore would find its inspiration neither in the hard look of the positivists, despite its offer of legitimacy, nor in that of the pre-Mendele writers, however much nostalgia they evoked, nor, for that matter, in Mendele himself, though his ethnographic talents were regarded as consummate. Jewish folklore found its inspiration in the folk-like form, 'packaged' by Peretz as *folkstimlekh*, a term and idea which he popularized in Yiddish.[74]

Jewish customs, beliefs, folk tales (especially Hasidic folk-tales) and folk songs became the inspiration for Peretz's masterworks and dramas such as the *Folkstimlikhe geshikhten* (1907), *Khsidish* (1908), and *Bay nakht oyfn altn mark* (1907), which he later subtitled a *folkstimlikhe dramatishe dikhtung*.[75] The sources of these works were mainly literary, drawn from traditional midrashic and Hasidic stories, as well as the classics of European folklore.[76] Here Peretz played more the role of the poet than that of the folklorist. In his use of folk songs, though they also served the poet's needs, he was equally a collector and purveyor of the material, acting more in the role of the folklorist proper. Moreover, in this case his sources were oral.

Sh. Niger observed that for Peretz and for writers such as Anski and Bialik, the oral lore began to assume the dimensions of a new oral law (*Tora sheb'al Peh*) which in turn, in writings such as *Khsidish* and the *Folkstimlikhe geshikhten*, became a new 'Scripture' (*Torah shebikhtav*). Niger thus amplified Selig Kalmanovitsh's interpretation of literature as a new source of secular Torah.[77] However, this interpretation can be traced to Peretz's own generation. His personal secretary and confidante, H.D. Nomberg, for example, described the impact on Peretz of Yiddish folk songs as 'prophetic revelation'. Following the example of his master, Nomberg resorted to religious language to describe the social *iberdikhtung* he witnessed.[78] As the language of, in Weinreich's apt term, *derekh hashas*, Yiddish itself determined that this *iberdikhtung* would have a popular resonance. The Bundist A. Litvak reported that in Peretz's time, secularized leftist workers came to regard his writings as 'holy'.[79]

In Yiddish folk songs, Peretz found what folklorists since Herder believed that folklore was supposed to reveal: the true picture of the folk. Hope in God, at least since Rousseau's *volonté général*, had been displaced by hope in the people. Through folk songs, the people could assume their proper place at the forefront of history, where, under the impact of nationalism, it was felt that they rightfully belonged. Introducing a series of folk tales by an anonymous writer, *Der Yid*, the Warsaw bi-weekly (edited by Ravnitsky), commented in 1899, that folklore mirrored the real life of the people: its 'character, spirit and soul'. To know the people, it advised, it is necessary to know their folklore. 'It is said that a Yiddish expression is a Torah, but to teach the people, a Yiddish song, a Yiddish tale is also real Torah'.[80] If the oral lore was Torah, its *iberdikhtung* was the all-embracing process of *midrash*.

But, in Peretz's reading of scripture not everything was to be revealed, studied, and transmuted; certainly not the people's Orthodoxy. Yet despite these imposing limitations on Jewish folklore, Peretz contended that the quotidian, when examined for its underlying secular universal values, was different in Jewish life from the folklore of other peoples. This difference, as Peretz saw it, was its *raison d'être*. Whereas previous Haskala writers and thinkers, including Ahad Haam, apologized for the 'uncivilized' state of the Jews by pointing to the ethical tradition of Judaism from the prophetic writings to medieval ethical literature, Peretz found the source of a living Jewish ethic in the spurned folk. Indeed, like Buber, he located this ethic in precisely that group most deplored by the enlightened, the *Hasidim*.[81] It was not just Judaism, in other words, that was superior to Christianity in its role as a 'light unto the nations', but it was the Jews themselves. The very people who were characterized by their Christian and Jewish defenders as immoral, Peretz elevated, with great national pride, above all their self-righteous neighbours and 'hosts'.[82] In his letter to estranged Jews returning to the people, Peretz wrote: 'Did you ever compare our folk songs with theirs? Our folk tales, for example, with those collected by the Brothers Grimm? Can you find among us those thieves, those cunning frauds of the seven league boots?' This was written around 1910.[83] But already in 1896, as we shall see, in a selection of folk songs prepared for publication, Peretz showed the same secular moralistic bias.

Peretz's folklorism was generally construed in Soviet criticism as part and parcel of his romantic shift away from radicalism and socialism, toward his *in shul arayn* (back to tradition) philosophy and newfound appreciation of tradition. However, coming one year after the appearance of the *Yontiv bletlekh*, the journal with which his socialist period is most precisely identified, his collection of 1896 demonstrated the mixture of tendencies, the 'contradictions', typical of his entire literary career. If folklorism represented a reactionary step backward it was also, owing to its secularism, just as much a manifestation of his radicalism. Secularism with its maskilic anti clericalism per se was recognizably radical vis-à-vis the Orthodox world. Although this too was a constant of his work, it by no means represented the extent of his radicalism. Peretz's work, as Miron put it, 'confronted reality with a revolutionary idealism, with a demanding humanistic system of norms, which is in essence alien to the authentic folk mentality and the historical reality of Hasidism'.[84] Prisoners of their own methodology, Soviet critics could not understand a radicalism tinged with a personal romantic nationalism, much less a tragic modernism in terms other than material contradictions.

The 1896 collection was rediscovered in 1937 in the Yivo archives in Wilno.[85] Kahan, Peretz's disciple and himself a victim of Soviet recrimination – though in the late 1920's his suggestions were solicited by Shtif for a programme of Soviet ethnography – said that his mentor did not think of his folklorism as a 'contradiction to his artistic and radical ideas of that period'.[86] On the contrary, Peretz saw the 'Yiddish secular folk song which was created and sung by the so-called lower folk strata as a progressive phenomenon, a mass expression of pure secularism' and a refutation of the widespread notion that Jews lacked a sense of 'love, beauty and poetry'.[87] Most important, folk songs also came to constitute an argument that, while Jews are indeed a nation like other nations, they possessed a moral superiority that was nourished by their historical culture.[88] Peretz brought this consoling message to the people in the guise of a prophet, a romantic pose to which he was long susceptible, rather than in the rebuking voice of the Maskil.[89] Equally romantic were the songs Peretz favoured, such as those he published in *Urquell* in 1898: love songs, songs of disappointed love, songs of loneliness and longing, and anti-religious maskilic songs. These were mainly songs of tragic dénouement.[90] In their pathos and sentimentality, they preached a moralism no orthodox Soviet critic could abide. Although they were impermissible contradictions of a rigid Marxism, for Peretz they were perfectly consistent with his modernistic ambivalence and the contradictions of his soul.[91] Thus, in the same so-called radical period, Peretz began to view the healthy revival of the folk as contingent on its tie to a secularly transmuted, morally grounded folklorism. These views were also behind 'Jewish Life according to Yiddish Folk songs', his poetic reflections on Ginsburg's and Marek's collection of Yiddish folk songs that came out in 1901.[92]

Peretz's need to transform folklore into a programmatic art lay behind his folkloristic études as much as his literary works. The *Urquell* songs, and the songs in the essay tracing the life of the Jew from cradle to grave, are unflawed and show no evidence of folk crudeness.[93] Quite obviously, they were polished to fit the poetic taste of Peretz's European romantic and moral sensibilities. What David Roskies described as the 'creative betrayal of the Yiddish folk tale' in Peretz's literary process applies equally to his interest in folklore.[94] In his stories and folk songs the folk was *fartaytsht un farbesert*, 'translated and improved'. This was an old tradition in the literary transmission of Jewish texts and of classic European folklore. The most notable of the packaged European works was the *Kinder und Hausmärchen*. Like the *Folkstimlekhe geshikhten*, it was intended primarily for adults but deliberately made suitable for children and it served as a primer in their national education.[95] It was only natural for Peretz, who was aware of and employed midrashic techniques, even though he tried to europeanize them, to continue the process and shape it to his own vision.[96] Soon it would become the working model for Bialik and Ravnitsky, Berdichevsky, Louis Ginsburg, and Martin Buber.

Even after the question of what constituted real Jewish folk songs arose in a spirited debate between Sholem Aleichem and Joel Engel (occasioned by the appearance of Mark Varshavsky's *Yidishe folkslider* in 1901), Peretz's views remained unchanged. Representing Peretz's position at a discussion of the issue in the Zamir chorale in 1909, Nomberg charged the specialist with the task of collecting the material and 'refining' it for the public.[97] Shortly before his death, Peretz must have felt a certain vindication in learning that his literary versions of children's folk songs were popular among Warsaw's homeless war orphans. Sholem Aleichem, too, had had the satisfaction of finding one of his own literary creations presented as an authentic anonymous folk song in Ginsburg's and Marek's classic collection.[98]

However great his writings, the main source of Peretz's influence on the Jewish intelligentsia of all stripes came from his many personal contacts and his charisma. 'Peretz', Ansky said, 'was an argument, a banner' whom nobody could deny. To a lost generation seeking a road to cultural recovery, folklore became in Peretz's presence an object of secular veneration.[99]

From as far away as America, writers, would-be writers, intellectuals, and community leaders made their pilgrimages to Warsaw, 'and going to Warsaw meant going to Peretz'.[100] His admirers spoke of themselves and each other as his Hasidim, and he was their *rebbe*. Appropriately, then, they held court at his home, his *shtub*, on Sabbath afternoons and chanted a *niggun*, '*rebbenyu, oy, oy, rebbenyu*'.[101] Sitting regally in his evening jacket, Peretz '*darshened*' to them on secular *Torah*, that is, literature. Towards evening, they sang the latest folk songs brought to Peretz's attention by one of the servant girls in the neighbourhood or by one of his agents, such as Reisin and Sholom Asch.[102] Always favoured were the songs discovered by Yehudah Leib Kahan, then a teenager, in the dance halls where the youth passed their time even on the Sabbath or in the shops where young seamstresses sang to the rhythms of their work.[103] (Later, these places became the subject of investigations into the secular history of the Jews.)[104] 'The songs of the street', Asch recalled, 'sounded sacred in Peretz's home and carried us off in an exalted mood'.[105]

Nomberg said that those present 'all had the impression that a fresh, vital, and effervescent well had opened up'.[106] The mood, another writer said, was 'mystical'.[107] Instead of God, however, the assembled felt themselves closer to the people.[108] Indeed, a sense of common purpose gave them a sense of being closer to one another. Peretz had written in 1890 that writers felt no connection to one another, that there was 'no foundation'.[109] At Peretz's apartment, a few years later, came the great change, the making of a literary community. On Sabbath afternoons, Scholem Asch wrote, 'one could come to know . . . all who work in the field of Yiddish. Peretz's apartment at Ceglana 1 was a centre for the Jewish radical idea. There the foundation was laid for the new Yiddish literature, not as a means but as an end unto itself. From this apartment came the idea of Yiddish; the poetic rebirth of Hasidism, the love of the folk song and the folk tale'.[110]

Echoing the sentiments of Henryk Lucjan Kohn, Peretz later exhorted repentant intellectuals in search of an aesthetic connection to the people to engage in a celebration of folklore. 'Collect, transcribe and inscribe. Come together and learn to read, sing together, recite, enjoy, create the atmosphere for the artistic . . . Later, genius will come and create'.[111] Kohn's remarkably similar plea in *Izraelita* in 1901 found repeated expression in Peretz's home. There the experience fulfilled its own vision and served as a model for the tradition's successful transmutation into a secular celebration.[112] These rituals of secular Yiddishism were reproduced again and again for decades to come in the Soviet Union, Poland, Palestine, Argentina, and the United States.[113]

Perhaps the best and clearest indication of the widespread excitement generated by Peretz was the secular ritualization of folklore research in its stylized celebration at the annual Purim ball in *fin de siècle* Warsaw.[114] Peretz helped plan and presided over these elaborate affairs. They were held in the grand ballroom of the elegant *Szwajcarska Dolina* on the aristocratic *Aleje Ujazdowskie*. There was music and dancing, feasting and acting. The masquerade was initiated by Peretz in order to set up a fund for the growing community of writers. As this would have been illegal under tsarist restrictions of cultural life, the Purim ball was conceived as a ruse and organized secretly. Tickets were sold for two rubles a person.[115] In keeping with the spirit of the Purim *shpiler*, the folk theatre troupes in which Yiddishists were to see the roots of their secular movement, the guests either came in costumes and masks or dressed formally.[116] Peretz's task was to ensure the Jewish character of the masquerade.[117] Zionists in their student uniforms, Bundists, Yiddishists, Hebraists, and assimilated admirers or Peretz, young and old, all attended.[118]

In 1902, the Zionist Berthold Feiwel, Herzl's associate, and the Beardsleyan artist, E.M. Lilien, came from Berlin to symbolize the union of east and west. With Sokolow as toastmaster, a banquet was given in their honour. The custom was imported from the literary avant-garde in Paris.[119] Unlike the Parisian affairs, however, whose creative figures 'often went astray and lost touch with the human values', participants at the Purim balls possessed a profound sense of their social responsibility. As he watched the *karakhod* – the circle dance – grow larger and sweep out across the floor, Avrom Reisin saw the ambience of the ball taking on 'a different character, *folkstimlekh*, cheerful, a portent of something, and a call to the people'.[120]

The high point of the evening came as the guests watched the scene of the blind beggar being led dutifully about the hall by a girl as they sang and collected folk songs from the guests.[121] The participation of the audience in this ritualized depiction of the state of folklore suggests a new popularity for this trend. What was obvious to those present, however, may now require some interpretation.

We may gather that the blind beggar symbolized the alienated intellectual returning to the people. The girl personified the folklorist's bridge to the folk traditions, whose real value he had not previously seen and whose sudden revelation now moved him to grope in the dark. The girl is the proverbial source for the folklorist, the *dinstmeydl*, the servant girl or perhaps the seamstress. The fateful transition which she, like others, made, from the village to the city, spelled the end of traditional folklore and the conditions in which it had thrived. While the ravages of time on tradition were unavoidable, folklore could be rescued from oblivion by the folklorist. Armed with the girl's songs, the folklorist could go out in the field. By showing that he already knew some of the songs, the folklorist hoped to win the trust of his sources and elicit more songs from them. Thus the beggar sings before he can collect.[122]

The people to whom he comes see him as odd, a beggar after trifles. This was how the folklorist thought of and depicted himself. What may at first seem like an unheroic image, however, was *de rigueur* in the romantic setting in which it was staged. The lonely seeker, ready to assume the burden of going to the people, was an image still fresh from the days of the *narodniki* in the mid-1870s and harked back to the classics of European folklore and the figures of Herder, Grimm, Pushkin, Percy, Mickiewicz, and others. Like the *narodniki*, the folklorists prepared themselves for going to the people by learning some of their folk customs and manners.[123] In the case of Sh. Ansky, the transition was personal; a Russian *narodnik* in the 1870s, he later became the most famous Jewish folklorist.[124] But whether as *narodnik* or folklorist, the sudden appearance of the 'city slicker' among the folk was not particularly welcome. Sensing their inherent condescension, the folk saw the folklorists as outsiders and intruders. The folklorists were certainly more successful than the *narodniki* in making some headway among, and gaining a measure of respect from, the people, though perhaps more for themselves than for their work. To be sure, their aims were also more modest. In Peretz's perception both were tragic heroes, the Jewish *narodnik* seeking redemption from the alien gods of the Russian village and the Jewish folklorist returning to native ground, doomed always to seek.

Just as important to the scene, though more subtle and complex in their meanings, are the mask and Purim, the holiday itself. The history of both was largely written in the years between the wars by secular Yiddishist historians in Poland, the Soviet Union, and the United States as part of their search for a usable past.[125] For secular Judaism, the importance of Purim was its longstanding tradition of worldly amusement. Although Purim was part of the religious calendar, its celebration assumed some of the social and cultural aspects of carnival, which it imitated in combining the sacred and the profane.[126] That this attitude drew the disapproval of rabbis and respectable community leaders for what they thought were its vulgar excesses, actually enhanced the secular stature of Purim. Since the fifteenth century the holiday had been celebrated with masquerades and impromptu performances. As Europe developed a secular theatre at the close of the Middle Ages, especially in Italy, Germany, and Holland, where Jews lived at the end of the sixteenth century, a Jewish – and more significantly a Yiddish theatre began to take shape.[127]

As early as 1770, Purim balls had begun to replace plays among the well-to-do Ashkenazim in Holland. What the use of masks represented came into relief when they were displaced. As Schipper put it: 'The new style leads away from *folkstimlekhkayt* and from masks. It leads to art and drama and the actor artist who brings individuality to the fore'.[128] If Schipper was correct, then the return to the use of the theatrical mask by the intelligentsia as well as the resumption of the Purim balls conversely represented a conscious and artistic effort to recapture a tradition suited to new and larger objectives. Purim, the secular holiday, became the holiday of secularism. It celebrated not just the victory over Haman but, more to the point, the way in which the folk celebrated it. In other words, it celebrated not just a historical event but folk history.

The meaning of this process of cultural recovery and *iberdikhtung*, which began so dramatically with Peretz, was explained by another exponent of secularism, Raphael Mahler, in his comments on Schipper's *History of Jewish Theatre Art and Drama*. 'More than its scholarly value,' he says, 'it revolutionized our understanding of our cultural past.... We have here living proof that both our modern theatre culture and our secular folk culture are not new ... but a continuation of a rich, colourful tradition, pleasing to the eye and heart, and dating back hundreds of years'.[129]

If secular history was thought to date back hundreds of years and thus able to grant legitimacy to the secular enterprise in traditional terms, the origins of that consciousness began with Peretz.

Certainly he was not alone in bringing about the new awareness. In the case of folklore, others contributed to the growing interest in the field, but Peretz was first in bringing it to the centre of a movement organized around himself and focused on the idea of a national revival. It remained for the intelligentsia to bring Peretz's literary mission to the folk by pointing out the areas of folk tradition that needed to be conserved, contemplated, and celebrated.[130]

The honour of marking the realization of Peretz's vision fell, appropriately enough, to Avrom Reisin. Reisin's own premonitions of a Jewish folklore movement occurred in the sight of the intelligentsia folk-dancing. *Mir zamlen*, his poem of 1931, can be read as an answer to Peretz's charge 'to collect'.[131] It was dedicated to Yivo, which, unlike the Soviet higher institutions of Yiddish studies, had been created without benefit of government, a Jewish university of and by the people. It was an achievement perhaps beyond Peretz's expectations, but certainly not beyond his Nietzschean appreciation of the heroic capabilities of Jewish gratitude and of Jewish self-esteem.

> We collect everything dear to us
> On our long journey till now,
> A page from then, a book from the present,
> Let all with love be prized.
>
> . . .
>
> The first quiet works in Yiddish
> When we still wrote 'es var'
> The *maysebukh*, what a surprise,
> A copy from the first press.
>
> . . .
>
> And seek out all the rich treasures
> The treasures which the folk creates
> All the proverbs, and expressions
> Which gives our lives its passion.
>
> And all the dreams and jokes
> And all the songs from long ago
> Let them sing in the masses
> In a renewed and youthful tone.
>
> And every word from quiet creation
> In most distant land and generation,
> No more need for silent hesitation,
> Let resound in the chorus of nations.

NOTES

Abbreviations:  *Yivo Bleter*, YB
                *Leo Baeck Institute Yearbook*, LBIYB

For their helpful suggestions, I would like to thank David S. Roskies and Chanan Kiel – both of whom keep the inspiration of Peretz as a living legacy – and also Eric Lowenkron and Eli Lederhendler.

1 Y. L. Kahan, 'Y.l. peretz, der zamler fun yidishe folkslider,' in, idem, *Shtudyes vegn yidisher folksshafung*, ed., M. Weinreich (New York, 1952), p. 107 (herein, Kahan, *Shtudyes*). I translated *daytshe*, as 'modern type'. Literally 'German', it was the colloquialism for Jews dressed in the fashionable European short jacket, see Yudl Mark, 'Vos iz tyidisher folklor?', *Idisher kemfer* (April 20, 1951), p. 67.
2 Y. L. Peretz, *Briv un redes*, ed. N. Mayzl (New York, 1945), p. 202; Kahan too, sold his folksongs to Peretz, see Y. Dineson's letter to H. Aleksandrov, YB (May-June, 1945), p. 452.
3 Rolf Wilhelm Brednich, 'The Song as a Commodity,' in James R. Dow and Hannjost Lixfield, eds. and trans. *German Volkskunde: A Decade of Theoretical Debate and Reorientation (1967–1977)*, (Bloomington, 1986) p. 210; cf. Mark Slobin, 'The Uses of Printed Versions in Studying the Song Repertoire of East European Jews,' in M. Herzog, et. al., *The Field of Yiddish*, vol.4 (Philadelphia, 1960), pp. 329–71.
4 Brednich, p. 210.
5 Ibid., p. 205: 'The folksong possessed its original functional value in a pre-literate society. It was a symbol of certain functional ties, a part of the communications system of the traditional community, and as an oral tradition it did not need to be fixed in writing since it had no functional value outside traditional rites. Its performance outside these rites, which were always based on strong customs, was regarded as an offense.' While we might better speak of a more literate society in which Jewish folksongs were produced, the functional explanation remains valid, for the Jewish case. On Jewish literacy in Eastern Europe see Shaul Stampfer, 'Yediat kro ukhtuv etsel yehudei mizrah eiropa betkufa hahadasha: heksher, mekoret vehashlakhot', in Shmuel Almog et al, eds., *Transition and Change in Modern Jewish History: Essays Presented in Honor of Shmuel Ettinger* (Jerusalem, 1987), pp. 459–83.
6 Jacob Katz, *From Prejudice to Destruction: Anti-Semitism, 1700–1933* (Cambridge, 1980), pp. 231, 237. The Warsaw writers, A.B. Reuf and Gustav Makman, displayed talent in using modern literary means to defend Orthodoxy. Theirs was a liberal, tolerant orthodoxy which defended all three classes of religious Jews, *hasidim, misnagdim* and *daytshe*. It is not clear however that they intended 'to defend the truth of religion in its folkloristic manifestation'. (Dan Miron, 'Folklore and Antifolklore in the Yiddish Fiction of the Haskala,' ed. Frank Talmage, *Studies in Jewish Folklore* [Cambridge, 1980], p. 247. On these writers see, N. Oislender, 'Varshever mekhabrim in di 50er un 60er yorn,' ed. Y. Lieberberg, *Bibliologisher zamlbukh* [Moscow, Kharkov, Kiev, 1930], pp. 172–85; Jacob Shatzky, *Geshikhte fun yidn in varshe*, vol. 3 [New York, 1953], p. 334 [hereafter, *Geshikhte*]; see also, Arnold J. Band, 'Folklore and Literature,' Talmage, pp. 33–5).
7 Jacob Katz, 'German Culture and the Jews, *Commentary* (Feb. 1984); idem., *Out of the Ghetto: The Social Background of Jewish Emancipation* (Cambridge, 1973), pp. 214–15; H.R. Schmidt, 'The Terms of Emancipation, 1770–1800,' *LBIYB*,

vol.1 (1956), pp. 29–45; Simon Dubnow, *Nationalism and History: Essays in Old and New Judaism* (Philadelphia, 1958), p. 144. The first book on Jewish folklore was Richard Andree's *Zur Volkskunde der Juden* (Bielefeld, Leipzig, 1881). Though, remarkably, it was praised by such advocates of Jewish folklore as Joseph Jacobs (*Jewish Encyclopedia*, vol.1, p. 580) Max Grünwald (discussed in, *Der Urquell* [1896] p. 27,) and others (*Revue des Études Juives*, vol.3–[1881], p. 131), the book was more a racial anthropology than *Volkskunde*, and was suffused with anti-semitic stereotypes. It certainly must have raised the hackles of Jews worried about folklore playing into the hands of their enemies, though in fact, Andree himself, at odds with his own findings, advocated emancipation for the Jews. The fact that Andree's work went unchallenged even by Jews engaged in the field, may be an indication of how great the need was for an outside authority to bestow respectability on the field of Jewish folklore or how deeply internalised and accepted were Jewish stereotypes. However in his own journal of folklore, *Der Urquell*, Friedrich Krauss (see below) did point out the threat he thought Andree's 'wertlose tückische Hetzschriften' posed. (*Der Urquell*, ibid.). Although he had predecessors, like Mosei Berlin, Ilya Orshanski, Szymon Dankiewicz, Feliks Cohn and Krauss, it was Peretz who first gave impetus to the idea of using contemporary Jewish folklore to counter negative stereotypes of Jews, particularly such stereotypes as Jews themselves internalised.

8 Michael A. Meyer, *The Origins of the Modern Jew: Jewish Identity and European Culture, 1749–1824* (Detroit, 1967), pp. 121–43; Alexander Marx, *Essays in Jewish Bibliography* (Philadephia, 1947), p. 119; Raphael Mahler, *Hasidism and the Jewish Enlightenment: Their Confrontation in Galicia and Poland in the First Half of the Nineteenth Century*, trans. E. Orenstein, A. Klein and J. M. Klein (Philadephia, 1985), chapter 2; Shatzky, *Geshikhte*, vol. 2, p. 254; idem, *Yidishe bildungs politik in poyln: 1806–1866* (New York, 1943), pp. 218–21; Yisroel Tsinberg, *Di geshikhte fun der literatur bay yidn* (New York, 1966), vol. 11, pp. 93ff.

9 Abraham Berger, 'The Literature of Jewish Folklore,' *Journal of Jewish Bibliography*, vol.1 (Oct. 1938), pp. 12–20, (Jan. 1939), pp. 40–9; Eli Yassif, 'Mehkar hafolklor umadaei hayahadut: kivunim umagamot', *Yedion haiqud haolami lemdaei hayahadut* (Winter, 1987), no. 27, pt. 1, pp. 3–26, pt. 2, pp. 3–26.

10 Miron, passim.

11 To cite a few examples: Leopold Dukes, *Zur rabbinischen Spruchkunde: Eine Sammlung rabbinischer Sentenzen, Sprichwörter, und sprichwörtlichen Redensarten* (Vienna, 1851); Alexander Kohut, *Über die jüdische Angelogie und Daemonologie in ihrer Abhängigkeit vom Parsismus*, (Leipzig, 1866); Adolf Brüll, *Fremdsprachliche Redensarten in den Talmuden und Midraschim, Eine philologische Studie* (Leipzig, 1869); idem, *Trachten der Juden im nachbiblische Alterthume, ein Beitrag zur allgemeinen Kostümenkunde* (Frankfurt A/M, 1873); Perles' investigations into post-Biblical wedding and burial customs were subtitled 'archaeological investigations' (*Hebrew Characteristics: Miscellaneous papers from the German* [New York, 1875]. pp. 47, 72; Leopold Löw's *Lebensalter in der jüdischen Literatur; von physiologischen, Rechts-sitten und religionsgeschichtlichen standpünkte betrachtet* (Szegedin, 1875), was intended as a contribution to *jüdischer Alterthumskunde*. While it is certainly the case that the various subjects of folklore were legitimate parts of other fields, they were also already regarded as components of a folklore canon. (cf. Bernhard Heller, 'Hovot haetnografia vehafolklor hayehudi bikhlal uveeretz hakodesh bifrat,' *Zion*, 4 [1930], p. 72).

12 Dov Noy, 'Eighty Years of Jewish Folkloristics: Achievements and Tasks,' Talmage, pp. 2–3. Abraham Tendlau's *Sprichwörter und Redensarten Deutsch-jüdischer Vorzeit als Beitrag zur Volks, Sprach und Sprichwörter kunde* (Frankfort Am

Main, 1860), was somewhat exceptional in using *Volks-kunde* in the title, though the *Vorzeit* and the apologetic introduction qualify the bold assertion by placing the subject, somewhat disingenuously, into a vague 'hoary' past, and presenting it as a contribution to *Germanistik* (p. vii). Other exceptions are: Moisei Berlin's *Ocherk etnografii evreiskago narodonaseleniia v rossi* (St. Petersburg, 1861); Ilya Orshanski, 'Prostonarodnaya Piesni,' *Gakarmel* (Jan. 20, 27, 1866), pp. 131–5, 137–9; Abraham Berliner, *Beiträge zur Geographie und Etnographie Babyloniens im Talmud und Midrasch* (Berlin, 1884). In using the term 'folklore' interchangeably with the more appropriate 'folklore material,' in the context of his discussion of maskilic fiction, Miron attributes to the latter the sense of the former's conceptual nature. He implies, that is, a definite folkloristric interest on the part of the *maskilim*. While this may be true concerning their fictive claim to have preserved the past for posterity's edification, a motive force of folkloristics, their intentions were in fact more parodic, critical and positivistic. Where Miron reads 'folklore', the writers used the traditional terms *minhogim, zabobones* and *tseremonyes*. Their ambivalence may thus be said to extend to the modern term. (Miron, pp. 221, 229, 248; idem, *Der imazh fun shtetl: dray literarishe shtudyes* [Tel Aviv, 1981], pp. 121–38 (Herein, *Der imazh*); Y. Shatzky, 'Peretz shtudyes,' YB, vol. 28 (1946) pp. 46–7.

13 On *Wissenschaft* historians' sense of Jewish identity see Ismar Schorsch, 'The Emergence of Historical Consciousness in Modern Judaism,' LBIYB, vol. 28 (1983), pp. 413–37.
14 Dow and Lixfield (see note 3), Introduction, p. 5.
15 Schorsch, p. 429. On the German 'misunderstanding' of the *Rechtsstaat*, see Ralf Dahrendorf, *Society and Democracy in Germany* (Garden City, 1969), pp. 67–8, 196; cf. Reinhard Rürup, 'Jewish Emancipation and Bourgeois Society,' LBIYB, vol. 14 (1969), pp. 67–91.
16 The term is Genz's, Peter Genz, *Jacob Grimm's Concept of German Studies* (Oxford, 1973), p. 10. The term *Deutsche Wissenschaft* was coined by Jakob Grimm, see Genz, ibid.
17 Genz, p. 12; Giuseppe Cocchiara, *The History of Folklore in Europe*, trans. John N. McDaniel (Philadelphia, 1981), pp. 195, 202.
18 Richard Beitl and Klaus Beitl, *Wörterbuch der deutschen Volkskunde*, third edition, (Stuttgart, 1974), pp. 879–80. On the image of the Jew in the volkish awakening, see George L. Mosse, *The Crisis of the German Ideology: Intellectual Origins of the Third Reich* (New York, 1964), pt. 1. Gerhard Lutz, *Volkskunde: Ein Handbuch zur Geschichte ihre Probleme* (Berlin, 1958), p. 14–37.
19 Tendlau, p. vi, cf. N. Veynig's sympathetic comments, 'Geshikhte un problemen fun der yidisher paremiografia,' YB, vol. 8. no. 24 (1935), pp. 359–61.
20 Shatzky, 'Peretz shtudyes,' p. 47; idem, *Geshikhte*, vol. 2, p. 254; idem *Yidishe bildungs politik*, pp. 218–21; Tsinberg, *Geshikhte fun literatur*, vol. 11, pp. 93ff; cf. Robert Seltzer, *Simon Dubnow: A Critical Biography of His Early Years,* unpublished Columbia Ph.D. dissertation (Ann Arbor, 1973), p. 209.
21 *Der Urquell* (1897), H.8, pp. 284–5. See also, Shatzky, 'Peretz shtudyes,' pp. 78–81, reprinted from the *Journal of American Folklore*, vol.7 (1894), pp. 72–5, and Richard Andree's reply in *Globus*, vol.65 (June, 1894), p. 363; L.Vints, 'Starie voprosi i novya sadatski,' *Voskhod*, vol. 10 (1892), no. 2. pp. 12–13.
22 'Die Wissenschaft hat mit Antisemitismus, Urgermanentum, und Urslaventum und ahnlich Rassen und Klassenhasszuchtereien nichts gemein. Unsere alte und so oft erfolglos hervorgehobene grundlehre [ist] dass es keine "Wilden" gibt ... ' (*Am Urquell*, [1890], vol.1, no.11, p. 190). Reading *Urquell*, a Jewish correspondent from Istanbul had the impression that 'Die Welt ist eine Stadt'. (*Am Urquell* [1891], vol.2, H.1, pp. 26–7.)

23 L. Peretz, 'Judendeutsche Volkslieder aus Russland,' *Der Urguell* (1898), vol. 2,H.8, pp. 27–9; reprinted in the Soviet Union by Kh. Nadel, *Sovietish literatur*, 10 (1940), pp. 145–51.
24 See note 7.
25 N. Veynig, called him *der altmayster fun der yidisher etnografiya*, 'Binyomin Volf Zegl:1866–1931,' YB, vol. 3 (1932), p. 91; idem, 'Bibliografia fun b. v. zegls etnografishe arbetn,' ibid. pp. 92–3. On Segel's views on Yiddish and the question of minority rights in Poland, see, idem., *Die Polnische Judenfrage* (Berlin,1916). On Segel, see Zalman Shazar, *Or ishim*, vol. 1 (Jerusalem, 1973), pp. 177–83; Reizin, *Leksikon fun der yidisher literatur, presse, un filologye* (Wilno: Kletskin, 1928), vol. 1, clmns. 1095–7.
26 On Jacobs and Gaster see, Brian E. Maidment, 'Joseph Jacobs and English Folklore in the 1890's,' and Venetia Newall, 'The English Folklore Society under the Presidency of Haham Dr. Moses Gaster,' both in Dov Noy and I. Ben Ami, eds. *Studies in the Cultural Life of the Jews in England*, vol. 5, in the *Folklore Research Center Studies* (Jerusalem, 1975), pp. 185–96, and 197–225. Jacobs, too, showed a pronounced ambivalence about a Jewish folklore, akin to Krauss's, in his early piece, 'Jewish Diffusion of Folk Tales' (1888), in his *Jewish Ideals and other Essays* (London, 1896), pp. 138–139, and his article on 'Folk-lore', in the *Jewish Encyclopedia* (1903), in which he said, 'It is difficult to deal with the subject from a Jewish point of view, since in essence there is no Jewish folklore; yet practically ... there have been survivals of folklore among Jews in all stages of its development.' (vol. 5, p. 423).
27 Alexander Scheiber, 'Le folklore juif dans le *Revue des Études juives*,' *Revue des Études Juives*, vol. 139, 1–3 (Jan.-Sept, 1980), pp. 11–37; cf. Krauss's qualifications to Loeb's conception of Jewish folklore, *Am Urquell* (1891), vol. 7, H.2, pp. 233–4.
28 Maxim N. Vinaver, 'When Lawyers Studied History,' ed. Lucy S. Dawidowicz, *The Golden Tradition: Jewish Life and Thought in Eastern Europe* (Boston, 1968), pp. 242–8.
29 Olga Goldberg-Mulkiewicz, 'Source Material on Jewish Culture in Polish Ethnographic Literature,' *Soviet Jewish Affairs*, vol. 5, no. 1 (1975), pp. 95–102; Shatzky, 'Peretz shtudyes,' pp. 46–58.
30 Richard M. Dorson, *The British Folklorists: A History* (Chicago, 1968). On the difference between liberal attitudes in England and conservative attitudes in Germany and Jewish Budapest toward folkloristic scholarship which challenged the social and religious *status quo*, see the reactions to Ignaz Goldziher's, 'ill advised', as Patai put it, *Der Mythos bei den Hebräern* (1876, and translated a year later into English) in Goldziher's, *Tagebuch* (Leiden, 1978), p. 423; R.Patai, *Ignaz Goldziherland his Oriental Diary* (Detroit, 1987), p. 31.
31 Haim Schwarzbaum, 'Terumatam shel hohmei yisrael beanglia leheker hafolklor hayehudi vehaklali,' Noy, Ben Ami, pp. 84–110. Gaster's landmark article was his 'Beiträge zur vergleichende Sagen und Marchenkunde', *Monatschrift für die Geschichte und Wissenschaft des Judenthums* (1880), reprinted in, Moses Gaster, *Studies and Texts in Folklore, Magic, Medieval Romance, Hebrew Apocrypha and Samaritan Archaeology* (New York, 1971), vol. 1, pp. 1187–293.
32 Seltzer, *Dubnow Biography*, pp. 207–8.
33 Mark Vishnitzer, 'Shimon Dubnov, der organizator fun idisher geshikhtsvisenshaft in rusland,' *Di tsukunft*, 1 (1931), p. 58; Dubnow's own views were set out in Russian and Hebrew pamphlets: *Ob izuchenii istorii russkikh evreev i uchrezhdenii istoricheskago obshestva* (St. Petersburg, 1891); *Nahpesa venahkora, kol koray leesof homer levinyan toldot yisrael bepolin verusia* (Odessa, 1892).
34 Vishnitzer, p. 57.

35 Robert Seltzer, 'Coming Home: The Personal Basis of Simon Dubnow's Ideology,' *Association for Jewish Studies*, vol. 1 (1976), p. 295; Vishnitzer, p. 58.
36 Güdemann too, referred to the Jews as a *Volk*, but nevertheless denied that they were one, and accepted instead the idea of a universal Jewish mission. Ismar Schorsch, 'Moritz Güdemann: Rabbi, Historian, Apologist,' *LBIYB*, vol.11 (1966), pp. 42–3, 53, 57; Yishayahu Volfsberg, 'Professor Avraham Berliner,' ed. Simon Federbush, *Hokhmat yisrael bemaarav eiropa* (Jerusalem, 1958), pp. 103–8. While duly recognizing the binding force of ethnicity (*Stammesgenossenschaft*), Leopold Löw's formulation of a legitimate subjective basis for a non-dogmatic Judaism denied the possibility of a romantic Jewish folklorism on any grounds other than academic, 'Dogmen, d. i. Lehren, die nicht handgreiflich und demonstrabel sind, und nur aus sittlichen, gemüthlichen, historischen Grunden für wahr gehalten werden, kenne ich nicht ... Mein Judethum ist meine moralische Gessinung und die demselbe conforme Lebensweise ... ,' *Gesamelte Schriften* (Szegedin, 1889), vol. 1, p. 175; see there also, his temperate review of Moses Hess' *Rome and Jerusalem*, pp. 332–55 and, vol. 4 (1898), inter alia; under the pseudonym, Leon de Modena Redivivus, *Die jüdische Wirren in Ungarn* (Leipzig, 1868).
37 Dubnow himself was anticipated by Orshanski, who in 1865 urged the Society for the Promotion of Enlightenment Among Jews (OPE), to collect and publish Jewish folksongs in Russia as a basis for a projected history of the masses, that would serve to dispel harmful stereotypes. Uri Finkel, 'Der onheyber fun der yidisher folkloristic in rusland,' *Heymland: literarish kinstlerisher almanakh*, vol. 6 (July-Aug, 1948), pp. 121–8; cf. above, n. 7.
38 Quoted in, Julian Krzyzanowski, *A History of Polish Literature*, trans. Doris Ronowicz (Warsaw, 1978), p. 452.
39 Avrom Reisin, *Di lider* (New York, 1935), p. 255.
40 Dov Noy, 'Dr. Max Grunwald, The Founder of Jewish Folkloristics,' ed. Noy, *Max Grunwald, Tales, Songs and Folkways of Sephardic Jews: Texts and Studies*, vol. 6 in the *Folklore Research Center Studies* (Jerusalem, 1982), pp. ix-xiv.
41 In his own paean to Peretz, Grünwald wrote: 'Noch weit höher als sein Wert als Dichter steht, so meine ich, seine Bedeutung als einer der berufensten Führer, und als einer der edelsten Söhne des jüdischen Volkes.' Grunwald, 'Der Dichter J.L.Perez als schilderers des ostjüdischen Lebens,' *Jahrbuch für jüdischer Volkskunde* (1924/25), p. 401.
42 Chone Shmeruk, 'Shtrikhn tsu der geshikhte fun dem yidishn lebn in varshe,' *Di goldene keyt* vol.110–111 (1983), p. 59 (hereafter 'Shtrikhn').
43 I follow here Shatzky's view (Peretz shtudyes) rather than Mayzl's (*Y.L.Peretz: zein lebn un shafn* [New York, 1945] pp. 170–9), that Peretz's interest in Jewish folklore originates in his contracts with Poles and polonized Jews at *Wisła*, rather than the rich folkloric life of his native Zamość. As Shatzky pointed out, with some overstatement, all Yiddish writers of that generation had folklore in their background, but only Peretz developed an interest in the field as such. The reason was the impact on Peretz of Warsaw. (Whether Peretz's interest was truly unique cf. Niger's reservations, *Y.L.Peretz* [Buenos Aires, 1952] p. 267).

Mayzl's view is interesting nonetheless, if not as good history then certainly as an example of the history of Peretz's great influence on leading Yiddish writers and critics. Mayzl heralded Peretz as the Jewish Pushkin. Both were heroic folk poets who instinctively and spontaneously recognized the native folk genius. Like the romanticist theory that the source of Pushkin's interest in folklore was the lesson he learned on his nanny's knee, more so than the larger intellectual currents of the day, Mayzl saw Peretz's folklorism as unmediated by the outside world. Mayzl's view was also based, in part, on too literal a reading of Peretz's memoirs, where, incidentally, Peretz talks of the great impact his invalid brother's Polish nurse had on his interest in Polish folklore (*My Memoirs: Isaac Leib Peretz*, trans. Fred Goldberg [New York, 1964], pp. 54–5).

Rather than a simple autobiography, Peretz's memoirs, as he himself hinted, contain something very much like a literary theory of modernism, in the form of a dynamic interplay between psyche and symbol. (David H. Roskies, 'A shlisl tsu Peretzes zikhroynes,' *Di goldene keyt*, vol. 99 [1979], pp. 132–59). Meizl, falling under the romantic spell of the memoirs, took as fact what Peretz intended as a 'higher truth.' Niger, with more justification, saw the beginnings of Peretz's folkloric interests in his statistical expedition (pp. 266–7). On the transition from positivism to neo-Romanticism as a general European phenomenon, see H.Stuart Hughes, *Consciousness and Society: The Reorientation of European Social Thought, 1890–1930* (New York, 1961), ch. 2; For Poland, see Aleksander Posern Zickiński, 'Kształtowanie się etnografii Polskiej jako samodzielnej dyscyplini naukowej do 1939r,' ed. Małgorzata Terlecka, *Historia Etnografii Polskiej* (Wrocław-Warsaw-Kraków-Gdańsk, 1973), pp. 52ff, 327–8; Julian Krzyżanowski, *Neoromantyzm polski* (Warsaw-Kraków, 1963). On Pushkin and some obvious similarities to Peretz see, Roman Jacobson, *Pushkin and His Sculptural Myth*, trans. and ed. John Burbank (The Hague, 1975), pp. 47, 58–62, 66.

44 Stanisław A. Blejwas, 'Polish Positivism and the Jews,' *Jewish Social Studies* (Winter, 1984), pp. 27–31; Shatzky, 'Peretz shtudyes,' pp. 48–51; idem, *Geshikhte*, vol.3, pp. 27–36, 227, 231, 319–21,406–7; Nahum Sokolov, *Perzenlekhkaytn*, trans. Moshe Sendrey (Buenos Aires, 1948), p. 40.

45 On Bernstein, see Hans Peter Althaus's introduction to Ignaz Bernstein's *Jüdische Sprichwörter und Redensarten: Im anhang Erotica und Rustica* (Hildesheim,1969), pp. xviii-xxii; Shatzky, 'Peretz shtudyes,' pp. 48–51, 56; idem, *Geshikhte*, vol. 3, pp. 325–8, 381, 387, 412–13; Veynig, 'Geshikhte un problemen fun der yidisher paremiografia,' pp. 361–3; cf. Goldberg-Mulkiewicz, p. 100–1, 102, n. 20. M.Spektor played a generally overlooked but very important role in Jewish folkloristics, not only for what he published in his journal, but also for what he discovered in the process of collecting folksayings. Aside from publishing the first major public appeal for a specific genre of folklore in 1878, Spektor found a great public interest in the subject. To his great amazement, nearly a thousand letters with folksayings poured in from Russia and Poland and from as far away as Africa, and Australia. His success, however, had probably more to do with the specific interest in a genre which had long enjoyed a special status in Jewish life, than with any popular interest in folklore as such. (See Spektor's introduction to Bernshtein's *Yidishe sprikhverter* [Warsaw, 1888], pp. 1–2. On post-Biblical Jewish paremiology see Yisroel Davidson, 'Nokhbiblishe literatur fun glaykhvertlekh: a bibliografye,' *YB*, [March-April, 1938] vol. 13, pp. 355–72).

46 Samuel Adalberg, 'Przyslowia Żydowskie,' *Wisła*, vol. 4 (1890), pp. 166–7; Julian Krzyżanowski, ed. *Słownik Folkloria Polskiego* (Wiedza, 1965), pp. 11–12; Dov Noy, 'Adalberg, Samuel' *Encyclopaedia Judaica*, vol. 2, p. 234.

47 Shatzky, 'Peretz shtudyes,' pp. 48–50.

48 Roman Zawiliński, 'O sposobie gromadzenia materiałów etnograficznych' *Wisła* vol. 1 (1887), p.3.'How ridiculous,' Bolesław Prus wrote, 'that we ... do not study the customs, religion and life of almost a million of our fellow citizens, who will sooner or later be fused with us into a uniform society.' Quoted in Norman Davies, *God's Playground: A History of Poland*, vol. 2 (New York, 1982) p. 257; cf. Shatzky, 'Peretz shtudyes,' p. 49.

49 Shatzky, 'Peretz shtudyes', pp. 52–4; Goldberg-Milkiewicz, pp. 98–9. On *Izrael-*

*ita*, see Shatzky, *Geshikhte*, vol. 2. p. 252, vol. 3. pp. 320–1; M. Fuks, *Prasa Żydowska w Warszawie 1823–1939* (Warsaw, 1979), ch. 5; Ch. Shmeruk, 'Ha'itonut hayehudit hatlat leshonit bevarsha,' (review of Fuks), *Hasifrut* (April, 1981), p. 196.

50 Krzyzanowski, *Słownik*, 'Lilientowa, Regina,' p. 203; Shatzky, 'Peretz shtudyes,' p. 53; Goldberg Miliewicz, p. 99; Zalman Reisin, *Leksikon fun der yidisher literatur prese un filologye*, vol. 2. (Vilna, 1927), pp. 162–5.

51 Goldberg-Mulkiewicz, p. 98; Shatzky, 'Peretz shtudyes,' p. 50; idem, *Geshikhte*, vol. 3, pp. 278–88, 306,311, 320–1; N.Sokolow, 'Nasza oświata ludowa,' *Izraelita* (1890), no. 49, pp. 485–6; Y.L.Peretz, 'Bildung' (1891), *Alle verk*, vol. 8 (New York, 1947), pp. 3–17; see also Shatzky's criticisms of Rosentsveyg's treatment of Peretz's 'Bildung' in relation to Sokolow and to Polish developments, 'Referatn un retzenzyes,' YB, vol. 12 (1935?), pp. 350–1. On the emerging literary community, see Shmeruk, 'Shtrikhn.'

52 Shatzky, *Geshikhte*, vol. 3, p. 278; Sokolow, 'Nasza oświata ludowa,' pp. 485–6; Czesław Miłosz, *The History of Polish Literature* (Berkeley, 1983), 2nd edn. pp. 303–23ff; Shatzky, overstating the case, said that Kohn, more than Berliner, Orshansky, 'or even Max Grünwald,' must be considered the 'first Jewish national folklorist': 'Peretz shtudyes' pp. 54–6.

53 Alina Cała, 'The Question of the Assimilation of the Jews in the Polish Kingdom (1864–1899): An Interpretive Essay,' *Polin*, vol. 1 (1986), pp. 130–50; Prus too, finally urged the Jews to convert (Shatzky, *Geshikhte*, vol. 3, p. 422).

54 Blejwas, pp. 29–33; Y.Shatzky, 'Di yidn in poyln fun 1772 biz 1914,' in, *Di yidn in poyln fun der ershter tsayt biz der tsveyter velt milkhome* (New York, 1946), vol.1, pp. 654–96; Meizl, *Peretz: zayn lebn un shafn*, pp. 317–22. See Davies on the Polish notion of an *Urvolk*, *God's Playground*, vol. 2, p. 28.

55 It was Russian positivism that had a greater impact on Jewish life than Polish positivism: see generally, James Billington, 'The Intelligentsia and the Religion of Humanity', *American Historical Review* vol. 65 (July, 1960), pp. 807–21; and particularly, on Dubnow, see Seltzer, 'Coming Home.'

56 Shatzky, 'Peretz shtudyes,' pp. 54–6; Goldberg-Mulkiewicz. pp. 98–101.

57 Blejwas, pp. 21–2, 33–4, n. 4; Niger, *Peretz*. 482ff.

58 Peretz's disappointment was, in the Nietzschean sense, tragically sublimated or *aufgehoben* into his dramatic masterpiece *Bei nakht oifn alten mark*, the subject of Khone Shmeruk's *Peretzes yeeush-vizye* (New York, 1971), see especially, pp. 195, 200ff (herein, *yeeush vizye*); Peretz' 'Hope and Fear' expresses a Nietzschean fear of mass movements (trans. Nathan Halper, *Voices from the Yiddish: Essays, Memoirs, Diaries*, ed. Irving Howe and Eliezer Greenberg [Ann Arbor, 1972], pp. 22–4). Mendele foresaw the disappointment in positivism in his epic of the Jew, *Yidl*, published in 1875, (*Ale verk fun mendele, yubileum oisgabe* [Kraków, 1911], vol. 4, pp. 19–25, esp. p. 22). Far from advocating the field of folklore, as Miron suggests, Mendele seems to have seen no point in it. For Mendele, Mindl, who represents the oral law and lore, is dying of old age, she is not youth reborn. What Miron translates as 'monuments' (*matseyvis*), may also be read as an ironic and pathetic contrast to the pyramids, not as an inspirational symbol of revival, but quite literally a 'tombstone. (Miron, 'Folkore-Antifolklore,' p. 239.

59 Ahad Haam, 'Riv Lishnot,' *Al parashat derakhim* (Berlin, 1921), vol. 4, p. 104; David Davidovich, 'Ishim vehashkafotam'al heker hafolklor hayehudi,' *Yeda'am* (1984), 51, 52, pp. 158–9; Nachman Mayzl, *Peretz un zeyn dor shreiber* (New York, 1951), pp. 322–37 (Hereafter, *Dor shrayber*).

60 Robert Seltzer, 'Ahad Ha-Am and Dubnow: Friends and Adversaries,' ed. Jacques Kornberg, *At the Crossroads: Essays on Ahad Ha-Am* (Albany, 1983), pp. 60–72, also there, Arnold J. Band, 'The Ahad Ha-Am and Berdyczewski Polarity,'

pp. 45–59. On Dubnow's positivism, Robert Seltzer, 'Coming Home: The personal Basis of Shimon Dubnow's Ideology,' *Annual of Jewish Studies*, vol. 1 (1976), pp. 283–301.

These writers, including Berdichevsky, the Jewish Nietzschean, advanced a concept of a Jewish ethical will to counterpose the will to power in its vulgar sense. Berdichevsky challenged Ahad Haam on this point in the guise of the *enfant terrible* of the Jewish renaissance, demanding a new individualism. He was more sensitive than the others to the creative needs of the writer, just as he was more rigorously secular in his iconoclasm. Ahad Haam and Peretz admired Berdichevsky's talent, but they disagreed with what they took for his revolt against Jewish values in his advocacy of the Nietzschean (Shmeruk, *Yeush-vizye*, p. 194). Berdichevsky was perhaps misunderstood because his critics misunderstood Nietzsche; though in reacting to how his volkish admirers understood him, they may have been more sensitivie to the urgent social issues. That Berdichevsky sought the Nietzschean in Hasidism was never duly appreciated by his critics who, like Dubnow and Peretz, rather professed admiration for the mass movement's ostensible democratic tendencies (Bal Makhshoves, *Geklibene shriften* [New York, 1953], p. 216; Seltzer, 'The Secular Appropriation of Hasidism by an Eastern Intellectual: Dubnow, Renan, the Besht,' *Polin*, vol. 1, [1986], pp. 151–62).

Peretz, obviously, was also deeply affected by Nietzsche, and cannot be accused of misunderstanding him. Like Berdichevsky, Peretz was openminded and could appreciate the positive even in the likes of Wagner, whose anti-semitism Nietzsche frequently excoriated (Gershon Levin, *Peretz: a bisl zikhroynes* [Warsaw, 1919], p. 28). In his last Hebrew poem, Peretz identified with Prince Vogelfrei, Nietzsche's *alter ego*, as he revealed himself in *Ecce Homo*, the penultimulate strophe of the prelude to *Die fröhliche Wissenschaft*, (Shmeruk, *Yeush-vizye*, p. 196; cf. F. Nietzsche, *The Gay Science*, trans. W. Kaufmann [New York, 1974], p. 67). Peretz's differences with Berdichevsky's Nietzscheanism needs further analysis. On these writers see Meisel, *Dor shrayber*, passim.

61 Dan Miron, 'Modern Hebrew Literature: Zionist Perspectives and Israeli Realities,' *Prooftexts*, Vol. 4 (Jan. 1984), pp. 52–7.
62 Peretz, *Alle verk*, vol. 9, pp. 159–60; Micha Josef Bin Gorian [Berdyczewski], *Yidishe ksovim fun a vaytn koriv*, ed. Shmuel Verses (Jerusalem, 1981), p. xii.
63 Mayzl, *Dor shrayber*, pp. 123–30, 322–37; Shmeruk, *yeush-vizye*, pp. 44, 199.
64 Leon Simon, *Ahad Ha-am* (Philadelphia, 1960), p. 85.
65 *Ibid.* pp. 137–46; A. Rosentsveyg, *Der radikaler peryod in Peretzes shafn, di yontif bletlekh* (Kharkov, Kiev, 1934).
66 Mayzl, *Dor shrayber*, passim; Niger, p. 279. Bialik's views in particular bear a closer look. Bialik wanted to do for the legacy of Hebrew culture and the Hebrew language, essentially, what Peretz had in mind for Yiddish culture and the Yiddish language: to collect, preserve and revitalize the best the culture and language had to offer. Bialik's *Sefer Haagada* (1908) constitutes his *iberdikhtung* of what he uncritically regarded as the folk literature of the Jews. This classic work assumed a position of importance in modern Hebrew culture comparable to the *Kinder und Hausmärchen* in Germany, much as the *Folkstimlekhe geshikhten* had done in Yiddish life at the same time. Unlike Peretz however, whose conception of Yiddish culture quite definitely opposed the exclusion of the Hebrew legacy, Bialik proclaimed the obsolescence of Yiddish, and specifically included the secularization of *halakha* in his vision of the folk's spiritual revival. As opposed as their views were in this regard, their cultural ambivalence allowed for a great and fruitful relationship. Bialik, after all, made significant contributions to Yiddish literature, while Peretz was also interested in achieving a secularized folk practice. The

precedent, if not inspiration, for Bialik's *Oneg Shabat* could be found in the regular Sabbath celebrations of the Jewish culture in Peretz's home. (See Ernst Simon, *Chajjim Bialik: Eine Einführung in sein Leben und sein Werk* [Berlin, 1935], pp. 98–9; Shmuel Verses, *Bikoret habikoret: haarakhot vegilguleihen* [Tel Aviv, 1982], pp. 108–9, 124; Nathan Rotenstreich, *Tradition and Reality: The Impact of History on Modern Jewish Thought* [New York, 1972], pp. 103–8; Eliyohu Shulman, 'Khaim Nakhman Bialik: zayne originele yidishe lieder, zayne ibersetsungen un zayn batsiyung tsu der shprakh frage,' *Pinkes far der forshung fun der yidishe literatur un prese*, [New York, 1975], vol. 3, pp. 50–107).

67 Shmeruk, *Yeush-vizye*, p. 6; Mayzl, *Dor shrayber*, pp. 141–6; Bal Makhshoves, *Geklibene verk* (New York, 1953), p. 196; Maurice Samuel, *Prince of the Ghetto* (New York, 1973), pp. 121–32; Nokhum Oislender, *Grundshtrikhn fun yidishn realizm* (Kiev, 1919), p. 77.

68 Mikhl Rabinovitsh, 'Peretzes shtelung tsu yidish in 1891,' YB, vol. 28, no. 1, p. 200; Niger, *Peretz*, pp. 210–11.

69 Nachman Mayzl, *Peretz zayn lebn un shafn*, pp. 110–18; Sokolow, *Perezenlekhkeytn*, pp. 252–3; idem, 'Jan Bloch: The Loyal Convert,' Dawidowicz, pp. 344–9; Niger, *Peretz*, pp. 200–3; *Bilder fun a provints rayze in tomashover paviat um 1890 yor*, *Yidishe biblotek*, vol. 2 (1891), in *Alle verk*, vol. 2, pp. 117–209.

70 Berlin, pp. ix-x, 46–7; Orshanski, *Gakarmel* (Jan. 20, 1866), p. 133; S. M. Ginsburg and Saul Marek, *Evreiskie narodnye piesni v rossi: sobrany i izdany* (St. Petersburg, 1901), p. iv.

71 Shatzky, 'Peretz shtudyes,' p. 66; Jonathan Frankel, *Prophecy and Politics: Socialism, Nationalism and the Russian Jews, 1962–1917* (Cambridge, 1981), ch. 2.

72 Shatzky, 'Peretz shtudyes,' p. 56; M. Khmelnitski, 'Y. L. Peretzes meditsinisher broshur: az men vil nisht shtarbt men nisht fun kholere,' YB, vol. 28, no. 1, pp. 146–52; cf. Goldberg-Milkiewicz, p. 99, 102, nn. 14, 15 for another early interest, also positivist, by B. Kowski in 1897. Older medieval Jewish folk medicine was already a subject of *Wissenschaft*, see sources cited in Jacob's 'Folk Medicine,' *Jewish Encyclopedia*, vol. 5, pp. 426–7; also Gideon Brecher, *Die transcendentale Magie und Magische Heilarten im Talmud* (Vienna, 1850); L. Low, 'Zur Medicien und Hygenie,' *Gesamelte Schriften*, vol. 3 (Szegedin, 1893), pp. 367–405; see also Dov Noy, 'Yahas haagada lerefua', *Mahanayim* (1970), 122, pp. 78–93.

73 Nokhum Oislender, 'Peretzes "shtet un shtetlakh",' *Tsaytshrift*, (Minsk), vol. 1 (1926), pp. 61–72; cf. Peretz, *Shtet un shtetlekh: Ale verk*, vol. 8, pp. 161–363; Miron, *Der imazh*, pp. 104–17.

74 Shatzky, 'Peretz shtudyes,' p. 66; Blejwas, p. 23; Goldberg-Mulkiewicz, p. 97. The differences between the positivistic concerns of Polish ethnography and Peretz's artistic approach to his material is evident, of course, in his *Rayzebilder*, as well. Cf., as Shatzky suggested, the earlier statistical study of Lashtshev, that appeared in *Lud*, B. Koskowski, 'O mieszkaniach i żywieniu się Żydów małomiasteczkowych w Królestwie Polskim,' (1897), pp. 314–29, with Peretz's artistic impressions of Jewish poverty' in the same *shtetl* (Shatzky's review of Meisel's biography of Peretz, YB, vol. 28 [1946], p. 173: see also Miron, *Der imazh*, pp. 44, 117). On the term *folkstimlekh*, which 'some say,' Peretz introduced to Yiddish, see Sh. e., 'Vos iz teitsh folkstimlekh,' and M. Sh., 'Folkish un poshit folkish,' *Yidishe Shprakh*, vol. 33 (1974), pp. 511–52 and 52–5 respectively.

75 Shmeruk, *Peretzes yeush-vizye*, pp. 130–44, particularly p. 141, for Peretz's use of folksongs in other dramas. The *Folkstimlekhe geshikhten* as well as *Khsidish* were most recently reprinted by Cyco, – 1984, 1987 respectively.

76 Bibliograhy for Peretz' sources discussed by Niger, *Peretz*, pp. 130–44; Menashe Unger, 'Mekoirim fun Peretzes folkstimlekhe geshikhtn,' *Idishe Kultur* (April-May, 1951), pp. 22–6.

77 Niger, *Peretz*, p. 273; Sh. Anski, *Gesamlte shriftn*, vol. 15 (Warsaw, 1925), p. 202; idem, *Dos yidishe etnografishe program* (Petrograd, 1915), p. 9; Zelig Kalmanovitsh, 'Y. L. Peretzes kuk oif der literatur.' YB, vol. 33 (1942), pp. 49–61; idem (continuation), *Di goldene keyt*, vol. 2 (1949), pp. 114–26. These articles were written in the Wilno ghetto and published posthumously. On Peretz's secularism see, Yakov Glatshtein, *In tokh genumen* (New York, 1947), inter alia, pp. 484–514. Peretz's literary secularism was not unlike that of Matthew Arnold's as described by Lionel Trilling (*Matthew Arnold*, [New York, 1975], pp. 441–3). On the same process of secularization in Germany in the works of Klopstock and generally, Dorthee Solle, 'Die übernahme des säkularisierungs Begriff in die Literwissenschaft,' ed. Heinz Horst Schrey, *Säkularisierung* (Darmstadt, 1981), pp. 91–105. Shikl Fishman's, 'Der tsushtayer fun veltlekhkayt tsum yidishn lebn' offers a lucid discussion of Jewish secularism, by defining secularism in its specifically historical Jewish context. (*Di tsukunft*, vol. 92 [Nov-Dec, 1986], pp. 201–8).

78 H. D. Nomberg, *Y. L. Peretz* (Buenos Aires, 1946), p. 78, portions translated as, 'Master of a Generation,' Dawidowicz, pp. 295, 297.

79 A. Litvak, *Vos geven: etudn un zikhroynes* (Vilna, 1925), p. 83. On Yiddish as *derekh hashas*, see M. Weinreich, *Geshikhte fun der yidisher shprakh*, vol. 1 (New York, 1973), ch. 3.

80 Niger, *Peretz*, p. 273; Shmeruk, *Yeush-vizye*, p. 121.

81 Nathan Rotenstreich, *Jewish Philosophy in Modern Times: From Mendelssohn to Franz Rosenzweig* (New York, 1968), chaps. 1–4. On the negative image of the Jews by their enlightened defenders, see Arthur Hertzberg, *The French Enlightenment and the Jews* (New York, 1968), chs. 9–10, pp. 273–9; Jacob Goldberg, 'The Attitude of Polish Society Towards the Jews in the Time of Enlightenment,' *Proceedings of the Conference on Poles and Jews: Myth and Reality in the Historical Context*, ed. J. Micgiel, R. Scott, H. B. Segel (Columbia University typescript, 1986), p. 176, also in the same volume: Harold B. Segel, 'Images of the Jew in Polish Literature,' pp. 292, 297–301, 310; Magdalena Opalski, 'Jewish Reformers of Polish Society and their Programs in Nineteenth Century Polish Fiction,' p. 328; for the assimilation of negative images into Jewish national thought, see Y. Kaufmann, 'Anti-Semitic Stereotypes in Zionism,' *Commentary* (March, 1949), pp. 239–45. An early defence of the Jewish 'morality' in England and Germany in the form of edifying tales when the word folk and nation were not yet fully out of favour, was Hyman Hurwitz's *Hebrew Tales: The Writings of the Ancient Hebrew Sages* (London, 1826), translated two years later as *Sagen der Ebräer: aus den Schriften den alten ebräischen Weissen* (Dettingen-Hainfarth, 1828).

82 Güdeman had argued the same about medieval Jewry. (Schorsch, 'Güdeman,' p. 58).

83 Peretz, 'Far di tsurikgekumene, a dritte eytse,' *Alle verk*, vol. 7, p. 129.

84 Miron, *Der imazh*, pp. 113–14; Meisel, *Dor shrayber*, pp. 143–6; Rosentsveyg, passim; On Peretz' anti-Orthodoxy, see the character of the *nakhtvekhter* and his parody of a rabbinic song, *Alle verk*, vol. 1, pp. 138–9.

85 Shmul Zanvil Pipe, 'Di zamlung yidishe folkslider fun Y. L. Peretz,' YB, vol. 12 (1937), pp. 286–90.

86 Kahan was unaware of the Peretz ms. until its rediscovery. He died before he completed his article. Some of the songs in the collection appeared in the *Urquell* in 1898 (see note 24). The original ms. was lost during the war; it survives in the Yivo archives, in the ms. copy transcribed by Pipe and sent to Kahan (Y. L. Kahan, 'Y. L. Peretz der zamler fun yidishe folkslider, 'Kahan, *Shtudyes*, p. 110). On the program Shtif solicited, see ibid. pp. 129–40.

87 Kahan, *Shtudyes*, p. 109; Nomberg, p. 70; Dawidowicz, p. 296. Peretz dealt with these perceptions in his *Monish*, *Alle verk*, vol. 1, pp. 3–27.

88 Peretz, *Alle verk*, vol. 8 p. 68–70; Ansky, *Gesamlte shriftn*, vol. 10, p. 54.
89 Peretz, *Ale verk*, vol. 1, p. 143, vol. 8, pp. 68–70; Glatshtein, pp. 494–5; Niger, *Peretz*. p. 212. On Peretz's understanding of the prophetic mission and its relation to the role of the poet, see Shmeruk, *Yeush vizye*, pp. 100–24.
90 Shmeruk, *Peretzes yeush-vizye*, p. 135. Y. Y. Lerner wrote a more explicit statement of Yiddishist romantic nationalism on the basis of Yiddish folksongs which came out the same year as the *Urquell* article. See 'Di yidishe muze' *Hoyzfraynd* (1898), pp. 182–98.
91 Cf. Samuel's description of Peretz 'The Confused Revolutionary,' pp. 171–6. Bal Makhsoves, *Geklibene verk* p. 196.
92 Shmeruk, *Yeush-vizye*, pp. 133–5; Pipe, pp. 286–90; Peretz, 'Dos yidishe lebn loyt di yidishe folkslider,' YB, vol. 12 (1937), pp. 291–9, *Alle verk*, vol. 7, pp. 129–57.
93 Shatzky, 'Peretz shtudyes,' p. 58; cf. Shmeruk's comments on Peretz' collection of poems published as *Romansero*, *Yeush-vizye*, p. 134.
94 Dovid H. Roskes, 'Peretzes shaferisher farat fun der yidisher folksmayse,' *Proceedings of the World Congress of Jewish Studies*, Division C (Jerusalem, 1982), pp. 349–55.
95 'It was said that all the *folkstimlekhe geshikhten* before they were written down, Peretz first told them to Janek [his grandson]. He told them in Polish because Janek did not understand Yiddish.' (Y. Y. Trunk, *Poyln: zikhroynes un bilder* [New York, 1949] p. 76). On Grimm see, 'Why not 'Old Marie' . . . or someone very much like her? A reassessment of the question about the Grimms' contributors from a social historical perspective,' *Social History*, vol. 13, no. 1 (Jan. 1988), pp. 3–4, 21.
96 See now, Maria Tatar, *The Hard Facts of the Grimm's Fairy Tales* (Princeton, 1987); Cocchiara, pp. 225–6. On Peretz's use of midrashic techniques, specifically allusion and quotation and their relation to his use of folklore, see Shmeruk, pp. 124–44. On Peretz's europeanization of Yiddish literature, see Glatshtein, relevant sections translated by Ronald Sanders as 'Peretz and the Jewish Nineteenth Century,' in Howe and Greenberg, pp. 51–63.
97 Sholem Aleichem, 'Letter to Joel Engel of the *Voskhod*,' *Der Yid*, no. 24 (1901), reprinted in *Forverts*, (June 1, 1984), p. 19, and (June 15, 1984), p. 19; Kahan, *Shtudyes*, pp. 194–201; Shatzky, 'Peretz shtudyes,' p. 5.
98 Sholem Aleichem, *Forverts*, p. 19, Kahan, *Shtudyes*, 194–201; Shmeruk, *Peretzes Yeush-vizye*, pp. 140–1, n. 34.
99 Anski writes further; 'In his own works, youth studied the Jewish people, and Judaism. Because of him assimilated boys and girls studied Yiddish.' Anski, vol. 10, p. 154; cf. Glatshtein, pp. 494–5. Peretz had a direct influence on Leo Wiener's interest in Yiddish folklore. This son of East European immigrants, who became a Harvard professor of Slavic languages, travelled to Warsaw, in 1898, having been told of Peretz's interest in Yiddish folksongs by Krauss. Peretz lent him a collection of Yiddish folksongs, which, he later lamented, Wiener never returned, and which ended up in Kahan's possession (Kahan, *Shtudyes*, p. 105). Wiener used the material for some of his early articles on Yiddish folklore and his *History of Yiddish Literature in the Nineteenth Century*. (Reprinted by Sepher Hermon Press, [New York, 1972] with an introduction on the author, by E. Schulman, pp. vii–xxiii). Though Wiener was neither a Yiddishist nor a Jewish nationalist, the positive light in which he cast his subject, in his still useful work, elicited the criticism of B. W. Segel, who felt, 'Es gibt in der Welt keine Volkersschaft die sich Jidden oder Yidden nennen.' (*Die Polnische Judenfrage*, p. 25); On Wiener see also Shatzky, 'Peretz shtudyes,' p. 60–1; idem, 'Leo Viner,' YB, vol. 15 [1940], pp. 247–56 (includes bibliography).

100 Reisin, 'Mayn bakantshaft mit Y. L. Peretz,' *Di tsukunft* (July, 1915), p. 651; idem, *Epizodn fun mayn lebn: literarishe erinerungen* (Wilno, 1929), vol. 1, pp. 203, 220ff; 'Dos yidishe folklid,' Kahan, *Shtudyes*, p. 42; Bal makhshoves, *Geklibene verk*, p. 205; Ansky, *Gesamlte shriftn*, vol. 10, p. 163; Sholem Asch, 'Mayn ershte bekantshaft mit peretzn,' *Di tsukunft* (May, 1915), p. 459; Shmeruk, 'Shtrikhn,' pp. 59, 61–2, n. 35.

101 Levin, p. 77; Asch, p. 467; Bal Makhshoves, *Geklibene verk*, pp. 192, 207; for Dubnow's criticism of Peretz's *rebbe* posturing, see Meisel, *Dor shrayber*, p. 155.

102 Levin, pp. 455–6; Reisen, 'Mayn bekantshaft', pp. 649–50; idem, *Epizodn*, vol. 1, pp. 53–4, vol. 3, pp. 73–4; Peretz, *Briv un redes*, letter to Y.Y. Propus, c. 1898–1900, p. 102. The servant was also the source for many of the songs Reisin collected for Saul Marek while travelling around the country in the Russian army orchestra, circa, 1898–1900. In Kovno, between performances, Reisin took a seat on a park bench next to 'the pretty girl who would come with the child of her rich employers, a servant girl, poor thing, though in fact she looked prettier and better off than all the bourgeois girls in the garden ... From this darling *folksmeydl*,' says Reisin, scarcely concealing his amorous delight, 'I was able to get, at first with great difficulty, later more easily, the most beautiful Yiddish folksongs, in particular those of deceived lovers.' How did Reisin achieve his folkloristic success? 'She was taken with my friendly manner towards her, though I would not deny that now and then I would kiss her, especially when she impressed me with a folksong.' Though Reisin did not think he was condescending to the 'simple folk,' he was sensitive to a patronizing attitude in others from his station, when it was directed to his work. (*Epizodn*, vol. 1, pp. 163–4). For a picture of one of Peretz's maids see Trunk, p. 113.

103 Shatzky, 'Y. L. Kahan (1881–1937): materialen far a biografia,' *Yorbukh fun amopteyl*, vol. 1, ed. J. Shatzky, A. Mukdoni (New York, 1938), pp. 11–12 (hereafter 'Kahan'); Reisin *Epizodn*, vol. 3, pp. 73–4; Pipe, 'Y. L. Peretz vegn y.l.kahans folkslieder,' YB, vol. 12 (1937), pp. 300–2; Nomberg, p. 78; Dawidowicz, p. 101. Trunk shows the lasting impact of Peretz by mistakenly attributing a pioneering role in the folk awakening to the young Boreisha, who first came to Peretz a generation later in 1905 (p. 24).

104 Shatzky, 'Peretz shtudyes,' p. 57; Moritz Güdemann, *Geschichte des Erziehungswesens und der Kultur der abendländischen Juden*, vol. 3. *Juden in Deutschlanden während des xiv und xv jahrhunderts* (Amsterdam, 1966), pp. 138–40; A. Berliner, *Aus den innern Leben der deutschen Juden in Mittelalter; nach gedruckten und ungedruckten Quellen: zugleich ein Beitrag fur des deutsche Kulturgeschichte* (Berlin 1871), pp. 8, 9, 52; idem, *Aus dem Leben deutschen Juden im Mittelalter* (Berlin, 1900) pp. 16–18, 121–2, 136; see also recently, Zvi Friedhaber, 'Beit hamekholot behayeha shel ashkenaz beyimey habeinayim', *Mehkarei yerushalayim befolklor yehudi* (1984), vol. 7, pp. 49–60.

105 Asch, p. 602.

106 Nomberg, p. 10; Dawidowicz, p. 295.

107 Levin, p. 46.

108 Reisin *Epizodn*, vol. 1, p. 203.

109 Peretz, 'Gedanken in der velt arein,' (1910–1911), *Ale verk*, vol. 9, p. 155.

110 Asch, p. 66; Reisin, 'Di shabosim by peretzn,' *Di lieder*, p. 255.

111 Peretz, 'Gedanken in der velt arein,' p. 152; cf. prescription for a Jewish folkloristics and art by Henryk Lucjan Kohn, Shatzky, 'Peretz shtudyes' p. 55.

112 Nomberg, p. 72; Dawidowicz, p. 296.

113 F. M. Kaufmann, *Vier Essais über ostjüdische Dichtung und Kultur* (Berlin, 1919), pp. 48–64; Steven E. Aschheim, 'The East European Jew and German Jewish Identity,' *Studies in Contemporary Jewry*, vol. 1, (1984), p. 20; Kahan, *Shtudyes*,

pp. 364–5. After my presentation of an earlier version of this paper at the 1987 Yivo conference, I was approached by a gentleman who informed me that he participated in such gatherings in pre-war Belgium. The ambience and legend of these Peretz Sabbaths were captured by Reisin in his poem *Varshe*, to which the foregoing may be considered a commentary (Reisin, *Di lider*, p. 256, recently reprinted in the *Forverb* [July 11, 1986], p. 19).

114 Shatzky, 'Kahan,' p. 17; Reisin, *Epizodn*, vol. 2, pp. 17–22; Bal Makhshoves, *Geklibene shriftn*, vol. 3, pp. 455–7.
115 Reisin, *Epizodn*, vol. 2, pp. 17–18.
116 Ibid. p. 18.
117 Levin, p. 82.
118 Reisin, *Epizodn*, vol. 2, p. 18.
119 Ibid. pp. 67–9.
120 Ibid. p. 22. Warsaw followed the example of Paris where, Roger Shattuck says, banquets had become 'the supreme rite' of the literary *avant-garde*. The Paris, and we may say the Warsaw banquets too, 'grew out of nonconformist tendencies of the romantic movement,' and both 'called for gaiety and scorn of convention, an assimilation of popular art forms and a full aliveness to the present moment'. Most importantly, what Shattuck said of the banquets, that 'this was the setting for a great regeneration of the arts,' was equally true for the Purim balls and banquets. (Roger Shattuck, *The Banquet Years: The Origins of the Literary Avant-garde in France; 1885 to World War I* [New York, 1969], pp. 3, 24, 26). The banquet fad soon spread to the bourgeoisie where it was put to less noble purposes. Morris Winchevsky sarcastically defined a ball as a place were, 'idlers acquire the taste for showing off' (*an ort vu leydikgeyer farzukhn dem tam fun shvitsn*, quoted in Reisin, *Epizodn*, vol. 2, p. 194; similarly, Bal Makhshoves, 'A yidisher ball').
121 Shatzky, 'Kahan' p. 17. Shatzky's information came from an undated clipping taken from the Lwów Zionist newspaper *Wschód*, that he found in the pre-war Kahan archive. Shatzky dates it 1899 or 1900. A different version of the event is described by the clipping found by Weinreich (see note, 120).
122 Kahan himself actually played the role of the beggar on at least one occasion as reported by *Der Yid* in Kraków (March 14, 1901). Though the place of the ball was not mentioned, the paper, most likely, reported on the festivities in Warsaw. Here the description suggests that the beggar might not be the folklorist but rather his source, the simple man of the folk who touches the heart of the more 'civilized' people with his sad songs. Still it was the folklorist who assumed the part as an expression of his identification with the folk. The clipping was placed by Weinreich at the end of the first article of Kahan's *Shtudyes* (p. 43). Titled, 'Purim Evening for the Jewish Literati,' the clipping reads:
' ... Mainly it was the truly original and impressive mask which made a great sensation: A poor blind Jewish man with a tragic weary face, on his head a hat with a long visor that blocks the glare from his sickly eyes, a little girl leads him by the hand. The blind man and his girl stand each time before a different circle of people and sing Yiddish folksongs with Yiddish folk melodies. The blind man sings about Jewish troubles, about Jewish mercy – it breaks the heart – and the girl holding his hand helps him with her fragile, thin but lovely, sweet voice. Who lives among Jews, especially in the provinces, and is not familiar with this picture? Which pious Jewish heart has the poor blind man not broken with his sad folksongs and melodies? And wherever the blind man and the girl stopped, they elicited a "bravo". It is noteworthy that Mr. K. who wore the mask ... is himself a great lover and collector of Yiddish folksongs and melodies, and no one could have performed the role as well as he.'

123 Mark W. Kiel, 'The Jewish Narodnik,' *Judaism* (Summer, 1970), p. 308.
124 Dov Noy, 'Mekomo shel Sh. An-ski bafolkloristika hayehudit', *Mehkarei yerushalayim befolklor yehudi* (1982), vol. 2, pp. 94–107. Vicot Tchernov, 'Sh. anski-rapaport,' H. A. Abramson, ed. *Vitebsk amol* (New York, 1956), pp. 247–62; also there, J. Shatzky, 'Sh. Ansky der folklorist,' pp. 263–74. Elias Shulman provides a useful survey of the major issues in Yiddishist scholarship in 'Veltlikhe motivn in der alter yidisher literatur,' *Bay zikh*, no. 21 (1982), pp. 78–93.
125 Samuel, pp. 122–3; Henry Malter, 'Purim,' *Jewish Encyclopedia*, vol. 19, pp. 279–80.
126 Jacob Shatzky, 'Yidish teater: di geshikhte fun yidisher teater,' *Yidn*, vol. B (New York, 1940), pp. 389–414. For the secularization of Russian folk ritual into theatre and the use of masks, cf. Elizabeth Wainer, *The Russian Folk Theater* (The Hague, 1977), pp. 14–18.
127 Jacob Shatzky, 'Purim shpiln un letsim in amsterdamer geto,' YB, vol. 19, no. 2 (1942), pp. 218.
128 Yitskhok (Ignacy) Shipper, *Geshikhte fun yidisher teater kunst un drama* (Warsaw, 1927), vol. 2, p. 225, quoted in Shulman, p. 64.
129 Raphael Mahler, *Historiker un vegvayzer: geshikhte, zikhroynes, khurbn* (Tel Aviv, 1967), pp. 269–70.
130 Glatshtein, p. 488.
131 A. Reisin, 'Mir zamlen,' *Literarishe bleter* (May 1, 1931), p. 337, *Di lieder*, p. 264, recently in *Forverts* (March 22, 1985), p. 23.

# THE LINAS-HATSEDEK CHARITABLE FRATERNITY IN BIAŁYSTOK, 1885–1939

Tomasz Wiśniewski

Śpiewa – jak Szczerszyński
Zgrabny – jak ułan z Dziesiątki
Zgrał sie – jak rzeka Biała
Złe – Jak bruki białostockie
Drogie – jak swiatło elektryczne
Punktualnie – jak w Pogotowiu Linas Hatsedek ...

He sings like Szczerszyński
He is as handsome as an uhlan from the tenth regiment
He is as melodious as the Biała river
As bad as Białystok's pavements
As expensive as electric light
As punctual as the *Linas Hatsedek* Emergency service...

(Białystok proverbs)

'As punctual as the *Linas Hatsedek* Emergency Service' was a pre-war saying in Białystok about the society for medical help, as well as about one part of it, the fast (night) emergency service. In this short paper I will describe the organization's history and discuss its more important achievements.

For centuries Jews have followed their ancestors' traditional belief in a duty to care for the poor, the needy and the sick. The first institutions of this type on Polish territories were the community-hospital committees, *Gabai Tsedaka*, or *Komisje Miłosierdzia* (Charity Committees). At first they functioned under the authority of the Synagogue and its officials, becoming independent from them in the seventeenth century. The *Komisja Miłosierdzia* supervised the activities of other charitable organisations like the *Hevra Kadisha* (Funeral Fraternity) and the *Hekdesh* (The old people's home).[1]

There were a very large number of active organizations, fraternities and charity communities – medical and philanthropic – to help those in need in the inter-war period. In the Białystok province, there were 136 registered relief organisations, 80 of which were Jewish; in addition there were 36 interest-free loan funds, the so-called *Gmilut Hasodim*.[2] Dozens of other smaller organizations and fraternities also existed with no legal basis, usually as branches of the larger registered societies.[3]

Of the societies with a charitable-medical, social-welfare and similar character the *Linas Hatsedek* fraternity, the first of this type, formed in Białystok at the end of the nineteenth century, was one of the most impressive. Similar organizations were formed, patterned after it, in many towns in the Russian Empire and Polish Kingdom. The inter-war period saw the *Linas Hatsedek* organization active in nearly every town inhabited by Jews in the Second Republic.

## The birth of *Linas Hatsedek*

*Linas Hatsedek* was founded in 1885 to help and care for poor Jews. The *Linas Hatsedek* fraternity, also known as the *Żydowskie Towarzystwo Dobroczynne* [Jewish Charity Society] was formed out of the similar older *Bikkur Kchoylim* fraternity. Białystok's Jewish community decided to reorganize the latter because it had proved unsatisfactory. *Linas Hatsedek* also acquired its accommodation from it. According to Abraham Samuel Herszberg, *Linas hatsedek* was born accidentally: Mejer Szochet, a hospital attendant fell sick, and had no one to look after him. When he died, on his own, this shocked the Jewish community. *Linas Hatsedek* was formed, therefore, to care for the isolated sick who needed a bed for the night.[4]

Henryk Mościcki, however, maintains that the fraternity was founded because of the incident of an isolated Jew who was bitten to death by rats. In Hebrew *Linas* (*linat* in modern pronunciation) *Hatsedek* means literally 'a charitable refuge', and, in practice a place of refuge to the poor and sick: the fraternity's main aim was indeed to care for the isolated sick.[5]

The *Linas Hatsedek* society in Białystok was the first social-welfare institution of its type. It was only several years later that similar bodies were set up in the Russian territories and the Congress Kingdom of Poland. In Brańsk, near to Białystok, a *Linas Hatsedek* was formed in 1893,[6] but one was not registered in Warsaw till 1901. In 1907 *Linas Hatsedek*'s so-called second ward was set up.[7]

*Linas Hatsedek* in Białystok functioned at first without legal registration, only by the permission of the governor. Its statutes and regulations were confirmed by its legal registration in 1898,[8] through the work of Abram Niemcow, who was elected its president at the end of the nineteenth century. A. Tilleman described this: ' . . . and a miracle happened, one of those Russian miracles. In 1899, the Grodno governor validated its statutes' and the *Linas Hatsedek* fraternity could then function legally.[9]

Dr Josef Chazanowicz, an eminent physician, educator and propagator of Zionism, played the main role in forming and consolidating the young organisation. He worked as a doctor in Białystok and emigrated to Palestine, where he founded a library in 1892, which was to become the National and University Library of Israel. Until the Second World War, there was a street in Białystok named after him, near the Large Synagogue.[10] Moshe Berl Bezim and Joshua Heschel Klementynowski were others involved in setting up this organization.[11]

At first, Chazanowicz managed to have all services and medical help provided by the *Linas Hatsedek* free of charge. Chazanowicz himself, popularly known as 'the man who cannot leave his cab', travelled constantly among the sick, accepting only minimal fees for his services, and charging the poorest nothing. The Tsarist authorities even honoured him by appointing him city doctor. The Govenor personally thanked him for his medical work during the Białystok cholera epidemic of 1896. It was due to Chazanowicz that *Linas Hatsedek* received so much help, both from the Jewish community, and from the town.[12]

One essential innovation in the organization was that, unlike all the earlier Jewish ones, which were directly, or indirectly, subject to the Jewish community, *Linas Hatsedek*, was the first to be entirely independent of both it and of all synagogues. At the beginning, this was rather a drawback because some of its activities were hindered by the reluctant attitude of the community's authorities. The fraternity's funds were provided by Chazanowicz himself and representatives of Białystok's Jewish élite. In 1899 the influential and rich Barasz family gave its house on Różańska Street (which no longer exists) to the fraternity, which was used till 1939 as the organisation's headquarters,[13] and in 1902 other accommodation in a house on Nowogrodzka Street.[14] Despite having two branches, at first *Linas Hatsedek* did not provide medical supplies, as it was largely dependent on interest-free loans. The events at the beginning of the twentieth century, the 1905 Revolution and the 1906 pogroms in Białystok, were to stimulate its members to greater activity.

*Linas Hatsedek*'s aims and activities

From the very beginning, the fraternity aimed at providing medical aid for the Jewish poor in Białystok. At first, medicine, as well as services, were free, but later on small charges, depending on the income of those treated, were imposed. The most significant feature of *Linas Hatsedek* was that its members had to remain on duty overnight to help the sick. All the members of the fraternity, whatever their functions or wealth, had to take on these duties, but, over time the rich paid the poorer members to act for them. Despite this development, *Linas Hatsedek* was regarded as one of the most democratic of Jewish welfare societies. Many of the fraternity members voluntarily took on overnight duties for the sick, in the inter-war period as well. There was even some rivalry among the members: A group of so-called *linists* (*Lina* in Hebr. means 'staying the night') competed with one another over who took on the most duties in a year, and there were prizes for those who won.[15]

*Linas Hatsedek* began life as an institution to help Jews, but at the turn of the nineteenth and twentieth centuries began to serve all, regardless of faith, nationality or class. In his speech at the 50th anniversary of the fraternity Dr Nahum Pryłucki said: '. . . you must have noticed, ladies and gentlemen, that throughout my speech, in describing the work and achievements of the *Linas Hatsedek* society, I have never used the word *Jew*, *Jewish* etc. This was deliberate, since, although it was founded and directed by Jews, is supported by funds from the Jewish community, and bears a Jewish name, *no one is ever asked about his faith or nationality*'.[16] In reality during its first years (till 1914) *Linas Hatsedek* mainly served the Jewish community, and it only served all, regardless of nationality in the inter-war period. It was also then helped from city funds.

In 1893, another institution, with similar character and aims, was founded; a largely Zionist organisation, *Mishmores Khoylim* (Help for the Poor). Many leading members of the Jewish community in Białystok helped to found it, but because the new fraternity functioned badly, and a number of its members, like Jechijel Ber Wolkowyski and his son Eber, stopped cooperating with it. Consequently, some members of *Linas Hatsedek* decided to help it by joining it. Conflicts in both institutions eventually led to a new one emerging: the *Linas Khoylim* (Refuge for the Sick). In effect two organizations *Linas Hatsedek* and *Linas Khoylim*, with similar aims and activities, now operated in the city. Because of their hostility to each other the fraternities were called 'Dwa Jakuby' (The two Jacobs). Their squabbles led to a severe warning by the famous Białystok rabbi, Szmuel Mohilewer, but even this did not lead to a reconciliation. This caused the rabbi, who was sick at the time, to say: 'You are not doing your work, although there is a real need'.[17] In reality these squabbles were short-lived, and eventually the two fraternities started to co-operate. For example during the inter-war period many doctors, such as Dr Herc Neumark, worked for both *Linas Hatsedek* and *Linas Khoylim*.[18]

## *Linas Hatsedek*'s activities before the First World War

At the beginning, financial difficulties and conflicts within the fraternity meant that *Linas Hatsedek* did not provide medical supplies and just supplemented the activities of various medical and philanthropic institutions. Many of these had been set up at the turn of the nineteenth and twentieth centuries. At that time, Białystok was developing fast, becoming a Jewish industrial and commercial town. In 1897, 41,905 of the 66,032 population were Jews. In 1911, the total population (including the suburbs) was 84,000, and two years later 99,000. Over 70 per cent of the population were Jews.[19]

Just after acquiring new accommodation from Fiszel Barasz in 1902, the society organized a free service for hiring medical equipment, and an outpatients' clinic, which started to operate in 1904. The out-patients' clinic was created by its later long-serving director, Dr Josef Rubinsztejn.[20]

In 1908, J. B. Rubinsztejn was president of *Linas Hatsedek*, and among it leading members were S.M. Cytron, F.A. Bloch, I.J. Barasz, Z. Chajet, N[?]. Bakszt, I.N. Nieważski, L.Kaplan and J.S. Rozental. M. Elbaum was the secretary. That such Białystok financiers and bankers as A.B. Wolkowycki, M. Gordon, and Z. Weinreich were members of the rival fraternity *Linas Khoylim*, is a sign of the rather poor position of *Linas Hatsedek* at that time, although they also gave money to *Linas Hatsedek* as well.[21]

The fastest growth of the *Linas Hatsedek* charity took place in the years 1910–1914. In 1911 the fraternity opened its own pharmacy with the help of the Wielbuszewicz and Perlis families, who were pharmacists and contributed 4,000 roubles to the enterprise. The weekly *Tempo* reported that up to 6,000 roubles were contributed by the Wilbuszewicz family to the pharmacy. In 1913, it helped provide medicines to 29,032 sick people.[22]

In 1912 members of *Linas Hatsedek* organized an ice cellar, which supplied practically all the Białystok hospitals. This ice cellar was named after one of the fraternity's dead members, Abram Kohn. According to the 1930 reports, all the city hospitals, as well as some smaller clinics, used the ice cellar.[23]

In 1913 Samuel Aronowicz Goldberg was president, and the eminent oculist, Leon Pines, director of *Linas Hatsedek*. On its Council were Iser Mscibowski, Jeoncz Gurwicz, Zalman Weinreich, Jowel Gordon, Abram Lewin, Abel Milecki, Mejer Smigielski, Josef Kagan, Hersz Ginzburg, Gordon [C.H.?], Lejb Makowski, Jakow Woroszylski, Dawid Potocki, Jerucham Mowszowicz, Hersz Rozenberg and others. The names of manufacturers and financiers like Gordon and Weinreich show that the fraternity had become an important institution, with access to considerable funds. Its budget a year earlier, in 1912, was the relatively large sum of 15,000 roubles. The fraternity had five honorary and 1,820 ordinary members.[24]

The greatest development of the fraternity took place around the year 1914, when *Linas Hatsedek* opened a number of new branches, ran another outpatient's clinic, imported modern medical equipment, and even discussed opening a small hospital. Maks Fiszel Barasz was elected its president in 1914 and these representatives of Białystok financial circles were on its Council: E. Trilling, Sz. Cytron, G. Beloch, A.J. Treszczanski, N. A. Einhorn, and others.[25]

## The period of the First World War

We possess only fragmentary information about *Linas Hatsedek*'s activities during the first World War. The constantly changing political situation and the proximity of the front resulted in the fraternity increasing its activities. The Barasz family above all, particularly Maks Fiszel Barasz, showed great initiative in this. The society's headquarters on Różańska Street were turned into a shelter for refugees, and a free soup kitchen was organized. The unemployed were either helped to find jobs, or given small benefits.

A. Tilleman claimed, with some exasperation, that during the German occupation of the town. ... 'There was some idea within the Society of organizing the Jewish community in Białystok to oppose German plans for Germanisation ... '. What seem to have happened, however, was that *Linas Hatsedek* managed to overcome many obstacles and to organise cooperatives to supply food and free soup kitchen to the poor. In 1920, during the massive confiscations by the Soviet army, much of the fraternity's equipment and both the pharmacy and outpatients' clinics were left untouched. After the Soviet army was forced to retreat *Linas Hatsedek*'s quarters were used as a field hospital for the Polish army.[26]

## *Linas Hatsedek* in the inter-war period

Polish independence saw a further development of the organization. The fraternity was immediately reactivated in Białystok, as well as in other towns of the Białystok region: Augustów, Krynki, Wolkowysk, Zabłudów, Szczuczyn and elsewhere.[27] In the reborn state, *Linas Hatsedek* took the lead in the sphere of medical charity work and incorporated many smaller organisations. Several respected members of the Jewish élite led the fraternity during the period: H. Efros, N. Perelson, I. Fried, G. Gerszuni, Ch. Gerc, A. Binhorn, Sz. Bramson, I. Lew, Z. Szuster, R. Kagan, I. Fajnsod, I. Boskies, Ch. Szaps, N. Polak, A. Frejdkies, Sz. Lin, H. Grochowski, C. Grinberg and others.[28]

The organization's facilities, including the outpatients' clinic, where doctors of various specialities worked, were constantly developed. The outpatients' clinic was open from 10 a.m. to 8 p.m. In 1929 there were 2,138 patients' visits; a year later 13,923 patients were treated and a further 11,126 were given various forms of help. 2,667 people were given injections; 250 operations were carried out, 142 of the more difficult ones in Warsaw, and 108 in Białystok. Dr M. Szacki was director of the outpatients' clinic, and 11 doctors worked there.[29]

In 1928 a radio-therapy consulting room, with much previously unknown specialist equipment, was opened. It became the city's pride. In 1930 9,677 persons were treated there. Under the direction of Herc Nejmark another consulting room, popularly called the *Nejmark* was opened. This initiative was financed by Zalman Weinreich.[30]

The *Linas Hatsedek* pharmacy was active as well, and in 1929 above 27,676 prescriptions were dispensed there. Many medicines were provided at lower prices, and in special cases free of charge. The pharmacy was also open overnight, and according to the daily, *Dziennik Białostocki*, in 1934/35 it was on night duty 118 times. All the medical institutions in the city, as well as some private doctors, co-operated with *Linas Hatsedek*. For example a private eye clinic with a national reputation, run by Dr Leon Pines was among them; the annual report of 1934 shows that the outpatients clinic in Różańska Street treated 10,332 patients, doctors paid 1,093 home visits, and admitted 585 sick, while the pharmacy dispensed 19,912 prescriptions.[32]

### The *Linas Hatsedek* night Emergency Service

The older inhabitants of Białystok remember very well the *Linas Hatsedek* night Emergency service. As we have observed, its punctuality and speed led to the expression 'as fast as the *Linas Hatsedek* Emergency Service'. A very fast emergency service was planned as early as 1899. This was to be a horse-drawn cart, always on call for the sick. But the plan could not be carried out at that time, and in an emergency one of the many horse-drawn cabs in the town was ordered.[33]

In the 1920s an attempt was made to organise a fast emergency service by using hired cars, a few of which were already in the town. But it was only in 1928 that a special branch of *Linas Hatsedek*, the so-called 'Fast Night Emergency Service' was organized. During the day time it still used horse-drawn cabs or taxis. At the start, the service had one car at its disposal donated by a bus company owner, Zelikowicz. The ceremonial opening of the emergency service took place on 26 February 1928 and by mid-1928 the fraternity already had two cars specially adapted for going to patients. Cars had identification emblems, three-tone horns, a compartment for the sick, spare wheels, special signal flags and organisational signs. In 1929 1,980 call-outs were registered.[34]

The 'Night Emergency Service' had its headquarters at 3, Różańska Street, where there were three garages for the cars.[35] As Tilleman said ' ... Białystok became one of those towns where the sick could be helped in an emergency'.[36] The service was often called out to emergencies during the day as well. The town authorities provided financial help so that the town could benefit from it in the daytime. The daily, *Dziennik Białostocki*, highly praised the three years' activity of the fast emergency service, especially stressing how it acted 'for all, regardless of faith and nationality'. Dr Chaim Lukachewski was the head of the motor section of the *Linas Hatsedek* Emergency Services.[37]

## Other activities of *Linas Hatsedek* in Białystok

Beside its main medical activities, *Linas Hatsedek* worked in other areas. In 1929, the interest-free loan fund, *Gmilut Hasodim*, which had previously been provided from within various synagogues, was renewed within the organization. The *Gmilut Hasodim* had been organized within the fraternity in 1890 and was directed at the beginning by Fejwel Bloch. In 1900 it was joined to a similar institution operated by one of the synagogues; its influence and funds grew proportionally. By 1935 this section was lending a total of 38,525 zloty.[38]

Besides loans, which could often not be repaid, *Linas Hatsedek*'s members distributed free food and clothing, often acquired from donations and wills, above all from the strong Jewish emigrants' organizations in Canada and the U.S.A.

*Linas Hatsedek* was also very active in the cultural and educational field. The weekly, *Prożektor*, reported in 1926 that the fraternity financed the establishment of the Jewish *Gilarino* theatre, which was also known as the *Glorina*. The theatre produced plays until 1939. Its directors, W. Bubryk and J. Różaniecki, were accommodated by the fraternity at 5 Sienkiewicz Street.[39] *Linas Hatsedek* was also responsible for inviting various musical and theatrical groups to Białystok, including, a cabaret participated in by the Warsaw Jewish *Azazel*.[41]

*Linas Hatsedek* had its own prayer house on the first floor in Różańska Street. This philanthropic synagogue (all prayers ended with money collections) was situated near the *Mishmar Beth Midras* synagogue, and rivalled it. Numbered collection boxes for each member of the fraternity were placed in the vestibule of the synagogue, which meant that everyone's actual generosity and charity could be seen by the contents of his collection box. *Linas Hatsedek*'s members who used other synagogues had their own collection boxes there. Some of those have miraculously survived.

## The attitude of Białystok's inhabitants towards *Linas Hatsedek*

Whatever their faith, the inhabitants of Białystok appreciated *Linas Hatsedek*'s activities. All those who still remember the working of the organization have fond memories of its employees. Most of *Linas Hatsedek*'s members were assimilated Jews, who knew the Polish language, traditions and culture very well.

The town authorities respected the activities of the fraternity and helped it financially. In the financial reports for 1927/28 we find that the organization was given the considerable sum of 4,800 zloty, that is 400 zloty a month. A year later the fraternity received 7,200 zloty, 3,600 of which was to help the pharmacy. The increased sum was because of the formation of the 'Night Emergency Service' in 1928 by *Linas Hatsedek*.[42]

In 1935 the town council remitted the fraternity's charges for using the municipal sewerage system. As the town lacked a proper daytime emergency service, it asked *Linas Hatsedek* to provide emergency service during the day as well, till a daytime emergency service could be set up. The town council paid an adequate amount for these services. In fact the 'Night Emergency Service' had operated during the day from the very beginning. When the sick needed help, there was no choice but for the cars to go out. Several drivers worked on day or night duties. Although the town council often discussed setting up its own emergency service, it never did so because of financial difficulties. Consequently the Health Department subsidised *Linas Hatsedek*'s emergency service's daytime work. For example in the quarter 1 April to 1 July of 1935 1,125 zloty were provided.[43] In 1935, on the occasion of *Linas Hatsedek*'s 50th anniversary, the town gave the fraternity a single, non-repayable sum of 200 zloty, to show its gratitude for its previous work.[44]

Although the fraternity was an apolitical organization, many of its members were involved in various political factions and groups. Therefore all the fraternity's activities were closely watched by the authorities, just like those of such Jewish political parties in Białystok as *Poalei Tsion*, the *Bund*, *Aguda* and so on.[45]

## Conclusion

On 17 November 1935, the *Linas Hatsedek* fraternity celebrated its 50th anniversary. Representatives of the town authorities, and leaders and members of the fraternity took part in the celebration. Dr Leon Pines, who had moved to Warsaw, came especially for the occasion, which was a splendid one. The president of the organization, I.D. Szpira, welcomed all the guests, then the mayor, S. Nowakowski, deputy *voivode*, M. Zgrzebniak, the head of the Jewish community in Białystok, Abraham Tytkin, the state rabbi, Dr Gedali Rozenman, the town council employee, Dr Alexander Rajgrodzki, Colonel M. Kawelin and many others, delivered speeches. Music was then played by an orchestra conducted by Szwarc. A *Linas Hatsedek* anniversary anthem was performed and the choir of the Great Synagogue sang the Alleluia from Handel's *Messiah*. The violinist, A. Kriegel, played some of Wieniawski's pieces, and Kopelman-Hirszhorn sang a number of songs. During a money collection for the fraternity an industrialist, A. Sokol, gave 500 zloty, I.D. Szpiro 1,000 zloty, Dr Leon Pines 200 zloty, the Jewish community in Białystok 500 zloty, that in Wasilków 25 zloty, and the Rudnicki firm 100 zloty.[46]

*Linas Hatsedek* functioned during the Soviet and then the Nazi occupation of Białystok during the Second World War. Its headquarters and the outpatients' clinic in Różańska Street were from 1 August 1941, inside the ghetto set up in the town. The fraternity carried on till the tragic end, 16 August 1943, when an uprising in the ghetto led to the liquidation of the Jewish quarter and the murder of all its inhabitants.[47]

### APPENDIX

The Jewish medical charity institutions in Białystok
Eighteenth century (1772) Jewish hospital;
1821 *Hevra Kadisha;*
1826 *Bikkur Khoylim;*
1828 *Gemilut Hasodim;*
1830 Refuge for the incurably sick;
1840 Jewish hospital founded by Sender Bloch;
1852 Refuge house;
1869 *Tzedaka Gedolah;*
1872 Refuge for the old people;
1879 Committee for helping the poor;
1880 *Bikkur Khoylim* (reactivated);
1882 Jewish hospital, opening of the old people's home;
1885 *Linas Hatsedek;*
1888 Refuge for the old and paralysed;
1893 *Mishmores Khoylim* (Later called *Linas Khoylim*);
1901 Cheap kitchen;
1905 *Żydowskie Towarzystwo Dobroczynności* (Jewish Charity Society) (philanthropic);
1906 *Towarzystwo popierania sierot i opuszczonych dzieci* [Society to help orphans and abandoned children], later known as *Białostockie Towarzystwo Opieki nad sierotami żydowskimi* [Białystok Society to care for Jewish orphans].

The inter-war period *Towarzystwo Ochrony Zdrowia* [Society for Safeguarding Health]; *Żydowskie Towarzystwo Ochrony Kobiet* [Jewish Society for the Protection of Women]; *Towarzystwo wzajemnej pomocy na wypadek śmierci* [Society for mutual help in case of death]; *Żydowski Dom Starców* [Jewish Home for Old People]; *Ezroas Jesojmin* [Refuge for orphans]; *Miejski Zakład dla dzieci żydowskich* [Municipal institution for Jewish Children]; *Linas Orchim* [Care for travellers]; *Towarzystwo Przeciwgruźlicze 'Marpe'* [Anti-tuberculosis Society]; *Towarzystwo Ochrony Ludności Żydowskiej* [Society for the protection of the Jewish Population]; *Towarzystwo Bezpłatnej kolonii dla dzieci w Druskiennikach* [Society for free children's summer camps in Druskienniki] and others.

## NOTES

1 M. Bałaban, 'Ustrój Gminy Żydowskiej w Polsce w XVI-XX', *Głos Gminy Żydowskiej* (Warsaw, 1937) no. 6, pp. 129–30.
2 Białystok *voivode* Marian Zyndram-Kościałkowski's report for the period 1 April 1931 to 1 April 1932 (Białystok 1933), p. 11.
3 Many of these organizations were set up because of the failure of the municipality in this field. Some of them are listed in the table at the end of the paper.
4 According to *Yevreyskaya Entsiklopedia* (further YE.), Vol. V (St. Petersburg), p. 175 the *Linas Hatsedek* fraternity was founded in 1880, which is wrong. A.S. Herszberg, *Pinkas Bialistok*, vol. II (New York, 1950), pp. 330–1; The Story about M. Szochet is in *Echo Białostockie* (1935) no. 314.
5 H. Mościcki, *Białystok Zarys Historyczny* (Białystok, 1933), pp. 192–266.
6 A. Leszczyński, 'Struktura społeczna ludności żydowskiej miast i miasteczek dawnego Obwodu Białostockiego w latach 1864–1914', *Biuletyn ŻIH* (1984) no. 3–4, p. 62.
7 H. Kroszczor, 'Żydowskie organizacje społeczne w latach 1907–1915', *BŻIH* (1976), pp. 63–4; Informator Kalendarz. Gruźlica największa Plaga Ludności. Żydowska Liga Przeciwgruźlicka ATIL w 1928, pp. 37–8.
8 *Spravochny Kalendar* po g. *Bielastokie na 1913* god (Białystok, 1913), p. 7.
9 A. Tilleman, 'Geneza i znaczenie "Linas Hatsedek". Przemówienie z okazji jubileuszu 50 lecia (dokończenie)' *Praca Twórcza, Czasopismo Obozu Żydowskiej Pracy Twórczej w Białymstoku*, 1936 (August), p. 4.
10 Chazanowicz was born in Grodno in 1844. He studied medicine in Königsberg (present day Kaliningrad). He was a Zionist and Haskala sympathiser. *Almanach Literacki* (Warsaw, 1931), p. 183; L. Rozental, 'Dr Josef Chazanowicz – a profile', *Bialystoker Memorial Book* (New York, 1982), pp. 13–14; A. S. Herszberg, pp. 331–6; Plan of Białystok, 1:10 000, Z. Daszuta, printed by *Lechia* (Białystok, 1938).
11 *Białystok Bilder Album* op. cit. pp. 30, 84.
12 A. S. Herszberg, pp. 332–4.
13 A. Tilleman, p. 4.
14 The house still stands today. Until 1939 it belonged to the Barasz family. In the period of the ghetto Efroim Barasz, president of *Judenrat* in the Białystok ghetto, lived there; B. Mark, *Ruch oporu w getcie białostockim* (Warsaw, 1952), p. 72; H. Mościcki, p. 192. Relations of the following persons: E. Kracowska of July 1987, J. Nechumowicz of September 1986, E. Kisler of September 1987, pp. 331–5 *Echo Białostockie* (1935), no. 314.
15 A. S. Herszberg, pp. 331–5; *Echo Białostockie* (1935) no. 314. Gold medals were awarded to linists after a 100 night duties in a year. N. Pryłucki, 'Przemówienie na uroczystej Akademii z okazji jubileuszu 50-lecia *Linas Hatsedek*', *Praca Twórcza*, p. 6.
16 N. Pryłucki, p. 6.
17 A. S. Herszberg, pp. 33–336.
18 *Dziennik Białostocki* (1935) no. 309. *Linas Khoylim* was also approved of by the town authorities.
19 *J. Enc.* p. 174. *Bielastoksij Adres-Kalendar na 1914 Fabrichny Bielastok* (Białystok, 1914), p. 13. Cf the table.
20 N. Pryłucki, op. cit.; Dr Josef/Josip Rubinsztejn also worked later with TOZ *(Towarzystwo Ochrony Zdrowia). Bialystoker Bilder Album*, op. cit. 87.
21 *Pamiatnaya knizka Grodnienskoy Guberni na 1908 god* (Grodno, 1908), p. 163; *Bialystoker Bilder Album* op. cit., p. 96.

22 H. Mościcki, p. 192; *Spravochny kalendar*, p. 64; *Dziennik Białostocki* (1935) no. 319; *Tempo* (1935), no. 9.
23 A. S. Herszberg, p. 334.
24 *Sprawochny Kalendar*, pp. 64–5.
25 *Bielastokski Adres-Kalendar*, pp. 81–2.
26 A. Tilleman, p. 5.
27 Cf. *Dziennik Urzędowy Województwa Białostockiego* 1922–1924 subsequent.
28 *Prożektor* (1926), no. 24. The List of *Linas Hatsedek*'s Council for 1932 is published in *Bialystoker Bilder Album* op. cit., p. 126.
29 A. S. Herszberg, pp. 330–6; *Echo Białostockie* (1935), no. 314.
30 A. S. Herszberg, pp. 335–6. It is worth mentioning that Z. Weinreich was the president of *Linas Khoylim* in 1928 which did not prevent him from co-operation with *Linas Hatsedek Prożektor* (1928), no. 5.
31 The pharmacy gave out 50 medicines daily *Echo Białostockie* (1935), no. 314 *Dziennik Białostocki* (1935), no. 319; N. Prylucki, pp. 5–6; A. S. Herszberg, pp. 335–6.
32 A. Tilleman, p. 5, I. D. Szpiro was the president of the clothing section of the Chamber of Commerce in Białystok *(Związek Przemysłowców)*, as well as a consultant to the Industrial and Commercial Chamber in Wilno. *Reflektor* (1935), no. 14; *Bialystoker Bilder Album*, op. cit., p. 94.
33 A. Tilleman, p. 4.
34 A. S. Herszberg, p. 332; *Image Before My Eyes. A photographic History of Jewish Life in Poland 1864–1939*, ed. L. Dobroszycki, B. Kirszenblatt-Gimblett, (1977), p. 180; *Prożektor* (1928), nos. 5 & 7.
35 *Spis Abonentów Białostockiej Sieci Telefonów Polskiej Akcyjnej Spółki Telefonicznej* (Białystok, 1929), K. II and p. 23, Tel. 503.
36 A. Tilleman, p. 5 In 1934 the Emergency Service was called out 1,942 times. N. Pryłucki, pp. 5–6.
37 *Dziennik Białostocki*, 26th February 1931; *Bialystoker Bilder Album* op. cit., p. 88.
38 *Tempo* (1935), no. 9 and *Dziennik Białostocki* (1935), no. 319.
39 S. Zak maintained that, as well as W. Bubryk, Jacob Tepicer founded the *Gilah-Rinaht* theatre. M. Szaberman was the musical director. S. Zak, 'The Jewish Theater 1919–39', *Bialystoker Memorial Book*, op. cit., p. 34; *Prożektor* (1926), nos 42, 44, 46. The photograph was published in *Bialystoker Bilder Album*, op. cit., p. 126.
40 *Prożektor* (1926) no. 36.
41 *Sprawozdanie Wojewody*, p. 85.
42 *Budżet miasta Białegostoku na rok 1927–28* (Białystok, 1928), p. 82; *Budżet . . . na 1928/29* (Białystok, 1929), p. 94.
43 *Dziennik Białostocki* (1935) no. 191.
44 Minute of the meetings of Białystok Town Council for the year 1935, *Archiwum Państwowe w Białymstoku* (APB), *Akta Miasta Bialegostoku*, shelfmark 115.
45 Miesięczne Sprawozdanie Wojewody Białostockiego, APB, Akta Bezpieczeństwa Publicznego 1935, p. 18.
46 *Dziennik Białostocki* (1935), no. 32.
47 B. Mark, p. 71.

# THE JEWISH PRESS IN KRAKÓW
# (1918–1939)
Czesław Brzoza

There was a Jewish population associated with Kraków for centuries. During the inter-war period it was the only national minority of any considerable size. Its number in the period under discussion grew steadily, both in absolute terms and as a proportion of the city's total population. The position for the years 1910–1935 is presented in Table 1.

There are no reliable data for later years, yet one can assume that this development continued, and even accelerated as a result of immigration from Germany. By tradition, Jews inhabited several districts, especially Kazimierz, Stradom and Podgórze. But the inter-war years saw them moving towards the city centre. The election of a Jew to the Town Council in the *Śródmieście* ('centre of town') district, in the 1938 elections, is proof of this.

Jews exerted considerable influence in many walks of life. They were relatively active in, *inter alia*, the field of newspaper publishing. It is not yet possible to present their achievements in this sphere in their entirety, owing to the state of source material in existence, the current stage of research, and, finally, the fact that many periodicals have not survived. I have prepared a file based on accessible archives and published bibliographies. It consists of almost 80 titles of periodicals, or publications which publishers intended to come out regularly, and about 90 titles of special single issues.[1] These data should be treated as approximate, as there is no detailed information on many of these publications. In some cases only publishers' applications for permission to issue a journal have survived, and it is hard to say, today, whether the advertised papers ever appeared. This applies, for example, to the following titles: (the date in brackets is the date of the publisher's announcement): *Der Arbayter* (9 February 1929), *Arbayter Tsaytung* (17 February 1921), *Yad Halutsim* (10 March 1934), *Unabhengige Shtime* (19 February 1923), *Unzer Tsaytung* (27 November 1931) and *Unzer Shtern* (4 December 1924). Sources confirm that some other periodicals, such as *Biuletyn Stowarzyszenia Adwokatów Żydów Okręgu*

## TABLE 1: JEWISH POPULATION IN KRAKÓW

| Year | City's total population | Jewish population | |
|---|---|---|---|
| | | number | percentage |
| 1910 | 151,884 | 32,321 | 21.3 |
| 1921 | 183,706 | 45,229 | 24.6 |
| 1926 | 189,843 | 49,181 | 26.0 |
| 1931 | 219,286 | 56,540 | 25.8 |
| 1935 | 245,304 | 70,254 | 28.6 |

*Source*: I. Grinbaum, 'Żydzi w Małopolsce', *Nowy Dziennik*, no. 101, 6 May 1925; *Rocznik Statystyki Miast Polskich*, Warsaw 1928, p. 5; Drugi powszechny spis ludności z dn. 9 XII 1931, *Statystyka Polski*, Serie C, fasc.64, p. 11; State police lists of population, 1926, 1935, Wojewódzkie Archiwum Państwowe w Krakowie, Urząd Wojewódzki Krakowski – 146.

*Izby Adwokackiej w Krakowie* were published, but no copies have yet been found. Other publications are known from various references in memoirs, or in the contemporary press – both Polish and Jewish – but their existence is not verified by sources, library indexes, or bibliographies published hitherto. Awareness of the large gaps in collections of the Jewish press, the dates between which newspapers were published may in some cases be open to doubt and argument. Jewish publishing activity in the years 1918–1939, as well as the duration of various periodicals are presented in Table 2.

As was indicated above, data entered in this table must be considered as approximate. Only 66 titles have full source documentation. In this paper I have omitted Kraków supplements to periodicals which were published in other towns, for example, Lwów's *Chwila* and Warsaw's *Unzer Ekspress*. However, I have considered periodicals which were initially published in other towns, but had offices in Kraków, as was the case with the assimilationist *Zjednoczenie* (1919), or the Zionist *Moriah* (1919). Magazines founded in Kraków which were transferred to other towns, such as the *Bund*'s *Walka*, have been included as well.

It is not really possible to classify the periodicals published in the period under discussion unequivocally. The relatively simplest division would be based on strictly formal criteria, such as language, or frequency of publishing, yet even then we come across obstacles. The most accurate data available are presented in Table 3.

The problems mentioned are particularly caused by the fact that some of the publications published over a relatively long period of time frequently changed their character. Most often, they were changed from weekly into fortnightly, or monthly publications. The reverse was very

## TABLE 2: THE DYNAMICS OF JEWISH PUBLICATIONS IN THE YEARS 1918–1939

| Year | no* | 18 | 19 | 20 | 21 | 22 | 23 | 24 | 25 | 26 | 27 | 28 | 29 | 30 | 31 | 32 | 33 | 34 | 35 | 36 | 37 | 38 | 39 |
|---|---|---|---|---|---|---|---|---|---|---|---|---|---|---|---|---|---|---|---|---|---|---|---|
| | | | | | | | | | | year of liquidation 19-- | | | | | | | | | | | | |
| 1918 | 2 | – | 1 | – | – | – | – | – | – | – | – | – | – | – | – | – | – | – | – | – | – | – | 1 |
| 1919 | 10 | | 7 | – | 1 | 1 | – | – | – | – | – | – | – | – | – | – | – | – | – | – | – | – | 1 |
| 1920 | – | | | – | – | – | – | – | – | – | – | – | – | – | – | – | – | – | – | – | – | – | – |
| 1921 | 3 | | | | 3 | 1 | – | – | – | – | – | – | – | – | – | – | – | – | – | – | – | – | – |
| 1922 | 4 | | | | | 3 | – | 1 | – | – | – | – | – | – | – | – | – | – | – | – | – | – | – |
| 1923 | 2 | | | | | | – | 1 | – | – | – | – | – | – | – | – | – | – | – | – | 1 | – | – |
| 1924 | 2 | | | | | | | 1 | – | – | – | 1 | – | – | – | – | – | – | – | – | – | – | – |
| 1925 | 4 | | | | | | | | 2 | 1 | – | – | – | – | – | – | – | – | – | – | – | – | 1 |
| 1926 | 3 | | | | | | | | | 2 | – | – | – | – | – | – | – | – | – | – | 1 | – | – |
| 1927 | 3 | | | | | | | | | | 2 | – | 1 | – | – | – | – | – | – | – | – | – | – |
| 1928 | 5 | | | | | | | | | | | 4 | 1 | – | – | – | – | – | – | – | – | – | – |
| 1929 | 2 | | | | | | | | | | | | 1 | – | – | – | – | – | – | – | – | – | 1 |
| 1930 | 1 | | | | | | | | | | | | | 1 | – | – | – | – | – | – | – | – | – |
| 1931 | 4 | | | | | | | | | | | | | | 4 | – | – | – | – | – | – | – | – |
| 1932 | 1 | | | | | | | | | | | | | | | 1 | – | – | – | – | – | – | – |
| 1933 | 1 | | | | | | | | | | | | | | | | – | – | – | – | – | 1 | – |
| 1934 | 6 | | | | | | | | | | | | | | | | | 3 | – | – | 1 | 1 | 1 |
| 1935 | 7 | | | | | | | | | | | | | | | | | | 5 | 1 | 1 | – | – |
| 1936 | 2 | | | | | | | | | | | | | | | | | | | 1 | 1 | – | – |
| 1937 | 7 | | | | | | | | | | | | | | | | | | | | 2 | 1 | 4 |
| 1938 | 3 | | | | | | | | | | | | | | | | | | | | | 2 | 1 |
| 1939 | 1 | | | | | | | | | | | | | | | | | | | | | | 1 |
| Total | – | – | 8 | – | 3 | 5 | 1 | 3 | 2 | 3 | 2 | 5 | 3 | 1 | 4 | 1 | – | 3 | 5 | 2 | 7 | 5 | 11 |

* Number of newly established periodicals

## TABLE 3: THE JEWISH PRESS IN KRAKÓW

| Language publication | daily | weekly | Frequency of appearance fortnightly | monthly | other | total |
|---|---|---|---|---|---|---|
| Polish | 3 | 7 | 5 | 16 | 3 | 34 |
| Yiddish | 3 | 13 | 3 | 3 | 2 | 24 |
| Hebrew | – | 3 | 1 | 1 | – | 5 |
| Polish-Yiddish | – | – | 1 | 1 | – | 2 |
| Polish-Hebrew | – | – | – | – | 1 | 1 |
| Total | 6 | 23 | 10 | 21 | 6 | 66 |

rare. These purely formal changes were usually mentioned by the publisher. Yet often, something completely different happened. A double or triple edition of a title would be published, but it would be the same size. Thus it appeared less often than was stated in the editorial declaration of intention. This phenomenon can easily be detected in the case of *Inwalida Żydowski*, or the *Bund*'s *Walka*. Other papers would appear irregularly without any explanation, for example, *Czasopismo Chemiczne*, *Trybuna Makkabi*, or *Unzer Vort*. The last, formally weekly, was in fact published once a month, or even less often. Therefore including these publications in this or that category is a formality rather than a representation of reality.

Classification according to linguistic criteria rouses similar doubts. Some periodicals published in Polish would occasionally add supplements in Yiddish. On the other hand, papers in Yiddish would, now and then, publish texts in Polish, or even appear in both languages. So for this categorisation as well, including one of these papers in any of the groups indicates the predominant trend, rather than a hard-and-fast statement.

The Jews were a people that used many languages. In all countries of the Diaspora they utilised, to a greater or lesser extent, Hebrew, Yiddish and the local language (Polish in the case of Kraków). These three languages also determined the ways in which their culture and press developed. Every language had its determined advocates, and equally determined enemies. The main advocates of Hebrew were Zionists of various orientations, which was shown in state censuses. Yiddish was propagated by the *Bund*, and by Orthodox Jews, albeit for different reasons. Assimilationists or, as they called themselves, 'Poles of Mosaic faith', backed the Polish language. Conflicts over language could be very vehement. It would be inappropriate to judge the merits of these different linguistic orientations, but any study of the press must assess which predominated in the newspaper world.

For Kraków Jews it is clear that publications in the Polish language were pre-eminent. This conclusion is based on the fact that not only were over 50 per cent of the 66 titles mentioned published in that language, but also that these periodicals had the largest circulation, and were the most stable. The Zionist *Nowy Dziennik*, the most important Jewish publication in Kraków published over the 20-year period, appeared in Polish. The main organ of the Zionist-Revisionists, *Trybuna Narodowa*, was published in Polish in 1934–1939. Other periodicals in Polish were: *Przegląd Kupiecki* (1919–1939), *Rękodzieło i Przemysł* (1923–1936), *Informator dla Właścicieli Realności* (1929–1939) and *Inwalida Żydowski* (1926–1937).

Between the papers published in Polish and Yiddish stood those published in two languages, Polish and Yiddish. Their publication followed various models. Some, essentially in Polish, would have supplements in Yiddish. This was the policy of the editors of *Rękodzieło i Przemysł*, and *Inwalida Żydowski*. Others, such as *Der Lustiger Yid* (1921) were founded as bilingual papers. Then again, papers such as *Dos Yidishe Vort* would add supplements in Polish, and eventually, after a few years of functioning, turn bilingual. But even if a paper was published in Yiddish, the whole advertisement section, or at least a large part of it, would typically be in Polish.

Yiddish was still, undoubtedly, the main vernacular language. Memoirs, archival sources, and evidence from the contemporary press, both in Polish and Yiddish, testify to this. Yet this fact did not find its expression in the press policy of Kraków Jews. The two attempts in 1919 to publish a Yiddish daily failed. Only some publications by the Communists (*Dos Lebn*, *Unzer Vort*). the Bund (*Der Sotsyaldemokrat*, *Der Veker*) and Poale-Zion (*Arbaytervort*, *Di Yugent Fon*) were consistently published in Yiddish, but none survived long, or had a large circulation.

During the second general census of 1931, almost 40 per cent of Kraków Jews indicated Hebrew as their mother tongue. But this was more a manifestation of national feeling, or Zionist consciousness, than a reflection of the real situation. Declaration of one's mother tongue was treated as a sign of nationality, in response to the appeals of Ozjasz Thon and other Kraków Zionist leaders, and people identified themselves with the Hebrew language, regardless of how well they knew it. In reality it was not very popular, and was used seldom – and then mainly for religious purposes. This is confirmed by the fact that in the years 1918–1939, Hebrew publications appeared very rarely and for short periods of time. A literary-political weekly *Hamitspe*, published in the years 1919–1921, was the first. After its failure, there were several attempts to bring weeklies and monthlies onto the market, but none of them lasted more than three months. The following publications appeared in the 1920s: *Shvuon*, a weekly, in 1925; *Hayarden*, a monthly, in 1922; and *Avuka*, a fortnightly, in 1928. In the Thirties, the question of a Hebrew publication was discussed many times at the local conferences of General Zionist organizations, and meetings of the Culturo-Educational Society *Tarbut*, but without concrete results.

The number of publications, relatively large in view of the size of Kraków, and their diversity, reflected political social and professional divisions. Politically, the Jewish population was divided almost as much as the Polish, and every party, faction and organization strove, with varying results, to demonstrate its existence by publishing its own press organ, or at least special issues of it. The achievements of various groups in this field are presented in Table 4.

At the end of the 19th century, and the beginning of Poland's period of independence, a relatively important part was played by the assimilationist movement, whose leaders included Dr Adolf Gross. After 1918 it was represented in Kraków by the following organizations: *Związek Niezawistych Żydów* (the Organization of Independent Jews), *Koło*

## TABLE 4: JEWISH POLITICAL PRESS

| Organization* | No. of periodicals | No. of special issues | Total |
|---|---|---|---|
| Assimilationists | 1 | – | 1 |
| Agudas Israel | 7 | 1 | 8 |
| Mizrachi | 2 | 7 | 9 |
| General Zionists | 19 | 38 | 57 |
| Hitachdut | 1 | 4 | 5 |
| Po'alei Tsion (Right Wing) | 1 | 1 | 2 |
| Revisionist Zionists | 4 | 4 | 8 |
| Bund** | 4 | 2 | 6 |
| Kombund | – | 1 | 1 |
| Communists | 3 | 27 | 30 |
| Total | 42 | 85 | 127 |

\* Including press of these parties' youth organisations
\*\* Including publications of the Jewish Social Democratic Party

*Młodzieży Polskiej im. Berka Joselewicza* (The Berek Joselewicz Circle of Polish Youth), and *Związek Młodzieży Studenckiej 'Zagiew'* (Organization of Student Youth 'Zagiew'). After 1919, these organizations united to form *Związek Polaków Wyznania Mojżeszowego* (the Organization of Poles of Mosaic Faith). At first, they published *Zgoda* as their organ in Warsaw and Kraków, simultaneously, but it stopped appearing after a few weeks. A similar fate befell the monthly *Zjednoczenie*, the editorial office of which was transferred to Kraków, simultaneously, but it stopped appearing after a few weeks. A similar fate befell the monthly *Zjednoczenie*, the editorial office of which was transferred to Kraków from Lwów. These failures were connected with the loss of popularity in the assimilationist movement. The Polish nationalists did not trust its representatives, while the Zionists, who, at that time, were gaining ground, regarded the assimilationists as their main rivals, and fought them in every way possible. As a result of these attacks the number of groups and their level of activity steadily declined. At the end of the 1920s, *Związek Polaków Wyznania Mojżeszowego* consisted of only 20 members and did not even have any offices. In the 1930s, trends close to assimilationism were represented by *Biuletyn Śląsko-Krakowskiego Okręgu Związku Żydów Uczestników Walkę o Niepodległość Polski*. It was a typical combatants' organ, which, as well as dealing with strictly organizational matters, concentrated on all aspects of Polish-Jewish co-operation, especially on brotherhood-in-arms during the national insurrections, the fights of the legions in the First World War, and the struggle for Poland's borders after the war. It included appeals to Jews to join Polish social organizations, especially the Polish Red Cross, *Liga Obrony Przeciwpożarowej* (League of Firefighters) and *Związek Harcerstwa Polskiego* (Polish Boy Scouts).

The Orthodox constituted the conservative right-wing of Jewish society in the inter-war period. They were represented politically by *Agudas Israel*, which in Kraków, and Małopolska was called *Shlome Emuney Israel* for many years. Organizationally, it resembled a classic-19th century party. Its leaders were well known, but it lacked a mass membership. It never established a stable periodical in Kraków, although there were a number of attempts to do so. In 1919 when, for a short period of time, the Zionist *Nowy Dziennik* lost its right of circulation, the *Krakover Togblat*, which was published and edited by one of the best known Orthodox activists, Isaac Deutscher, appeared, but it only lasted for several months. However, it was not an official organ of the Orthodox faction, even though it was connected with that movement through its publisher. The first paper clearly to stress its Orthodox character was the weekly *Der Yidisher Veg*, which was published between May and August 1926. A year later, the Kraków branch of the *Shlome Emuney Israel* started to publish another weekly, whose title, *Unzer Yidisher Veg* referred to the previous one. It also lasted for only three months. At the end of 1927, a new weekly appeared, *Di Yidishe Shtime*, which was more successful and came out for almost two years.

The most powerful political force in inter-war Kraków was represented by the Zionist movement. The movement was not homogeneous. As well as the General Zionists, it was made up of *Organizacja Syjonistów Ortodoksów 'Mizrahi'* (The organization of Orthodox Zionists 'Mizrachi'), *Syjonistyczna Partia Pracy 'Hitachdut'* (Zionist Labour Party 'Hitachdut') and the right-wing of *Poalei Tsion*. Kraków Zionists dominated the 'Jewish Street' as they themselves called it, through their great organisational efficiency, the attractiveness of their slogans, and well-organised propaganda. No wonder that a considerable number of publishing initiatives were connected with them.

The conservative right wing consisted of '*Mizrahi*', who were not very numerous in Kraków. The weekly *Dos Yidishe Vort*, which was associated with *Mizrahi*, was the only Yiddish periodical which survived more than 15 years. Over the whole period, it was edited and published by Samuel Probst. Its editors did not publish particularly controversial political material, and what was included was very balanced. Thanks to this policy, it rarely found itself in conflict with the Kraków censors. At *Mizrahi*'s inspiration, about weekly, *Di Tsayt* appeared at the beginning of 1937, but this attempt was not successful and the paper was liquidated after a few editions.

The most important organ of the General Zionists was *Nowy Dziennik*, the first Jewish daily in the Polish language in Kraków. It was founded in early July 1918, and came out until the outbreak of the Second World War. In its last years, it even broadened the range of its influence by bringing out an evening edition with a rather sensational content. The Jewish elite, not only in Kraków but in the whole province, revolved around this periodical. Dr Ojasz Thon, Dr Wilhelm Berkelhammer, Dr Moses Kanfer, Dr Salomon Wahrhaftig, Dr Chaim Hilfstein, Zygfryg Moses and Henryk Leser were among those whose writing appeared in it. Bernard Singer was the paper's Warsaw correspondent. The history of *Nowy Dziennik*, especially in its early days, was rather stormy. At the beginning of 1919, its right of circulation in Galicia was suspended, because of the sharp tone of its articles and reports. Instead, *Gazeta Żydowska* began to be published; like *Dziennik* it was printed in Moravska Ostrava in Czechoslavakia. The outbreak of the conflict between Poles and Czechs over Cieszyn, Silesia, brought about its demise. Then *Dziennik* appeared, just once, for it was closed for breaching the press laws. In February 1919, permission was granted for *Nowy Dziennik* to be published again, and a year later, for a publishing house to be opened. Later on, there was only one break in the paper's appearance, for one day, following a bomb attack on the editorial office and publishing house in May 1923. The editors responded to the lack of specialist publications by bringing out supplements, which appeared over several years, in some cases for more than ten. The most important were: *Lekarz Domowy* (1926–1939); *Dzienniczek dla Dzieci i Młodzieży* (1928–1939); *Literatura i Sztuka*, which later changed its name to *Literatura, Sztuka i Nauka*, *Głos Kobiety Żydowskiej*, the WIZO (Women's International Zionist Organization) organ for western Little Poland and Silesia; *Informator Palestyński*; and *Dom i Szkoła*. Many more appeared, but were of an ephemeral character.

The General Zionists were also behind a number of other publishing initiatives, most of which were unsuccessful. An attempt to bring out a Yiddish daily, *Di Tsayt*, in 1919 was a failure. The fortnightly *Der Ruf*, established in March 1934, appeared for several months only. Several other papers, such as *Di Naye Tsayt*, which had been set up during the 1928 parliamentary elections, and had been intended to appear regularly, met a similar fate. Zionists were also behind moves to establish a number of Hebrew periodicals, but, as was mentioned above, these attempts were short-lived.

A number of youth organizations, which either published their own periodicals, or were given hospitality by *Nowy Dziennik*, were associated with the General Zionists. *Przegląd Akademicki*, which appeared irregularly as a supplement to *Nowy Dziennik* between 1934 and 1939, served as the joint publication of student confederations. The activity of other organizations showed more initiative and independence. This was especially true of the boy-scouts, who, as well as numerous special issues, published the following periodicals: *Tsofim* (1925–1926), *Hano'ar* (1926), *Tseirim* (1934–1936), and *Divrey Akiba* (1936–1939). Zionists also had influence, through personal ties, on papers with which they were not linked formally. Examples of this were *Przegląd Kupiecki*, published by *Krakowskie Stowarzyszenie Kupców Żydowskich* (the Kraków Association of Jewish Merchants), *Głos Detalisty* published by *Stowarzyszenie Drobnych Kupców* (the Association of Small Merchants), or the publication of Jewish combatants, *Inwalida Żydowski*. The only periodical for children, published between 1927 and 1939, *Okienko na Świat*, also propagated Zionist ideology.

The leftist Zionist party, *Hitachdut*, did not have many members, at least in Kraków. In 1927, it established a weekly, *Przegląd Żydowski*, which stopped appearing after two numbers. An attempt ten years later was somewhat more successful. A weekly, *Nasza Walka*, appeared regularly for eight months. Another leftist group, *Żydowska Syjonistyczna Partia Robotnicza Poale Syjon* (Jewish Zionist Workers' Party *Po'alei Tsion*) started to publish a fortnightly, *Der Kemfer*, which survived for several months only. Its failure was probably related to inner-party conflicts, which resulted in the party dividing into leftist and rightist factions. After the split, the rightist wing, under the name of *Żydowska Niezależna Socjaldemokratyczna Partia Robotnicza Po'ale Syjon* (Jewish Independent Social Democratic Workers' Party *Po'alei Tsion*), started to publish a weekly, *Arbayter Vort*. It even became the party's main organ, but existed for only a year.

The Revisionists constituted the radical wing of the Zionist movement. In Kraków they began organized activity in 1926, but had no publications at first: that was not necessary, however, as long as they fell within the Zionist camp, in the broadly understood sense. They published topical information in *Nowy Dziennik*, having representatives on the publication's supervisory council. In the 1930s, when the Revisionists stopped being a faction, and started to organize their own party, further co-operation proved impossible. Despite the fact that the new party described itself as Zionist in its title, it broke completely with the programme and tactics of the General Zionists and even started to combat them. In 1934, as a result of the common endeavours of the Kraków, Lwów and Warsaw branches, a general organ of this party, the weekly *Trybuna Narodowa* was established in Kraków. Palestinian topics, along with the struggle against the General Zionists, predominated. *Trybuna Narodowa* published a regular supplement, *Trybuna Betaru*, for their youth organization, Brith Trumpeldor. Right from its inception, *Trybuna Narodowa* had to cope with financial problems, and there were constant appeals for new subscribers and contributions to meet the publishing house's debts, and the like. Probably to gain publicity, the last three numbers of *Trybuna Narodowa* came out as special issues: *Myśl Syjonu* (11 August 1939), *Zew Syjonu* (18 August 1939), and *Zew Narodu* (25 August 1939). An attempt to publish a separate youth periodical, *Ku Wolności* undertaken in 1938, failed after a few numbers, due to financial problems.

The trends towards division within the Zionist movement which, *inter alia*, were demonstrated by the founding of *Nowa Organizacja Synonistyczna 'rewizjoniści'* (the New Zionist Organization 'Revisionists'), and especially in the ruthless internal struggle connected with the 1935 parliamentary elections, resulted in some activists from the General Zionist faction attempting to reunite the movement. Such was the principal aim of the weekly *Głos Jedności*, established in 1938, and later renamed *Tsofim*. Yet the paper's sharp criticism of both Revisionists and General Zionists seems to indicate, rather, that it saw itself becoming the nucleus of a new party. This process was stopped by the outbreak of war.

At the beginning of this period, the most important workers' party in Kraków was *Żydowska Partia Socjaldemokratyczna* – ZPSD (the Jewish Social Democratic Party) which later united with the *Ogólnożydowski Związek Robotniczy Bund* (the General Jewish Workers' Union *Bund*). In 1904, ZPSD had set up a weekly, *Der Sotsyaldemokrat*, which was its principal organ in Galicia and Bukovina. After 1918, this periodical encountered financial problems, which finally led to its collapse in 1921. At the end of 1918, ZPSD started to publish a weekly, *Nowe Życie*, which was addressed not only to Jews, but also to Polish readers. The radical character of publications, as well as of the party, resulted in official repression, which manifested itself in numerous confiscations. March 1919 saw the establishment of the Warsaw publication *Głos Bundu*, whose aims converged with those of the Kraków's weekly. An agreement was therefore signed between the two editorial staffs, under which *Nowe Życie* ceased to exist, and its subscribers started to receive the paper published in Warsaw. This agreement was followed by the merger of the two parties, and the Kraków *Bund* did not take up another publishing initiative for five years. In May 1924, a monthly, *Walka*, devoted mainly to political programmes, and theoretical problems, started to appear. But this periodical also had numerous problems, as was evident from its irregular publication. In 1928, the publication was transferred to Warsaw, where it appeared for several years more under a slightly different title (*Nasza Walka*). The *Bund*'s last effort to establish their own paper was connected with the 1928 parliamentary elections. Following a resolution by the Kraków Committee, a weekly, *Der Veker*, started to appear but the first edition was confiscated owing to its radical character. A similar fate befell the second issue, and no more were ever published.

After it split with the rightists, the *Żydowska Socjaldemokratyczna Partia Robotnicza Po'alei Tsion* (leftist wing) published a weekly, *Unzer Arbetervelt*, for several months in 1922, that was liquidated as a result of financial problems. The weekly youth publication connected with this party, *Di Yugnt Fon*, which appeared for three years (1922–1924), was more successful.

A considerable number of members of the Communist Party, both in Kraków and throughout Poland, were Jews; and some Yiddish publications appearing in Kraków were addressed to them. It should be stressed that the 'Krakówness' of these publications is open to doubt. This is because the whole publication activity of the *Komunistyczna Partia Robotnicza Polski* – after 1925, *Komunistyczna Partia Polski* (Polish Workers' Communist Party – after 1925, Polish Communist Party), was directed by a secret Central Editorial Office, which selected all texts, prepared them, and even supplied ready page-layouts. Periodicals were published where conditions were favourable. After Communist papers were banned in Warsaw, the Central Editorial Office turned its attention to Kraków. After several special issues appeared without any obstacles, it was decided to set up a regular publication. In 1923, the weekly *Dos Lebn* started to appear. It ceased to exist that November, in unexplained circumstances. According to certain sources, it was closed by the public prosecutor's office; according to another, the withdrawal of the publisher was the reason. A number of special issues started to appear in place of *Dos Lebn* with similar covers and headlines to the defunct periodical; and at the same time, steps were taken to publish it again. Despite the fact that the authorities had no doubts as to the character of the periodical, permission was granted, and it started to appear in January 1924. *Dos Lebn's* unceasing attacks on the bourgeois order in Poland, constant emphasis on the reactionary nature of the Polish authorities, and simultaneous praise for Soviet Russia, resulted in action by the state authorities and innumerable confiscations. In April 1924, the police arrested the person who was responsible for contacts with the Central Editorial Office, i.e. passing the supply of texts, and of money for publishing and circulation. This brought about the collapse of the paper. The next Communist paper, *Unzer Wort* appeared four years later. In several months, only five numbers were published, almost all of which were confiscated, and finally the responsible editor and publisher were arrested. In the following years, Communists tried to publish a number of special issues, but their efforts had little effect.

There were many other periodicals in inter-war Kraków, which do not have so strongly marked a political orientation, above all of a cultural and literary character. The Hebrew periodicals mentioned above were of this type. Cultural and literary periodicals also appeared in Polish and Yiddish. In chronological order, we can cite the following: *Der Lustiger Yid* (1921), *Unzer Shtern* (1924), *Klangen* (1925), *Wiadomości Teatralne* (1927), *Getsaylte Werter* (1929–1930), *Tsvishen Vindmilen* (1931), *Sztuka i Życie Współczesne* (1934), *Rzut* (1934), *Der Reflektor* (1935), and *Di Post* (1937–1939). All except *Di Post*, which appeared for two years, were short-lived, regardless of which language they were published in. Depending on their finances, they functioned for between several weeks and several months.

Some publications were devoted to more specialist problems, and addressed to small circles of readers. 'Professional' publications may be listed among them. Owing to the considerable role played in the life of the Jewish community by trade and craftsmanship, a number of special publications were devoted to these issues. At the end of April 1919, *Przegląd Kupiecki* started to appear as an organ of the *Krakowskie Stowarzyszenie Kupców* (the Kraków Merchants' Association). In 1922 it became an organ of the *Związek Stowarzyszeń Kupieckich Małopolski Zachodniej* (Corporation of Southern Poland Merchants' Associations), and, in the final phase of its existence (1938–1939), also covered Silesia. This weekly, along with *Nowy Dziennik*, was the Kraków Jewish periodical which appeared most regularly and had the longest life. *Przegląd* concentrated on purely professional matters, and political overtones were very seldom to be traced in it even though most of the editorial staff were connected with the Zionist camp. *Głos Detalisty*, which was published in Kraków between 1937 and 1939, and an organ of the *Stowarzyszenie Drobnych Kupców w Krakowie* (Corporation of Small Merchants in Kraków) was similar in character. In theory, it had been intended to be a monthly, but in practice it never developed to be a regular publication; only five or six numbers appeared up till March 1939. *Głos Kupiecki*, established in 1935, represented a different political orientation, and was a professional paper in name only. In reality, as far as we can tell from the first and only surviving issue, it was devoted to the struggle against the 'Jewish national democrats', as it called the Zionists.

The most important paper for craftsmen was *Rękodzieło i Przemysł*, published between 1923 and 1936. According to its founding declaration, it was to be monthly, but it appeared irregularly. It also did not touch on political matters, but was devoted to providing information about the organizations problems of the *Stowarzyszenie Rękodzielników Żydowskich w Krakowie* (the Corporation of Jewish Craftsmen in Kraków). For several years, it had a two-page Yiddish supplement, *Der Yudisze Handverker*.

The *Informator dla Właścicieli Realności*, was of an even more specialist character. Despite the fact that its publishers announced that it would be a fortnightly, it appeared very irregularly. Some numbers were not even printed, but prepared on a duplicating machine. Theoretically, it was an organ of the society of all the proprietors of real estate, regardless of nationality and religion. In reality, Christians had their own organization and periodical. The number of copies published was not high, as it was aimed at the members of the society, which in 1929 numbered only about 400, and two years later (1931), 750.

*Czasopismo Chemiczne*, an organ of the *Krakowski Oddział Związku Chemików Żydów w Polsce* (Kraków Branch of the Society of Jewish Chemists in Poland), was published for an equally small group of readers. With its highly scientific character, it was intended for people with at least university or polytechnic education. Formally it was a monthly periodical, but only five numbers (one of them a double issue) were published in the years 1937–1939.

*Biuletyn Urzędniczy*, an official organ of the *Związek Zawodowy Żydowskich*

*Pracowników Umysłowych* (Labour Union of the Jewish Workers), was published irregularly between 1934 and 1939. Initially prepared on cyclostyle, it was only printed after 1936. In fact, this periodical should be included among internal organizational bulletins, as it was not sold to the general public.

Jewish combatants' organizations also had their own periodicals. The *Związek Żydowskich Inwalidów, Wdów i Sierot Wojennych* (Organization of Jewish War Disabled, Widows and Orphans) started to publish a monthly, *Inwalida Wojenny*, in mid-1921. Only one or two numbers appeared at first, and it was relaunched five years later, in autumn 1926. It appeared very irregularly, sometimes in double, or even quadruple issues, till autumn 1937. In the years 1926–29, it had a double page supplement in Yiddish, *Der Judiszer Inwalid*. The *Związek Żydów Uczestników Walk o Niepodległość Polski* (Organization of Jewish Participants in the Fight for Poland's Independence), established at the end of 1933, represented assimilationist tendencies, and in 1934–38 published an irregular *Biuletyn*.

The *Związek Stowarzyszeń Humanitarnych B'nai B'rith* (Corporation of Humanitarian Organizations B'nai B'rith) had an exceptional position among the tens of various types of organisations. It had a branch in Kraków: Solidarność. The periodical *B'nai B'rith*, published from the end of 1928, was the principal organ of the corporation. It was published in Polish, but sometimes articles in German were included as well, to make it more accessible to members of the organization in Silesia. This periodical survived for half a year, and was liquidated for unknown reasons. Nine years later, an attempt was undertaken to establish it again, under a slightly different title, but the attempt ended at the first edition.

To recapitulate, one can point to some characteristic features of the Jewish press in Kraków. It developed rather slowly but, as time went by, the number of publications grew steadily. Thus, while there were barely two or three titles in 1918, the second half of the 1930s saw the publication of a dozen or so. The peak was reached in 1935, when 17 periodicals were on the market.

Publications in Polish predominated in the Jewish press. This applies to both the total of papers published and the numbers that appeared each year. Only in the year 1922 did more titles appear in Yiddish and Hebrew than in Polish, while even by the 1930s these proportions had completely changed. In 1935, 14 of the 17 titles were in Polish. Moreover, publications in Polish came out in the largest number of copies and survived longer.

In most cases, Jewish publications were not very stable. Of the 66 titles investigated, as many as 45 did not survive even a year, and in 13 cases only the first number appeared. Furthermore, almost all papers which were published for a longer period of time appeared very irregularly, except *Nowy Dziennik* and *Przegląd Kupiecki*.

It is a paper's circulation that determines its potential influence. In this respect, the Jewish press was not in a very good position. Many Jewish publications appeared only in several hundred copies, and therefore had to be subsidised; when patronage failed, papers had to be liquidated for financial reasons. In this respect, *Nowy Dziennik*, 6,000–8,000 copies of which appeared each day on a par with most of Kraków's daily press (with the exception of *Ilustrowany Kurier Codzienny* of course), was in the best situation. *Nowy Dziennik* achieved the peak of its potential in 1929, when its circulation reached 11,000–18,000 copies. At the other extreme was *Dos Yudishe Vort* which, in its 15 years of existence, never exceeded 600 copies.

Jews constituted about 25 per cent of all Kraków's inhabitants, but their press, according to sketchy calculations, accounted for only about 10–15 per cent of all publications. This disproportion was probably the result of Jews making extensive use of the Polish press, especially *Nowa Reforma*, *Ilustrowany Kurier Codzienny* and, at the end of 1930s, *Krakowski Kurier Poranny*. The more stable Jewish papers published in other towns, especially Warsaw, also had a role of some importance.

What should be stressed in conclusion is that despite its faults, its transitory nature and the fact that it has not survived in the best condition, the Jewish press is a very important – and in many cases the only – source for the history of the Jewish population in inter-war Kraków.

NOTE

1 In preparing the index of all publications most of the sources I used came from the *Wojewódzkie Archiwum w Krakowie* (Kraków State Provincial Archive). The most useful were reports of the press department of the Kraków *Starostwo Grodzkie*. Much information was also gleaned from the files of the *Urząd Wojewódzki Krakowski* (Kraków Provincial Offices), including monthly reports on the situation prepared by the *voivode*. More information is to be found in police and court files. Archival information was supplemented with published contemporary bibliographies, lists and catalogues. One should mention Paul Glikson's *Preliminary Inventory of the Jewish Daily and Periodical Press in the Polish Language 1823–1982* (Jerusalem, 1983); Jechiel Szeintuch's *Preliminary Inventory of Yiddish Dailies and Periodicals Published in Poland between the Two World Wars* (Jerusalem, 1986); Israel Szajna's *Bibliografia wydawnictw żydowskich partii robotniczych w Polsce w latach 1918–1939* (Warsaw, 1963); idem, *Bibliografia dzienników i czasopism żydowskich wydawanych w Polsce w latach 1918–1939*, *Biuletyn Żydowskiego Instytutu Historycznego*, henceforth *BŻIH*, 1971, fasc. 2, pp. 107–132; idem, *Bibliografia żydowskiej prasy młodzieżowej wydawanej w Polsce w latach 1918–1939 w języku polskim*, *BŻIH* (1975), fasc. 2, pp. 103–13; Marian Fuks's *Materiały do bibliografii żydowskiej prasy robotniczej i socjalistycznej wydawanej w Polsce w latach 1918–1939*, *BŻIH* (1977), fasc. 3, pp. 75–98, and 1978, fasc. 2, pp. 59–89; Danuta Dębicka's *Prasa socjalistyczna w Polsce 1918–1939, Katalog* (Warsaw, 1974); and Maria Krych's *Polska prasa rewolucyjna 1918–1939. Katalog* (Warsaw, 1965). Some additional information was supplied by the press itself, especially by *Nowy Dziennik*.

# RITUAL SLAUGHTER AS A POLITICAL ISSUE

Szymon Rudnicki

During the years leading up to World War Two, the issue of ritual slaughter became part of a power struggle between Polish political factions, and it was just one front on which attack against the Jewish minority was conducted in Poland. It is an issue which enables us to examine the mechanisms of both power struggle and the movement against the Jews.

A new dimension was given to the Jewish problem by the economic crisis. The National Party (*Endecja*) was well aware that the crisis encouraged anti-semitic propaganda. Anti-semitism became the fundamental factor of propaganda, a common denominator to which all other problems were reduced. For the National Party it was a convenient point of departure for stimulating chauvinism and an anti-government campaign. The anti-semitic atmosphere in Poland was also intensified by Hitler's success in Germany.[1]

The figure of the Jew, crudely painted but easily recognizable, was made to personify the source of social injustice. For the majority of people who accepted anti-semitic propaganda, the battle against the Jews meant taking over their stalls, or the hope that expulsion of the Jews from economic life, and then to an ever-greater degree from Poland, would mean a sudden improvement of their own situation; this applied especially to the peasantry, who constituted two-thirds of Polish society.[2] During the crisis the slogans began to reach not only the *petite bourgeoisie* but also, to a lesser extent, the villages. Anti-semitism involved increasingly wider groups of people, although, at the very outset, one must note that a considerable part of Polish society remained immune to the propaganda.

The anti-semitic campaign intensified in 1935, after the death of Piłsudski, when, for a brief period, the National Party counted on taking over power. According to Ludwik Krzywicki, 'the National Democrats understood that anti-semitic slogans were a convenient means of influencing the emotions of the mob, while the university students were to play the part of a vanguard in attacks directed against the government by means of slogans aimed at the Jews'. The conservative periodical *Czas* wrote with irony that the National Democrats wished to return to power via Nalewki (the Jewish quarter in Warsaw).[3]

Anti-semitic slogans were widely used to attack the government for its supposed philo-semitism and the left wing for its role as an agent of 'international Jewry'. It was then that a campaign was launched in favour of the 'ghetto bench' which, in the course of time, to a considerable degree paralysed institutions of higher learning and led to an even greater lowering of mores. There also took place several massive anti-Jewish demonstrations, such as the one in Grodno. On 25 November the Minister of the Interior informed a session of the Council of Ministers about the disturbances in the Lwów and Kielce voivodeships. In December the number of bomb attacks was put at nine, and there occurred 46 cases of serious bodily assault and one murder, as well as uncounted crimes against property. The anti-Jewish campaign was not carried out everywhere simultaneously; for example, in the Białystok voivodeship, the National Party did not launch a wide-scale campaign until the second half of 1936. Incidents resulted in a death toll of three, and 99 cases of assault.[4]

The two pogroms, which, alongside the seizure of Myślenice by Doboszyński (22 June 1936), became symbols of the anti-Jewish campaign, were the incidents in Przytyk (9 March 1936) and Mińsk Mazowiecki (2 April 1936). From that time on the National Democratic Party began promoting the idea that the two nations were divided by spilt blood.

This was the atmosphere in which the problem of ritual slaughter arose. The problem was by no means specifically Polish; during the nineteenth century a number of countries had witnessed attempts to use ritual slaughter as a way of attacking the Jews. In Switzerland, ritual slaughter was forbidden in 1892. In Norway, a similar decision was taken in 1929, and in Germany, a prohibition was introduced immediately after Hitler's rise to power. In many other countries petitions concerning this question were either dismissed by the courts (as in Great Britain) or were not pursued by the government (as in Russia).

In Poland, the right of the Jews to perform ritual slaughter had remained unquestioned. It is true that prior to World War One the matter was examined twice. The first to raise the matter, in 1878, was the League for the Protection of Animals in Warsaw. The second, in 1914, was Andrzej Niemojewski in his book *The Jewish Soul in the Light of the Talmud* which was a general attack against the Jewish religion. On neither occasion was the issue taken seriously.

In independent Poland even the rabid anti-semites appeared to forget the matter for quite a few years. As one of the leaders of *Rozwój* (an organization established to protect Polish tradesmen and craftsmen from Jewish competition) admitted, 'up to 1923 work in this sphere amounted to zero'.[5]

The problem of ritual slaughter emerged again with the growing tide of anti-semitism produced by the National Democrats' struggle for power. On 26 May 1923 two deputies connected with *Rozwój* presented in the *Sejm* a motion for a total prohibition of ritual slaughter. The justification included all the arguments which were usually raised on similar occasions. The motion was relegated to the archives of the parliamentary commission of industry and commerce, which showed that there was little interest in the question. A motion to introduce the so-called *numerus clausus* principle in the enrolment of new students met with a similar fate. Nonetheless, the evil genie had been let out of the bottle.

In 1928 the local authority in Warsaw established a special commission to examine the meat market and, above all, the question of ritual slaughter. It had been demanded that ritual slaughter should be restricted to meat produced for the Jewish community while meat for the rest of the population would be produced by a system 'accepted in the whole civilized world'. The spokesman of the commission rejected the charge that ritual slaughter was not humanitarian, and, on the contrary, recognized it as 'least at variance with humanitarian demands'.[6] The commission made two statements: first, that kosher meat was more expensive than the better quality meat consumed by non-Jews, and, second, that both the sale and the slaughter of cattle constituted a Jewish monopoly. The *Gazeta Przemysłu Mięsnego* wrote that even in the slaughterhouse belonging to *Rozwój* the animals were slaughtered in the ritual manner.[7] The newspaper itself had ten pages in Yiddish out of a total of 12.

The next stage of the struggle against slaughter was of a different nature. In 1935 the campaign was joined for the first time by the ruling party, *Sanacja*. The whole situation started with attempts by the local authorities, headed by Stefan Starzyński, to lower meat prices. I doubt whether Starzyński had any other purpose or foresaw the outcome of his actions. He first attempted to reduce the number of slaughterers and to employ only slaughterers who agreed to accept wages reduced by a half. The main difficulty lay in the fact that the slaughterers were not recognized by the rabbinate. The administration of the slaughterhouse demanded a declaration from the slaughterers that they would accept lower payment for ritual slaughter. The slaughterers, supported by the Union of the Rabbis of the Republic, rejected these demands.[8]

The local authority then embarked upon an attempt to restrict ritual slaughter and chose the simplest way of doing this. Journalists were invited to a slaughterhouse to witness that mechanical slaughter is more efficient than the ritual method. The goal was attained, although *Nasz Przegląd* charged that the exhibition was carried out in a tendentious manner.[9]

The effects of this operation were greater than anticipated. The campaign now involved the press, not only the National Democratic press but also that of *Sanacja*. The leading *Sanacja* daily, *Gazeta Polska*, called for an immediate abolition of this 'barbarous regulation', emphasizing, however, its economic aspects. The Catholic Press Agency went even further, demanding that 'ritual slaughter, or rather murder, should once and for all be prohibited as a disgusting superstition under the threat of severe punishment'. The statement was eagerly seized on by the well known Jew-baiter, Father Stanisław Trzeciak, who broadened the attack and tried to prove that the laws of the Jewish religion provided no justification for ritual slaughter.[10] In the meantime, the original object of the campaign ceased to matter as the costs of slaughtering cattle were now as low as those for pigs.[11] In December a session of the temporary city council unanimously agreed that the whole issue should be treated exclusively as an economic one and that ritual slaughter should be reduced to meet the needs of the Jewish community by a gradual increase of mechanical slaughter.[12] But soon afterwards, in the *Sejm*, both sides went further in their demands, and rejected the compromise solution. Some wished to retain the status quo in the meat industry while others strove towards a total prohibition of ritual slaughter.

On 7 February 1936 there was motion in the *Sejm* concerning the slaughter of farm animals.[13] It was seen as especially important as it was proposed by Janina Prystorowa, whose husband had been one of the closest associates of Piłsudski and was currently speaker of the Senate. The proposal included two points which would outlaw ritual slaughter: first, that cattle should be stunned before being bled, and, second, that the carcase should be divided into half lengthwise. Both these points excluded ritual slaughter. Prystorowa maintained that her concerns were purely humanitarian, but it is difficult to see why a carcase should worry about the way it was divided.

The motion was instantly supported by *Gazeta Warszawska*,[14] but the government, believing that the entire question would soon be forgotten, refused to take a stand, and thus allowed the development of a propaganda campaign. This was curious considering that in 1934, when the German government wanted to abolish ritual slaughter in part of Upper Silesia, a Polish government delegate protested, with the result that ritual slaughter was maintained in that region.

The fact that the administrative-legal commission of the *Sejm*, which examined Prystorowa's motion, invited Father Trzeciak as an expert was a clear indication of its stand. It did not follow the advice of Emil Sommerstein who requested that the motion be forwarded to the rules commission in order to ascertain whether it corresponded with the constitution. Neither was notice taken of the view of the Vice-Minister of Religious Affairs and Public Education that the proposals should be changed to accord with the constitution (article 110, 111, 113 and 114). Disavowing this proposal, deputy Duch claimed that he had been told in the Ministry of the Interior that the Government had not taken any stand as regards the whole issue. On the other hand, an expert representing the Ministry of Industry and Commerce declared that ritual slaughter hindered the organization of the meat trade.[15] Such attitudes of the government and of the press encouraged the opponents of ritual slaughter. The only votes against in the commission were those of the sole Jewish representative and two Ukrainian representatives who regarded the project as a fundamental violation of the Jewish religion.[16]

During the parliamentary debate Juliusz Poniatowski, the Minister of Agriculture, proposed an amendment to permit the sale of kosher meat only in shops with an official licence and in those which sold only that one product. Moreover, in administrative regions where the Jews constituted less than three per cent of the population, permission would have to be granted by the local authority and subsequently confirmed by the voivode for slaughter to take place.[17] It is clear that the restrictions were considerable, making it impossible to perform ritual slaughter in the voivodeships of the former Prussian territory.

In order that the law should be passed during the session, the speaker of the *Sejm* requested an urgent meeting with the chairman of the commission. The commission accepted the government amendments despite the protests of several deputies, and on 20 March the question was examined by a plenary session of the *Sejm*. Deputy Dudziński, a member of the commission and representative of the *Jutro Pracy* group, spoke, on the one hand, as someone who wished to enable the Jews to purchase the better, healthier hind cuts of meat, and, on the other, as someone who saw the economic necessity of abolishing ritual slaughter. Dudziński stated that the kahals obtained 28 million zlotys for ritual slaughter.

The same amount of money was lost due to the damaged hides which supposedly resulted from that method of slaughter. These arguments persuaded him to stand by Prystorowa's motion.[18] In response to the first charge, Mojzesz Schorr stated that the budget of all the 817 kahals in Poland amounted to 38–40 million zlotys and that therefore they could not possibly make a profit from the slaughter equal to the sum quoted by Dudziński.[19] The humanitarian attitude towards animals was mentioned, but economic concerns dominated the debate. It was no longer concealed that the intention of the law was to limit Jewish participation in economic life. The battle now was for the acceptance or rejection of the government amendments. The opinions of the Jewish deputies could have no influence, but Sommerstein did point out that it was not mere coincidence that the motion appeared at a moment of great intensification of anti-semitism, which it further inflamed. He stated that the authors of the motion were in no way inspired by humanitarianism, but by a desire to attack the Jewish religion and community.[20] Other Jewish deputies drew attention to the inconsistency of the motion with the constitution and to the economic consequences of its acceptance.

It is possible that Sommerstein was inclined to become over-excited. But Deputy Józef Morawski also maintained that 'under domestic pressure we attempt to outbid each other on the question of anti-semitism'. Anti-semitic sentiments were present in opinions expressed by a number of deputies. Dudziński declared that if he were to become minister of agriculture, then 'these moans of Israel would change into a lament heard throughout the Republic'.[21]

From 1930 the *Sejm* passed all laws in the form in which they were proposed by the government. This case was no exception, althought it was passed only by a small majority, a fact which enabled Bernard Singer to joke that: 'The honour of the parliament was saved by the ox and humanitarianism . . . The ritual blood of the cattle had aroused those gathered here', and 'in the course of the last five years the fate of the government had never hung so strangely by a hair.'[22]

On 27 March the law was discussed by the Senate. Despite resistance from some of the senators, it was accepted in the version proposed by the *Sejm*. Again, the discussion concentrated on the economic aspects but, in contrast to the *Sejm* discussion, only one voice attacked the Jewish population as such.[23] Both houses passed the law with unprecedented speed.

To overcome the prohibition law, the Jews organized protests and a propaganda campaign. They established a Committee for the Protection of Ritual Slaughter and held a convention of rabbis from all over Poland. On 11 March 800 representatives of Jewish kahals from 290 small towns and hamlets met in Warsaw. Even the *Bund*, which up to that time had remained aloof from religious questions, aligned itself with the defence of ritual slaughter. It saw the attack on ritual slaughter as another aspect of the anti-Jewish campaign. On 17 March the whole Jewish population in Warsaw and several other towns participated in a strike organized by the *Bund*. The struggle for the right to perform ritual slaughter united the fragmented Jewish community in the realization that, unlike other anti-semitic acts, this prohibition was directed against religion, which Ozjasz Thon described as 'our last bastion'.[24]

A series of pamphlets, articles and parliamentary speeches attempted to rebut the charges of the opponents of ritual slaughter. Their most important point was that ritual slaughter was not simply an accepted custom but, as the Warsaw rabbinate declared, 'one of the main principles of the Jewish religion'.[25] Once this point had been accepted, the Jews were able to refer to the constitution which guaranteed freedom of conscience and religion and the right to observe religious regulations (article 111). The opponents of ritual slaughter had derived support from being able to point to other countries which had introduced a prohibition. To counteract this, the Committee for the Protection of Ritual Slaughter collected official declarations from 17 European countries and from the USA where the procedure was carried out without any limitations. Another point of issue, discussed in the press and in the *Sejm*, was whether the burden of the charge for ritual slaughter was partly carried by the non-Jews. It was argued that the non-Jews did not lose anything but, on the contrary, profited from ritual slaughter. The Jews published meat prices which showed unambiguously that in the whole country the better hind cut of meat was cheaper than kosher meat. They also pointed out that ritual slaughter did not mean a waste of either blood or hide.

Most campaigning literature stressed that the struggle against ritual slaughter was, above all, of a political nature. The representatives of the kahals mentioned above regarded 'the attack on ritual slaughter in Poland as part of an anti-semitic campaign whose intention was to deprive the Jewish population of equal rights and to bring about the ruin of the national, religious and economic centres of Polish Jewry'.[26] The literature also pointed out that the campaign against ritual slaughter had been initiated by the National Democratic Party whose purpose it predominantly served. It drew the government's attention to the fact that the campaign was also directed against it.

Prime Minister Kościałkowski was well aware of this, and he declared in the *Sejm* that the National Democrats were exploiting the country's economic difficulties to cause unrest which would strike at the base of law and order. This opinion was shared by the Minister of the Interior, who proclaimed that in its struggle for power the National Party was willing to use all possible measures, including a campaign to set Poles against Jews which had already claimed many victims.[27] The *Sejm* took no immediate notice of these statements, although numerous condemnations were heard in the Senate. Let us note that this Senate session took place on 9 March, the day of the pogrom in Przytyk. During the session of the *Sejm* at that time all the speakers condemned the exploitation of anti-semitism by the National Democrats as an instrument of political struggle. Konstanty Terlikowski announced that 'in this respect the government Party will not enter into competition with the National Democrats'.[28]

Unfortunately, events did not bear out this optimism. After Piłsudski's death his party needed a new programme and sought ways of winning over young people. For this purpose some of its members were willing to adopt nationalist slogans, including anti-semitic ones which up to then had been propagated only by the National Democratic Party. At the same time, a struggle for power was taking place within the government. In the *Sejm* the anti-semitic campaign was carried out particularly by the *Jutro Pracy* group and deputies from central and northern parts of Poland. They succeeded in undermining the position of the relatively liberal Kościałkowski, for whom the ritual slaughter law became a stumbling block.[29] Soon after the proclamation of the law the government collapsed and Kościałkowski was replaced by Felicjan Slawoj-Skladkowski. This was a victory for those who were ready to adopt right-wing solutions.

In his inaugural speech in the *Sejm*, Slawoj said: 'Economic struggle – yes, but injury – no.' That 'yes' was understood to advocate economic boycott, and this interpretation was confirmed during a meeting with a delegation of the Supreme Council of Jewish Merchants in Poland.[30] In 1937 the government party founded a new political organization – the Camp of National Unity (*OZON*) – whose manifesto for the first time made a distinction between the Jewish community and all other ethnic minorities. It also confirmed and extended the interpretation of the 'yes' formula. It declared: 'The instinct of a cultural self-defence and the natural striving of Polish society towards economic independence is understandable.' This was now to be the official government view.

It was a view which coincided with that expressed by the highest dignitaries of the Catholic Church who, on the one hand, condemned anti-Jewish excesses and on the other advised people to patronize Polish shops and to avoid Jewish shops.[31] Many of the priests absolved members of armed groups since, as Father Błotnicki wrote, 'a serious illness sometimes requires strong medicine'.[32]

The National Party complained that the government party was increasingly stealing its clothing in its campaign against the Jews. In order to outbid the *Sanacja*, the National Democrats with their radical wing employed more and more brutal methods: there were numerous cases of bombing, arson and destruction of property. Life for the Jews became increasingly difficult. Often they were forced to abandon the villages and small towns where they had lived for generations. The armed campaign actively involved young people, and even schoolchildren. The *Warszawski Dziennik Narodowy* wrote quite openly about the use of knives, pieces of metal and similar instruments by thugs. This was not surprising considering that the thugs often came from the very bottom of society, but similar scenes also took place in the institutions of higher learning. 'Polish students threw themselves at the Jews and communists, hitting them with chairs, sticks, desks – whatever was handy. Escape was useless. Those fleeing were chased and further beaten. Scores of people were seriously injured.' This description of events at the Warsaw Polytechnic was published in an approving fashion by the *Warszawski Dziennik Narodowy* on 2 May 1936. The illegal leaflets of the radical groups openly called for a 'bloody showdown with Jews and their lackeys'.[33]

The organizers of these incidents were well aware of the fact that quite a few people would have doubts about the persecution of the Jewish poor. But in order to prevent even a flicker of compassion or doubt about the correctness of the anti-Jewish activities, an appeal to the Polish youth sounded:

Remember the Jew is your enemy! Even that poor little man who stands behind the counter in his miserable shop, whom you know well, and who you know has done no wrong and himself goes hungry. Even he is an enemy of your country because behind him stands world Jewry ... He who gives his money to his enemy, the Jew, is unworthy to call himself a Pole.[34]

The economic battle was fought in the marketplace. First the market was divided into two parts: Polish and Jewish. Then, in order to make trade impossible for the Jews, all trade was shifted to Saturdays and to areas outside the marketplaces where the Jews had their shops or stalls. Jews were also refused places in the new markets, and when that did not prove effective, the stalls were simply overturned or other means were employed to prevent all trade. The most frequently used method was picketing the shops, often intimidating customers by violence or threats. The local anti-semitic press also published the names of people buying in Jewish stores.

In certain places Jews were defended by the local Poles, peasants and workers who, as Deputy Sommerstein said in the *Sejm*, usually also opposed the pickets who as a rule came from outside. *Nasz Przegląd* was therefore able to write: 'The assurances of the National Democrats that all Poles have accepted anti-semitism have no basis in reality.'[35] Jews were defended above all by the workers' parties and the more radical offshoots of the peasant movement. On the right, only the conservative *Czas* consistently opposed anti-Jewish excesses.

The socialist *Tydzień Robotnika* wrote about the campaign to abolish ritual slaughter: 'It has become part of a nationalist drive, a further stage in the discrimination against the Jews and a boycott of the work of the Jewish proletariat.'[36] Even before the discussion in the *Sejm* came to an end, the National Party attempted to force through motions about the abolition of ritual slaughter in local authorities. Wherever the nationalists enjoyed a majority, the resolutions were passed easily enough.[37] In such cases the socialists voted together with the Jews, while councillors connected with the ruling camp voted together with members of the National Party or tried to delay the resolution until the law was passed by the *Sejm*. On 4 June 1936 the Silesian legislature prohibited ritual slaughter in its voivodeship.[38]

The law took effect from 1 January 1937. Initially there were difficulties with obtaining licences for running kosher butchers and determining quotas. In January 1937, every Jew in Warsaw was entitled to 2.4 kg of beef and veal. With time the situation improved but it remained much worse in the small provincial towns where the rabbis raised additional difficulties.[39] The limitation of ritual slaughter had an adverse effect on the financial situation of the *kehillot*. Data from Kraków show that two-thirds of the income from the slaughter of cattle was lost.[40] The drop in income of the *kehillot* adversely influenced Jewish schools, health services and so on; this effect was often compounded by the local authorities' restrictions on funding for these institutions.

Even though slaughter in the Warsaw slaughterhouses was carried out according to the law, the Union of Christian Butchers appealed to the authorities, calling for a complete abolition of ritual slaughter. *Jutro*, which was connected with the ONR, demanded the prohibition of the ritual slaughter of poultry. The Jews were also immediately accused of breaking the law. Since hind cuts were still sold cheaper, *Jutro* expressed the fear that certain non-Jews would buy meat from Jewish butchers. It also demanded the introduction of a total prohibition of ritual slaughter.[41]

In March 1938 Dudziński presented a new motion for total abolition. In it he claimed that the law of 1936 had not fulfilled its task of taking over the meat trade from the Jews, a trade with an annual turnover of four billion zlotys producing 10 per cent per profit. Mrs Prystorowa also no longer mentioned the humanitarian aspects of the question but concentrated on the millions of zlotys which could be made from the meat trade.[42] Meanwhile, according to official figures, the actual turnover amounted to only 1.6 billion zlotys. But in this game every move was acceptable.[43] This time the government was much better prepared for the discussion. It defended the article of the law which permitted limited ritual slaughter. It also warned that regulating religious matters by means of secular legislation was setting a dangerous precedent, and that the abolition of ritual slaughter would not solve the problems of the meat market. The government pointed to the decline in the amount of meat consumed by the Jews and the fact that the costs of the slaughter were borne exclusively by them. They also presented a number of other economic arguments.[44] After Tadeusz Schaetzel, Deputy Speaker of the *Sejm*, declared that the law did not contradict the constitution, the Deputies rejected all government amendments. The majority of the deputies apparently did not want to take part in the procedure and there were only 70 deputies present out of a total of 199. The law was opposed by Jewish and Ukrainian deputies together with five Polish deputies, including Andrzej Wierzbicki, chairman of the Central Union of Polish Industry, Mining, Commerce and Finance.

The day that the law was passed by the *Sejm* was also the last day of the Senate session, which was to meet again in July. What was discussed on this occasion was not the law passed by the *Sejm* but a new project to submit the whole meat trade to the control of the Ministry of Agriculture. Many deputies in the Agrarian Commission did not conceal their criticism of this project, fearing excessive government control and an increase in meat prices. They also did not hide the fact that ultimately they would support the project since it would make it possible to eliminate Jews from that particular branch of the economy. The political aspects therefore clearly dominated the economic ones.[45] Soon the *Sejm* was dissolved and the new one never returned to this question during the ten months of its existence. This time the Jews did not undertake the kind of protest they had conducted two years earlier. The only protest was a day-long fast by the Polish Jewish community. The Jews were also aware of the fact that those senators who spoke about a growing tide of anti-semitism and the unavoidable deterioration of the Jewish situation were correct.[46]

In September 1937 the rectors of institutions of higher learning were allowed to introduce separate benches for Polish and Jewish students. This decision did nothing to calm the situation in Universities and Polytechnics. The number of Jewish students rapidly declined from 20.4 per cent in the 1928–29 academic year to 7.5 per cent in 1937–38. Nationalist students also began a campaign for the introduction of the *numerus nullus* principle with regard to lecturers. The whole issue quickly went beyond the universities. A growing number of organisations and associations of engineers, doctors, architects and journalists introduced the so-called 'Aryan paragraph'. Exclusion from these organizations made it difficult or impossible to work in the professions they represented. There were more and more initiatives whose main feature was to limit the rights of Jews. Similar tendencies also appeared in the *Sejm*. At the same session during which Dudziński presented his motion for the abolition of ritual slaughter, his colleague Wacław Budzyński suggested that the full name of every shopkeeper should be written on the signboard. Jan Hoppe proposed a law regarding citizenship, accepted by the Senate on 29 March 1938, which stated that all persons who stayed five years abroad and lost contact with Polish statehood should be deprived of citizenship. By using this law, as a pretext, the Nazi government in Germany expelled many thousands of Polish Jews from the Reich. Attempts were made to harass the Jews in various ways; for example, the law concerning tax reductions on the production and sale of wine excluded raisin wine.

Several projects of this kind never went further than the *Sejm* commissions and were outvoted. This was the case when Józef Bakon proposed that Jews be excluded from military service, or when Franciszek Stoch suggested that Jewish property be taken over for purposes of compulsory Jewish emigration. Let us note that Bakon, who presented more than one anti-Jewish proposal, had been chosen by Jewish voters as well. The government prepared a whole series of anti-Jewish laws which, however, never went beyond the stage of projects.[47]

Generally speaking, the majority of Polish political parties and the government held the view that Jewish emigration from Poland was the only way to 'solve' the Jewish question. The differences concerned only the pace, methods of forcing the Jews to leave, finances and so on. Bogusław Miedziński wrote: 'There is no other solution than a planned, organized emigration.'[48]

As will be clear, the problem of ritual slaughter is a paradigm case marking the course on which Polish-Jewish relations in pre-war Poland were irreversibly set. No great leap of imagination is required to fathom whither this was leading, when the fate of both nations was so cruelly altered by the outbreak of war.

NOTES

1 S.H. (Hirzhorn): 'Szanse endecji', *Nasz Przegląd* 7.1.1936; 'The anti-semitic movement in Germany has contributed to a great measure to the intensification of anti-semitic moods in Poland. This symptom should be regarded as favourable since up to now all versions of reaction towards the Jewry were hampered by concern for Western opinion. See also, W. Zawilec, *Bez kompromisów i bez uprzedzeń* (Warsaw, 1939), p. 80.
2 R. Wapiński, *Narodowa Demokracja 1893–1939* (Wrocław, 1980), p. 307.
3 L. Krzywicki: *Wspomnienia* V.III, (Warsaw, 1959), p. 292; H. Lubieński, 'Pozytywny program w sprawie żydowskiej', *Czas* 10.IV, 1936: 'They are riding Jewish horse towards power; by means of violence applied to the weak and helpless Jews, they reach for power, held by the strong and armed'. M. Schorr, speech in the budget debate, *Sprawozdanie stenograficzne z posiedzenia Senatu (SSSen)* 9.III. 1936 Col. 72: P.Korzec: *Juifs en Pologne* (Paris, 1980), p. 244.
4 Wład. Raczkiewicz in J. Szembek, *Diariusz i teki*, V.I (London, 1964), pp. 421–2; H. Jaroszewiczowa, *SSSen*, 9.III. 1936 Col. 22; F. Sławoj Składkowski in a speech at the budgetary committee of the *Sejm*, *Nasz Przegląd*, 14.1.1987.
5 E. Zajączek, 'Rytualny ubój bydła a społeczeństwo polskie', *Rozwój* 2.VIII. 1924 p. 7.
6 Z. Bychowski, *Ubój rytualny z punktu widzenia humanitarnego i sanitarnego. Referat wygłoszony na Komisji Specjalnej Rady Miejskiej m.st. Warszawy dn. 22 Lutego 1928 r.* (Warsaw, 1936), p. 16.
7 A.L., 'W sprawie uboju rytualnego'. *Gazeta Przemysłu Mięsnego* no. 2 (1928), pp. 11–12; On the discussion in the City Council, see: W. Fabierkiewicz, 'Sprawa normalizacji handlem mięsem na terenie Warszawy', *Kronika Warszawy* no. 4, (1934), pp. 135–62; *Ubój rytualny ze stanowiska gospodarczego* (Warsaw, 1936), pp. 6–7.
8 'Konflikt w sprawie uboju rytualnego zaostrza się', *Nasz Przegląd*, 30.1.1935; 'Sprawa uboju rytualnego', ibid., 1.3.1935.
9 'W rzeźni miejskiej', ibid., 23.2.1935; 'Na marginesie akcji przeciwko ubojowi rytualnemu', ibid., 5.5.1935.
10 'Należy znieść ubój rytualny bydła', *Gazeta Polska*, 28.3.1935; Kommunikat KAP, 25.3.1935; S.Trzeciak, *Ubój rytualny w świetle Biblii i Talmudu* (Warsaw, 1935).
11 W. Fabierkiewicz, op. cit., p. 64.
12 'Z Tymczasowej Rady Miejskiej', *Nasz Przegląd*, 20.12.1935.
13 *Druk sejmowy* no. 59.
14 'Opinia społeczna za wnioskiem Prystorowej', *Gazeta Polska*, 19.11.1936.
15 'Wniosek o uchwalenie uboju rytualnego uchwalony przez komisję sejmową', *Warszawski Dziennik Narodowy*, 6.3.1936.
16 'Oświadczenie ukrainskiej reprezentacji parlamentarnej', *Nasz Przegląd*, 6.3.1936.
17 'Ustawa o uboju zwierząt gospodarskich w rzeźniach', 18.3.1936, *Druk sejmowy* no. 143, J. Poniatowski, *Sprawozdanie stenograficzne Sejmu (SSSejm)* no. 21, vols. 74–9.
18 J. Dudziński, *SSSejm* no. 21 (1936), cols. 61–74. Others mentioned even higher payments made by the Christian population to the Jewish Kahals; 'For example over 80 mln zloty annually and almost 15 billion zloty during the 17 years of

independence. We could have built a navy.' *Warszawski Dziennik Narodowy*, 21.3.1936.
19 M. Shorr, *SSSen*, 5, 27.3.1936.
20 R. Sommerstein, *SSSejm*, no. 22, 20.3.1936, col. 30-1.
21 J. Morawski, ibid., col. 24; J. Dudziński, ibid., col. 59.
22 Regnis (R. Singer): 'Pod znakiem Apisa', *Nasz Przegląd*, 23.3.1936.
23 The Jews were always an uncertain element, on which we were never able to rely, and despite gained benefits they reacted and still react to the Polish nation negatively. They were and remain an immature element as regards the state, uncreative, devoid of state and civic ideals', R. Kornke, *SSSen*, no. 15, 27.3.1936, col. 62.
24 O. Thon, 'Tanie zwycięstwo, które jednak drogo może kosztowac' *Nasz Przegląd*, 8.3.1936.
25 For the text of the declaration: *Ubój rytualny ze stanowiska gospodarczego*, p. 3.
26 'Całe żydostwo polskie protestuje przeciwko zamachowi na religię', *Nasz Przegląd*, 12.3.1936. The aspects of ritual slaughter were discussed in the following brochures: N. Asz, *W obronie uboju rytualnego* (Warsaw, 1936); E. Majzel, *Prawda o żydowskim uboju rytualnym* (Łódź, 1936); G. Rozenman, *Zagadnienie uboju rytualnego* (Białystok, 1936).
27 M. Kościałkowski, *SSSejm*, no. 10, 17.2.1936 col. 26; W. Raczkiewicz, ibid., no. 16, 24.2.1936. Col. 8-11.
28 R. Terlikowski, *SSSejm*. no. 8, 9.3.1936, cols. 5-6.
29 'Sprawa uboju rytualnego w komisji', *Warszawski Dziennik Narodowy*, 19-3-1936; 'Sensacyjne wyjaśnienie referenta o motywach zgłoszenia wniosku Prystorowej' *Nasz Przegląd*, 19.3.1936.
30 F. Slawoj-Skladkowski, *SSSejm*, no. 26, 4.6.1936, col.7; 'Żydzi u premiera', *Warszawski Dziennik Narodowy*, 13.7.1936.
31 Pastoral list of Cardinal Augusta Hlonda of 29.2.1936 in: A. Hlond, *Listy pasterskie* (Poznań, 1936); Appeal of the Prince Metropolitan Adam of 12.3.1936; (*Odezwa Ks. Metropolity Adama Sapiehy*) *Warszawski Dziennik Narodowy*, 3.6.1936.
32 F. Błotnicki. 'Antysemityzm a religia' ibid., 7.7.1936.
33 AAN. ONR. *Archiwum Akt Nowych, Druki ulotne* vol. 154.
34 J.G. (Jędrzej Giertych), 'Żydzi w małych miastach', *Warszawski Dziennik Narodowy*, 29.4.1936. 'Młodzieży Polska'. *Gazeta Narodowa*, 12.9.1937.
35 E. Sommerstein, *SSSejm*. 60, 1-2.7.1936, col.129; 'Szlachetny katecheta i dyrektor', *Nasz Przegląd*, 8.1.1936.
36 Quoted in *Nasz Przegląd*, 25.3.1936.
37 'Rada Miejska w Kaliszu uchwala nagłość wniosku przeciw ubojowi rytualnemu', *Warszawski Dziennik Narodowy*', 23.2.1936.
38 *Śląski Dziennik Urzędowy*, 15.6.1936, no. 13, doc. 29.
39 'Uchwały zjazdu rabinów w sprawie trybowania', *Nasz Przegląd*' 20.1.1937.
40 *Akta gminy Krakowa*, Arch. ŻIH, t.1147.
41 'Dookoła uboju rytualnego', *Nasz Przegląd*, 2.3.1937. *Jutro* 10.1.1937; 'Zabobon i okrucieństwo kapłanów "szechity"', ibid., 6.1.1937.
42 *Druk sejmowy* no, 792, 22.3.1938; Dudziński, *SSSejm*, no. 8, 25.3.1938, col. 120-4; J.Prystorowa, ibid., col. 145-6.
43 According to calculations favourable for Dudziński, and taking into consideration the weight and prices in eight largest towns in Poland, the slaughtering of cattle in 1937 gave a profit of 580 milion zlotys brutto, and of pigs – one billion zlotys. Calculations according to the *Mały Rocznik Statystyczny 1938*, p. 149, table 10 and p. 237, table 8.
44 Untitled memorandum from 21.2.1938, p. 12, *AAN Akta F. Potockiego*, vol. 13; the

Declaration of the Deputy Secretary of State J. Alexandrowicz presented to the administrative-Self-government Commission of the *Sejm* on 17.3.1938; Ibid., the Speech of the Deputy Secretary of State in the Ministry of Agriculture and Land Reform, *SSSejm*, 25.3.1938, col. 126–7.

45 J. Trockenheim, *SSSen*, 14.7.1938, col. 38–9.
46 T. Petrazycki, ibid., no. 41, 7.3.1938, col. K. Fudakowski, ibid., no. 43, 9.3.1938, col. 38.
47 A. Chojnowski: *Koncepcje polityki narodowściowej rządów polskich w latach 1921–1939*, (Wrocław 1979), pp. 225–6
48 B. Miedziński, *Uwagi w sprawie żydowskiej*, (Warsaw, 1938), p. 16.

# BRITAIN AND THE JEWISH EXODUS FROM POLAND FOLLOWING THE SECOND WORLD WAR

Ariel Joseph Kochavi

One strand in the skein of Anglo-Polish relations in the period immediately following the Second World War was the problem of the Jews of Poland, the majority of whom had no wish to remain in that country. About 140,000 Jews had fled Poland after the liberation, most of them having departed by October 1946. The greatest number made their way to DP camps in Germany, Austria, and Italy. The United States, at Truman's direction, had put pressure on the British government to allow the immigration of 100,000 Jews to Palestine. At the same time, British prestige in the United States and relations between the two countries were being undermined by reports in the American press concerning the wretched conditions of Jewish displaced persons, and by British rejection of Truman's request to open up Palestine to a substantial number of Jews from Europe. Britain for its part made the transfer of Jewish refugees to Palestine contingent on a comprehensive solution to the Palestine question. Whitehall was moreover intent on preventing any significant increase in the population of displaced Jews in the West, who were the principal source of recruitment for the clandestine embarkations of illegal immigrants to Palestine. In line with this, Poland became a major target of British diplomatic efforts, since it was from there that most Jewish refugees were now arriving in Western Europe. In this article I shall therefore be considering the course of negotiations between London and Warsaw on the issue of Polish Jewry, and attempt to evaluate the factors that accounted for British failure to bring a halt to the Jewish exodus from Poland.

Postwar Poland was in ruins and the country was deeply divided politically. The new régime was identified with Moscow, whose troops were stationed in the country, and was regarded with hostility by large segments of the populace and the Polish Catholic Church. Various opposition groups had organised themselves into an underground and resorted to violent action with the purpose of bringing down the government, which had managed to assert its control primarily in the large cities. In the rest of the country, however, armed anti-government groups were able to operate with a fair measure of success. In the course of the struggle, the underground had killed over 10,000 Polish civilians, soldiers, and policemen; of these, as many as seventy per cent had died during 1945 and 1946. The casualties among the underground in the three years following the conclusion of the war are estimated to have been approximately 7,000 dead and 2,000 injured.[1]

Only about 380,000 Polish Jews had survived out of the three and a quarter million who had been living in Poland prior to the outbreak of the war. Roughly seventy per cent of the survivors consisted of Jews who had fled the country, principally to the Soviet Union, either before the onset of hostilities or during the initial months of German occupation; included among these were the Jews who were evacuated by the Red Army to the Soviet Union after Poland had been divided as a result of the Ribbentrop-Molotov agreement. Some fifteen per cent of the Polish Jews who survived were liberated from German extermination, concentration, and forced-labour camps. The remainder, comprising another fifteen per cent, had made it through the war by assuming non-Jewish identities and hiding among Poles, or as partisan fighters.[2]

In mid-September 1945 the Foreign Office received a report from the British ambassador to Warsaw, Victor Cavendish-Bentinck, on the scale of the destruction of Polish Jewry during the war. Poland, as the ambassador was at pains to point out, had been virtually emptied of its Jewish population. In the country's villages, where Jews had been highly visible in their capacity as tradesmen prior to the war, there were now no Jews to be seen at all. According to information furnished by the Polish government, there were about 50,000 Jews living in Poland as of August 1945, and another 200,000 were expected to arrive from Soviet Russia. Cavendish-Bentinck thought the latter figure excessive, himself reckoning that no more than 150,000 were likely to return. His visit to Auschwitz had convinced him that the reports of atrocities at the camp were undoubtedly true, including that of the extraction of fat from the corpses of victims for the purpose of manufacturing soap. He estimated that fully six million people had perished in German concentration and death camps, and that at least four million of them were Jews. In Poland itself, more than three million Jews had been killed.[3] About two months later the ambassador reported that Polish policy was to encourage Jews to emigrate while preventing Poles from doing the same.[4]

Towards the end of 1945, reports were being received by Whitehall from British occupation authorities in Germany and Austria concerning the infiltration of thousands of Jews from Poland into the British zones who claimed to be seeking asylum from persecution in their native country.

According to the refugees' testimony, the persecutions were not being instigated by the government but were the result of popular hostility, and economic motives played no part in the exodus. They moreover made no secret of their intention of going on to Palestine. They also estimated that 40,000 more Jews intended to leave Poland, although with the onset of winter, the movement might be interrupted between December and the coming spring. The British Control Commission for Germany believed the departure of Jews from Poland to be part of a concerted plan to increase the number of potential immigrants to Palestine in Germany.[5] Early in December 1945 the British embassy in Prague reported that between 15,000 and 20,000 refugees from Poland, most of them Jews, had passed through Czechoslovakia on their way to the American zones in Austria and Germany; and that at any given time there were anywhere from 2,000 to 3,000 Polish refugees in the country. The grand total of those who had already left or were intending to leave was thought to be 70,000.[6]

The British embassy in Poland considered that the departure of Polish Jews was spontaneous and the consequence of Jews being universally disliked by Poles. Cavendish-Bentinck maintained that Poles were just as anti-semitic now as they had been twenty-five years earlier. The exodus was not taking place in consequence of any policy of the régime, notwithstanding the fact that the Polish government was granting passports to Jews which were valid for a single crossing of the border in exchange for a thousand zlotys. But many were also leaving without passports. The preferred method of departure was to obtain a permit for crossing the border to visit family relations in the Soviet zone in Germany, and then simply not to go back. Many Jews were arriving from Poland through Berlin on their way to Munich, where the Americans had established camps to receive them. Cavendish-Bentinck did not think that there was any evidence at this stage of direct Zionist influence on the exodus. Nor did he believe that there was a specific organization which was responsible for the murders being perpetrated against Jews throughout the country, particularly in small towns and villages. These he regarded as being attributable to widespead anti-semitism among the populace, and to the fact that Jews were prominent in the government and among the hated security authorities. He rejected the claim of Polish authorities that the killings and other acts of violence were the work of reactionary groups which had infiltrated the country. In any case, Polish Jews were unanimous in wanting to get out of the country and there was no way of stopping them from carrying out their intention. In only a few years Poland was destined to become the only country in the world in which not a single Jew could be found.[7] The view in America at the time was that the Polish government was too weak to act against the anti-semitism which was running rampant in the country, and that it was being passive in its response to the Jewish exodus.[8]

A very different view of the situation was presented by Frederick E. Morgan, the British general who headed UNRRA in Germany. At a press conference on 2 January 1946, Morgan pronounced that there was no factual basis for the stories of pogroms and violence against Jews in Poland, and that such reports were part of a Jewish scheme to force the United Nations to grant the Jews a permanent home. The general dismissed the testimony of Jewish refugees from Poland about anti-Jewish violence in the country. He maintained that the Jews who were daily arriving by train from Poland were well dressed and had come carrying substantial sums of money.[9] Alarmed by the angry response of the American press to Morgan's interview, the Foreign Office sent an urgent request to its embassy in Warsaw for information concerning the renewal of anti-Jewish violence. Additionally, Ambassador Cavendish-Bentinck was asked for his assessment of the motives behind the current exodus of Polish Jews, and for his opinion as to whether the departure of Jews from the country was connected with the issue of Palestine or had come about because of the actions of Poles who wished to be rid of Jews for economic and political reasons.[10]

Robin A. Hankey, chargé d'affaires at the Warsaw embassy, was of the opinion that economic and psychological factors were largely responsible for Jews leaving the country. Economic chaos and the imposition of the communist system had turned Poland into a country where it was becoming exceedingly difficult to make money. Zionist motives, too, were at work and many of those who were leaving were persuaded that by their departure they would increase the pressure for the settlement of Jews in Palestine. Information concerning the organization that was arranging the departure of Polish Jews was hard to come by, but Hankey had no doubt that this was in fact an organized movement. He argued that despite the killings, Polish Jews did not face a physical threat on so great a scale as to warrant their fleeing the country en masse. After all, pogroms were no longer taking place. Jews were afraid of living in small towns and villages because of the hostility of Polish peasants, who refused to return Jewish property they had taken possession of during the war. Hankey moreover maintained that not all the murders of Jews had been inspired by anti-semitism. According to his information, some three hundred Jews had been killed in the period between the end of the German occupation and November 1945. He was however unable to determine if Polish authorities had a hand in the movement, and whether such involvement was official or stemmed from the corruption of certain government personnel. In any case, a bottle of vodka sufficed to get one past the frontier. Hankey suggested that it might be possible to threaten Polish authorities with postponement of the reception in Germany of Germans living in Poland if the departure of Jews from the country was allowed to continue.[11] For his part Cavendish-Bentinck reported that, in contrast to the situation in the past, very few Polish Jews were now asking to go to the United States. This would appear to give some support to rumours that the current movement was part of an effort to bring pressure to bear on the Anglo-American Committee of Enquiry regarding the problem of European Jewry and Palestine by creating a large concentration of Jewish refugees in Germany demanding to be allowed to immigrate to Palestine.[12]

Thus it would seem that the embassy in Warsaw had come round to the opinion of Whitehall and of British occupation authorities in Germany and Austria that the departure of Jews was part of Zionist strategy. As a result, the embassy's report did not accommodate the views of A. J. Banks, head of its consular section, who argued that Jews wanted to leave Poland primarily because of fears for their physical safety. Banks could understand that Jews should want to leave a country in which they had been made to suffer unspeakable afflictions in body and mind. He pointed out, too, that many of the survivors had been left without either kin or community, so that they had no hope of being able to rebuild their lives and businesses in Poland.[13]

At the Foreign Office there was some difference of opinion as to the course of action to be followed in dealing with the Poles in the matter of the exodus of Polish Jews. Ian L. Henderson of the Refugee Department concluded from the Warsaw embassy's reports that the Polish government wanted to rid itself of the problem of Jews in the country by their expulsion to Palestine. He conceded, however, that there was some doubt as to the extent of the government's involvement in the organization of the movement. Henderson did not think that any good would come of approaching the Polish government in the matter.[14] Nor did P. P. Hancock, an official of the Northern Department, who considered that the central government in Poland exercised very little authority in the country, and that the movement of Jews through the frontier could not be stopped. Sir George Rendel, who had formerly been at the head of the Eastern Department, advised that American cooperation might be solicited in bringing pressure to bear on the Polish government to halt the exit of Jews.[15] Setting out his views in a memorandum to Hector McNeil, the Parliamentary under-secretary of state for foreign affairs, Rendel argued that he was unable to accept Jewish claims that the exodus was entirely a result of the intolerable conditions of Jews in the areas in which they were living, and that their present circumstances were no different from those they had experienced under the Nazis. He warned that the Zionist were taking unscrupulous advantage of the understandable apprehensions of Jews, and the movement was largely a consequence of Zionist propaganda, which was encouraging Jews to migrate westward and in the direction of the Mediterranean coast in the belief that they could thereby compel the British government to allow them into Palestine. Rendel maintained that since the departure of Polish Jews could not be accounted for by persecution, the only explanation for the exodus was that those leaving the country had been made part of the Zionist plan in the struggle against Britain for Palestine.[16] McNeil took issue with Rendel. The movement did not seem to him to be sufficiently organized to be a result of Zionist machinations, although the Zionists were undoubtedly exploiting it for their own ends.[17]

Ernest Bevin, on the other hand, was of the same opinion as Rendel. In a memorandum to the Cabinet Overseas Reconstruction Committee, the foreign secretary maintained that the departures from Poland were directly connected with illegal immigration to Palestine and the work being done by the Anglo-American Committee of Enquiry. There was almost no persecution of Jews in Poland, and certainly none of the sort that could justify Jews quitting the country. He thought the best way to handle the situation was to stop the flow at the source, although this would be very difficult to do. However no serious attempt had as yet been made to try to persuade the Polish government to take effective action against the movement.[18] At the Cabinet Committee's meeting on 25 January 1946, John B. Hynd, Chancellor of the Duchy of Lancaster, who headed the Control Office for Germany and Austria, reported that the British Parliamentary mission visiting Poland had concluded that there existed an organized movement of Jews to leave the country. Hynd warned against allowing the entry of a large number of Jews into Palestine. The likely outcome would be to encourage the exodus to continue, and even the Jews in DP camps who were now prepared to be repatriated to Poland might be persuaded, as a result, to change their minds. Bevin spoke of the difficulties involved in approaching the Poles about the conditions of the Jews in Poland. He thought that the Polish government would undoubtedly deny the charge that anti-semitism was rife in the country. Lord Nathan, Parliamentary undersecretary of state for war, doubted if there was an organized evacuation of Polish Jews taking place. He countered the claim by calling attention to the changed situation of the Jewish people as a result of their decimation in the war. In the past the Zionists had hoped to create a Jewish majority in Palestine by settling a million Jews in the country from a reserve of five million. However this original source of potential immigrants no longer existed, and to achieve a majority in Palestine at this juncture would require bringing in all of the survivors in Europe. Nathan suggested that the Russians might be approached in order to forestall the repatriation of Jews to Poland from the Soviet Union. At the end of the meeting it was decided that an approach should be made to the Polish government, but that the British ambassador would not bring up the subject of the maltreatment of Jews in Poland.[19]

Early in February 1946 the Foreign Office instructed its ambassador in Warsaw to convey to the Polish government British appreciation of the Polish foreign minister's warning against illegal immigration, and of the assurances given that Jews who remained in Poland would obtain special treatment. However, the ambassador was asked also to make a point of the fact that many Jews had managed to leave Poland for the American and British zones in Austria and Germany, as well as for Italy, in order to set out clandestinely for Palestine.[20] An attempt to obtain American cooperation in approaching the Poles ended in failure. The Americans contended that, short of resorting to serious military measures, the movement of Jews out of Poland could not be halted.[21]

In conversation with Cavendish-Bentinck on 7 February, M. Olszewski, the secretary-general of the Polish foreign ministry, emphasized that his government was making every effort to prevent all illegal departures from the country, including those of the Jews. Indeed, these efforts had resulted in a substantial decrease in illegal emigrations in recent months. Olszewski assured the ambassador that very few exit visas had been issued to private persons during the course of 1945 – no more than two or three hundred all told. Passports were approved only if an applicant was able to show that he was in possession of a visa or visa of entry to some other country. Cavendish-Bentinck asked for discretion to be exercised in the whole matter of issuing visas to Polish Jews. Olszewski put the number of Jews that had left Poland since the liberation at about 20,000. The British ambassador concluded from his talk with Olszewski that the Polish government was unable to prevent Jews from leaving the country illegally.[22]

In a letter to Christopher Warner, head of the Northern Department, Cavendish-Bentinck expressed the view that Jews wanted to leave Poland because of internal conditions in the country. The Poles were determined to keep control of all enterprise, including petty trade. Jewish welfare organizations and religious institutions were on the verge of collapse, partly because of the government's prohibition against maintaining religious organizations, and these had in the past made it easier to deal with persecutions and other manifestations of anti-semitism. The renewal of contact with the Gentile population in the places where Jews had lived prior to the war had brought home to them the hazards of attempting to re-establish themselves in their former neighbourhoods. To be taken into account, as well, was the general unpopularity of the government, some of whose more prominent members were of Jewish origin – a circumstance which added fuel to the hatred of Jews. These, then, were the obstacles that Polish Jews faced in trying to rehabilitate their lives in a country which they had come to regard as a graveyard. The ambassador thought that at the very least 120,000 Jews would leave Poland by January 1948, and that the figure was more likely to be between 160,000 and 170,000. The Jews were determined to leave and no power on earth could stand in their way. He also stressed that there was no evidence that the desire of Jews to depart from Poland was being exploited by the Zionist organization.[23]

Cavendish-Bentinck delivered himself of this sombre prediction, notwithstanding the sharp decline in the number of Jews leaving Poland since January 1946. During the first four months of the year only 3,000 Jews left Poland, as opposed to 33,000 in the latter half of 1945.[24] The sharp decline in Jewish departures resulted from a number of causes – improved security in consequence of drastic measures implemented by the Polish government; difficulties of travel during the winter season; tightened Russian surveillance; and reports of hardship experienced by Polish Jews in Germany, and of expected difficulties for emigration in the future.[25] However, the introduction of tighter control of borders seems not to have come as a result of British urgings. Cavendish-Bentinck had approached the Poles on the matter only in February 1946, whereas difficulties were already being put in the way of crossing the border two months earlier – as Olszewski had pointed out to the British ambassador. The stricter security along the frontier was in fact connected with the Polish government's war against the underground opposition. In any event, the British had avoided turning the matter into a major issue in the relations between the two countries, and had not followed Hankey's recommendation to threaten the Poles with retaliation in order to obtain their cooperation.

The turning point in the Polish government's policy on Jewish emigration came with the pogrom in Kielce on 4 July 1946, in which forty-two Jews were murdered, out of a total of 250 that had come to live in the town after the war. Following the massacre, an unofficial understanding was struck between Zionist representatives of Jews in Poland and the Polish minister of defence, General Marian Spychalski, that Jews would be allowed to leave the country without visas or exit permits. Assembly and transit points were established at the frontier with Czechoslovakia, and on 30 July 1946 the Polish border was opened to Jews wishing to leave. The arrangement was to last for only a month of two, but in practice the frontier was allowed to remain open until the end of February 1947.[26] However the pace of departures had already begun to be stepped up two months prior to the agreement. About 3,500 Jews left the country in the second half of May; by June the figure had risen to around 11,000. Movement on such a scale could not have taken place without the knowledge of the Polish authorities. Although they had as yet given no formal undertaking, the authorities were plainly giving their consent to the movement by their non-interference. At this time, too, Jewish repatriates to Poland from the Soviet Union were being gathered at special assembly points in the country. The great majority of them had no desire to be integrated into the Polish nation, and their continued presence in the country was bound to have undesirable repercussions – politically, economically and culturally, as well as for security. Quite likely the Polish government was aware of the potential risks of having the repatriates remain in Poland, and therefore took no overt action to prevent their departure, but without extending its cooperation at an official level at this stage of the game.[27]

Reports of departures from Poland on a considerable scale were received by the Foreign Office during August. Schuckburgh, at the British embassy in Czechoslovakia, reported that a steady stream of Jews was entering the country from Poland at the rate of 1,800 daily, and that 35,000 had already arrived between 1 July and 9 August, with another 70,000 expected to follow at their heels.[28] The American Ambassador in Warsaw, Arthur Bliss Lane, informed the State Department that the rate at which Jews were leaving Poland had risen from about seventy a week, prior to the Kielce pogrom, to an average of 700 per day; and the prospect was that as many as 100,000 more would eventually leave the country. It was also noted that Polish border guards were allowing the departure to take place.[29] In mid-August the Americans informed the British that according to General Mark Clark, commander of United States forces in Austria, some 60,000 Jews would leave Poland in the coming three months.[30]

News of the massacre at Kielce produced no change of attitude at the Foreign Office, which persisted in maintaining that the Jewish exodus from Poland was organized rather than spontaneous, and part of a plan to encourage illegal immigration to Palestine so as to have an effect on British policy in that region.[31] This was the view held by Clement Attlee, as well. Thus when the prime minister spoke with Fiorello LaGuardia, then secretary-general of UNRRA, he declared that he did not accept that Jews were unable to remain in Poland.[32] Nevertheless the assessment at the British embassy in Warsaw remained at odds with opinion in London. John Russell, for instance, wrote to inform the head of the Foreign Office's Eastern Department, Charles Baxter, that ninety-nine per cent of the 120,000 Jews in Poland wanted to get out – where to, was a matter of indifference to them so long as they left the country. There were a variety of groups dispersed along Poland's southern and western borders whose purpose was smuggling Jews into the West, past the Polish frontier. These groups were largely semi-autonomous and not necessarily operating under Jewish control, their motives being mercenary. The embassy had no evidence of there being an organization that was controlling or arranging local departures. Most of the movement was in the direction of the south, towards Czechoslovakia, whence it proceeded to the American zone in Germany. Russell observed that conditions in Poland were intolerable for Jews, and the Kielce pogrom had convinced those who until then had been reluctant to leave that they should get out now. For the moment, persecutions had died down and incidents in kind were very rare. But Polish Jews had been living in a state of terror since the German savageries and, more recently, the deadly violence at Kielce. Conditions being what they were, the rate of 1,000 Jewish departures daily from Poland could therefore be expected to continue unabated.[33]

Where the Foreign Office and the Warsaw embassy did agree in their evaluations was that now, in the aftermath of the Kielce pogrom, the Polish government was prepared to permit the exit of Jews from the country.[34] The embassy had received word of unimpeded mass crossings of the border, without documents and with the consent of Polish authorities. According to an eyewitness account, departures were taking place in broad daylight from Poland to Czechoslovakia. Groups ready to depart would arrive bearing a list of names and the document of a Jewish organization to affirm that all persons on the list were Jewish. After Polish military personnel had verified that no non-Jews had managed to slip in among the group, permission was given to proceed to the other side. John Dickenson of the British consulate in Szczecin reported that the authorities were making no effort to hide the fact that the movement was taking place, and had even put up temporary customs checkpoints to deal with the traffic of Jewish emigrants.[35]

The question at issue in the Foreign Office by the end of August was whether it was worthwhile submitting a protest to the Polish government, and demanding that it should act to suppress anti-semitism in the country and the illegal departure of Jews from Poland. It was thought that such a submission would be ineffective, and that making it public would only arouse the ire of Polish authorities.[36] Some days earlier Britain and the United States had made an official protest to Poland over irregularities in the referendum of 30 June and in the preparations for the first Polish general elections to be held since the war. The Poles responded by charging the two Western powers with interfering in the internal affairs of a sovereign state.[37] There was also another reason for the Foreign Office's hesitancy in deciding on a course of action. At the meeting between Cavendish-Bentinck and Olszewski, the secretary-general of the Polish foreign ministry claimed that his government preferred that the Jews should remain in Poland, especially those among them who were craftsmen. A special office had been established to settle repatriated Jews in the former German territories in Silesia. However the incident in Kielce had greatly alarmed Jews in Poland, and the nation's frontier was too extensive for Polish authorities to be able to stop Jews from fleeing the country. Olszewski believed that illegal immigrations might be halted if each month a given number of Jews were allowed to emigrate to other countries. Cavendish-Bentinck rejected the proposal on the grounds that no refuge could be offered to Jews now in Poland without first solving the problem of the great number of homeless Jews in Germany, Austria, Italy, and Cyprus.[38]

Cavendish-Bentinck concluded from his interview with Olszewski that the Poles were powerless to prevent Jews from leaving the country illegally, because policy on this matter was determined in Moscow. He doubted if approaching Polish authorities in secret or publicly would do any good.

Any attempt to suggest to the Poles that they should act against antisemitism in their country was likely to be met with the counterclaim that it was the agents of British-backed General Władysław Anders who were instigating anti-semitism and violence against Jews in Poland. According to the ambassador, the Polish difficulties in Palestine, and the corruption of the Polish security police and border guards had made it possible for Jews to slip out of the country. He also entertained serious doubts concerning the efforts of officials at the foreign office to bring a halt to the exodus, which he believed was unstoppable. The driving force behind the flight of Jews from Poland was anti-semitism, he noted, which only the Polish bishops had the power to restrain; however they themselves were fundamentally anti-semitic.[39]

Despite his misgivings, Cavendish-Bentinck approached Olszewski once again at the beginning of September in order to lay before him the evidence that border authorities were neglecting to respond to the movement of Jews out of the country, and to remind him of the assurances that had been made that Jews not in possession of the necessary documents would be prevented from leaving.[40] By now, however, there was a steep drop in the number of refugees from Poland, following the waves of mass departures that had been going on since June. From October 1946 to February 1947 no more than 10,000 Jews had left the country.[41] One reason that the rate of departures had fallen off was that a very substantial number of Jews had fled in the panic created by the Kielce pogrom. Later, when relative calm had been restored, many of those who were left behind had begun to settle down to a semblance of normal existence. The latter group consisted principally of Jews who settled in Silesia. The setting in of winter weather played its part, as well, in curbing traffic out of the country. Finally, rumours of difficult conditions in the DP camps, and waning hopes of a solution that would clear the way for immigration, to Palestine or elsewere, exerted no small influence in discouraging attempts to leave. In February 1947, Polish borders were closed to Jewish emigration. The closure of the frontier was one of the measures implemented by the régime to assert its control over the country, following the victory of the government bloc in the elections of 19 January 1947.

Britain's failure to persuade Polish authorities to act in order to prevent the departure of Jews from Poland derived from a number of circumstances. One of these was the widespread anti-semitism in Poland that furnished the setting for the murders of Jews and for a number of pogroms. Also, the Polish government had no interest in keeping Jews in the country against their will, particularly at a time when their departure suited the internal needs of the régime. The Soviets for their part sought to aggravate the problem of Jewish refugees in Germany and Austria, since this issue was putting a serious strain on relations between Britain and the United

States, which was demanding that the refugees be allowed to immigrate to Palestine. Moreover relations between London and Warsaw were at a low ebb as a result of Poland's having joined the Soviet bloc, and because of British connection with the leader of the Polish opposition, Stanisław Mikołajczyk.[42] And, finally, the surviving remnant of Jews in Poland had an overwhelming desire to leave – an aspiration in which they were encouraged, and which they were assisted in realizing, by Zionist emissaries.

That Britain had very little leverage to apply in its efforts to influence Polish authorities is made manifest by the inefficacy with which it protested against the suppressions of Mikołajczyk's adherents, and questioned the results of both the June 1946 referendum and the January 1947 elections. Illustrative of Britain's low standing in Poland is the arrest of Cavendish-Bentinck at the end of 1946, when the ambassador was visiting his friend, Count Grocholski. After his release from detention, Cavendish-Bentinck learnt that Grocholski had in the meantime been executed on charges which included giving information to the ambassador of a foreign power.[43] However, before hastening to judge Britain's performance in trying to obtain Polish cooperation to bring a halt to the Jewish exodus, we have to remember that for the Polish régime the struggle against the opposition under Mikołajczyk's leadership was of vital significance to the very survival of communist rule in Poland. The question of the departure of Polish Jews could hardly be weighed on the same scales.

For the Foreign Office it was a matter of policy interest that the conditions of Jews in Poland should be improved, and especially that Polish Jews be made to feel that their security was not in jeopardy. But the Foreign Office also faced something of a quandary in bringing pressure to bear on the Polish government in the matter. This was, after all, a government in which Jews held senior positions and which was itself opposed to anti-semitism. Anti-semitic agitation and violence were primarily the work of persons and groups associated with the opposition, which was itself exploiting the Jewish issue in its campaign to defeat the government. Moreover, key elements in the opposition, chief among them Mikołajczyk, had close links with Britain, which was sympathetic to their cause. And though the Catholic Church in Poland might have exerted its influence in order to restrain anti-semitism in the country, it was itself (as Cavendish-Bentinck had noted) no less anti-semitically inclined than were ordinary Poles; what is more, anti-semitism served the purposes of the Polish opposition, to which the Church was favourably disposed.

Although bringing an end to the Jewish exodus from Poland had been treated as a matter of the utmost urgency in London, the issue was laid aside for a while, until August 1946. The Foreign Office was pinning its hopes on a joint Anglo-American solution for Palestine that would also resolve the problem of Jewish refugees.⁴⁴ The issue aroused the concern of the British government once more when negotiations with the Americans had broken down, and in consequence of a huge surge in Jewish departures from Poland. By this time, however, the situation had got out of hand. Even so, the British refrained from putting any ultimatums to the Polish government, possibly because of their uncertainty about both the extent of their own power to influence the Polish régime and the capacity of the latter to take effective action in the matter. The British were also reluctant to exacerbate relations with Polish authorities, since this might result in losing touch with the opposition, with which they preferred to remain in contact at least until the elections in Poland. Britain was also discouraged in its efforts by American refusal to join in the attempt to prevail upon the Poles to put a stop to the exodus of Jews from their country. When the Polish government finally did halt the free movement of Jews out of the country after the January 1947 elections, it was motivated to do so by internal considerations.

Thus it was almost inevitable that the British should fail in their endeavour to prevent the mass departure of Jews from Poland — unless possibly they were prepared to throw their full weight behind such an effort. But even then the outcome would have remained in doubt.

NOTES

1 Susanne S. Lotarski, 'The Communist Takeover in Poland', *The Anatomy of Communist Takeovers*, ed. Thomas T. Hammond (New Haven, London, 1975), pp. 339–67; Geir Lundestad, *The American Non-Policy towards Eastern Europe 1943–1947* (New York, 1975), pp. 225–56; John Coutouvidis and Jaime Reynolds, *Poland 1939–1947* (Leicester, 1986), pp. 215–21.
2 Yisrael Gutman, *Hayehudim be-polin akharei milhemet ha-olam ha-shniya* (Jerusalem, 1985), pp. 11–14.
3 Cavendish-Bentinck to Charles W. Baxter, 17 September 1945, Public Record Office, Kew, United Kingdom (hereafter cited as PRO), Foreign Office (hereafter cited as FO), 688/31, file no. 48.
4 Cavendish-Bentinck to FO, no. 956, 19 November 1945, PRO, FO371/51127, WR 3418.
5 Control Commission for Germany to War Office, no. 224, 8 December 1945, PRO, FO943/699; Sir William Strang, Political Adviser to Commander-in-Chief, Germany to FO, no. 44, 15 December 1945, PRO, Cabinet (hereafter cited as CAB), 134/595.
6 Shuckburgh, British Embassy Prague, to Bevin, no. 252, 8 December 1945, PRO, FO371/51129, WR3735.
7 Cavendish-Bentinck to Bevin, 18 December 1945, Chargé d'Affaires at Warsaw, to Baxter, 8 December 1945, PRO, FO688/31, file no. 48; Hankey to Hilary Young, Political Division, Control Commission for Germany, 18 December 1945, PRO, FO688/31, file no. 46.
8 Memorandum of Conversation, by George L. Warren, the Adviser on Refugees and

Displaced Persons, 21 December 1945, US Department of State, *Foreign Relations of the United States* (hereafter cited as FRUS), (Washington, 1967), Vol. 2, p. 1218.

9 Earl of Halifax to FO, no. 15, 2 January 1946, PRO, FO945/655; *New York Times*, 3 January 1945; Yehuda Bauer, *Flight and Rescue: Brichah* (New York, 1970), pp. 194–8.

10 FO to Warsaw, no. 50, 6 January 1946, PRO, FO371/37684, WR65; FO to Warsaw, no. 27, 4 January 1946, PRO, FO371/57684, WR64.

11 Warsaw to FO, nos. 53, 54, 55, 9 January 1946, PRO, FO0371/57684, WR213.

12 Cavendish-Bentinck to FO, no. 70, 10 January 1946, PRO, FO371/57684, WR111; about the Anglo-American Committee see: Amikam Nachmani, *Great Power Discord in Palestine: The Anglo-American Committee for Palestine* (London, 1987); Michael J. Cohen, *Palestine and the Great Powers 1945–1847* (New Jersey, 1982), pp. 60–7, 100–15; Zvi Ganin, *Truman, American Jewry, and Israel 1945–48* (New York, London, 1979), pp. 49–64; Wm. Roger Louis, *The British Empire in the Middle East 1945–1951* (Oxford, 1984), pp. 397–419.

13 Memorandum by Banks, 8 January 1946, PRO, FO688/34.

14 Memorandum by Henderson, 11 January 1946, PRO, FO371/57684, WR88.

15 Record of a Meeting held at Refugee Department, FO, 7 January 1946, PRO, FO371/57684, WR75.

16 Memorandum by Rendel, 'Treatment of New Jewish Refugees in British Zone in Germany', 9 January 1946, PRO, FO945/655.

17 Memorandum by McNeil, 9 January 1946, PRO, FO371/57689, WR 839.

18 Memorandum by the Secretary of State for Foreign Affairs to the Cabinet Overseas Reconstruction Committee, O.R.C. (46) 9, 20 January 1946, PRO, FO371/57685, WR212; Draft memorandum for the Cabinet Reconstruction Committee, 15 January 1946, PRO, FO371/57686, WR264.

19 Cabinet Overseas Reconstruction Committee, O.R.C. (46) 2nd mtg., 25 January 1946, PRO, CAB134/595.

20 FO to Warsaw, nos. 242, 243, 2 February 1946, PRO, FO375/57687, WR54; Memorandum by Rendel, 30 January 1946, PRO, FO371/57686, WR267.

21 FO to Washington, no. 1110, 2 February 1946, PRO, FO371/57686, WR267; Halifax to FO, no. 1163, 21 February 1946, PRO, FO371/52626, WR7855.

22 Cavendish-Bentinck to FO, no. 237, 7 February 1946, PRO, FO945/655.

23 Cavendish-Bentinck to Warner, 20 February 1946, PRO, FO371/57688, WR736.

24 Gutman, op. cit., pp. 48–9; Bauer, op. cit., p. 126.

25 Steel to Warsaw, no. 31, 9 February 1946, PRO, FO371/57687, WR396; Jewish Telegraphic Agency, 5 February 1946, PRO, FO371/57687, WR403.

26 Bauer, op. cit., pp. 205–12, 219–23; Gutman, op. cit., 34–41, 44–53; Michael Chęcinski, *Poland* (New York, 1982), pp. 21–34.

27 About the repatriation to Poland see: Joseph B. Schechtman, *Postwar Population Transfers in Europe 1945–1951* (Philadelphia, 1962), Chap. 8; Gutman, op. cit., pp. 20–6.

28 Shuckburgh to FO, no. 904, 7 August 1946, PRO, FO371/57697, E7723; Shuckburgh to FO, no. 947, 15 August 1946, PRO, FO371/52629, E8141; Cavendish-Bentinck to FO, no. 1312, 25 August 1946, PRO, FO371/57694, WR2287.

29 Lane to the Secretary of State, 25 July 1946, FRUS, Vol. 5, p. 174; Erhardt to the Secretary of State, 3 August 1946, 3 September 1946, *FRUS*, Vol. 5, pp. 175–6, 185–7; Dean Acheson, the Acting Secretary of State, to Lane, 12 August 1946; *FRUS*, Vol. 5, p. 178.

30 Cabot Coville, American embassy in London, to Baxter, 15 August 1946, PRO FO371/57694, WR2206; Acheson to Key, Chargé d'Affaires at Rome, 14 August 1946, *FRUS*, Vol. 5, p. 179.

31 Memorandum by C. J. Edmonds, FO, 27 August 1946, PRO. FO 371/57693, WR2067.
32 Note of Mr. LaGuardia's Interview with the Prime Minister, 5 September 1946, PRO. FO 371/57769, WR2494.
33 Russell to Baxter, 21 August 1946, PRO, FO371/52630, E8422; Memorandum by Warner, 21 August 1946, PRO, FO371/57698, WR 2662; Cavendish-Bentinck to FO, no. 1312, 25 August 1946, PRO, FO371/57694, WR2287.
34 Memorandum by Robin M. A. Hankey, at the time Head of Northern Department, FO, 9 August 1946, PRO, FO371/56534, N10434; Cavendish-Bentinck to FO, no. 270, 11 September 1946, PRO, FO371/56534, N11739; FO to Washington, no. 9307, 25 September 1946, CAB 127/280; Lane to the Secretary of State, 3 September 1946, *FRUS*, Vol. 5, pp. 186–7.
35 Cavendish-Bentinck to British Consulate, Katowice, no. 39, 31 August 1946, PRO, FO371/56534, N11440; British Consulate, Katowice to Cavendish-Bentinck, no. 1, 6 September 1946, PRO, FO688/34; Memorandum by Banks, 10 September 1946, PRO, FO688/34.
36 FO to Warsaw, no. 1446, 27 August 1946, PRO, FO371/56534, N10434.
37 Lunestad, op. cit., p. 214.
38 Cavendish-Bentinck to FO, no. 1291, 21 August 1946, PRO, FO371/52630, E8339.
39 Cavendish-Bentinck to FO, no. 1291, 21 August 1946, PRO, FO371/52630, E8339; Cavendish-Bentinck to FO, no. 1344, 31 August 1946, PRO, FO371/56534, N11209; Cavendish-Bentinck to Hankey, 1 September 1946, PRO, FO371/56534, N11440; Cavendish-Bentinck to FO, no. 1332, 29 August 1946, PRO, FO371/57694, WR2335; Arieh J. Kochavi, 'The Catholic Church and Anti-semitism in Poland following World War II as reflected in British Diplomatic Documents', *GAL-ED*, eds. Emanuel Melzer, David Engel (Tel Aviv, 1989), Vol. XI, pp. 116–28.
40 Cavendish-Bentinck to Olszewski, no. 309, 11 September 1946, PRO, FO688/34.
41 Allied Commission for Austria to German Department, FO, 17 December 1946, PRO, FO371/57778, WR3953; Bauer, op. cit., p. 287.
42 Stanislaw Mikolajczyk, *The Rape of Poland* (Connecticut, 1948).
43 Victor Rothwell, *Britain and the Cold War 1941–1947* (London, 1982), p. 364.
44 Cohen, op. cit., pp. 116–32; Ganin, op. cit., pp. 65–109.

# HENRYK GRYNBERG CALLS POLAND TO ACCOUNT

Józef Wróbel

The themes in Grynberg's work can be reduced to a few basic questions. They are distinctive in their thematic and artistic unity. This unity is accentuated by the consistent identification of the hero and the narrator throughout most of his work, a literary autobiography of almost forty years of Polish-Jewish co-existence.

Henryk Grynberg is perhaps the last writer for whom being a Pole and a Jew was both a human and artistic drama. Jewish emigration after the Second World War meant escape from the terrible memory of the millions who had been murdered. Later, after October 1956 and in 1968, the need to flee from growing anti-semitic attitudes meant that emigration also involved escaping Polishness. The latter produced a negative complex which could only be removed by assimilating to another culture. Grynberg's calling Poland and the Poles to account was bitter, but free of bigotry. However, acculturation was impossible for him as a writer. The Polish language was the only one in which he could write on the theme of the interconnections of Polish and Jewish destiny.

Grynberg is also the last Polish-Jewish writer to examine the theme of Jewish martyrdom, a martyrdom which was also part of his own life. He regards it his duty, because of his own survival, to keep alive the memory, and to bear witness to those who were killed, starved and gassed, and who thus somehow saved his life:

> My family was young on the whole. Around ninety people gathered to celebrate an engagement. Today I go and search for any traces of them at the sites of our great loss, amongst the graves in the fields. I look at the finger prints on the walls of the gas chambers. People filled all the gas chambers, all the mass graves; they caused the gun-barrels to be pointed towards themselves to attract attention away from me, so there would be no time or space left for me. I was only six years old

and could be completely overlooked. (*Ekipa 'Antygona'* ['Antigone's Team] p. 41)¹

He wrote the above in the story *Pełnomocnictwo* (Plenipotentiary Powers) which should be interpreted symbolically. Plenipotentiary powers mean here the right and obligation to speak for those who did not survive and for those who could not defend themselves later on. In 1968, attempts were made to deprive him of these powers in a lampoon which described *Żydowska wojna* (The Jewish War) ironically as a 'semi-autobiographical' novel, and which tried to invalidate the author's own experience by changing his date of birth from 1936 to 1941.²

Like Oriana Fallaci, Grynberg described his duty to his murdered family and to all the Jews destroyed by the war in *Prawda nieartystyczna* (Unartistic Truth), as 'doing something to make the dead less dead'.³ This was the path chosen by the hero in his story *Jidit*, when he decided to return from Israel to Poland in order to become the 'guardian of the graves' there. Unable to explain this to a Dutch Jewess, the Jidit of the title, he only said to her: 'I have various things to settle there' (*Ekipa 'Antygona'* p.84). The same hero saw this in a slightly different light in *Życie osobiste* (Personal Life) when he tried to revive the Jewish world and language in Jewish theatre.

Grynberg's novels and stories are made up of his own and his hero's life stories and encompass his pre-war rural childhood in *Sielanka-Sia* (Pastoral-Past), his wartime experiences in *Żydowska wojna* (The Jewish War) (1965), travels after the war in *Zwycięstwo* (Victory) (1969), the Stalinist period of indoctrination in school and at university in *Życie ideologiczne* (The ideological life) (1975), the years spent working in the Jewish theatre in *Życie osobiste* (Personal Life) (1979), the dramatic break with Poland in *Ojczyzna* (Fatherland) (1970–71), and finally his emigration to America in *Kadisz* (Kaddish) (1987). The Israeli stories from *Ekipa 'Antygona'* and *Buszujący po drogach* (Rampaging along the Roads) have to be included between *Życie osobiste* and *Ojczyzna*, if only to fill a gap in the author's life. We will ignore *Życie codzienne i artystyczne* (Daily and Artistic Life) as this has a different, non-Jewish hero.

The chronological order of these works does not correspond to that of the hero's life. It seems, however, that the author had a definite chronological order in mind, although he did not keep to this in writing the works. The farewell to the desecrated grave of his father constitutes a clear break, and certain declarations seem impossible after it. It is difficult to imagine Grynberg making his hero say later on:

> And even if they strike their tents and depart into the past for ever, then one can still stay and listen to what the old names have to say, to what the gravestones whisper, to what the woods murmur around

Treblinka and to what the anti-semites hiss. Someone should keep watch, stay on guard. Even over this emptiness. It's good that I am a Jew. If I were a Frenchman I would be bored to tears. As it is, I always have plenty to do. (*Życie ideologiczne*, pp. 105-6)

These works are further linked together by their concern with fundamental individual existential problems, such as choosing and acquiring Jewish identity, the mental rejection of 'Aryan papers', their concern with the collective problems of martyrdom, the disintegration of the Polish form of Jewish culture and the complicated issue of Polish-Jewish relations.

The first chapter of *Prawda nieartystyczna*, which is a kind of internal autobiography, is called 'Życie jako dezintegracja' (Life as disintegration). This life almost completely coincides with the biography of the hero created by Grynberg. It begins in *Żydowska wojna* from 1942. The title of this story is of course an inversion of that of Flavius and Feuchtwagner. The shift of emphasis onto the first part of the title indicates the kind of experience that the Holocaust was. The term 'war' is used ironically: only one side is at war, since the other neither fights, nor kills, and is continually fleeing. The six-year old narrator observes this war with all the naivety of his age, more with surprise than with terror. He depicts his experience and that of those nearest to him in the simplest of narrative forms, sometimes including an adult's point of view and enriching it with a brief psychological or philosophical comment. Short, laconic, dispassionate sentences are doubly justified here: psychologically and artistically. The first is the result of seeing through the eyes of the child protagonist, the second is the result of the conviction which was part of all post-war literature: that it was impossible to express and convey the extent of bestiality and suffering, and that the language of literature must return to the simplest and truest sentences, since these would somehow unconsciously convey the greatest terror. Jarosław Iwaszkiewicz drew attention to the relation between this prose and that of Zofia Nałkowska's *Medaliony* (Medallions),[4] but here the inhabited world is seen from within, surrounding someone incapable of understanding it and helpless before it. The value of human life is devalued: money becomes more important. The hero's father died because of it, although he had hidden it for a rainy day and believed that it would help him survive. But he was killed by a robber's axe precisely because he had money. This is one black paradox; another is constructed around it:

> But he was right to save money so obstinately. He used it to buy bread which he carried under his cloak. It seems money can be relied on. Money proves that one is a human being, he thought. And if one is killed for it then at least it is not like an animal! For money – like a man ... (*Żydowska wojna*, pp.44-45)

Here the author's commentary needs adding:

> But money, which was more valuable than human life in the conditions of 'the Jewish war', was not only a way of salvation (as in the ghetto): it also had fatal properties. Death for money in the conditions of the Holocaust meant a human death, death with honour, because it was for a reason.[5]

This Jewish death at Polish hands is an obsessive theme in Grynberg's work, a death for which neither the murderer nor Poland is brought to account, a death around which there is a pact of silence, although everyone knows the murderer's identity. His father died because he was a Jew and could not help being one:

> For my father spoke in an unrepeatable and unique mixture of Mazovian dialect ('un' or 'tun' instead of 'on'), with a Jewish sing-song accent and simplified declensions. He knew no other way of speaking Polish and did not need to, for everyone understood him perfectly. (*Żydowska wojna*, pp.37–38)

Survival for the mother and son meant denying everything that was Jewish: not only their appearance had to be changed but also their surroundings and their very past. A mythologised world is created around the hero, in which he plays an assumed role, losing his psychic and cultural identity.

> I had a grandmother who played the piano and a grandfather who died of cancer of the stomach, the noble disease of noble people, and my mother was in mourning. I did not need to conjure up myths like other children. I had my own, complete and beautiful. My own mother provided me with it every day. She spoke about it, she lived through it with me and she did it all quite seriously ... She was the best companion and partner of my childhood game. (*Żydowska wojna*, p. 69).

The consequence of being a non-Jew was being a Pole – and if a Pole, then a Christian, which meant going to communion and having a Catholic upbringing, though without being christened, a completely artificial life. Confusion in so young a mind had far-reaching effects for the psyche, with repercussions for one's whole life, making one less sincere, more secretive, distant, even fearful. It would not be inappropriate to quote Grynberg's own admission here:

None of the wonderful girls I knew ever found out if I loved them or not. And I myself do not know to this day. I unknowingly misled people by controlling my facial expressions and showing no one my suffering. Even my own mother, my partner in the game we played together during the occupation, who should have known me inside out, was amazed when I began to publish my stories. 'He was always a happy boy', she said, with surprise, when she talked about it to her Californian neighbours and friends. 'I go on living and continually discover more bad things' – and this seems to be the maxim of my life.[6]

His hero is similarly reticent: he describes situations and describes himself in situations, but he rarely betrays his thoughts and experiences. This happens only once, on leaving his father's grave, and testifying to the strength of that experience.

In describing his own suffering and that of his whole nation, he often uses figures and situations from the New Testament. These recall the Polish romantic messianic tradition on the one hand and overlap with his Catholic religious education on the other. The history of Christ's childhood is repeated in the history of the hero:

The most moving story was about Jesus. Though he was the son of God himself, immediately after his birth, having received the homage and gifts given so willingly to every newborn child, he and his distressed young mother had to flee Herod's soldiers and hide everywhere in fear of being betrayed. (*Żydowska wojna*, p. 77)

His brother Buciek perished 'when he was betrayed and found in hiding at a farmer's where his mother had hidden him from Herod's lackeys'. (*Kadisz*, p. 42). Grandfather Jeszije was crucified 'on an invisible cross with invisible gas, in a gas chamber filled with martyrs, in September or October at a Golgotha called Treblinka in the unforgettable year of martyrdom 1942 or 5702/3'. (*Kadisz*, p. 40). 'At Easter, my mother said that she wanted to take me to the cathedral on the other side of the Vistula to show me the tomb of Jesus. The "tomb" turned out to be a great, smoking fire, which could be seen even from Praga. But my mother wanted me to see it from close up.' (*Żydowska wojna*, p. 51). Christ was after all 'exceptionally lucky: only one out of thirteen was a traitor'. (*Żydowska wojna*, p.78). In describing the nation's torment through Christ's torment, Grynberg does not link it with any hope for the moral rebirth of the world as is the case in Polish tradition: suffering is not historically justified. In this way, he accuses the indifferent Christian world of not seeing that the essence of redemption is suffering. God redeems the world through every person who suffers – to help this person is to help Christ.

The tragedy of Occupation continued for the Jews beyond the years 1939–1945. As soon as freedom was regained, the tragedy of the hero's family became the tragedy of the hero's consciousness. Born into and for Jewish society, he was deprived of it doubly: by his upbringing in a Christian social, ethical and religious system and by the physical annihilation of Jewish society. A feeling that he had betrayed his own nation developed within him and life became somehow unreal. Just as the hero of the Tomb had his own grave where his own remains had not come to rest purely by chance, so he had his place in the transport to Treblinka and in the gas chamber. By chance, he had survived his own death. The price was a change of personality, its visible manifestation a change of name: in the tradition of the Old and New Testaments, this had enormous significance as names are given by God himself. And God would use these names to summon members of the chosen people to himself at the moment of death.

> The people among whom we were born and among whom we lived were dead: they had died driven along other earlier roads where we were not with them, and they had died under their own names. If we had died, no one would have known our own real names. There were only the two of us. (*Żydowska wojna*, p. 68)

The tragedy of losing a name which describes one's individuality, and its replacement by a number is the subject of a lament by Joshua Perl, the text of which has survived in Ringelblum's archive.

> A person's name is part of a living organism; intangible and invisible, but one cannot live without it ... It was I and I was it. It learnt to walk beside me; it learnt to walk as I did. When I was called, it took notice. When I suffered, it shared my suffering. It shared my joy, wept with my tears, laughed with my laughter and dreamt my dreams.[7]

The eponymous victory of the next novel of the cycle should be considered ironically or as posing a rhetorical question. The events of war were not over and settled for good: history has trodden a well-worn path that can be repeated at any moment. History obviously does repeat itself, not in the totality of occupation, but in individual situations, reminding the young hero of the war:

> One thing made me wonder. Uszer was once again in prison. Mama again rushed around the strange town, hiding illegal clothing coupons in her case, bribing guards to take parcels to the prison. My father was lying in the ground near Radoszyna. By the side of the road. The grass grows higher there and has a quite

different colour – and people pass by there everyday, from field to field. And no one had the courage to say – who killed him? Oh, no one even had the courage to ask ... So how did the war end in the end? (*Zwycięstwo*, p. 92)

When his mother attempted to find Adek, who was dragged off the train by the National Armed Forces (*NSZ*) together with some communists and then shot, she received this reply from the investigating officer: 'We have grown used to Jews being killed ... ' (*Zwycięstwo*, p. 61). In the *Jewish War*, the landowner Podorewski had even found a philosophical justification for handing two Jews over to the Gestapo ' ... Podorewski was a philosopher. Is there any way of helping them, he thought. Perhaps only by shortening their suffering? And there was the question of the money that would be left after them. What if the Germans were to get their hands on it, or if it were to be lost completely ... Yes, Podorewski was a philosopher.' (*Żydowska wojna*, p. 32). Sometimes a peasant helped. 'The peasants were ignorant and superstitious. They said it was a sin not to help.' (*Żydowska wojna*, p. 32)

The repulsive *szmalcownicy*, traitors, clear murderers, despite all their disgusting behaviour, did not treat the Jews as objects. Tomaszkiewicz's apparently indifferent response to the death of Bolek's mother, one of the survivors of the slaughter, is related as if with a justificatory sub-text and arouses a sense of menace:

> Tomaszkiewicz neither gave her up nor betrayed her, and he was not, in fact, responsible for her death. Tomaszkiewicz was passing by in a cart, when a gendarme stopped him and ordered him to take the Jewess to Węgrów. It was late autumn. Tomaszkiewicz certainly did not feel like travelling so many kilometres during foul weather and he was sorry for his horse. He asked the gendarme to shoot the woman on the spot, in the nearby forest, offering to bury her himself. Apparently he also stood the gendarme a vodka. (*Zwycięstwo*, p. 26).

Bolek later killed him while trying to escape arrest by the *NKVD*, which Bolek had joined to ensure those who had harmed the Jews were punished. Here Grynberg barely touches on the contentious issue of the Jews making common cause with communism. People like Bolek had the chance to take revenge for the war period; others such as Nusen joined the party because they felt more secure in having at least one ally – the authorities.

This picture of Poland and the Poles in Grynberg is not the product of any kind of prejudice or resentment. In *Prawda nieartystyczna*, he directly defends Poland against the falsifications of propaganda: 'To accuse Poles of collaboration in crucifying the Jews contradicts the truth and is as tendentious as accusing the Jews of crucifying the Messiah, or God himself. In both cases, historical circumstances are distorted.'[8] He reminds us of the criminal acts of the anti-semitic French police and the extermination activities of the Slovak authorities. But a reading of the texts leaves one with a different impression, that of the psychological truth experienced by the hero, the result of feeling constantly under threat. Lost by his mother in the town, the hero cannot rationalise his fear or describe the direction from which danger comes, and is even afraid to cry. 'That is just what they were waiting for. Who? I did not know, but I knew *they* were there. They were definitely around me. They were everywhere! They were in the sound of the feet on the pavement.' (*Żydowska wojna*, p. 52) If Grynberg feels bitterness towards the Poles, and he does, then it is less because of their hatred than for their lack of compassion.

The key words in *Zwycięstwo* and *Życie ideologiczne* are phrases associated with fear. It is characteristic that they do not appear so strongly in *Żydowska wojna*. This is not because Grynberg maintains that the nightmare of the post-war years was worse than that of the occupation, but because as the hero grows up, he becomes more aware of the times he lived through and what he experienced. Previously, he had understood these feelings only through his interaction with his parents. Death was not terrible, because it only meant disappearance and absence and one grew accustomed to it. The post-war world was something new. Now he was richer in understanding and convinced that history could repeat itself, that Jewish history was a treadmill of suffering and persecution. He learned this truth in his first lessons at a Jewish school: 'History filled us with fear.' (*Życie ideologiczne*, p. 9) The Jews hid their traditions, not wanting to provoke hostility or hatred. 'The wedding of Belcia and Moniek did not take place outside, as custom demanded, but inside. People did not have the courage to take their Jewish customs onto the street.' (*Życie ideologiczne*, p. 55). Their fear made them change Jewish names to Polish ones:

> Almost everyone did it. Even actors in the Jewish theatre. Meir Melman was written on one side of the poster and *Marian* on the other. On one side Moyshe Szwejlich in Hebrew letters and on the other *Michał*. On one Israel, on the other *Izydor*. On one Itshak, on the other *Juliusz*. Everyone did it and no one bothered to ask why?' (*Życie ideologiczne*, p. 55).

The emigration of 1957 was accompanied by feelings of panic and threat. In describing these events, Grynberg even resorts to the language of the Occupation, not because he wanted to stress the actual similarity between the two situations, which were not comparable, but because every event reminded the Jews 'that history had by no means finished with them'.[9] On leaving, the Jews had to pay: they paid carpenters for trunks, customs officials for turning a blind eye, and waiters for a last meal in a restaurant. They paid everyone who asked, just as they had paid what had been demanded during the Occupation. 'Everyone paid. The rich and the poor, the mean and the generous. They paid the pleasant and the unpleasant. Those paid who had reason to be afraid and those who did not. They did not even have a clear idea whom or what they were afraid of, but they were in fear and – they paid (*szmalcowali*)' (*Życie ideologiczne*, p. 107).

In *Życie osobiste* Grynberg describes the making of a film near Sokołów Podlaski. The actors from the Jewish theatre played war victims, while Polish actors played Germans:

> In elegant sheepskins, with weapons on their arms and in their belts, they stalked about straight-backed and cocksure, unable to hide their disdain as they looked at our rags. Nor could they control their authoritative tone when talking to us: when getting in and out of their vans, they ordered us around without second thoughts, even though we were all just actors.' (*Życie osobiste*, p. 71)

Were the roles played here a continuation of the occupation or a vague presentiment of a future which could become reality at any moment? Anti-semitism is a demonic, irrational force, which keeps alive the stereotype of the Jew and hatred for him even among a generation which has never seen one. Adolescents mocked these actors, although not reacting at all to the strange nineteenth-century garb or even to Gypsies. 'Institutionalised' anti-semitism, its use a trumpcard in political games and everything else that went with it, as well as a certain silent compliance in the face of its individualised manifestations, led the hero of *Ojczyzna* to part painfully with Poland and necessitated an evaluation of the concept of fatherland. Visiting his family home, Radoszyna in 1967, he found human excrement on his father's grave. The shock he suffered affected his loyalty to Jewish graves. His homeland now ceased to be Poland and became the internalised heritage of the Jews.

Grynberg's first volume of verse written in emigration is called *Antynostalgia* (*Anti-nostalgia*). His dispute with Poland now becomes one with Polish history and not a struggle with contemporary reality:

> I was soaked and started to shiver. I shivered with cold, nothing else.
> The peasant standing by me thought I was suffering. But I felt relief.
> My task was accomplished. ('Ojczyzna', *Kultura* (1971), 1:83)

The hero's fundamental problem is to choose and discover his Jewish identity, or as Sartre put it, his authenticity[10]. The child hero had demanded his mother's reassurance that he would never be a Jew again, not of course understanding what he was asking.

> It was only when I was small that I really did not want to be a Jew. I said to my mother: 'Mama, when the war ends, I will never be a Jew again. I won't have to be, will I?' 'We'll see,' said my mother. 'If you want to, then you will be.' 'But I don't want to be! Do you hear, I don't want to.' ('Buszujący po drogach' *Twórczość* (1967), 7:30)

There is, indeed, hardly anything to link him with Jewishness, apart from his circumcision. However, that, at the most, is an external sign of belonging to the Jewish people. Knowing neither Hebrew nor Yiddish, he has no authentic cultural background: his world had been carefully swept away. Before he can grow to accept being Jewish, he is defined as such from the outside by the imposition of irrational stigmata. This was when he began to be entrusted in *ZMP* (Youth) organisations with the *agitprop* work which was always assigned to Jews, and when he began to be reminded of his real name: Hersh vel Hershek, and especially when a guest at a ball in the Europejski Hotel remarked to him:

> 'I don't like Semites at all' . . . It was only then that we noticed that all of us looked like Jews. If someone has ever thought about what it means 'to look like a Jew', then he would have seen it at that moment. Because suddenly we all looked like Jews. This is how Jews are made: Jews are not born themselves. What made me think, though, was the fact that we had all found ourselves together, only 'us' and no one else with us. ('Ojczyzna', *Kultura* (1970), 12:39)

A section from Sartre's *Thoughts on the Jewish Question* seems to provide a commentary on this scene:

> Everywhere that a Jew makes his way in, fleeing his Jewish reality, they still accept him as a Jew, and he feels at every moment that he is thought of as a Jew. His presence among Christians is no reprieve: it by no means ensures him the anonymity he so desires. On the contrary, there is a constant tension – in his pitiful chasing after man, the Jew cannot escape the effigy which constantly stalks him. It is this which creates a deep solidarity among all Jews, based not on their activities, not on common interests, but on their common situation . . . For a Jew, another Jew is the only person with whom he can say 'we'.[11]

This feeling of being alien, foreign and even exotic is experienced by the hero during a student festival in Warsaw, when he is treated as a foreigner simply because of his physiognomy. Deprived of fatherland, family, and tradition, but carrying with him the stigma of Jewishness, he defines being a Jew as extra-national, extra-cultural, ethical – it involves choosing the fate of, and solidarity with, people like himself: rejected, persecuted, disinherited, threatened and rebelling against external causes, that is against the injustice of the world which imposes them. The following reflection occurs to him when he is beaten up during the student strikes of 1957:

> There were only a few of us there, in front of the student hostel, but no one was alone. We were faced by greater forces and had no chance – this was traditional in this town. But here on the pavement, where the brute could smash me with a single blow of his heavy stick, I was once again a Jew – that is an isolated, defenceless individual calling for justice. To whom? Mainly to heaven. (*Życie ideologiczne*, p. 112)

He makes a similar ethical declaration to his friend Opala who, having been brought up as a Jew and applying to the Israeli embassy for a visa, finds out he is the son of a peasant woman from near Białystok. He rejoices, not because he has found his mother, but because he is free of his Jewish fate. The hero remonstrates with him:

> You see Opala, if there were as many Jews as there are Christians, or as few Christians as there are Jews, if six million of *them* had been murdered and they had been threatened that, who knows, perhaps one day as many again might be murdered, if people shouted at them, 'Christians to Palestine', then I would immediately go over to their side. What is more, I think every true Jew should do so. So I am surprised that, given the existing opposite situation, the Christians have not come over to our side. (*Życie ideologiczne*, pp. 104–5)

Polish national mythology, which feeds on the stereotype of hopeless struggle, has no place for the Jewish attitude of martyrdom and resignation. During his school years, the hero of *Życie ideologiczne* submitted to historical-patriotic Polish emotions; after the tragedy of three and a half million, an emptiness remained.

> It is a pity – he thought bitterly – that Mama was not a courier during the occupation and did not hide underground leaflets or grenades, but just my circumcised penis. That my teenage aunts and thirteen-year-old uncle did not die at Starówka, or in Mokotów, but at Bidula near Dobry, and not up against the wall where there are now memorial plaques and flowers, but in a wood at the bottom of a trench, at a place peasant children keep well away from. (*Życie ideologiczne*, p. 98)

Grynberg does not describe the concept of fatherland and of national belonging in the sense in which these are normally experienced. They are philosophical constructs created by him during his search for identity in his disintegrated autobiography and disintegrated Jewish world. Jews no longer have a Polish fatherland: the surviving castaways create a different form of culture in the United States and a different one in Israel. In the story 'Nieznajomy' ('The Stranger') he wonders if 'he could live in a place where there were no old houses'. (*Ekipa 'Antygona'* p. 70). The paradoxical process of Jewish acculturation in Israel has also been the subject of Hemar's reflections:

> I am increasingly troubled by the thought that this strangest of the world's nations is threatened by the strangest of dangers. It is threatened – in its own state, on its own land – with denationalisation, with losing everything which for centuries constituted its face and character, essence and charm. Just one more generation of *Sabras*? And another twenty, another thirty years, and all the old people will have died out, everyone from Europe, everyone from Vienna and Lwów, from Paris and Warsaw, from Dresden and Frankfurt, everyone for whom literature was the literature of all civilisations, whose own languages were Polish and German, French and Russian, everyone who was a catalyst, who was at home in the wings of theatres, in the corridors of parliament, in the politics of the whole world, in its poetry, its editorial offices, film studios, in its philosophy, its scheming and intrigues, and its psychoanalysis – when their children and grandchildren come together on this bit of the Asiatic peninsula as a new, small Levantine nation, speaking the hermetic language of the East, using hermetic letters in papers and books read from right to left, when this happens and it is finally realised, when Jews are made into Israelis, it will be a great shame, an irreparable loss.[12]

The hero of the novel *Kadisz* collects data on people he knew for the Museum of Names in Jerusalem: he recreates the world which disappeared before his eyes. The information he can gather is as meagre as if it were ancient history. He can rarely give a date of birth and only an approximate date of death. He gives names in three languages: Hebrew, Yiddish and Polish. No one will ever address another with the Polish version again; no one will say Jankiel, Abramek, Dwojra. His mother searching further back in her memory can augment the list with more names, but they seem suspended in the air; some people she remembers she cannot name. 'Her non-memory – the hero states – filled me with fear, for I saw in it a manifestation of an annihilation without end.' (*Kadisz*, p. 39) This annihilation is the preservation of silence about Jews, the destruction of traces of their significant presence in Poland. In 1957 the hero could still look at property registers for traces of his ancestors. When he asked, in the seventies, if he could look through them, they could no longer be found.

The most moving parts of the novel are the pages dedicated to his mother, his love for her, helpless before the final death sentence of a doctor's diagnosis. She and a small circle of the Nowy Dwór Society are the hero's last links with the world of authentic Jewry which consists, above all, of people declaring and nurturing the human virtues of solidarity, compassion and sincerity, brought from their little Mazovian town.

> Red Indians from the Nowy-Dwór tribe, from the past, of whom apart from ourselves nothing is left, moved and gesticulated in a natural and unpretentious way, using warm, unpretentious words. They were old and I knew that before long I would be left alone: they understood this and so sat close to me, silently in a warm, family silence. (*Kadisz*, p.101)

Grynberg describes this Society as castaways on a boat who have escaped catastrophe, but are now threatened by a new danger. The boat is adrift on an alien, threatening sea, ruled by money. Horror at the nihilism of the modern world and modern man who has lost his sense of a system of basic moral values was an earlier dominant motif in *Poems from America*.

The hero's half-brother is the most ruthless and American of them; he can function according to modern techniques of manipulation and even employs them with those nearest to him. He is already a non-Jew for the little group who came to say kaddish at his house. The world of the past which is shared by the mother and hero is completely alien to American Jews. The rabbi preparing the eulogy of the deceased asks questions positively grotesque, because of their inappropriateness to the true content of her life. The resulting portrait is made up of the most banal features: she was a good housewife, liked growing flowers, loved her grandchildren.

His mother's death is, so to speak, a double tragedy for the hero, in the sense that death touches everyone who has lost a loved one, but also in a wider, existential sense:

> I felt fear. She was my last living link with that world which was truly ours. When she was gone, I was the only one left out of all those who had been annihilated, together with the records of their birth, existence and death. (*Kadisz*, p. 39)

His mother was the one person with whom he had any real ties; her death also freed him from *all* apparent and supposed ties. He had no brother, wife, or place on earth, and was suspended in a void:

I realised that I did not like this new house, but unlike my daughter I did not want to return to the old one either. (*Kadisz*, p. 142)

His new situation is thus the incarnation of the stock theme of the Eternal Wandering Jew.

A sentence appears for the first time in this novel which somehow brings to an end, even nullifies his attempt to call his Jewish-Polish past to account. In all his works, the question of his father's death recurs obsessively. Grynberg had said till now that he had died by a Polish hand, and thus the responsibility for his death fell on the whole nation. Now, in a discussion with his step-father, who remembered that his father had been killed by a Pole, the narrator contradicts him by saying that *Poles* saved his mother, but his father was killed by a *robber* [my italics, J.W.].

Grynberg's work, like that of other writers who base their view of the world on their Jewish descent, is linked with the need to find in the past what he had lost by being deprived of his original *milieu*. In no other writer, however, has the philosophical concept of rootedness, which Simone Weil has discussed, appeared so clearly in literary form. Let us first quote two thoughts of Simone Weil's:

> Rootedness is, perhaps, the most important and most necessary known need of the human soul. At the same time, this need is difficult to describe. The human being has roots, if he truly, actively and naturally takes part in the existence of the community which treasures some of the past and is aware of the future. Participation should be natural, that is it should occur automatically from place, birth, surroundings, occupation. Each human being needs various roots. He receives almost everything in his moral, intellectual and spiritual life because of the *milieux*, of which he is a natural part.[13]

Further:

> The future brings us nothing, gives us nothing. It is we who, in order to construct it, must give it everything, give it our very lives. But in order to give, one must possess, and we possess no other life, no other life-blood, no other treasure than that which the past has left us, absorbed, comprehended, re-created by us. Of all the needs of the human soul the most vital is the need for the past.[14]

The image of a growing tree and rootedness appears twice in Grynberg's prose:

> ... in Warsaw, our base [The Jewish Theatre] was inexpensive, made from a barracks in the ruins of the former palace of the former

Jew Kronenberg. In these ruins, behind our barracks, there was a chimney, and out of it – nourished by the fertile ashes – grew a little tree. This chimney and the tree growing out of it could be seen from a distance above the façade of our single-storeyed barracks. It was our emblem and most visible monument. (*Życie osobiste*, pp. 36–7)

In *Ojczyzna*, however, the hero visiting his ancestors' place of birth notes:

The place where my grandfather lived is overgrown with grass, and a boy in a school cap was grazing his cow there. Some chipped crockery from the burnt-out fire was lying in the grass, and there was bare brickwork where the stove had been. A small tree was growing out of the brickwork as out of the chimney, nourished by the old ashes. One must know what one grows out of, I thought with a smile. One must know what one grows out of and where one stands. And everything else will recur by itself. ('Ojczyzna', '*Kultura*' (1971), 1/2:73)

Grynberg's concept of rootedness, as expressed in this image, modifies that of Simone Weil for whom it was growth in time and space. With Grynberg only history is left, for all the survivors as well as for himself: it represents salvation for him, but only a partial salvation. This is why he refers constantly to the past and the need to preserve the traces and consciousness of the Jews' particular fate, which are beginning to fade on a universal scale through universalisation. He comments ironically, 'Everyone suffered, not only Jews. It is not only Christians who grasp this opiate, but Jews as well. For the former it acts as an escape from guilt, for the latter from fear.'[15] Consequently he demands that a clear distinction be made between the concentration camps and the death camps meant for Jews, and he rejects the wrongful appropriation of the term 'Holocaust' and its use to cover all Nazi crimes:

There have always been attempts to murder Jews, but never *all* Jews. This is the meaning of the Holocaust and the meaning which the morphology of the word clearly indicates. It is not a question of numbers or proportions, but of dimensions, of the extent, quality and range of this crime.[16]

And he also opposes erecting plaques at the places where Jews were murdered with the epithet: 'To citizens of Poland ...'. The Jews, he insists, did not die for that citizenship, but because they were Jews.

## NOTES

1 Quotations from Grynberg's works according to the editions: *Ekipa 'Antygona'* (Warsaw, 1963); *Żydowska wojna* (Warsaw, 1965); *Zwycięstwo* (Paris, 1969); *Życie ideologiczne* (London, 1975); *Życie osobiste* (London, 1979), *Kadisz* (Cracow, 1987).
2 '*100 słów*', '*Walka Młodych*', 1968, no. 3.
3 H. Grynberg, *Prawda nieartystyczna* (Berlin, 1984), pp. 23–24.
4 J. Iwaszkiewicz, '*Wojna żydowska*,' *Życie Warszawy*, 1966, no. 105.
5 H. Grynberg, *Prawda nieartystyczna*, p. 111.
6 Ibid., p. 8.
7 J. Perle, *Nr 4580*, in *Archiwum Ringelbluma. Getto warszawskie lipiec 1942 – styczeń 1943*, ed. R. Sakowska (Warsaw, 1980).
8 H. Grynberg, *Prawda nieartystyczne*, p. 48.
9 H. Grynberg, '*Samokrytyka*,' *Kultura* (Paris, 1976), no. 6, p. 130.
10 J. P. Sartre, *Rozważania o kwestii żydowskiej* (Warsaw, 1957), p. 95.
11 Ibid., s. 96.
12 M. Hemar, '*Świstki z podróży*', in *Awantury w rodzinie* (London, 1967), p. 275.
13 S. Weil, '*Zakorzenienie*', in *Wybór pism* (Paris, 1958), p. 247.
14 Ibid., p. 253.
15 H. Grynberg, *Prawda nieartystyczna*, p. 71.
16 Ibid., p. 71.

# LIFE IN NAZI-OCCUPIED WARSAW

## THREE GHETTO SKETCHES
Jan Marek Groński

### THE GHETTO JESTER

The flagstones of Shakespearean dramas, slippery with blood, echo the footsteps of a jester as he strolls across. Without the jester the tragedy would not be complete. He can see far beyond the backdrop. An obscene gesture is more telling than mere words. We are all admirers of the performance of Shakespearean jesters. Only the most famous of them all – Yorick – does not care for popularity; his entry into the play is not designed to make the audience burst into applause. His skull, picked up from the graveside by Prince Hamlet, belongs to the sphere of the shadows. It is through Hamlet's recall that his antics and witticisms are brought back to life. There was a time when these reflected contemporary life; the whole world found a reflection in the mirror of his laughter.

Now only his rotting skull remains – a familiar sight for multitudes of theatregoers. The jester who played on the stage marked out by the wall surrounding the Warsaw ghetto cannot even boast a grave of his own, let alone his bodily remains. The face of a man, eyes set wide apart, look back from a faded photograph. Mischief and professional arrogance clearly lurk in those eyes, which come to life when an audience gathers around him.

Houdini, the magician and renowned eccentric, looks very much the same on the photograph taken in 1926 shortly before he was due to be lowered in a tightly shut wooden box onto the bottom of the swimming pool in the New York Shelton Hotel where he was supposed to remain without air for an hour. Houdini, as a show business personality, was celebrated by many authors – Doctorow paid him special tribute in one of his novels. The showman from behind the ghetto wall has no biographer.

Nobody seems to know where he was born or what he did for a living before he ceased to be an anonymous person and became an institution as a street commentator. Not a single line was put down on paper. His dicta circulated by word of mouth, sometimes slightly distorted or modified according to taste. Whatever has survived was what was recorded by diarists. Remarkably, both the ghetto's mayor, Adam Czerniakow, and the great historian and archivist Emanuel Ringelblum refer to the man without giving him a name.

The ghetto jester's family name was Rubinsztajn. Simply Rubinsztajn. His first name had vanished, evaporated. There were scores of Rubinsztajns and Rubinsteins behind the ghetto wall, but no-one would ever have confused this one with anybody else. They used to say: 'Rubinsztajn said ...' – and that was enough. Everybody knew him. They knew he was mad. And as a madman he was free to look at events through his own peculiar perspective and express his views. He was immune because he was certifiable. Even the German sentries were amused by his antics.

Rubinsztajn must have been truly crazy, otherwise he would have been petrified by the armed 'supermen'. They could have put an end to his show with a single shot or a kick or a blow of a butt. He would approach closely without apparent fear. He would then taunt them. He changed their role of participants in murder into spectators of a street show. In a street show the clown traditionally picks on members of the audience in the front row; he insults them, makes fun of them. The rule is: however aggressive and unsavoury clown's behaviour becomes, the audience must remain passive, feigning amusement. To respond aggressively would be to recognise the clown as one's equal; sitting it out maintains the status quo. The show will soon be over; after all the clown is only playing a role. But Rubinsztajn's show was necessary if only to bring back a bit of colour to the dreary streets and a fleeting smile to people's gloomy faces. It is true, the laughter is that of a madman. The laughter of a lunatic, for only a lunatic would have the courage to laugh so close to the guardhouse, a spot where life and death were held in the balance.

Part of Rubinsztajn's popularity was due to his nonchalance in approaching the German sentries. In the situation when the very sight of a guard's uniform made one's heart miss a beat the jester remained cool and unconcerned. How strong the fear of the uniform was is illustrated in a verse in which Władysław Szlengel, the ghetto poet and satirist expressed his dream: 'He would pull on his dinner jacket, squeeze on his top hat and then slowly stroll across towards the sentries. Dressed up in his dinner jacket and top hat, nostalgic props belonging to his former life, he would feel a free man again.'

Rubinsztajn's rags passed for a dinner jacket, his broken peaked cap for a top hat. Dressed like this he would proceed to tempt fate; ruthless and cunning. When not sufficiently rewarded, he would stop in front of a richly dressed shop window and announce that if they didn't pay up, he would shout 'down with Hitler'.

Can a man who played the fool at what was, in fact, the funeral of tens of thousands of Warsaw Jews be regarded as mad? It is not easy to say. How are we to differentiate between madness and normality in a world created by hideous insanity? What is the norm and what the departure therefrom? Who has the right to pronounce? Those whose ashes are scattered in Treblinka, Sobibor and Auschwitz? We, who are still unable to encompass the everyday reality of that time, composed of fear, despair, hope and resignation?

This everyday reality deformed the psyche of the victims. Adam Czerniakow makes no reference to this in his diaries. The mayor was far too proud to dwell on his own humiliation The following anecdote was related by Marceli Reich Ranicki, at the time an official interpreter at the Judenrat office:

The Germans once ordered Mayor Czerniakow to arrange for the delivery of a chamber pot made of solid gold. The item was handmade in the ghetto workshops and duly delivered at the appointed time. After all pre-war Warsaw was renowned for its craftsmen and goldsmiths.

If Rubinsztajn was not really mad, then he did play his part. Lunacy provided a suitable form for the message he wanted to convey. Being certifiable gave him freedom from censorship and self-censorship. Everyone would put his rantings down to his insanity, seeking neither logic nor consistency in what he proclaimed. If Rubinsztajn did have a strategy it was certainly a good one as the numerous accounts of his street shows bear witness. He was seen as somebody unique, at the same time, typical. Collective consciousness finds expression in the voice of the madman. Supposing that Rubinsztajn's insanity was not pretended but genuine, it makes little difference in the end. Fluctuations between hysterical elation and extreme depression are clinical signs of psychosis. Being genuinely mad would not make any difference to the matter: as Stanisław Lec observed, 'Jokes told by lunatics often have surprisingly sober punch lines'.

But it was not the jokes and puns that made Rubinsztajn go down in the ghetto's history. Every showman worth his salt has some sort of idiosyncrasy that will identify him as the author of a particular quip or catchphrase. It could be virtually anything, a gesture, a tone of voice or a chorus line in a song. The turn of phrase, even though it passed into common parlance, was always connected with its original author.

Rubinsztajn's most famous saying was the phrase 'alle glaich' – all are equal. It may sound banal, but it must be remembered that it was first used in the spring of 1941. This apparently innocuous saying carried, in fact, the coded message: equal in death; in death worldly distinctions are worthless. Motel Pinkert, the funeral director, knew his business when he opened a new branch of his funeral parlour at Smocza Street. He offered a proper funeral service with all the trimmings including coffin and hearse. More and more corpses, however, were being picked up daily from the pavements, dumped on to a cart and driven away to the cemetery for burial in a mass grave. A wooden shed was stacked full of them, piled up high under the tarpaulin, awaiting their turn. The Germans began to visit the shed which quickly became a kind of a tourist attraction: there were even family outings, and snapshots were taken. Eventually the authorities banned the visits as they were allegedly affecting the morale of the troops.

'Alle glaich', shouted Rubinsztajn, pointing to the richly embroidered hearses of Pinkert's funeral fleet. 'Alle glaich', he mocked, waving his finger at the hunger-swollen legs of the corpses sticking out from under old newspapers – that makeshift shroud of the poor.

Black humour is not confined to high abstraction. It can easily mirror reality itself, exposing its absurdity. Rubinsztajn's mockery was aimed at the ideological fallacy, the travesty of the noble ideals and beliefs of humanity. Democratized death – that's what remained of the principle of equality, from its slogans, utopias, rhetorics.

Rubinsztajn's popularity reaches new heights, noted Ringelblum in May 1941, 'The Melody Palace has recently opened the new show 'ALLE GLAICH'. Rubinsztajn's jibe had caught on and had become the chorus line in a popular cabaret show. The show opened on the very same stage where, not long before, a beauty contest had been held. One should not be dismayed by this. After all, the ghetto community had to familiarise itself with the new reality where death was omnipresent. There was no other way – life had to go on.

The mocking of death would propitiate the change of fortune. That's why the vagabond Rubinsztajn, running through the streets shouting 'Alle glaich, alle glaich', commanded more interest than did the Wise Men. People would pay more attention to Rubinsztajn than to the rabbis who prophesied the imminent end of the war and Hitler's fall. They knew the Germans were not about to run away turned into rabbits by the sound of a magic horn, as one of the prophets from Kozienice had proclaimed.

Another catchphrase attributed to Rubinsztajn again dealt with the subject of death. Only the themes ever present in the consciousness of the public caught on in the street show. Rubinsztajn came up with an apt expression to illustrate the departure of an inhabitant of the ghetto – It's not death itself but its mechanism which is shown. Death came to take what is most valuable – the food ration coupons, the most precious possession. Rubinsztajn was saying 'Give up the coupons, give up the coupons to death.' This says it all.

'Rubinsztajn's concept caught on immediately' – noted Ringelblum. Indeed, the whole ghetto was soon resounding with Rubinsztajn's rhyme about not wanting to give up the coupons:

> The coupons, oh the coupons
> I won't give them up
> All I want is a scrap of bread
> That's all I need.

The jester with a madman's licence is not a mere joker; he speaks to the condition of the oppressed and the condemned. The catchphrases have little to do with the tradition of joking in the face of adversity. Far more with the heroes of the plays of Samuel Beckett where the protagonists are but one more element in the process of the decomposition of the world. Beckett places his heroes in terminal situations; nothing more can happen to them which would exceed their present condition. Human torsoes, bodies sinking into sand, do not try to make their jesting amusing. They mumble their lines out of force of habit. They care little for the niceties. This much they know. It's the rubbish heap and the empty skies, this is the end of the cycle and grey, leafless stumps of trees, bits of rubble is all that remains to serve as a source of laughter. Only laughter helps to recognise the landscape of destruction. Only laughter hovers over the wasteland.

Rubinsztajn's sayings and jokes, taken out of their context, lose their impetus; they become language games. Their comic force sprung from the clash between Polish and Yiddish. Moreover, a thing as volatile and transient as a joke is ill-suited for the written medium.

When the Red Army reconquered Rostov on the Don, Rubinsztajn would shout: 'Rosh-tov, Rosh-tov'. The slightly twisted name of the Russian town acquired a brand new meaning: 'a good beginning'.

Military operations on the Balkans inspired another witty comment: 'It all began in the corridor and now it's gonna end up on the balcony.'

At the time when the ghetto was riven by the death transports which on occasions could be postponed through bribery, Rubinsztajn advised, 'Better get rid of your last shirt (Westl) than to acquire a coffin (Kestl).

When Lejkin, diminutive chief of ghetto police, introduced a ban on peaked caps, Rubinsztajn quipped: 'Lejkin banned visors because his knees would get bruised on his as he walked...'

One day a rumour started (subsequently substantiated by the investigators of Nazi crimes) that soap was being manufactured out of the body-fat of those already exterminated. Whether or not people really believed the story, it became the subject of many jokes which served to devalue the horror. Rubinsztajn was not slow to comment: 'We shall meet in the shopwindow. We'll be made into ordinary grey soap but the bigwigs will be the de luxe toilet soap'.

On another occasion he would ask the public: 'Who's gonna survive the war?' and then answer it confidently to himself: 'Judenrat, number 13 and myself'. (Number 13 refers to 13 Leszno Street – headquarters of the Gestapo). 'Why them? That's obvious. And why me? Well, after all I am a loony...'

It is clear from his pronouncements that Rubinsztajn detested those who even then constituted the upper crust. The upheaval of the times failed to nullify social distinctions. What is more, the rich were no longer separated from the poor; they moved within each other's orbit. The owners of smart flats in Sienna Street brushed past a throng of beggars in the streets. The wives of the industrialists, merchants, doctors and lawyers frequently found it quite difficult to bring their shopping home intact. 'Snatchers' were commonplace; little kids would snatch away anything that could quell the hunger. Very shortly the shopping baskets with a solid wire mesh lid were introduced and the ghetto cabaret show Sztuke immediately picked on this ingenious invention featuring a well-dressed lady holding an egg on a chain.

Among Rubinsztajn's audience there were many from the professional classes thoroughly assimilated, with no links with Jewish culture, language or religion. This madman, this lunatic, suddenly brought back to them an echo of their past. But the bulk of his audience was always the poor, the lower strata of society. His view, from the bottom, typical for the Jewish humour, was what they understood best. Rubinsztajn was an anti-hero, mocking the high and mighty. The luckless, ill-starred fellow is a key figure in Jewish folklore. Looking at the person in rags gave them a feeling of superiority. They felt they still had a long way to go, after all they retained their common sense, their powers of anticipation and planning. So they still had some chance of survival while this vagrant could only be saved by a miracle. They still felt that it was good that Rubinsztajn was there – someone had to be out of his mind to set off the insanity of those days, their bloody absurdity.

Every ghetto community had its Rubinsztajn, says Lucjan Dobroszycki, a historian of the period. And in every ghetto the jester and the lunatic perished along with his audience, with all those who to the very last minute believed that their life-long experience would prevent them from making a false move and perishing in the extermination camps. They still believed in it when tightly packed into the lime-dusted cattle-trucks on their final journey.

### THE MAGIC LANTERN OF DREAMS

The sadness of discarded objects – a shoe which has lost its owner, a badly chipped saucepan, a pair of broken spectacles and the silence which hovers over ruins ... These are the images still to come. After ...

The ghetto was awhirl with throngs of people confined within a maze of narrow streets. It was filled with sounds of people shouting, wailing, stamping their feet, imploring, cursing. This is how eyewitnesses remembered it and wrote about it.

Only Curzio Malaparte, an officer of the Italian Army visiting the closed District, saw it as a zone of silence. This may have been due to the psychological shock he sustained embarking on this voyage of discovery – it was, in fact, a voyage in time – a walled-up district in the heart of the modern city, a throw-back to the Middle Ages with all its inhabitants wearing armbands emblazoned with the bright yellow star of Zion, all just a couple of hundred yards away from the posh Europejski Hotel where he had checked in as a correspondent of a friendly nation. Life behind the wall was of our age – the age of totalitarianism, although it also echoed a much more distant past.

Malaparte was touring a world in which the sudden appearance of Golem would have come as no surprise. Though it would have been a degraded Golem – wearing an armband with the yellow star of Zion. It would have been a Golem out of the ghetto poems, a fugitive, a man living off scraps, hiding in rubbish dumps . . .

But could the Golem, a helpless creature, become the stuff of legend? The legends of the Warsaw ghetto were different. We know little of its literature which was passed by word of mouth, in whispers. And yet the naive folk tales give us a glimpse of the psyche of the community turned into a vast amorphous mass.

### *The Legend of the Girl With the Plaits*

It begins like scores of other stories, exceptional and commonplace. It happened in many towns all over Poland, claims the narrator. A Jewish girl was queueing for bread. Suddenly a German appeared and told the Jews to step out. The girl ignored him. Someone pointed her out to the German. The German snipped off her plaits as a punishment. He laughs with derision, and so does the informer. The girl looked at them defiantly, without shedding a tear. 'My hair will grow back before you will see the end of this war,' she said.

### *The Legend of the Coming of the Messiah*

This story takes place in Kraków, for a change. At the graveyard beside the city synagogue there is a grave of the 16th century Talmud scholar – Moses Isserles, at one time the head of Kraków's Yeshiva. Every year the Jews gathered there on the anniversary of his death for prayers, seeking his intercession on the traditional scraps of paper. On that day, says the legend, the crowd of worshippers was bigger than ever: they had been ordered to abandon their homes and to move to the ghetto in Podgorze. Seeing the large crowd around, the Germans grew suspicious that this was the site of buried treasure. They dug up the grave but found nothing.

But then one of the Torah scholars came across a note in one of the old folios predicting that before the coming of the Messiah Jews would be expelled from Kraków. Before this the persecutors would dig up the grave of Isserles looking for gold. That was the sign. The Messiah might float down from the skies, or maybe, with the heavy step of a wanderer, shaking off the dust of the Milky Way from his sandals . . .

There were even those in the Warsaw ghetto who swore to have seen this prophecy written in the non-existent book.

* * *

An exercise in imagination: a magic lantern parlour on Smocza Street. Murky interior, thick, purple curtains – admission price: 20 groszy. Only then can you sit on the chair and look through the magic lens. In the background – sweet sounding melody of the Viennese waltz played on an ancient wind-up gramophone, then a tango, a hit from a pre-war review. You don't sing a tango, the cognoscenti maintain, you sob it. The pictures slowly moved in the peep hole – the lust thicket of tropical jungle giving way to the arid vastness of the sandy dunes in a desert, snow-dusted mountain peaks to be succeeded by sweeping panoramas of great foreign cities where there is no curfew and no blackout. This world appeared close and tangible. For a mere 20 groszy one could escape to the other side of the wall, beyond reality. End of the show – back to Smocza Street, one of the many streets in the closed quarter.

'Candy bars! Candy bars! Only 10 groszy! Softer than butter! Sweeter than sugar! Real bargain! Only 10 . . .'

'Blini! Blini! Only 40 groszy! Cheaper than bread . . .'[1]

'Jews! Don't let them walk over your heads – buy thick combs! Only 80 groszy each!'

Along with the tradesmen's shouts, curses abounded; new curses ingeniously fitting the reality:

'May your skin be the colour of your yellow armband!'

'Let Heaven remember you the way you have to remember to put on your armband!'

'I wish you what I wish you know who. Let Hitler's soup be like the one from the soup kitchen!'

'Let his star shine like our electricity plant.'

'May you fall into the hands of the Jewish police!'

Some escaped into the dream-world of magic lantern parlours, the majority, however, relied on memory to project their dreams on to everyday reality:

'Oh, Lord, may I become a fly so that I could eat what is displayed in the shopwindows . . .'

'Oh, Lord, may I become the son-in-law of the soup kitchen manager . . .'

'Oh Lord, may I now have as much bread as I used to have cakes.'

* * *

Still on Smocza Street. A thirteen year old street busker, Szlojme Elbojm, is onto his most popular number: *Girls*

> All girls the world over
> Know one thing for sure:
> No matter how much money
> Their husbands bring home
> It is never enough.
> But when a husband knows the score
> He will grab a cane
> And beat his wife
> Till she says:
> My dear, you're always right
> And I wish you well of it.

It follows a similar pattern for a few stanzas and ends unexpectedly like this:

> I would like to do the same
> I would show them what I'm made of
> But my strength
> Has ebbed away.

Another hit from the repertoire of street buskers: *Money*

> May our smugglers
> Always be on top form
> And may their luck
> Always hold
> May the Jerries go blind
> Whenever they spot them
> Money, money, money,
> The best of worldly things.
> Have no money, mate?
> You won't last a day
> You can only jump
> On Pinkert's wagon
> And be taken straight
> To the graveyard
> Money, money, money
> The best of worldly things.

This uncomplicated philosophy of the ghetto street stated a simple fact. Money could buy you time, prolong your survival. The old prayers were replaced by this imprecation:

'Oh, Lord, don't let it last as long as Jewish endurance.'

The street buskers (the most notorious of them all – fourteen year old Jakub Lejb Solnicki) always on the move, always dashing around, made the most of their relative freedom. 'The air could not be censored' – observed Michal Borwicz. In *The Jewish Tango* the singer assures his audience that 'the day will come when we shall all dance on the Germans' graves'. Another one pronounced: 'and yet we shall say kaddish for Hitler one day'.

The street songs sometimes carried encoded news bulletins; they signalled information not otherwise available to the ghetto inhabitants. 'Great frost approaches from Siberia.' The audience around the singer understood what he meant. They picked up the clues. For instance, a stanza from *Boots Worn to Shreds*:

> Half an inch thick was a slice of bread
> And kindling was weighed by the ounce
> It was all done for the common good
> Or so mighty Judenrat declared.

But it was not the actual commentary that made the street buskers so popular. It was their ability to bring back the familiar images of pre-war city life. They led their audience down memory lane, switching to the old hits, giving new meaning to old metaphors and clichés.

The chorus line from *When you come back after so many long years* evoked the image of one's home left behind outside the ghetto wall; *The Three Letters*, a sentimental song, was no longer a song about a ditched girlfriend, it was a letter mailed to oneself back in the past. The famous tango *The Last Sunday* brimmed with memories of the last Sunday of August 1939. The audience quite often participated in these shows supplying rhymes, prompting the long forgotten lines . . . For many, those sentimental songs offered access to the world of fantasy. As vivid as for them as the images in the magic lantern show.

The author of the catchy lyrics to many pre-war hits – Andrzej Wlast (Gustaw Baumritter) – himself ended up behind the wall with an armband on his sleeve. He was one of the most important personalities in pre-war show-business. He was derided for his rhymes, his cheap effects, for taking liberties with grammar and syntax. His craftsmanship as a lyric writer was of a dubious value and some even hailed him as the King of Musical Trash. Nonetheless, he was accepted as an epitome of success. People talked enviously of his earnings, his mistresses, luxury cars and skill in business. In the Forbidden District he became a tragic figure. Without his shows he was totally lost. He could no longer invent jokes, puns and quips. The death of his parents pushed him into the depths of depression. On the verge of madness, haggard, with burning eyes, he no longer amused; he repelled the public which was seeking a few hours of escape. In the end, he had to give up.

'But life goes on, my friends' – he declared in one of his last poems describing everyday life in the Warsaw ghetto.

Andrzej Wlast was swallowed up in the big round-ups of July 1942, abandoned, unprotected, packed into the cattle truck on the way to the happy ending.

It is difficult to imagine what torture it must have been for Wlast in the ghetto to hear snippets of his famous songs, coming to him from all quarters.

'In the summer of '42 a famous magician was performing in the streets of the Warsaw ghetto' – this was the introduction to a ballad which circulated in the ghetto in hundreds of copies, passed from hand to hand and became a part of performances – open and clandestine – of many literary evenings. What new tricks could a magician show an audience? Every member of the audience had himself to be a magician in order to survive. The author of the review called 'The Bird' treated the traditional acts like juggling, fire-eating, sword-swallowing as nothing out of the ordinary. It was the last act which was startling. A bird flies out from the top hat, rises above the clouds and soars freely over the walls.

> Into the skies the bird has flown
> Fleeing the magician's sorrowful gaze
> And into the blue it has long gone
> With crowds below in tearful daze.

It was this particular image that lent the ballad its enormous appeal. Many learned it by heart and recited it on social occasions. The ballad epitomised their dreams. Flight into the skies above the earth to freedom. The author conveyed the simple truth: dreams have wings . . .

Copies of the ballad survived. It was eventually included in an anthology with the accompanying note: 'author unknown'. The authorship was later established, though. It was apparently written by an eighteen year old. He survived the war and today lives in Warsaw, not far from the former ghetto wall.

An anecdote from 1942. Three Jews are discussing their plans for the first day of freedom.

'When it's all over I'll buy myself ten loaves of bread, two pounds of butter and then I'll eat and eat and eat . . .'

'And I'll go on a tour round the world to see all the cemeteries of Hitler's soldiers.'

'I'll just get myself a pushbike and go on a tour round Germany.'

'And some tour it will be' – comment his more ambitious friends – 'a pleasure for just half an hour . . .'

Not always were people's dreams associated with the future, frequently they reverted to the past. Sometimes they were rooted in the present.

Diana Blumenfield, an actress performing in many ghetto theatres had in her repertoire a moving *Ballad of a Parcel* written by Henryka Lazowert. The ballad tells about a starving family begging for a food parcel from their relatives. Neither those in Galicia nor uncle Salomon from America seem to be able to help them in their predicament. Suddenly, a miracle happens on Krochmalna Street: a parcel arrives for the grandmother, the initiator of the desperate letters, from someone who once knew her. Although many years had passed he still remembered the little town where both the Poles and Jews lived together.

> Bustling with people Krochmalna at noon
> The postman delivering their parcel
> Just as the hearse trundled by
> Taking grandmother on her final journey.

Isolation, loneliness, the futility of all efforts to bring succour gave rise to visions and dreams, fed not on fantastic improbabilities but on what was for others beyond the ghetto wall everyday reality: only a few hundred yards away, and a whole eternity.

It was possible to make a phone call to the other side.

The hero of Władysław Szlengel's poem *Telephone* indulges in a strange telephone 'conversation' with the speaking clock on the Aryan side of the wall. The recorded voice becomes the voice of all those who inhabit his memory, the speaking clock listens patiently to the ghostly monologue . . .

Let us go back to the magic lantern parlour on Smocza Street. The more hungry the ghetto inhabitants became, the more they wished for escape to exotic places, the further away the better. The fantasy was fed on images derived from cinema magazine illustrations, told by those who had or pretended to have been to such places. Images of the city on the other side of the wall did not quell their hunger for exotic places.

In Eldorado Theatre Dora Fakiel was singing *Black Jim on the Dancing Floor* while Sztuka, the very same venue where Andrzej Wlast failed to amuse the audience, successfully staged a fifteen-minute long musical hit *Her First Ball*. The music was composed by Władysław Szpilman and the lyrics were written by the already mentioned Władysław Szlengel. Every performance was ecstatically received. Wiera Gran, the first singer to perform it on stage, owes her success to this very hit. It made her a real star – the highest paid, separate dressing-room, all the trimmings.

An exercise in self-delusion: the circumstances in which the show was staged were forgotten; the show, the public, a normal theatrical event for ordinary people, not for a community condemned to death.

Years later, Gran wrote in a memoir:

'A little coffee shop with only casual custom suddenly became a sensation. Tables had to be booked days in advance. The huge demand exceeded all expectations.'

Why was *Her First Ball* such a success? Performed in a venue seating 200 people it echoed something very familiar from their former lives. It comprised variations on the waltz from the opera *Casanova* by Ludomire Rożycki, first staged in 1923. The waltz is first sung by the wife of the Prefect of Venice – Caton, a girlfriend of the seducer. *Caton Waltz* was in fact the only lively bit of the whole opera, and was soon included in the standard repertoire of the opera and operetta singers. Often it was performed as an orchestral piece. Everybody in the audience was familiar with it and was keen to supply the words.

The story line of the song borrows from the plot of the pre-war movie: *carnet du bal* in which the heroine finds the card with the names of her partners of long ago. She brings them back in her mind. This allows for the creation of five splendid characters.

It is said that Szlengel solved overnight the technical problems of staging the variety of scenes required by the score.

Szpilman could see that *Her First Ball* would appeal enormously to those imprisoned behind the ghetto wall if it took them on an exciting journey; hence the quick changes of rhythm and mood – from the rhumba to Tyrolean yodelling, from the moon over Tahiti to a familiar local landscape.

Just imagine the cabaret venue only yards from the German checkpoint. Wouldn't the following lines be like a powerful drug for the audience?

> Let me race the wind, let me win the race
> Let me see the world in a dreamlike daze
> Let me see Morocco
> And the Orinoco
> It feels so good to be alive
> See the world go slowly by
> Drinking bitter sweetness in the tropical night . . .

The bounty of nature, in contrast with what the inhabitants had – scanty grass, dying trees, listening to descriptions of palm trees, rippling water brought a lump to their throats. (In one of the lullabies a mother tries to explain to her son the meaning of the words like: forest, meadow, lush green grass, the smell of good earth.)

There are grounds to believe that the audience was moved most by the final chords which transformed the waltz by Rożycki into the one by Chopin.

Chopin's name is mentioned ostentatiously in the lyrics. The authors were aware of the consequences and bravely defied the ban on playing Chopin, the ban enforced equally rigorously on both sides of the wall. In the magic lantern of dreams Chopin was a fixed point for the memory, a link between the two separated parts of one city.

The café, Sztuka, at 2 Leszno Street. A sudden power failure. Why? A simple fault, an attempt to get a bribe for putting the lights on again? The Stuka waitresses were the prettiest girls in the ghetto, daughters of lawyers, doctors, businessmen. They were on first name terms with many of the patrons. Their job was not only a way of making a living as a continuation of their social life, the perpetuation of the little snobberies in the circles of the readers of *Wiadomosci Literackie* of the clientele of IPS café, of the lovers of the poetry of Tuwim, of the feuilletons of Boy and Słonimski. New names now appeared: the authors – Fokszanski, Szlengel, Teitelbaum. The hitherto unknown singer Pola Braun. The comedian Lipski – gingerhaired, squinting, irresistibly funny with his monologues spoken in the local Polish/Jewish dialect. And, last but not least, the pianists: Adolf Goldfeder and Władysław Szpilman – two virtuosi who, instead of performing in 'the capitals of Europe' were reduced to playing in front of the dying population of the ghetto. The main attraction of the show was the satirical news review. Such as:

> Daily worries – dump the lot
> Lucky coin in the slot
> Bunch of flowers, glass of juice
> Here comes your DAILY NEWS!!!

Still no lights. The carbide lamps had been placed around so as to cut short the unscheduled break. The shadows are dancing on the walls. In the background the pianist plays a waltz. Mina Tomkiewicz remembered this evening quite vividly:

'Wiera Gran, the favourite singer, saunters on to a small stage. A bit on the plump side, the hair swept back in a girlish fashion, dressed in a flowing crinoline with a low cut neckline . . .'

And we already know what follows, or at least, we think we do: the deep, throaty voice of the singer fills up the room:

> It's my first ever ball
> For sweethearts is this waltz

> It's my first ever ball
> A deeply cherished memory
> The waltzing throng but a brilliant blur
> The spinning walls, the whirling floor
> It's my first ever waltz
> It's my first ever ball

The next show was about to begin in the magic lantern parlour...

## A DAILY ALLOWANCE OF HOPE

How do jokes originate? Who is behind all those quips and witty comments? How do they soon become such common property, passed around, crossing frontiers and successfully adjusting to new cultural circumstances? These are obviously matters of debate.

Jokes of literary provenance reveal a fair amount of their historical background. They are devised by professionals who endeavour to imbue them with their own unique style – the vivid ribaldry of Rabelais, the heavy irony of Voltaire, the sharp paradoxes of Oscar Wilde, the dry sarcasm of Gogol.

But how can we trace the anonymous authors of so many of the other jokes in circulation, who do not seem to care much whether or not authorship is ascribed to them? Some were known to take great pains to obliterate the joke's origins altogether and succeeded so well that even the 'thought police' in the totalitarian states had to give up on ever tracking them down. Admittedly, people did get thrown in jail for passing around jokes which were openly detrimental to the regime, but this had nothing to do with the question of authorship; it was merely for publicising them. The true authors, who blended into anonymous crowds, were never caught or brought before any tribunal.

An anonymous joke could always sneak through borders and crawl under coils of barbed wire. It would always pop up in places where it was banned by decree. The experience of the Warsaw Ghetto is very instructive in this respect. The Nazi planners envisaged the ghetto wall as the ultimate seal around the Jewish district; it was designed to cut off all communication with the Aryan part of the city. The Ghetto was seen as a separate entity, its inhabitants completely alien to the rest of the town's population.

The plan was consistent with the most rudimentary laws of social psychology: the more obscure and inaccessible the object of public interest, the easier it is to promulgate certain myths about it, to stimulate animosity and prejudice. Its very inaccessibility would automatically, as it were, lend credibility to the picture of it that was propagated. The image promoted by the Nazi planners is well illustrated by posters and caricatures. The Jews are depicted as subhuman, a parasitic part of the human race rightly condemned to extermination.

An illuminating example – a poster equalising three things: Jews – lice – typhoid.

The very fact that jokes were still being passed around within the Ghetto walls, despite the ban, amounted to much more than just an expression of defiance. It was also a clear transgression of the policy of complete isolation of the Ghetto community, consistently pursued by the Germans. A joke entailed communication with the outside world, a running commentary on current events, a daily allowance of hope that stimulated the will to survive.

Were people aware at the time that the most optimistic anecdotes had hardly any roots in grim reality, being merely projections of their hopes and nothing more substantial than wishful thinking? They were, apparently, though that did not seem to have any bearing on their attitude. Quite often a simple question, 'What's new?' was answered with a quip: 'Can't you think something up yourself?' Rumour had it that the main news network was YIVA – *Yiden Vilen Azoy* : Jews Want it This Way. The competition was called JUDAS – Jewish Unrealistic Dreams and Self-delusions. The history of the Warsaw Ghetto can be reconstructed from the scraps of 'news bulletins' distributed by both agencies. Virtually no event passed without some apposite comment, from the very first days of the German occupation of Warsaw right up to the tragic end of the Ghetto. The German soldiers who entered the city in 1939 were immediately dubbed 'tourists' – short-term visitors who only popped in for a while – as everyone was expecting a joint Anglo-French military action on the Western front that would chase the Germans away. The first weeks of German rule in Warsaw brought the following story:

A German soldier, an avid reader of *Völkische Beobachter* and anti-semitic pamphlets whose knowledge of Jewish features is based solely on cartoons and caricatures, accosts a passer-by in the street who seems to look distinctly semitic and asks him: 'You're Jewish, aren't you?' To which the man replies sarcastically: 'And you think I look Turkish, don't you?' The dumbfounded soldier takes his reply at face value and says: 'Oh, so you're Turkish, I do apologise . . .'

That anecdote relates only to the initial, 'idyllic' period of German rule. The Nazis were slowly getting used to the idea that about half a million of 'untermenschen' just happened to be at their mercy. This species of the inferior race was portrayed in *Mein Kampf* as the source of all evil and perversion. The German Jews, long assimilated into German culture, were quite different from their East European brethren, who adhered to long-held traditions, both in appearance and orthodox religious ritual. Most Germans looked at their way of dressing (long black coats, fox fur caps with tails which marked out the rabbis, long beards and payes) as something utterly exotic and defying comprehension. They soon learned to recognise the inhabitants of Nalewki Street (traditionally the Jewish quarter, later to become the centre of the Warsaw Ghetto), and snipping off beards and payes soon became their favourite pastime. Punching passers-by in the face was simply a cheerful manifestation of high spirits.

The Polish-Jewish intelligentsia, however, was considerably more difficult to recognise in the street, for it did not fall into the over-simplified, picturesque category of shopkeepers, salesmen and small-time merchants portrayed by scores of anti-semitic brochures. Their language and clothing were no different from that of ethnic Poles. In order to facilitate ethnic differentiation, the Germans therefore decided to introduce compulsory armbands, which were also intended as an additional humiliation. The Jews wearing armbands emblazoned with the yellow Star of David were meant to feel like branded cattle; they were given the status of outlaws, banned from contact with the rest of the town's population. The death penalty was imposed on anyone defying this order.

'If you must buy this rag, better buy a clean one!' shouted small-time sellers of this new 'garment'. They were, in fact, doing a roaring trade. The armbands were made from all sorts of fabric, from the most luxurious to the plain, all designed to suit the individual budget. Some wit observed that 'Nalewki Street has much in common with Hollywood these days – stars wherever you like . . .'

In jail, a warden is beating up a Jew caught out not wearing an armband. 'I'll teach you to walk around without an armband, you rotten Yid,' shouts the warden.

'I am terribly sorry, but the order precisely stipulated that one may not wear an armband when at home and I do feel very much at home here . . .' interjects the Jew, between blows.

With rumours mounting that the Germans were planning to seal off the Jewish district and sever all communication with the rest of the city, the demand for papers showing 'Aryan' status soared. (The looming threat of genocide as Hitler's 'Final Solution' to the Jewish question, duly explained in *Mein Kampf*, had not even crossed anybody's mind at the time.) The forgery of relevant documents was soon a flourishing trade on a massive scale. There was a particularly big demand for Christian birth certificates. It has to be borne in mind, however, that although many selfless and righteous people did their best to help Jews, regardless of the high personal risk that this illicit activity entailed, many unprincipled hustlers and provocateurs seized the opportunity of making a quick buck by working for both sides. It was like striking gold – their customers quite willingly paid in dollars and jewellery.

Not surprisingly the wits soon started picking on this new social phenomenon: 'What is the 11th commandment that Moses left out? – Thou shalt baptize thy grandparents.'

They also claimed that Aryans could be divided into the horizontal and the vertical. The horizontal ones were, of course, those that had been carried into the church by their parents to be christened; the vertical ones went on their own.

When the Germans started implementing the long-planned eviction of Jews from the city centre and setting up the Ghetto (Jews were allowed only one suitcase each and were given far too little notice to have time to pack), some wits still managed to make light of it and came up with the following consolation: 'After the war we shall all be going on organised trips to Berlin. One of the attractions will be the guided tour "Let's Have one More Look at our Furniture".'

This witticism refers to the fact that the Jews were being openly robbed of their personal belongings. In due course, the Nazis would rob them of their lives as there would be nothing else left to take. Despite the oppressive and intimidating atmosphere, carefully stage-managed by the Germans so that it would develop in the Jewish community a Kafkaesque complex of guilt and fear of conviction by an unknown tribunal; and despite dramatically deteriorating living conditions and bleak prospects of survival, anonymous satirists managed successfully to expose to public ridicule Hitler's Aryan 'genius'.

The favourite setting for a Jewish joke was a tailor's workshop. A Jewish tailor is seen as the archetypal self-appointed folk philosopher who, for the sake of convenience, only masquerades as a tradesman. In his lifetime, he has seen too many celebrities with their trousers down, so to speak, to stoop to flattery.

The story has it that one day Hitler visited the Jewish tailor to have a suit made. The tailor measured him up and declared that he had bought just enough cloth for three suits. Hitler was clearly taken aback and said that other tailors were positive that it was hardly enough for one, even without a waistcoat. 'Well,' replied the tailor thoughtfully, 'you are clearly a very big man to them . . .'

'Work will sweeten up your life,' a German is trying to persuade a Jew, in another joke. 'Well, it's not for me then,' comes the reply, 'I don't really care much for sweets . . .'

The structure of that joke reflects not only mockery of the German propaganda machine geared to brainwash the meek and the naive into submission. It also hammers home the importance of pursuing survival tactics in all aspects of life. Those sort of jokes taught a vital scepticism towards all German promises and guarantees; they also drew heavily from the treasury of Jewish folk wisdom – that uniquely Jewish perception of reality which stems from centuries of hardship and persecution.

The jokes covered not only mundane matters of everyday existence. They also served as a running commentary on developments in the European theatre of war.

'The Germans have just made a search of one of the city synagogues,' another storyteller informs his audience. 'What were they after?' asks someone from the crowd. 'Well, apparently they were looking for Moses' walking-stick so that they could part the waters of the English Channel and step across to England without getting their feet wet.'

All major battlefields were always under the careful scrutiny of the witty commentators. Even the smallest set-back suffered by the German armies provided a glimmer of hope. When there weren't any in the offing, a quick scan of the obituaries would do nicely by way of a tonic. A simple 'killed in action' or 'fell for the Führer and the Fatherland' prompted the wits to dub them as 'mincemeat adverts' or 'fun pages'.

From the moral standpoint, that does indeed look dubious. After all, it was the fallen, the maimed and the injured who were the subject of their rejoicing. Were the Jews therefore really the bloodthirsty race portrayed in dark myths? Yet it has to be borne in mind that years of fascist persecution had eventually brought about this backlash of vindictiveness, burning hatred and an overwhelming wish for vengeance. The true evil of the fascist doctrine is its intrinsic ability to make all its followers ethically stunted and devoid of human emotion. Whoever had a close encounter with this ideology was contaminated for life. The black humour of Ghetto jokes also serves as a powerful indictment of this era.

The last years of pre-war Poland were not exactly an idyllic period for Jewish members of society, as the country was then troubled by ethnic unrest fomented by home-grown fascist sympathisers. Violence erupted at the universities; the immediate issue was the demand that Jewish students should not be allowed to share desks with their Aryan colleagues. Nor was incitement to pogroms unusual.

Despite the fact that nationalistic feelings had run extremely high at that time, it still seemed in retrospect like paradise compared to German rule in Warsaw. The following joke reflects the sentimental longing for the 'good old days' of the pre-war era: A Jew is laughing through his sleep. His wife turns on the bedside lamp and shakes him awake. 'What's going on? What are you laughing at?'

'I've just seen the poster calling on the government to "Send the Jews to Madagascar!" I've heard the students chanting "Down with the Ritual Slaughter!" and I've seen the prime minister giving his consent in parliament to the boycott of Jewish shops.'

'And all that made you laugh?' asks his wife incredulously.

'But can't you understand?' – he sits up in bed – 'it's our own people coming back!'

Horovitz and Moshele were nicknames given to Hitler and Mussolini respectively by those who thought up jokes. The nicknames served a dual purpose: they protected the authors of the jokes and also stripped the two leaders of their charisma, cutting them down to size, as it were.

The inseparable pair appear in scores of jokes and amusing anecdotes. One of the great Ghetto favourites:

The three leaders, Horowitz, Moshele and Stalovy (Joseph Stalin), meet for a conference. The place is then blown up by a bomb that has been planted. The inevitable question: who survived? – Humanity . . .

Mussolini seemed particularly liable to be the prime subject of public ridicule. His megalomaniac behaviour, predilection for grand poses and near-grotesque clumsiness made him an unrivalled favourite for many anecdotes.

At the time, Mussolini's Balkan campaign was far from successful and the wits seized the golden opportunity, coming up with this alleged quote from his cable to the Führer describing his military predicament in Greece.

'GREEKO BANDITO. TUTTO FINITO. MORALE – DITTO. NON CAPITO – BENITO?'

As another anecdote had it, once upon a time, two identical twins were born in Germany: Horovitz and Moshele. By mistake, they were swapped in hospital. As nobody could tell them apart, the advice of a rabbi was sought. The rabbi declared that whichever of them excreted first was bound to be Moshele . . .

Once, Moshele summoned all Italian Jews and asked them to help him escape from Egypt. Apparently they had managed it once before . . .

German air raids on London were greeted by the Ghetto wits with an ironic comment: it would work out much cheaper if the Germans bombed Berlin while the English bombed London themselves . . .

Hitler's military conquests of France, Holland, Belgium and Denmark, ominous as they must have appeared, were nevertheless acknowledged by the Ghetto community with a healthy dose of scepticism, reflected in the following anecdote:

Hitler steps off the train in a small Polish town and asks the Jew who just happens to be passing by if he could possibly lend him a 100-zloty note. The Jew digs into his wallet and hands over a note without a word.

'Aren't you worried that I might not give it back?' asks Hitler.

'Ah, Mr Hitler, what is the point of me worrying over a 100-zloty note if you will have to give back the whole of Europe one day?'

One of the anonymous anecdotes was honoured by being recorded in a widely acclaimed book, *Kaputt*. In its original version, supplied by a Jewish historian, it is set in the area of the would-be Warsaw Ghetto.

A Gestapo officer barges into the flat of a widow with a child. He carries out a thorough search of the premises and declares the confiscation of anything of value. The widow starts to despair. At that point, the Gestapo man decides to stage a little game. He promises not to take anything away on condition that her little son can guess which of his eyes is artificial. The sobbing boy points to his left eye straight away:

'How did you know?' asks the clearly surprised Gestapo officer. 'How did you guess that the left one is made of glass?'

'Because it has a human look about it,' promptly replies the kid.

In order fully to appreciate the work of a writer, one should first learn to appreciate the culture of his native country, according to folk wisdom. We must tune in to the voices of his childhood, soak up the landscapes of his youth, rise to the challenges of his mature years. Otherwise, our perception is conspicuously incomplete, superficial and lacking in the deeper insight that would allow us to grasp the merit of his work, to reach to the heart of the matter.

To understand the specific nature of Ghetto life and the type of humour it bred, one has to look at it from a somewhat different perspective. One has to acknowledge that the Warsaw Ghetto, apart from being the scene of Jewish martyrdom and extermination, was also a tightly-meshed fabric of everyday human life squeezed into the walled-up maze of narrow streets bustling with frantic activity. Its inhabitants would simply go about their daily business regardless of the circumstances, refusing to recognise the atrocious reality and seeking refuge in dreams. The Ghetto really meant not only the Umschlagplatz, sudden round-ups, Gestapo searches for those who holed themselves up in ingeniously camouflaged bunkers and behind false cupboard walls. It was not only numerous cases of deaths from starvation (incidents of cannibalism were reported), the looming spectre of Frankenstein – one of the particularly callous and sadistic German guards – but also the desperate and frequently futile attempts to adapt to this reality.

Life against all the odds – a salesman of party balloons on a street-corner in January 1941, another ingenious salesman offering prophylactics made of teats, women in wigs selling smuggled belly-pork on Krochmalna Street, the very location of many stories by I. B. Singer. Even at the time when nobody had any illusions left as to the Ghetto's future in Nazi hands, people were still learning foreign languages with great zeal. 'Millions of memorised new words and expressions had gone up through the smoke-stacks of the crematoria in the Nazi extermination camps,' Adolf Rudnicki, the survivor of the Holocaust, would later write. Theatres and cabaret shows were playing to full houses in the Forbidden District, and musical concerts and piano recitals were as popular as ever. A detail worth nothing: the ban on playing Aryan composers was not strictly observed in the Ghetto – Beethoven, Schubert, Bach and Mozart were simply introduced under made-up Jewish names. It was not unusual to introduce 'The Dream' by Schubert as by Chaim Blum, though part of the audience was at first strongly against this practice. There was also a marked revival of religiousness. Synagogues were full and so, for that matter, were the churches, as there were a great number of Catholic converts in the Ghetto community, some of whom had been well-assimilated into Polish cultural traditions for generations, and spoke no Yiddish. Many diarists describe Catholic services performed by priests wearing Ghetto armbands and giving Holy Communion to the similarly adorned congregation. A few blocks away, Rabbi Wajnberg presided over the orthodox Hasidic community that consisted of those evicted from small towns around Warsaw. His teachings proclaimed that the surrounding reality was totally unworthy of recognition and, as such, should be completely disregarded. Only true faith would deliver them from the evil of this world. God would stay the hand of the executioners and grind their vanity and arrogance into a fine dust.

Ghetto humour, feeding off all aspects of everyday reality, duly acknowledged the sudden upsurge in religious feeling in the community, responding to it with its usual scepticism. Jewish humour, in general, is not particularly given to mysticism and religious ecstasy; it is much closer to earth than heaven, to coin a phrase.

A Ghetto inmate is looking at the synagogue set alight by the Germans. He slowly averts his eyes and murmurs to himself: 'Let the Lord worry about it now . . .'

A man on his deathbed implores his relatives gathered around to fetch a Catholic priest. 'But why a priest, of all people?' they ask, clearly taken by surprise, some of them suspecting that he might well be delirious.

'In these hard times, one cannot afford to rely on one God only,' – explains the dying man.

Let us leave aside metaphysical questions. On the whole, Ghetto humour thrived on mundane matters: smuggling, trade and rampant corruption among the *Judenrat* bigwigs, the Ghetto police and even the Gestapo officers. The wits promptly came up with a name for it: 'feeding the juke-box'.

> 'Want things moving – don't stand still!
> Feed the juke-box – and they will . . .'

*Feeding the Juke-box* soon became the title of a successful revue show. 'May the smugglers' luck still hold . . .' went a line in one of the cabaret songs.

The very existence from day to day of the Ghetto community depended solely on their luck. The supply lines managed by smugglers were their lifelines. They had their own ingenious ways of getting food across the wall. Sometimes it was literally 'across' – requiring breathtaking acrobatics combined with sharp reflexes and unparalleled coolness. There were tunnels starting in the maze of basement passages and cellars and terminating in a similar fashion on the other side. Another way was to smuggle the foodstuffs strapped all over one's body on the way back from the cemetery which was located on the Aryan side. The constant body-searches hardly deterred anyone from having a go. The hunger proved a powerful incentive, more powerful than fear of the death penalty imposed on the smugglers. Many of the Ghetto's great fortunes originated in the smuggling enterprise. Sometimes a youngster with his wits about him and a bit of entrepreneurial spirit would support the whole family. One of those little streetwise kids eventually made it into a popular Ghetto ballad, though his luck eventually ran out on him in the last stanza – he got shot by the German sentries during one of his forays. Others, even younger and even more hungry, took over where he left off. The diary of Jack Eisner gives us an insight into the unsurpassed ingenuity of the young smugglers and their great efforts to keep their families alive.

A joke bordering on the grotesque captures the spirit of those days:

The daughter of the king of smugglers is getting married. The happy father, clearly surprised at his own generosity, announces that he is bequeathing her, as a dowry, a secret passage under the Ghetto wall which is open 24 hours a day.

The set-backs of the German armies on the Russian Front very soon coloured the political jokes passed around in the Ghetto.

The Lord dispatches an angel to Earth to see what the current situation is. The angel comes back and reports as follows: in Germany, Italy and Japan, everyone is dressed in military uniforms and talks about peace. In England, everybody is walking around in civilian clothes and talks about war. 'What about Poland?' asks the Lord. In Poland, everybody is walking barefoot and drivelling about victory . . .

Hitler is driving a car, in mechanic's overalls. A Jew gives him a passing glance and says under his breath:

'You're gonna run out of petrol, the axis will break up and they will eventually take away your driving licence . . .'

(Needless to say, the Axis – the military alliance of Germany, Italy and Japan – was a popular subject of many anecdotes.)

A donkey stubbornly refuses to budge although his owner desperately tries to force him off the road. A Jew happens to be passing by and offers to help the unfortunate man. He bends over to the donkey's ear and whispers something. The donkey promptly runs away. His incredulous owner begs the Jew to reveal the magic word. The Jew says that he has simply asked the stubborn beast to join the Axis . . .

'What did Napoleon take along for his Russian campaign?'
'Black shirt, in case he got injured.'
'And what did Hitler take?'
'Black long johns . . .'

After the German defeat at Stalingrad and the mourning by Goebbels, it was announced that a new organisation had been set up in the Ghetto,

'Kraft durch Schadenfreude'. The German newspaper *Deutsche Algemeine Zeitung* was said to have changed its name to *Deutsche Algemeine Tsores* (yid. – troubles).

Posters depicting German soldiers on the Russian Front were immediately inscribed with graffiti: '1812 – the year that Napoleon's army was defeated.'

The Gestapo officers are questioning a detained Jew: 'Who is going to win the war?'

'*Die Achse* [the Axis].'
'And who's gonna be the loser?'
'*Der Jid*.'

'Since even you are saying that it is the Jew that's going to lose it, we'll let you get away this time!'

The Jew can hardly believe his good fortune. On the way home he mutters to himself: 'The idiots didn't cotton on to it at all – *Der Jid* is short for the Axis: Japan, Italy and Deutschland ...'

A Ghetto joke had many functions. It served not only as a running commentary on events in the making but provided a glimmer of hope at the same time. On many occasions, the joke itself brought the news. One has to bear in mind that papers were banned (except *Gazeta Zydowska* published in Krakow, in Polish) and that listening to the radio was a serious offence, punishable by death. Clandestine publications from the other side were sporadic and, on the whole, had a rather restricted circulation. The news black-out was imposed by the Germans as part of their consistent policy of isolation. Ghetto jokes therefore doubled as news bulletins.

The idea of opening up the Western Front was slowly taking shape among Allied strategists. But for the Ghetto community, it was far too slow and their disappointment at the incomprehensible reluctance of the West to take decisive action is reflected in the following anecdote:

Winston Churchill is seeking advice on this matter from the Tsaddik of Góra Kalwaria (a small town south of Warsaw).

'There are two ways of invading Germany,' declares the learned Jew, 'The ordinary one and the miraculous one. The ordinary one is simple: the Lord will dispatch a million angels. The miracle would be if a million British troops parachuted into Germany ...'

One of the most hated symbols produced by German propaganda was the letter 'V', standing for Hitler's victory and invincibility. It was prominently displayed in all public places, painted on walls and posters, stencilled on military vehicles, decorating the porticos of official buildings. The monumental wooden model of the hated letter dominated the Saxon Square in the very centre of Warsaw. (It was subsequently burned down by a commando of the underground Home Army.) The Ghetto wits weren't far behind the Polish resistance in dealing with German military arrogance. One popular jibe at the generally despised symbol:

'What does it stand for, this "V"?' 'Well, you see, it's like the Fifth Class of the Lottery. But Jerry's number seems to be up, anyway . . .'

A personal jibe at Hitler's low military rank was slipped between the lines of the invocation to the statue of Frederick the Great in Berlin:

> *Komm herunter grosser Reiter*
> *Der Gefreiter kann nicht weiter!*
> [Come down, great horseman,
> The Corporal can do no more]

This rhyme clearly denigrates and shows venomous contempt for Hitler's blown-up sense of national pride, which quite evidently stands no comparison with the true genius of the actual maker of German and European history.

It is no coincidence that the two banned and highest priced best sellers in the Warsaw Ghetto were *War and Peace* by Leo Tolstoy and *The False Nero* by Leon Feuchtwanger. Feuchtwanger was avidly read for his satirical passion in exposing the tyrannical traits of an emperor so clearly evocative of Adolf Hitler himself. Tolstoy was appreciated for his epic rendering of the Battle of Borodino through the eyes of Prince Bolkonsky.

'One cannot wind up the clock with tears,' Adam Czerniakow, Mayor of the Forbidden District, quotes Dickens in his diary. He understood only too well the true value of humour for the Ghetto's inhabitants. It helped them through their ordeal, giving a glimmer of hope so vital in their struggle for survival. 'Only the Lord knows what pains I must take to keep that smile glued to my face at all times . . .' Czerniakow enters in his diary on another occasion.

If not for their sense of humour, the Ghetto community would never have been able to face up to the unbearable hardship of their daily existence behind the wall. Those who were scornful of witty comments and observations made by some ostensibly cheerful characters during funeral rites at the cemetery were obviously too restricted by self-righteous indignation to see the phenomenon in a broader perspective. Without this witty sarcasm and irony, the cemeteries would have remained but mournful monuments to sorrow and despair.

They couldn't yet have known that the Führer had already given the official seal of approval to the 'Final Solution to the Jewish Problem' in January 1942 in Wannsee. The Final Solution was to be facilitated by gas chambers and Zyklon B.

The supervision of the task was delegated to Adolf Eichmann. He promptly paid an official visit to the city to assess the technical and logistical problems posed by this assignment. As a diligent official of the Third Reich, he set about his task with cool efficiency. The number of railway trucks required to move the Jewish population to the extermination camps was quickly assessed, and the cubic capacity of stores, gas chambers and auxiliary buildings and the quantity of Zyklon B required for the actual implementation of the whole scheme were calculated and specified.

The objects of the 'Final Solution' were still holding out, drawing whatever hope and consolation they could manage from their own black humour and refusal to acknowledge the impending doom. Their laughter was disturbingly reminiscent of the biblical fight between David and Goliath. Just one example:

Another big round-up. The Germans are thoroughly combing the whole area, house by house, flat by flat, cellar by cellar, pulling everyone out into the street. Special passes and employment certificates cut no ice with the troops: no exceptions this time – everyone is to be shipped down to the camps. Behind the false back wall of the closet, a pregnant woman is hiding. When the stamping of soldiers' boots fades away, the woman suddenly goes into labour. In a short while, the shrill voice of a newborn baby can be heard: 'Mummy, can we get out now? Is the round-up over?'

A whole new language of code-words and double meanings was devised to cover the realm of everyday communication in a manner unintelligible to outsiders and so perfectly secure to the initiated. There were many informants and denunciators around, busily ferreting out anything that would please their employers at 13 Leszno Street (headquarters of the local Gestapo) and ultimately pave their way to freedom. Ironically enough, they were the last ones to be put into the railway trucks.

Many jokes openly warned against the traps set up by the paid informants and taught how to use 'double-speak'.

Two Jews meet in the street. 'What's new?' asks one. 'How can I tell you? One of us is working for *them* . . .'

Those in the Oneg Shabbat Group who documented events subsequently established that there had been around 4,000 active informants at the time.

'What's the news from the front?' asks someone, a touch too glibly to pass for being genuinely interested. 'Hard to say, really. I live round the back . . .' comes the guarded reply.

Jewish humour is, by nature, very down-to-earth, thriving on mundane, everyday matters, generally sympathetic to the human condition. The proverbial hard-luckers inhabiting the vast majority of Jewish anecdotes always manage to find a way out or stay on top, against all odds. Viewing themselves critically helps them a great deal as they blunder along. This way they pre-empt Fate, so to speak, disarm it with self-inflicted mockery and, not surprisingly, receive more benign treatment.

Tevye the milkman, the hero of Sholem Aleichem's novel *Fiddler on the Roof*, confesses to the reader that 'if he took up making umbrellas, it would surely never rain again ...' Here is the very quintessence of Jewish humour. Though Tevye is quite openly sceptical as to his ability to make it big in business, he is, nevertheless, set on plodding on undeterred by adversity. Maybe one day Fate would deal him a better card. He refuses to believe that life could all be sharp practice.

A measure of Jewish optimism: Two Jews meet under the gallows. One of them ventures a comment – 'It looks good, they're clearly running out of ammunition ...'

# MY RECOLLECTIONS OF THE DEPORTATION OF JANUSZ KORCZAK*

Marek Rudnicki

I have never talked about this in public – would not do so now except that Felek Scharf is pressing me and I trust him that he knows what is to be done. He understands me and also is familiar with these matters better than most, and he forces the story out of me syllable by syllable; sometimes the words are his, sometimes mine – I could not do this on my own. One could not even say that this is the opening of old wounds, the wounds have never healed and never will. All my life I have tried to put this behind me, in order to be like other people – but when my mind appears to let go of it, I am overcome by guilt and shame. To complicate matters further, when it dawns on me that the world forgets, that it is capable of forgetting – my hackles rise.

I am not a writer, I am used to pencil and brush, I think like a painter – in images. What often springs to my mind is that famous painting by Breughel, 'The Death of Icarus'. A rustic idyll, furrowed fields, peasants behind their ploughs – only in the corner, unnoticed, Icarus' legs sticking out from the sea – as he fell from the clear skies after his failed dash towards the sun. Breughel captures here, shrewdly, the indifference of the world towards a great event, a tragedy, death; everybody goes about his own pedestrian, everyday business; it has always been thus.

Events of those days, engraved on my memory, are inseparable from the nightmares which I dream with my eyes open. I cannot always distinguish what was a dream and what was reality, but I know that reality was the more terrible nightmare. Under Felek's questioning many more things surface to which I was a witness – but I must observe the bounds of his and your sensibility.

Nobody who was not there can – or ever will be able – to comprehend how it really was, and perhaps this is all to the good; except, that by now

---

* Talk given at a Korczak Symposium, at Rauischholzhausen, nr. Frankfurt, West Germany, October 1988. Translated from Polish by Rafael (Felek) Scharf.

there remain very few people who have a real grasp of it – maybe they have some special responsibility? I don't know.

Every Jew who survived owes this to some astonishing set of circumstances which border on the miraculous. I do not know to this day why I myself survived, I know that I have not striven to do so. I saw it then through the eyes of a fifteen-year old, it is impossible now to regain that perception. I know that I grew a skin and became hard, the gruesomeness began to be accepted as 'normal'.

Horror was commonplace, human corpses strewn on the pavements, covered with newspapers or naked, stripped of their rags and shoes, were an everyday occurrence; skeleton-like children with eyes bulging from hunger begged for bread. I was consumed with hatred of the Germans, the Ukrainians, the Latvians, I dreamt of acts of vengeance, I had hallucinations wherein I was tearing them apart with my own hands, I believed that this, indeed, would come to pass, soon; such thoughts kept me going. I had great, greater than ever love for my parents, my brother, my friends. When my brother died of typhoid I ran to the cemetery, searched for him midst the mountains of corpses, I found him, held him tight, cried out his name. My father, a doctor, has been friendly with Korczak over a long period of time. In the ghetto my father worked in the hospital on Leszno Street and often had some dealings with Korczak – one might guess that he was passing on to Korczak some medicines to which he had better access; but it was all too clear, in view of the dreadful shortages, that giving to one meant depriving another, decisions which no man should have to face.

My father knew already on 5 August, I don't know how, maybe this was common knowledge, that on the sixth the orphanages would be 'evacuated', including that of Korczak. Unable to leave his post my father charged me to go and see what was happening.

When, on 6 August, around 10 o'clock in the morning, I got to the house at Sienna Street 16, the children were already assembled, in fours, on the side-walk. They were neatly dressed and did not look starved; seemingly, Korczak always had managed to scrape enough to give them sufficient nourishment.

This scene is well known and has been described and reconstructed many times, not always accurately. I don't want to belittle or debunk, but I must truthfully say how I saw it.

The atmosphere was pervaded by some paralysing fatigue, numbness, apathy. There was no sign of agitation, no saluting (as some describe it) because here walked Korczak with his children, certainly there were no messengers from the *Judenrat* – nobody approached Korczak. There were no gestures, no singing, no proud spring in the step; I don't remember whether the children carried the Children's Home flag – some people say they did. There was an overwhelming, weary silence. Korczak dragged his feet with an effort, appeared smaller than usual, as if shrunk, mumbling something to himself.

When I think of this scene – which is all too often – I seem to recall that he mumbled the word 'why' – I was near enough to hear it. But this is surely a figment of my imagination, in retrospect. This was no time of philosophical reflections; it was time of dumb, bottomless despair; without questions to which there is no answer.

Those few grown-ups from the Children's Home, among them Stefa (Wilczyńska) walked close-by, as I did, or behind; the children, to begin with in fours, later in mixed ranks, in single file. One of the children hung on to Korczak, gripping his coat, perhaps his hand. They walked as if in a trance.

I followed them to the gate of the 'Umschlag' as we called it. I cannot describe the scene in front of our eyes, I lack adequate words, perhaps such words do not exist.

Since 22 July, when the so-called Great Deportation, in other words the liquidation of the ghetto, began, tens of thousands of people were driven daily to this square, at the corner of Dzika and Stawki. A heaving multitude in unspeakable confusion, wailing, groaning, howling. Some walked round as if demented shouting names in search of their families. Many took poison, whole families in common embrace. There was no established order of loading the trains, some groups hung around there already for a few days and nights.

The traffic was directed by the chief of the Jewish police of the *Umschlagplatz*, Szmerling and his cohorts – by screams, kicks and blows, under the watchful eye of the almighty SS officer Handtke, with the detachment of SS, Ukrainians and Latvians.

This sight was not new to me. I was at that spot nearly every day. At the behest of the *Judenrat* we brought here baskets with loaves of bread. At first we used to throw the loaves over the barbed wire fence surrounding the square, but they would have been grabbed by the stronger. The system was changed – we cut the loaves into slices and somebody would take the basket into the square and see to it that shares were fair. In my group there were three 'cutters' of bread – Wdowicki, myself and Zamenhof (yes, the grandson of the 'Esperanto' Zamenhof). The way from Sienna through the streets of Leszno, Karmelicka, Dzielna, Zamenhofa to Stawki seemed enormously long, it lasted about two hours – it was midday when we reached the *Umschlagplatz*.

The heat was overpowering, the sun beat down on us mercilessly. Korczak with the children, Stefa and the rest of the staff entered the Square. From where I halted, about 30 yards, away, one could see the railway sidings and the cattle trucks, some already loaded, some still open, with their windows sewn up with barbed wire. A noxious stench of chlorine, burning eyes and throat, drifts over the square. I can see lime on the floor of an open truck, also dripping from other trucks onto the railway line.

A representative of the *Judenrat* is busy on the Square – I now know that this was Nachum Remba, who of course knew Korczak and immediately came to speak to him. From his report (preserved in the Ringelblum archives) it would appear that Remba, in desperation, suggested to Korczak that they both go to the offices of the *Judenrat* in order, in some way, to 'intervene'. We know to-day that 'intervention' would have been totally futile, but in any event Korczak rejected the offer, did not want to leave the children for one moment.

Remba intended then, as he says, to steer the group to the periphery of the square, in order to delay their departure; such manoeuvre proved sometimes successful, but Szmerling prevented this and pointed the way – straight to the truck.

The children went up the sloping ramp and disappeared in the darkness. Korczak went after them, the last. I can see his hunched figure disappearing from view. Children from another orphanage were already pressing from behind. I waited a long time till the last struck was loaded. I waited till the train departed.

I am almost certain that many of those children suffocated in the train before reaching Treblinka. I am also convinced that Korczak did not survive the journey to Treblinka.

The greatest pain that can befall a human being on this earth is for a parent to watch, helplessly, the suffering of his or her child, unable to shield against such suffering or to relieve it. What Korczak felt, looking on the anguish of his children, the two hundred of his wards, during that last march and later in the stinking darkness, the terror, the crying when the door of the truck shut tight – human imagination cannot encompass. But it is enough to give this a thought – and this must leave a mark for life.

Two days later my parents shared the fate of Korczak – and hundreds of thousands of their kinsmen. On 8 August 1942, my parents were taken from their room in Nowolipki Street – and my mother was not even Jewish. When I returned home that day, after roaming aimlessly the empty alleys of the ghetto, and found the room empty, I knew instantly what had happened. I could not endure further ordeal and I cut my veins with a piece of glass. A Jewish policeman passing by dragged me to a hospital where they brought me back to life. A grotesque, irrational, senseless act in those circumstances – the saving, the prolonging of a single life, as it happens – mine. . . .

History is a continuum, an unbroken chain – it is not possible to say that such and such event began here and another ended there, all have their seamless antecedents and their consequences. However this one thing can be said with cruel precision: there, just there on the *Umschlagplatz*, the thousand-year history of Jews in Poland came to an end.

I think that even those – and, sadly, there were many, a great many of them – before, during and after the war, who dreamt of such 'Poland without Jews' – I think that even they have come to realise that what happened on the *Umschlagplatz* was not only the greatest calamity that has befallen the Jews throughout their history, but also a calamity for Poland and for our civilisation. Looking at the world which led to it and allowed it to happen – who can say for certain that this will never happen again?

# THE DEATH OF ADAM CZERNIAKÓW AND JANUSZ KORCZAK'S LAST JOURNEY
Jerzy Lewiński

Numerous accounts, memoirs, diaries, chronicles, and historical treatises about the Warsaw ghetto have already been written, particularly about the living conditions of its imprisoned, teeming Jewish population, about its progressive pauperisation and ever-increasing poverty, about its homeless and starving children, about disease and epidemics and the mortality which kept going up every month, about the Jewish Council and its activities, about the Jewish police, about the ghetto's cultural institutions and social self help, about the many people who sacrificed their lives by becoming involved in this type of activity, about the life of the various political organisations and the emerging resistance movement which culminated in the sudden heroic action of the ghetto fighters. Individual authors, first and foremost among them the eye-witnesses who were vital participants in the events of this tragic period, have provided us with accounts of their experiences, feelings, opinions, evaluations and even conclusions, but all these descriptions tend to be predominantly subjective, frequently one-sided, sometimes distorted or even inaccurate. However, such is the nature of things, that in all writings of this sort, the principal role in the evaluation of the events described is played by the authors' personalities and sociological and political views. It is because of this, that serious historians researching the past cannot be satisfied with just one source, however comprehensive. These testimonies reproduce an image of the past which is based on many original writings and surviving documentation, but all the same, their authors' researches and assessments are formed according to their own personal views. This is perfectly understandable. For an author has a right to judge the events he is describing, but he should not alter or bend any facts to fit his own views or convictions. Nonetheless, quite a number of examples of such conduct do exist.

As I have already said, writing about the Warsaw ghetto and the historical research based on it, is not only not free of one-sided subjective assessment, but often contains actual distortions of certain individual events. Some justification for this state of affairs can be found in the heightened emotional state of the writers, a perfectly understandable feeling when involved in a process of recreating the experiences of a population shut away in the ghetto and the terrible repressions it was forced to endure, the scale of which, if one includes in it the systematically organised genocide, was previously unknown in the annals of history, despite the fact that earlier Jewish history was not devoid of persecution and frequent painful discrimination. The Jews who found themselves under the domination of Nazi Germany were prepared to suffer persecution and discrimination. But they did not suspect, and therefore did not admit the possibility of – and they were not alone in this – genocide. As a result, all accounts put down in writing by the victims during the time of the perpetration of this crime against the Jewish nation, or those written down immediately after the tragedy by its few survivors, cannot really be expected to be free from emotional and subjective feelings and judgments.

As the fiftieth anniversary of the genocide inflicted on the population of the Warsaw ghetto approaches, it should provide an opportunity for those survivors who are still alive to attempt to leave behind a record of what they witnessed and lived through, now no longer written in the heat of the moment, but carefully considered from the perspective of time and in the full knowledge of all the circumstances and with complete respect for truth.

Personally, I lived through a great deal during the German occupation, and during my time in the Warsaw ghetto I witnessed events which have a particular historical significance, and this is why I would like to put them down in writing, following the principles mentioned above. I am in the process of preparing the materials in my possession. In the meantime, I would like to offer remembrances of the deaths of two outstanding personalities of the Warsaw ghetto, Adam Czerniaków and Janusz Korczak. Certainly, a lot has also been written about them, but in so many different ways, giving rise to numerous legends and inaccuracies, and even complete fabrications. Therefore, having an exact and largely direct knowledge of the facts connected with Adam Czerniaków's suicide and also of those leading up to Janusz Korczak's refusal to take advantage of the possibility of leaving the Umschlagplatz, I feel obliged to leave a permanent record.

As far as Adam Czerniaków's death is concerned, quite a few reminiscences and accounts actually contradict what he himself wrote in his diary[1] and the testimony left behind by his wife, Felicja Czerniaków. And this applies even to the seemingly indisputable fact of the date of his death (23 July, 1942). So Julian Kulski, vice-president and director of the Warsaw City Council during 1935–1944, writes in his *W wspomnieniu o Adamie Czerniaków* (Memoirs of Adam Czerniaków): 'Killing himself on 24 July, 1942, he was saving himself from the disgrace, imposed on him by an inhuman enemy, of having to participate in an action of destroying those same people whom he was so decisively determined to save'.[2] Kulski's Memoirs contain an introduction from the editor signed with the initials M.F., where we read: 'And when he realised the hopelessness of his isolated struggle, he committed suicide on the third day of the liquidation action of the Warsaw ghetto on 24 July, 1942'. The author of this introduction thus fails to correct Julian Kulski's incorrect date of Adam Czerniaków's death, and does this unequivocally, adding 'on the third day of the liquidation action'.

Similarly, in his famous conversation with Hanna Krall,[3] a prominent player in these ghetto events, Marek Edelman, makes a different, albeit equally erroneous statement: 'On the evening of the first day of the action, the Chairman of the Council Czerniaków committed suicide'. The inaccurate date of 24 July returns again in the notes to Ringelblum's *Kronika getta warszawskiego* (Chronicle of the Warsaw Ghetto), where it is claimed: 'the former chairman Adam Czerniaków, committed suicide on 24 July 1942'.[4] *Pamiętniki z getta warszawskiego* (The Memoirs from the Warsaw Ghetto) also contain several references which not only describe inaccurately the circumstances of Chairman Czerniaków's death, but also its date.[5] Thus though Leon Tyszka,[6] Chairman Czerniaków's colleague on the Council, gives the correct date of the suicide, he describes the time of his death incorrectly, and this completely distorts the sequence of events on 23 July 1942. Tyszka (who used his real surname Tenenbaum in the ghetto) gives a completely arbitrary account of the sequence of events on 22 July 1942, stating that 'at 9.00 o'clock in the morning, the Gestapo director of the Department for Jewish affairs, appeared in the Council surrounded by Gestapo and SS officers. All the counsellors who could be found are present. They assemble in the conference room'. Two pages further on he writes: 'Around noon, a number of high-ranking SS officers appear in the Council. They were led by Höfle, accompanied by Worthoff, and others whose names I do not recollect'. This is inaccurate. Nobody appeared at 9.00 a.m., or at noon. Sturmbannführer Herman Höfle did appear with some SS and Gestapo officers at 10.00 o'clock, which is conclusively verified by an entry in chairman Czerniaków's diary, dated 22 July 1942: 'At 10.00 o'clock Sturmbannführer Höfle appeared, accompanied by several other officers'. The latitude which Tyszka allows himself in the course of his reminiscences, results not only in discrepancies in the real course of the events of 22 July, but he also ends up contradicting himself when he writes: 'around noon – today is 22 July 1942 – the Chairman comes into my office and asks me to accompany him on a tour of the ghetto'. The tour of the ghetto did not and could not have taken place. One only has to read carefully the entry Chairman Czerniaków made in his diary on 22 July 1942, in order to understand that not only at noon, but even after Sturmbannführer Höfle and his colleagues left the Council, he was totally preoccupied with implementing – as Höfle had demanded – the order to resettle the population to the East instantly, with the threat of otherwise having his hostages shot. He was simultaneously involved in desperate efforts to mitigage the order, particularly to protect the children in the orphanages, and he also was asking for the release of the arrested Counsellors 'which I managed to get them to agree to', as he wrote in his diary.

As far as 23 July is concerned, Tyszka has got the Chairman's time of death wrong, when he wrote: 'about 4.00 p.m. a Security Service guard knocked on my door with the news that the Chairman had committed suicide in the Council office'. In actual fact, the events that were fundamentally to influence his decision to kill himself, occurred later. The Chairman only took the poison at about 8.00 p.m. in his office where he returned after 6.00 p.m. after having been summoned by the Germans.

Let me attempt to present the last days of Adam Czerniaków's life, basing myself on available facts, and in order to be able to understand the motives which led him to kill himself. I have to go back and examine events which occurred in April 1942. During the night of 17/18 April, incidents took place in the ghetto, which initiated the tragic period which led up to the decree of 22 July 1942, for the 'resettlement' of the Jewish population to the East. The ghetto population found out early on the morning of 18 April that officials of the Warsaw Gestapo had seized 52 men from their flats and that every one of them had been immediately shot in the street and their corpses had been left lying there. This bloody night shook the ghetto.

After identifying the victims of the hooded murders, the horrified population attempted to discover the reasons for this tragedy. Amongst the murder victims could be found people connected with the political underground and rich merchants who had given financial support to the illegal press, but there were also people who had nothing to do with political action and even individuals connected with the so-called No. 13 who had been in the service of the Germans.[7] The overriding opinion within the ghetto was that this was a blow directed at the group of people connected with the underground movement, although the composition of the group of the murder victims did not make it easy to evaluate unequivocally the Warsaw Gestapo's action. The population was not allowed a lot of time to solve the puzzle of the April tragedy. A few days later a dozen or so more persons were seized from their flats and murdered in the same way. These hooded murders now became quite a common sight in the ghetto. Jews who had been illegally living on the 'Aryan side' under assumed names were also brought in and killed in the streets of the ghetto. These events produced an almost continuous state of anxiety and agitation in the ghetto population.

Chairman Czerniaków, who had always felt responsible for the fate of the people imprisoned in the ghetto, was involved in numerous battles – which are also well documented in his diary of that period – to try to help his people to live through this new period of increasingly more threatening repression. And indeed, this was a very difficult period, with sporadic murders, the execution of 110 Jews in reprisal for disobeying German orders, increasing poverty, a growing number of homeless and starving children and also the resettlement of Jews from other places into the ghetto, which required gigantic efforts to try and absorb them, as well as the arrival of uniformed German film crews to make propaganda films. People were well aware of what was really going on; some reasonably dressed individuals were seized and scenes in the streets or in restaurants were staged, to imply a state of prosperity and indifference towards the starving beggars in the streets. More and more frequently rumours would appear that the propaganda action of the German film makers was a preamble to their intention to resettle a given number of people from the ghetto with an even tighter sealing of the ghetto walls. During all this, Chairman Czerniaków tried to keep up everyone's spirits. He opened orphanages, he supported the opening of Kindergartens, he made a speech at the opening ceremony of the Detention Chamber on Chłodna Street,[8] he made an appearance at a concert, but at the same time he bravely defied the German film makers who wanted him to take part in a staged ball. All this does not come easy to him and on 21 May 1942, he writes the following entry in his diary: 'Will I have the strength to continue to act honourably.' However, nothing seems to diminish the level of Chairman Czerniaków's activity: he never fails to campaign for improvement in the people's living conditions at every single official meeting with representatives of German authorities and he attempts to find out whether the previous month's repressions have a transitory character, or if they are harbingers of further tragic things to come. On 9 July 1942 we find the following entry in diary: 'At 8.00 a.m. I went to the little square at Ceglana Street where the night before they had brought about 800 evacuees from Rawa Mazowiecka and its surrounding districts. Small children, babies, women. This sight would have broken my heart, were it not so steeled against it all by the past 3 years of adversity'. These words indicate that the sufferings which Czerniaków had undergone had not managed to break him, and that he was quite ready to continue his struggle to lighten the misery of the ghetto inmates. Nevertheless, only two weeks later he commits suicide; but during these last days of his life Czerniaków's level of activity does not in any way diminish, as he is fully conscious of the difficult times which are in store for the ghetto. News was coming in from various sources that tens of thousands of Jews were to be evacuated from the ghetto, but nobody knew the destination or purpose of this evacuation. Czerniaków gives his utmost attention and concern to these reports even though, so far, they have not been officially confirmed.

Without neglecting any of his duties as Chairman of the Council, he makes every effort to contact the representatives of German authorities in charge of the ghetto. He is well aware of the fact that he is not very likely to get at the truth, but he might be able to get some idea of the murderers' real intentions from conversations with various members of the German bureaucracy, including the Gestapo. On Monday, 20 July, he sets off for Gestapo headquarters and he talks with every single official of the Jewish department. They all assure him that they have heard nothing and know nothing about any deportation plans for the ghetto population. Czerniaków is not satisfied with these answers and tries to obtain a concrete, official statement. Not having any other alternative, on 20 July he wrote in his diary: 'I went to see Scherer, the deputy director of section 3. He expressed surprise at the rumours and said that he too knew nothing about this. In the end I asked him if I could tell the people that there was nothing to worry about. He replied that I should go ahead, and that everything that was being rumoured was nothing but *Quatsch* and *Unsinn* (stuff and nonsense).' Other representatives of the German authorities expressed the same opinion. I know that Chairman Czerniaków thought hard about whether or not to communicate these answers to the people, and if so, in what form it would be best to do so. He wanted to avoid creating generally the impression that he was personally corroborating this news, but the intense panic in the ghetto made him instruct Lejkin, deputy head of the Jewish police, 'to inform the population, district by district.' (On 20 July he wrote in his diary that almost everyone knew that assurances from the Gestapo were not to be believed, but under the existing circumstances, they did give some measure of comfort.)

In the meantime Czerniaków did not miss any opportunity to attempt to obtain additional information from other departments of the German authorities, so he could compare it with the facts he had earlier obtained from the Gestapo. All reports confirmed the Gestapo's statements. During the three years that Czerniaków had carried out the duties as Chairman of the Council, he had become thoroughly familiar with the way that the Nazi authorities and administrators operated and the behaviour of their representatives did nothing to inspire confidence in the assurances he received from them. But not having any other sources of reliable information, he spent all of that Monday following up every possible contact in order to assess the situation. At the same time he continued his activities which he had planned for that day in the Council. These included talks and attempts to free the children who had been arrested by the German authorities. He managed to come to a positive arrangement about this matter, and the children were to be transferred to reformatories and temporary lodgings on Dzika street. The German commissar's attitude gave no indication that any radical changes in the ghetto were on the cards. However Czerniaków did not stop thinking about the possible danger threatening the population of the ghetto. This is how this very difficult day in the life of the Chairman of the Council ended. When he finally went home, Czerniaków could not stop thinking about what the next day might bring.

Chairman Czerniaków started work early in the morning on Tuesday. Suddenly, at noon, several secret policemen appeared and proceeded to arrest all the counsellors in the Chairman's office and simultaneously, they arrested members of the supplies' administration office. Czerniaków wanted to be taken along with the other arrested members, but he is told to stay in his office. He immediately starts an onslaught both on the commissar of the Jewish district and the Gestapo, to free the counsellors. He receives assurances that they will be freed the next day, which seems to indicate that the arrests are not a foreboding of some sinister action against the ghetto. But the Chairman is very suspicious of the fact that he was not given any reason for these arrests, which made him very anxious considering the existing atmosphere of menacing premonitions of danger to the continuing existence of the ghetto in its present form. During the evening, a piece of news from Dr. Milejkowski manages to relieve the anxiety to some extent. It appears that several Jewish doctors had asked an eminent Polish surgeon, Professor Franciszek Raszeja to come to the ghetto to examine a seriously ill, renowned antiquarian, Abe Gutnajer. The Gestapo granted the Professor an entry and exit pass to the ghetto without any problem, and he arrived at the patient's flat. This could be interpreted to mean that there was no immediate danger to the ghetto. But whilst evaluating these events in this way, at the same time Czerniaków was perfectly well aware that brute force, violence, the murder of his colleagues, lies, deceit and cunning devices dominated the criminal Nazi system, particularly in relationship to the Jews. Within such a system, every decision which Czerniaków had to undertake required an immense effort and a feeling of responsibility. However, he had already 'steeled his heart' and he started preparing a plan of action for the following day.

That day, Wednesday, 22 July, 1942 had an ominous beginning. Already during Tuesday night, members of the Gestapo and the SS carried out numerous murders in the streets of the ghetto, as well as in flats, among them in the flat of the patient Gutnajer, where they shot Professor Raszeja, some Jewish doctors, a nurse and the patient's relatives.

Czerniaków, already aware of the previous night's tragic events, headed for the Council at 7 a.m. and on his way he noticed, as he later wrote in his diary, that 'the boundary of the small ghetto now had an extra guard surrounding it, in addition to the normal one'. The first thing Czerniaków did when he arrived in the Council, was to try and find out what was going on. First he phoned Brandt and Auerswald, the commissar of the Jewish district. He was told they were out. He asked to speak to any other officials of these institutions and was told that they also were not there. In the meantime, panic and dejection spread throughout the ghetto, when news of the terrible events of the previous night and the encirclement of the small ghetto became known.

At about 10 o'clock, the manager of the 3rd district of the Jewish police, which at this time had its offices at No. 2 Leszno Street, telephoned the Council that eight passenger cars full of uniformed Germans with 'POL' painted on their sides, had just driven into the ghetto through the Leszno-Tłomackie gates. All the streets through which these motor cars were passing, became instantly deserted. At the same time a cordon of German police and military gendarmes, members of Lithuanian, Ukrainian and Latvian units and Polish policemen, was forming around the outside periphery of the ghetto walls. A few minutes later, ten field vehicles loaded with field gendarmes and members of the Sicherheitspolizei in full battle dress enter the ghetto. They shoot at anyone who happens to be on a balcony or to appear in a window. Despite this, news of these happenings spreads with lightning speed throughout the ghetto and everyone already knows that the passenger cars with the Germans have stopped in front of the Council building. The ghetto holds it breath and the terrified population waits for news of its fate. In a state of high tension, the Council workers observe how uniformed Germans enter the Council building – all around it the streets are totally deserted, like in a dead city.

It is 10 o'clock. SS-Sturmbannführer Herman Höfle (from the Lublin branch Einsatz Reinhard; plenipotentiary in charge of Jewish resettlement) together with several officers from the same unit, SS-Untersturmführer Karl Brandt and SS-Oberscharführer Gerhard Mende from the Jewish Department of the Warsaw Gestapo now enter Chairman Czerniaków's office. Czerniaków keeps his outer composure, despite feeling quite shocked and horrified.

Brandt, who for the past two days had, on several occasions, assured Czerniaków that the rumours concerning the deportation of the ghetto population were nothing but simple inventions, now explains the reason for his visit, without any trace of embarrassment and with self-assured foreknowledge. As soon as he finished, Herman Höfle begins to talk and slowly reads out the order entitled 'Eröffnungen and Auflagen für den Judenrat' (Information and Instructions to the Judenrat) about the resettlement to the East of the Jewish population from the Warsaw ghetto and instructions of how this is to be carried out by the Council. Höfle commands that the ghetto population be immediately informed of the contents of the order in the form of a proclamation. In connection with this, many different versions about Czerniaków's alleged refusal to sign the order dictated by Sturmbannführer Höfle have appeared in memoirs and historical treatises. The fact is that no order from the German authorities concerning the Jews required any oral or written agreement from the Judenrat, as the Germans used to call the Jewish Council. These orders were to be carried out unconditionally, with a list of punishments to be meted out in case they were not executed. The chairman of the Judenrat had a duty to inform the ghetto population of the order in the form of a proclamation. It is true that until 22 July 1942, the bilingual proclamations which were issued 'on the orders of the German authorities' and were signed 'the Chairman of the Jewish Council in Warsaw, eng. A. Czerniaków', and in the German text *'Der Obmann des Judenrates in Warschau, Dipl. Ing. A. Czerniaków'*. In this specific case, Chairman Czerniaków ordered a Council worker to prepare the proclamation about the deportation of the Jewish population to the East in such a way, that it would not, as it always had hitherto, include his name, but would only say: 'The Jewish Council in Warsaw' and only *'Der Judenrat in Warschau'* in the German text. It cannot therefore be maintained that Czerniaków refused to sign the order dictated by Höfle or that he could have had any influence whatsoever on the contents of the order. He had no choice whether to sign it or to refuse to do so, since the German authorities did not actually require his signature. However, I do not wish to minimise the significance of Chairman Czerniaków's decision not to place his name under the proclamation announcing the German order to resettle the ghetto population to the East. The same afternoon the proclamations did indeed appear on the walls of nearly all the ghetto streets, but the terrified people who read them did not actually notice the absence of Czerniaków's name. The Chairman was not really so much interested in the immediate effect of his decision, but he was conscious of the fact that fateful events were taking place, and he wanted to put on record his opposition in the only way available to him at that moment, both personally and as chairman of the Council of the largest conglomeration of Jews in occupied Europe.

Let us now return to what was happening in the Council. After having read out the order and the instructions for its implementation by the Judenrat, Höfle announced that 'in case of failure to carry out the orders and instructions one hundred percent, a designated number of hostages who will be held in the meantime, will be shot.' Apart from this announcement, the German text of the order and instructions contained entries which were headed *Strafen* (punishments), where the only anticipated punishment for Jews for any infringement of the orders was death by shooting. Consequently, the threat of this punishment applied to every member of the Jewish police, who were given the task of conveying the designated contingent of people to the Umschlagplatz (railway sidings). The sheer monstrosity of this order, even within the context of the German atrocities which were being inflicted on the Jewish people, escapes all attempts at rational judgment within the realm of moral values which have been evolved and handed down to us by history. Here one must add that the head of the Jewish police within the organisational structure of the Jewish Council was none other than its chairman! One should keep this fact in mind when passing judgment on Czerniaków's action after he had heard the contents of the German order and instructions. These anticipated that he must immediately, this very day, order the Jewish police to supply a designated contingent of people for resettlement in the East. The Chairman's question about where in the East these people were being resettled, remained unanswered and put Sturmbannführer Höfle into a temper. Even for a 'heart well-steeled' this was an immensely difficult moment.

Czerniaków was fully aware of the fact that the imprisoned and encircled ghetto population was completely defenceless and exhausted by past trials, and that no adequately organised political force which could provide any help existed in the ghetto. Neither could any such help be expected from the outside. Consequently, for the time being, there was no possibility of any resistance to the German orders and even the slightest attempt at merely postponing their execution might have resulted in incalculable consequences for which the Germans would put the burden of responsibility on the same Jews for whom Czerniaków felt himself responsible. The Chairman did not get any answer to his question about where the Jews were to be resettled and he had no knowledge of the full extent of the German intentions, but even passive resistance taking the form of inactivity would result in immediate repressions on a scale which was difficult to predict. Hitherto, no Jew throughout the whole history of his people which was, after all, accustomed to persecution and suffering, had found himself in quite such a situation. Assuming complete responsibility, he remained true to the basic principle of his previous actions, namely to do everything in his power to soften the impact of the German orders. Accordingly, not allowing himself to become antagonised by Sturmbannführer Höfle's state of irritation, he proceeded to discuss the subject of broadening the categories of persons to be exempted from the German resettlement order, to include officials of the Jewish Social Self-help group, of the Craftsmen Union and of other organisations involved in the day to day running of the ghetto 'to which I managed to get their agreement', as he wrote in his diary. He also asked for the Counsellors who were being held as hostages to be freed and, with the exception of Counsellor Rozen, he managed to get the Germans to agree to this. He had just finished making these arrangements, when, on leaving the building, the Germans reminded him again immediately to begin the action necessary to carry out their orders, including the vacating of the premises at 103 Żelazna Street, as this building was to be occupied by German officials from the resettlement headquarters (the so-called Befehlstelle). By now it was nearly noon, and the demanded action had to begin, without the hope of any further delay.

About 9.00 o'clock on the same morning, Dr Felicja Czerniaków, the Chairman's wife made her way to Centos, as she was a member of its committee. When she heard the news about the Germans barging into the

Council building, she moved to a friend's house on Żelazna Street and on her advice she did not return to her own flat. I was given this information and was asked by Mrs Czerniaków to pass it on to the Chairman at my earliest opportunity. As soon as I saw that the Germans were going away from Grzybowska Street, I headed for the Council. I met the lawyer Zygmunt Warman, the Council secretary in front of the Chairman's office and it was he who told me all about the terrible orders and all that had happened and added that the Chairman was very busy and was waiting for Jakub Lejkin, the acting head of the Jewish police. He did, however, agree to inform the Chairman that I had an important message from his wife. A few minutes later the Chairman came out into the hall and asked what was happening. He looked under great stress, but was in full control. I gave him the message. Without a moment's hesitation he said to me: 'Please go and tell my wife to return to our flat immediately. We have to be prepared in case the Germans come for her to take her as a hostage. In such a case, her absence might cause misfortune for other people'. I had the impression that this man had become completely preoccupied with one single thought, namely how to prevent suffering for the people for whom he had always felt responsible and all this without any thought as to the consequences which might befall himself or his wife. After hearing her husband's answer, Dr Czerniaków immediately returned to their flat on Chłodna Street. I then returned to the Council to inform him of this and to find out what else was happening. From Warman I found out that the Chairman had passed on the German instructions for the implementation of the order to Lejkin and that even today, 6,000 people were to be delivered for resettlement. The Chairman pointed out that he fully understood the tragic nature of the duties which were being imposed on the police, but a refusal to carry them out might result not only in cruel repressions, but might form the pretext for an imminent start of a complete liquidation of the ghetto. Czerniaków pointed out that in the present situation there was no other possible solution, except to attenuate the German orders and he advised them first and foremost to try and shield children and the intelligentsia, for whom the finding of jobs which would exempt them from deportation would prove very difficult. When evaluating this statement, once more one feels obliged to underline emphatically that Chairman Czerniaków had no knowledge of the final fate of the population to be deported, nor anything about what would become of the ghetto afterwards, and despite many previous unfortunate experiences, he could not be certain that the agreement to exemptions in the resettlement order was characteristic of the cynicism, lies and deceit which were part and parcel of the German machine designed to effect a total extermination of Jews.

I maintain that, despite what many people have written, during the initial period of resettlement, no one in the ghetto knew for sure that all Jews under German occupation were sentenced to total destruction. It is perfectly true that by then, for several months preceding these events, alarming news about the tragic fate of Jews who had been 'resettled' from other places had been reaching the Warsaw ghetto. It was said that several thousand Jews had been deported from the Łódź ghetto to Chelmno on Ner and nothing further had ever been heard of them. Yet the Łódź ghetto still continued to exist and had well over 100,000 residents, practically all of them working for the German war effort. Consequently, it was thought that because the war was dragging on, the Germans would want to keep the Warsaw ghetto going, albeit in a considerably whittled down state, as it had been exceptionally productive and that this was the reason why the Germans had decided to exempt people who were working for German enterprises and firms from the resettlement programme. The German criminals were well aware of the fact that the isolated and terrorised ghetto population was utterly defenceless and had been left to their own devices and, as a result, the treacherous and deceitful illusions which were designed to create some hope of survival, would prove effective. And this is exactly what did happen.

The illusion – psychologically perfectly understandable – that work in enterprises working for the German war effort would save one from deportation, resulted in some Jews undertaking precipitous action to form production points which were attached to German firms, the so-called sheds (*szopy*), resulting in a rush to obtain employment there. Some people who had no hope of finding legal work in the ghetto, even volunteered for resettlement. They thought that they would be sent to hard labour camps and if they somehow managed to adjust to the conditions there, they would survive. When passing judgment on such a mode of thinking and conduct, one must take into account the mental state of the Jewish population in the ghetto at that time. It was prepared to face persecution and suffering, but it could not believe that Germany, even Nazi Germany, was planning, in the middle of the twentieth century in the very centre of Europe, to murder the entire Jewish people under its domination and that the world would just look on passively. After all, both Polish and Jewish underground organisations were sending news to London about the ever-growing terror and activities in the camp in Chelmno on Ner. These Jews felt that they were justified in counting on the weight of public opinion, on the Pope's influence, on the sizeable conglomeration of Jews in England and, above all, on those in America, who would convince their governments and, with the support of the neutral countries, would act to stop Germany from destroying the Jewish nation. And at the same time, the destructive war was nearing the end of its third year without great success for the Germans and the course of events could change any day and the Jews who would manage to survive till then would be saved. It was also known that the Łódź ghetto continued to exist and today we know that if the attempt on Hitler's life on 20 July, 1944 had succeeded, or if the

Soviet offensive had not stopped then on the other side of the Vistula river, over seventy thousand Jews still imprisoned in the ghetto would indeed have been saved.

Therefore one must not judge the attitudes and conduct of the population of the Warsaw ghetto nor those who honourably and conscientiously ran the Council on the basis of what we know today about the Nazi genocide machine and the world's passivity towards the extermination of the Jews, but on the basis of what these Jews could have known, thought and felt after reading the proclamation about the resettlement of the population to the East. After giving Lejkin instructions how to carry out the ominous German order, Chairman Czerniaków began a campaign to get the Germans to agree to exempt orphan children from resettlement and to find some means of support for them under the new conditions. At the same time he was waiting for any information about the progress of the action to deliver people to the assembly point at the railway sidings (the Umschlagplatz) was progressing. He feared German provocations and killings. He wrote on his diary under the date of 22 July 42: 'This afternoon Lejkin sent me a message that apparently someone had thrown some glass into a German motorcar. I was warned that if this happens again, our hostages will be shot'. His feelings of anxiety about provocations and pretexts for committing murder, were thus well founded. The terrified population was also keeping track of events, both on the streets and in their flats and everyone was trying to find any means to join the category of persons who were exempted from the resettlement action. Only very few made the decision to go to the Umschlagplatz voluntarily. Consequently, Jewish police were having to make up groups of people from those arrested on Gęsia Street, those in shelters for refugees, in asylums, homeless people and beggars to take them to the Umschlagplatz. At 5.00 p.m. Lejkin reported to chairman Czerniaków, that the required resettlement contingent of 6,000 people had been delivered.

An hour later the Chairman made his last entry of the day in his diary, as follows: 'Sturmbannführer Höfle (Beauftragter for resettlement) asked me to come to his office and announced that for the time being my wife will remain free, but if the deportation action should go wrong, she will be the first hostage to be shot'. The Chairman returned home about 7.00 p.m., but did not mention this threat to her. However he told her that the required contingent for resettlement had been delivered, but it was difficult to tell whether tomorrow this would also be possible to achieve without interference from the SS and without bloodshed. His wife told him that she had had a visit from Messrs. Berman and Gitler from Centos and they had asked if he could give an order to the Jewish police to protect all the orphanages from deportation. The Chairman told his wife that already during the first discussion concerning the implementation of the German order he had instructed Lejkin to do this and that he had also set efforts in motion to persuade the German authorities to agree officially to exempt orphans from the resettlement action.

Following the day's events, on the evening of 22 July 1942, the Chairman felt completely exhausted and, at the same time, he was coming to the realisation that an entirely new period of Jewish suffering, perhaps the most disastrous the Jewish people has ever known, was beginning and he thought that on that day he had succeeded in doing everything that was possible to mitigate this suffering and to prevent the worst scenario from happening. His thoughts were preoccupied with the question whether, taking into account the terrible reality, the next day would make it possible for him to carry out his duties in the same way.

Thursday 23 July, started with a glimmer of hope when Worthoff from the Umsiedlungsamt (resettlement department) appeared in the Council, and Chairman Czerniaków managed to have a positive discussion with him about a number of problems. He succeeded in obtaining exemptions from resettlement for pupils of polytechnic schools and also for husbands of working wives. As far as the orphans were concerned – as the Chairman noted down in his diary – he was told to talk about it to Höfle. He was also told to talk to him about the craftsmen. In reply to his question how many days per week the action would be in force, he was informed that it would be seven days per week. In the ghetto, there was tremendous pressure to set up workshops. The slogan 'A sewing machine can save lives' summed up the general situation. The population of the ghetto believed that the Germans really needed the existing as well as the newly-set-up manufacturing establishments which were working for their war effort. This kind of thinking seemed entirely logical, as the war had now been going on for over three years, and the needs of the war economy were growing all the time, and here in the ghetto, hundreds of thousands of people were eager to do work which was practically unpaid. However the rules which guide logical thinking could not be applied in relation to the Jews. For the Germans considered their priority to be the so-called final solution of the Jewish question, which signified the extermination of the entire Jewish population in the shortest possible time. Consequently, German tactics also included psychological options within the framework of the scrupulously worked out mechanism of mass murder. One such psychological option included facilitating the setting-up of production establishments attached to German firms, a process which inspired confidence in the ghetto people, particularly as they had been living in total isolation from the rest of the world and, as I have already indicated, had been left to their own devices. One should keep in mind, while judging this state of affairs, the situation the ghetto population found itself in and that it was entirely impossible for them to be able to be aware of the machine which had been set up with such German precision to plan and carry out this criminal carnage. Even the Polish underground Home Army, which was very well informed about the methods of German terror and which had an efficient intelligence service at its disposal, did not realise what was happening. During the first week, while the Jewish population was being deported from the Warsaw ghetto, it not only failed to recognise the extent of the German intentions, but it could not even get hold of reliable information about the final fate of the deported people. Even such an authoritative person as General Tadeusz Bór-Komorowski, the Home Army commander, wrote in his book,[9] that the reports and accounts 'about the greatest act of barbarity ever carried out in our times' were only reaching him gradually. He used to forward all these accounts to London, but it took a long time for anyone to believe – and many never did – that the Germans were involved in a programme of criminal genocide of the entire Jewish nation which found itself living within their domain. This state of affairs had also been documented by another eye witness of German savagery in the Warsaw ghetto, Professor Jan Karski (real name Jan Kozielewski), who in 1943 in London in his capacity as a Polish Underground courier, describes giving direct accounts of what he had seen and meeting with total disbelief.[10] So, if it is at all possible to reproach anyone with not doing anything to prevent or even to hamper the realisation of the German extermination plan, then in any case, it is certainly not the people of the Warsaw ghetto, besieged and for several months completely defenceless and deprived of any meaningful help as they were.

Neither could any such a reproach be directed towards Chairman Czerniaków. He had no other alternative than to strive for any alleviation of the effects of the order for 'resettlement' with the then well-founded hope that the ghetto would not be liquidated altogether. Such hopes had been engendered during the morning conversation with the German official from the resettlement headquarters. But at the same time a new, alarming situation had arisen, namely the delivery of the required contingent of people to the Umschlagplatz for 23 July was running into serious difficulties. During the first day of the action, the people who were under arrest, in asylums or in refuges, did not actually resist, as their situation in the ghetto was so bad that they thought that resettlement to another place was not likely to worsen their circumstances. But on the second day, the situation changed. It was necessary to summon people from their flats to come down and to assemble in the courtyards, or even to go upstairs and take them by force and to convey them to the Umschlagplatz when they could not show any documents exempting them from resettlement. For the most part, people refused to obey the summons of the Jewish police and it was feared that it would prove impossible to carry out the German order in its entirety. Barely half of the 2000 official Jewish policemen appeared for duty in the morning, and many of them went straight home again after roll call in order to protect their own families. Others found jobs as guards in the workshops and many simply shirked such painful duties as having to take people to the Umschlagplatz. Admittedly, the Council did call out employees of Jewish institutions to help the Jewish police to deliver the numbers of people demanded by the German authorities 'so as to protect innocent victims' and to prevent German squadrons from joining in the action, but without success. In fact a large number of people from all walks of life did answer this call, but what they were mainly interested in was to obtain an arm-band which would exempt themselves from resettlement. For this reason it was decided to do without this help, and only the remaining few hundred Jewish policemen were left to carry out the action. This led to dramatic confrontations, with Jew fighting Jew, and the passing German patrols incited these fratricidal struggles with bellowing and shooting. These were terrifying scenes, but everyone preferred to fight with a Jewish policeman than to meet SS men or officials of the Nazi units face to face. German treachery had reached the summit of its criminal tactic.

Practically every Jew made attempts to remain in the ghetto, not merely because of the uncertainty connected with the 'resettlement' action, but also because the fate of his family, spouse, children, parents, brothers and sisters was at stake. There were some cases where the whole family decided to go to the Umschlagplatz together to avoid being separated. But the vast majority struggled hard to remain in the ghetto. Under these circumstances the Jewish police, not having any way of enforcing the law except by getting involved in these dramatic battles, was unable to deliver the required numbers to the Umschlagplatz. By 3.00 p.m. the number of people there was only about 4,000, with just one hour to go. Many of the police, unable to take the psychological strain involved in carrying out the action, simply escaped home. Chairman Czerniaków, who was periodically kept abreast of the progress of the action, reacted with anguish to these struggles between fellow Jews, but like everyone else he was waiting with great trepidation for the reaction of the German authorities. The present situation had no precedent in the history of Jewish persecution. The German instructions given to the Council were unequivocal: Every day, the Judenrat, using its executive organ (the Jewish police), was under obligation to deliver a designated contingent of people for resettlement to the Umschlagplatz. But the desperate population, uncertain about the real significance of this resettlement, was for the most part refusing to obey the summons of the Jewish police to be taken to the Umschlagplatz. What was to be done? Should one have refused to carry out the orders of the German authorities, or withdrawn the Jewish police from the action or dissolved it and simply waited for the reaction of the German resettlement squads? At such a time, no Jew with any sense of responsibility was prepared to make such a decision. This would have resulted not just in the threatened execution of the hostages, counsellors and the Chairman and his wife in retaliation for not carrying out German orders, but also in mass repressions, slaughter and the inevitable liquidation of the entire ghetto. I must reiterate that on 23 July, not a single Jew was in a position to know the Germans' extermination plans and the fact that the people who were being deported were being sent directly to gas chambers and that within a few months the ghetto would be totally liquidated. It is for this reason that the penultimate entry in Czerniaków's diary dated 23 July 42 reads as follows: 'It is 3.00 o'clock. At the moment there are 4,000 ready to go. To comply with the order, there have to be 9,000 by 4.00 o'clock.'

About a quarter of an hour after this diary entry, the Chairman was informed that it would be impossible for the police to come up with the required number of people at the Umschlagplatz by the appointed time. A situation was developing which, at any moment, threatened to become irreversible in its ramifications and consequences. Up till now, Chairman Czerniaków never broke down in any critical situation and always undertook the appropriate defensive action. He, therefore, decided to contact Höfle and to request a reduction in the designated contingent and also an extension of the delivery deadline. He fully realised that the hope for having this request granted was small, but he could not fail to take some sort of action. None of his associates, counsellors or social functionaries could find any alternative, more efficacious course of action.

His attempts to contact Höfle were interrupted by appalling news. It appears that as soon as it became evident that the designated contingent of people for resettlement would not be completed, a detachment of SS-men, Lithuanians and Ukrainians joined in the action. They opened fire from hand-held machine guns and drove several thousand terrified people into the courtyards of their multi-storey houses which bordered on the Umschlagplatz. They did not look at any documents and they did not allow anything to be brought along, and drove everyone to the Umschlagplatz, just as they stood, with only the shirts on their backs, with the help of frenzied terror and monstrous howling.

This disclosure made everyone break down, including the Chairman. All the concessions in connection with the resettlement action which he had managed to win that morning, instantly became nothing more than useless scraps of paper. For the German detachment had driven individuals from their homes regardless of sex, age or any exemption certificates in their possession. What this meant was, that if the contingent designated by the German authorities could not be made available for resettlement by the Jewish police, then this would be done by the SS, and all the exemptions included in the proclamation would be pronounced null and void and it would prove impossible to avoid the beatings and murders. And if the Chairman were to fail to obtain a reduction in the numbers of people to be brought to the Umschlagplatz tomorrow, there were bound to be further tragic consequences. In this case any activity Czerniaków might become involved in in his capacity as the chairman of the Council would become purposeless. He would no longer be able to defend anyone or to try and soften the cutting edge of German orders and he would simply end up as a helpless witness to the deportation of people to an unknown destination cruelly carried out by the German detachments. He could not come to terms with such a thought, and decided, the very next morning, to make another attempt to lessen the severity of the German resettlement order and to insist that they respect the exemptions which were part of that order. At 5.00 p.m. Czerniaków went home in a state of utter despair and pain. Before he had a chance to recover from the shocks of the previous few hours, he was told by telephone that the Germans required his immediate presence in the Jewish Council premises.

Chairman Czerniaków left home at 6.00 p.m. and told his anxious wife that, if possible, he would try and return very soon. On arriving in his office in the Council, he found two officials of the resettlement staff Einsatz Reinhard already waiting for him. The discussion started immediately after his arrival. We do not have all the details of this conversation. We only heard the stormy sounds reaching us from his office. Certainly the fact that the police had not fulfilled their delivery quota of people to the Umschlagplatz that day had now made the threat of repressions a reality. One of these was put into action immediately, namely that the police were now required to provide 10,000 people to the Umschlagplatz the very next day.[11] This signified a considerable increase on the contingent of 6,000 which had been fixed on 22 July. Clearly, all the Chairman's intentions of trying to ease the process of resettlement had lost their meaning. Before arriving for his meeting with officials of Einsatz Reinhard, his fear that if the resettlement action were directly taken over by German units – which is exactly what did happen shortly – he would lose what little influence he had on the course of events, was becoming a reality. Then he would be in no position to defend anyone and people would be sent to the Umschlagplatz by the application of terror and murder, as had been done today when the police failed to provide the full contingent of people as demanded.

In this situation, Czerniaków clearly realised that his role as Chairman of the Council, deprived of any possibility of action to lighten the tragic fate of his people, had come to an end. He could not, however, remain passive. This stance had been totally alien to him, throughout the whole of his time of attending to his duties as Chairman of the Council. As the previous several hours had demonstrated, he realised that now not only there was no chance of undertaking any active resistance in the ghetto, but even passive defiance was futile. For the ghetto was a prison-camp where not only grown men and women were held, but whole families. Family ties, alongside defencelessness in the face of brutal terror, comprised one additional factor which rendered one powerless to undertake any kind of resistance action, especially taking into account the fact that no one yet knew the whole truth about the plan for genocide. In such a situation, the intimidated ghetto Jews reacted in accordance with their human nature, namely they wanted to save their lives and those of their nearest and dearest, and they had no other prospects than to attempt to do this within the framework of the existing reality.

Chairman Czerniaków was no longer able to help his people, and so far as his own personal fate was concerned – as he proved more than once – this was linked to serving a mission which was assigned to him by history. He was not yet aware of the full extent of the murderous intentions of the German powers, but all that had happened during the previous two days and what the next day was likely to bring, demanded some sort of action from a man who had always carried out his duties with complete dedication and a feeling of responsibility. Fully aware of the fact that he had to react to the enemy's brutality, lonely and helpless in the face of a cruel adversary armed to the teeth, he willingly laid down his own life.

Immediately after the departure of the Einsatz Reinhard officials, Czerniaków writes a suicide note addressed to the Council Management, in which he informs them of the new ultimatum; he also writes a short farewell letter to his wife.[12] Next, clear as to his intentions, sitting behind the desk which he had occupied as Chairman of the Council, he takes poison from a phial of potassium cyanide in his possession.

The circumstances preceding the suicide and the place where it was carried out, unequivocally point to the nature of the deed. The situation was such that Czerniaków could no longer deal with the orders of the brutal enemy and as Chairman of the Council he decided to protest against the action of the Nazi criminals in the Warsaw ghetto. But also 'in the deep belief that his sacrifice would arouse the indifferent world and would help save his brothers' – as the Chairman's wife Dr Felicja Czerniaków wrote to Dr Henryk Szoskies in February 1948.[13] In the same letter she also observed: 'Czerniaków was the first ghetto uprising! When the time came, his brothers understood the call: they rose up and attacked the barbarians during the later, never-to-be-forgotten uprising'. Granted that these words belong to Chairman Czerniaków's wife, nonetheless the course of events following his death fully confirm their truth. The sacrifice of Czerniaków's life did not waken the indifferent world and it did not prevent the tragedy of the Warsaw ghetto, but it did become the seed of active resistance taken up by the heroic defenders of the ghetto who set out to vindicate Jewish dignity and honour. They went into their last battle in armed combat on 19 April 1943.

But that which happened on 19 April was not possible on 23 July 1942. During the following nine months, the situation in the ghetto changed radically. Gradually, the people began to find out the whole truth about the 'resettlement', which in reality signified organised genocide. Political organisations, and the Zionist youth moment in particular, were becoming more active. Money for the purchase of arms was being collected or procured, the population was becoming conscious of the consequences of believing the fraudulent German reassurances that there was no danger for those working in German production establishments and the idea of armed resistance was gaining more support. Towards the end of 1942, the Jewish Fighting Organisation (ŻOB), led by the 24-year old member of the top command of *Hashomer Hatsair* Mordechai Anielewicz, was founded. No longer were the proclamations given out by the Council on the orders of the German authorities wholly carried out. The population was now beginning to pay more attention to the proclamations and actions of the Jewish Fighting Organisation. And the Jewish fighters did rise up in armed battle to drive off the enemy, when on 19 April 1943, German detachments and police, accompanied by Ukrainian, Latvian and Lithuanian units, all armed to the teeth entered the ghetto in order to raze it to the ground. This act of heroic resistance continued for several weeks. There are very few examples in history of such an uneven contest led with such dedication in defence of dignity and honour.

On 8 May, German armed detachments surrounded the bunker occupied by the leaders of the Jewish Combat Organisation in their determination to capture the leaders of the uprising, even using gas weapons. There was no chance of any further defence. Not being prepared to surrender, Mordechai Anielewicz and his fellow combatants committed suicide.

And so, the death of the Chairman of the Council, Adam Czerniaków by suicide initiated the period of the destruction of the Warsaw ghetto, whilst the suicide of Mordechai Anielewicz, the leader of the Uprising closed the last episode of the struggle against the crime of genocide which was perpetrated on the population of that ghetto.

Adam Czerniaków did not have a chance to commit suicide in such heroic circumstances as Mordechai Anielewicz. But his act of protest on 23 July 1942 was a spark which, to a large extent, kindled the progressively intensifying popular resistance, culminating in the heroic Uprising against the Nazi murderers in April 1943. Both these deaths will therefore remain forever in history as a symbol of martyrdom and the fight in the cause of preserving life, the dignity of man and the honour of the Jewish population confined in the Warsaw ghetto by brutal force.

A great deal more has been written about Janusz Korczak's last journey than about Adam Czerniaków's death and there are also a great number of inaccuracies, liberties, embellishments and even straightforward inventions to be found in these writings. Some of the authors of memoirs and other accounts of Janusz Korczak's last journey, thought that the martyrdom of the children whom the great social functionary, writer and doctor led to the Umschlagplatz on that sweltering August day in 1942, required additional embellishment, pathos, loftiness and even fantasy, for it to be able to find its special place in the annals of the horrifying crime of genocide which was inflicted on the Jewish people. Yet the cruel reality of this march of these children accompanied by their teachers, to be loaded into the train waiting for them at the Umschlagplatz is in itself immensely tragic and moving, without the need for any fabrication or excessive pathos.

Before I describe my version of the course of events of August, 1942, I think that it might be useful to set my view of some of the memoirs and studies which have been published about Janusz Korczak's last journey. I have selected the memoirs of Adolf Berman,[14] Nachum Remba,[15] Marek Rudnicki[16] and Ida Merzan.[17]

I will begin with Ida Merzan's exemplary text which, whilst negating some of the earlier myths about Janusz Korczak's last journey, at the same time creates a new myth of its own. And so, Ida Merzan, an outstanding and well-respected educationist, Janusz Korczak's collaborator from pre-war years, uses accounts from eye witnesses about his last journey, and bases her own judgments on them. She writes as follows: 'there are a great number of literary visions describing that day, and in my opinion, one should not get involved in any polemical discussions with them'. She justifies these visions by saying that the writers have a perfect right to write 'as their imagination dictates'. But in the same article she continues: 'The only thing that makes me angry, is when a writer or a scenarist presents false facts as true ones'. But if she allows a writer to draw on his imagination, then this is exactly the source of these literary or cinematic visions which are largely based on deformations or simply on inventions about Janusz Korczak's last journey. If a writer has the right to draw on his imagination to describe Janusz Korczak's last journey, this clearly contributes to the creation of the various myths and legends.

And Ida Merzan creates a new myth herself. When referring to Hanna Mortkiewicz's description of how the children went to the Umschlagplatz 'calmly and in an orderly fashion', she draws the conclusion that the children's composure was not – as the poets tend to suppose – a result of Dr Korczak having made them believe that they were going to the country, but that 'the children knew that they were going to their death'. This conclusion contradicts not only the truth about the state of awareness of those who were being deported at the beginning of August 1942, but human nature as well. Even if we accept that – as the writer asserts – 'nearly every day Korczak kept telling the children that one must never give up one's humanity, even in the face of death . . .' is it likely that this kind of noble teaching could, in a relatively short time, transform the instinct of all the children so successfully as to be able to remove from them any trace of natural anxiety and fear of death. And besides, it would not have been possible to make their instinct of self-preservation disappear to such an extent that the children would march and mount the train, knowing 'that they were going to their death' in a state of complete composure and self-possession. To support her theory that the children were well aware of the fact that deportation meant certain death, Ida Merzan also refers to the fact that 'the children used to return to their family homes every week, so they were not really cut off from the general atmosphere within the ghetto and were fully aware of what was in store for them.' There is no shadow of a doubt that every succeeding day of the resettlement action – with the action being progressively taken over by detachments of the SS, Lithuanians, Latvians and Ukrainians – further intensified the feelings of extreme anxiety, fear and menace in the ghetto, but in spite of all this, during this period in the ghetto, allegations that deportation necessarily signified a direct road to a camp and instant extermination were still not believed. The vast majority of the people – and at the end of July/beginning of August 1942, there were still 300,000 inhabitants in the ghetto – thought that the people deported were sent to places like concentration camps, which did not necessarily mean instant annihilation. I recall that Tadeusz Bór-Komorowski wrote in his previously cited book *Armia Podziemna* (Underground Army) that the Home Army's intelligence was making efforts to obtain information about where the Jews from the Warsaw ghetto were being taken to and what was their fate. They found out quite quickly that the Jews were being taken to a place called Treblinka, but that 'the Germans made a special effort to prevent any news from the concentration camp in Treblinka reaching the outside world.' Bór-Komorowski writes that only towards the end of August did the Home Army intelligence service manage to obtain any reliable information about the existence of gas chambers in Treblinka and that Jews were being sent there after arrival. In any case, on 6 August 1942, no one in the ghetto could be certain about the fate of the deportees. Neither did Dr Korczak with whom I had a conversation on 3 August. He was trying to find out if we had succeeded in placing all the children from the Detention Chamber attached to the 3rd regional police station in orphanages. At that time we had no idea that in three days' time the deportation of children from the orphanages would begin.

And when the tragic day of 6 August did arrive, Dr Korczak did everything he could to keep the children quiet, and without having to be driven by the Nazi killers, they marched in columns of four to the Umschlagplatz. When they arrived there, Dr Korczak and the other teachers also made every effort to make the children remain calm and to create the optimum conditions for their journey under the brutal circumstances. This is how Dr Adolf Berman, the distinguished Centos official described the scene in his memoir: 'Dr Korczak was worried about the fact that the children who had been driven out without a moment's notice, had not managed to take anything along with them and they were wearing only thin summery shirts. With a friendly smile, Wiłczynska told the younger children that they were going on an outing and that, at last, they were going to see woods, fields and meadows'. From this account it appears that the children were being comforted and taken care of. It is known that Dr Korczak was involved in productive efforts to provide the children with some food and water for the journey and – according to Dr Berman – 'the Jewish police managed to get more carriages for them, to make their journey more comfortable'. In the inhuman conditions of the Umschlagplatz, with the continual threat of German terror, such efforts and pains about the children's welfare and relative comfort would not have been undertaken if it had been known that they were going straight to their death. Everything points to the fact that Dr Korczak was concerned about the children arriving at their destination in a relatively good physical state. This outstanding educationalist and social functionary remained hopeful that he would continue to be able to be of help to these children, even in the most dire circumstances, but he was certainly not getting them ready 'to go to their deaths' and they were supposedly accepting this in a totally calm state. May I say again that Ida Merzan's conclusion is entirely erroneous and based on some arbitrarily selected accounts which had been given to her and evaluated ex post facto.

In addition, in order to support her conclusions further, Ida Merzan refers to the memoir of Nachum Remba, an eye witness of the children's march to the train at the Umschlagplatz, led by Dr Korczak and other teachers. From his memoir it may be surmised that while boarding the train the deportees were aware that they were going straight to their deaths. But the fact remains, that Nachum Remba was writing his memoir at a time when this horrible truth was already widely known, and clearly, he applies this later knowledge to the situation which existed on 6 August 1942.

Nachum Remba exhibited exceptional courage and dedication during the deportation action, frequently following the convoy of deportees, sometimes all the way to the Umschlagplatz which was so carefully guarded by the particularly cruel SS-men, Lithuanians, Ukrainians and Latvians. The object was to find the right moment to try and extricate and save – just in the nick of time, as it turned out in many cases – some people of distinction. I have no doubt that Remba also wanted to do everything in his power to save the children and their teachers from deportation. This is how he describes the situation in his memoir: 'I proposed to Korczak to go with me to the Council to convince them to intervene on their behalf.' Aside from the fact that just getting out of the Umschlagplatz for someone finding himself as part of a convoy which had just arrived there was not a simple proposition, by then the intervention by the Council could not only have no effect, but even such an undertaking had, by this time, ceased to be a realistic proposal. And besides, elsewhere in his memoir Remba remarks: 'A wave of deep pain swept over me at the thought that now we are so helpless and that I cannot do anything but stand around idly and watch the carnage.' It is precisely this deep pain and the heart-rending experience connected with witnessing the children along with Dr Korczak and the other teachers boarding the train, which linked up with the later disclosure of the truth about their fate which influenced the content of Nachum Remba's memoir. It is for this reason that his moving memoir has an especially personal and emotional character and is far from free from adornments and unrealistic embellishments, similarly it is characterised by a superfluous and very detrimental evaluation of the demeanour of the remaining deportees, who are described as 'a herded mass going like cattle to the slaughter'.

Every so often, new publications and films about Dr Korczak's life and his final journey keep materialising. In October 1988, at the Korczak symposium in Germany, the memoir of Marek Rudnicki, a well-known painter living and working in Paris since 1957 was read. This memoir was acclaimed as a revelation because it departs completely from any previous publications; it has no embellishments and is totally devoid of any pathos. Below is a quote from Marek Rudnicki's memoir:

> This scene is well known and has been described and reconstructed many times, not always accurately. I don't want to belittle or debunk, but I must truthfully say how I saw it.
> 
> The atmosphere was pervaded by some paralysing fatigue, numbness, apathy. There was no sign of agitation, no saluting (as some describe it) because here walked Korczak with his children, certainly there were no messengers from the Judenrat – nobody has approached Korczak. There were no gestures, no singing, no proud spring in the step; I don't remember whether the children carried the Children's Home flag – some people say they did. There was an overwhelming, weary silence. Korczak dragged his feet with an effort, appeared smaller than usual, as if shrunk, mumbling something to himself.[16]

Rudnicki recalls that he accompanied the convoy right up to the Umschlagplatz gate where he went 'nearly every day' bringing baskets of bread loaves sent by the Judenrat for the deportees. From a distance of about 30 metres, he writes, he observed how the children mounted the train and that 'Korczak was last. I can see his hunched silhouette disappearing from view.' Rudnicki also recalls the presence of a Judenrat official in the square, and says 'now I know that this was Nachum Remba' and he believes that his account is the only authentic testimony of an eye witness. I am aware of the fact, that some people consider this statement as seriously undermining the validity of Rudnicki's memoir which, after all, stands in stark contrast to Nachum Remba's account. In December, 1988 in London, I had the opportunity of discussing this subject with a well-known Korczak expert, Rafael Scharf, who wrote down the Rudnicki memoir. He told me that he himself pointed out to Rudnicki that the Judenrat official's name was Nachum Remba. And yet, Marek Rudnicki did not know about Nachum Remba's memoir when describing what he had seen.

I think that one should not separate the true course of events of 6 August 1942 from the tragic situation of the whole besieged Warsaw ghetto population. This was the sixteenth day of the so-called resettlement of the Jews to the East and the mood of the Jewish people was shifting every day.

During the first two days of the resettlement action, the prevailing opinion was that the carrying out of the German order about delivery of a designated contingent of unemployed people for resettlement would make it possible to keep the ghetto going albeit in a whittled down form. But Czerniaków's sudden suicide, a man whom the population basically trusted, increased the state of anxiety and insecurity which already existed. But at that time the only reigning principle in the ghetto was to hope against hope. Consequently, everyone tried to obtain any sort of a job which would provide them with a work document. These documents were acceptable to the Jewish police. When, however, it emerged that the police – whose numbers were decreasing every day – were not able to deliver the full contingent demanded to the Umschlagplatz, the Germans themselves took over the implementation of the resettlement action. This resulted in a fundamental change in the general situation. No longer was there any possibility of disobeying the people in charge of the action with impunity and furthermore any intervention on the part of the Council officials had no effect on the SS-men, Lithuanians, Latvians and Ukrainians. This was the start of many tragedies connected with families being separated, it also became pointless to make efforts to protect the intelligentsia and work papers were no longer always respected, but the orphanages still existed and it was assumed that maybe the resettlement action was coming to an end. For this reason, individuals who did not have jobs in the workshops tried every day to find out where the Einsatz Reinhard detachments leading the resettlement action were located, to be able to have time to escape to another part of the ghetto or to try and find a reliable hiding place. During the action, as a rule, the streets were quite empty.

August 1942 was exceptionally hot. But it was not the heat which determined the frame of mind of people, for whom the basic problem was to avoid resettlement and all their thoughts and efforts were directed to this end. As soon as morning came, everyone waited for news in a state of the highest tension. About 9.00 o'clock, reports that the German detachments were heading for the orphanages spread throughout the ghetto with lightning speed. This development was interpreted in several different ways: some said that the Germans were simply continuing to carry out their announced plan to resettle all non-working individuals, whilst others saw it as an evil omen for the continued existence of the ghetto. The psychological state of the people was subjected to further unbearable strain. About 10 o'clock it was being said up and down the ghetto that the orphanage in No. 16 Sienna Street was also being surrounded.

And this is exactly what was happening. Dr Janusz Korczak and his colleagues did not want to allow the Nazi assassins to drive the children out of the orphanage building using their customary brutal tactics. For this reason, immediately after the orphanage was surrounded, the teachers told the children to go outside. There they arranged them in columns of four, comforting and keeping them under control as best as they could. These children trusted their teachers, and they set off to the Umschlagplatz with Dr Korczak at the head of the marching columns, a scene described so often in so many different ways, so colourfully, frequently with a large amount of pathos and simple imagination. But, after all, this was not the first forced march of Jews to the Umschlagplatz. It is true that it was the first procession involving children, and this fact did evoke special pain in view of their age and particular defencelessness. The streets were empty, and many people had the opportunity to observe this tragic procession, and those who really did see it, reported that the children marched quietly and that the teachers made a point of keeping them well-disciplined. Dr Korczak, in a state of severe depression, walked at the head of the procession, clearly considering in his mind what was in store for these children and how he would be able to help them in these new circumstances. There is no need to embellish this children's march to the Umschlagplatz. Their road was strewn with thorns and the desperate helplessness of the Jewish people, a road of those who were defenceless, abandoned and subjected to a barbaric force. On 6 August 1942, Jewish children and their teachers marched along this road.

The arrival of the children and Dr Janusz Korczak at the Umschlagplatz did not arouse any interest. I was told all about it by a Jewish policeman who had arrived there early that morning to try and rescue his sister-in-law. The German, Lithuanian, Ukrainian and Latvian detachments which guarded the Umschlagplatz were particularly vicious. But on that day, the excessive heat seemed to dampen their zeal a little, and they were being a bit less cruel than normal. As a result, Dr Korczak and Stefania Wiłczynska were able to provide the children with some food and water without being harassed, and they also were able to make the time the children had to spend in this inhuman place somewhat easier while waiting for their impending journey. The children were first to climb into the cattle trucks, followed by the teachers, and last of all by Dr Janusz Korczak.

Of course, everyone in the Council was well aware of what was going on, but there was no possibility of any realistic intervention any longer, and no one was considering – as Dr Izrael Milejkowski claims[18] – any attempt to separate Dr Korczak from the children. Such a thought would never have occurred to anyone who knew this outstanding educationist and children's friend, already legendary in his lifetime.

Among the many ridiculous fabrications are the different versions of how a German officer offered to release Dr Korczak from the Umschlagplatz. We know that Dr Korczak would never have agreed to leave the children, but we know, too, that for several days preceding this incident, many outstanding Jews from almost all walks of life were being driven from this inhuman place into the cattle trucks. Not one of the German ruffians, regardless of his rank, ever offered to free any one of them. In their eyes they were simply creatures called 'Jude', regardless of their personality, sex or age. And this designation determined the way the German criminals behaved towards them. The assertion that a German officer offered to release this outstanding personality, Dr Korczak, from the Umschlagplatz belongs to the realm of fantasy, and totally contradicts the barbaric reality of that place. It also devalues the tragedy of the last journey of every other Jew, including the Jewish children and their beloved teacher. It amounts to an attempt to ascribe humane gestures to the behaviour of Nazi criminals, whose actions were a negation of any form of humanity.

The cruel fate of the children, who were led, on what turned out to be their last journey, by this outstanding social activist, writer, doctor, and educationist on 6 August 1942, does not require any additional colouring, pathos, or embellishment in order to embody an eternal monument to martyrdom, more durable than bronze, that martyrdom which was inflicted on a great but defenceless educationist, on his worthy team of collaborators and on his beloved children by the Nazi criminals, for no other reason than that they were born Jews.

## NOTES

1 Ed. M. Fuks, *Adama Czerniakowa dziennik getta warszawskiego 6.9.1939–23.8.1942*, (Warsaw, 1983).
2 *Biuletyn Żydowskiego Instytutu Historycznego* (henceforth BZIH), January–March 1972, No. 1.
3 Hanna Krall, *Zdążyć przed Panem Bogiem* (Kraków, 1977).
4 Emanuel Ringelblum, *Kronika getta warszawskiego* (Warsaw, 1983) p. 406.
5 *Pamiętniki z getta warszawskiego*, ed. Michal Grynberg (Warsaw, 1988), where, for example, Jan Mawult mistakenly says that chairman Czerniaków committed suicide on the third day of the resettlement action (p. 54), and Samuel Puterman invents the date and circumstances surrounding Czerniaków's death (pp. 90–91).
6 Leon Tyszka, *Sukcesy i klęski jednego życia* (London, 1984).
7 At No. 13 Leszno Street in the Ghetto, the Gestapo had organised their own agents

who called themselves 'Commission for Combating Usury and Speculation'. People would refer to this institution as 'No. 13', from the Leszno street number but everyone was well aware of the fact that those who were established there worked for the Gestapo.
8 The duty of the Jewish police force was to detain any person found in the streets after the curfew. In general, only beggar children failed to obey this curfew. The Jewish police had no suitable building to put them in and a passing German police patrol could easily shoot these children dead. There were also other dangers. Homeless and severely starved children who were left in the streets overnight, would generally be dead by the next morning. Following the initiative of several lawyer colleagues from the 3rd local police department and with the support of Rachela Auerbach, a prominent social worker in charge of the soup kitchen at 40 Leszno Street, where the 3rd local police station was located, and the paediatrician Jan Przedborski, with the greatest difficulty, we managed to find the necessary shelter. We adapted it, obtaining sufficient finance to house and feed the detained children. After 2-3 days we made attempts to find them places in orphanages. And we considered our shelter for detained children as complementing the official local police station, hence its name: 'The detention chamber of the 3rd local police station'. Following our example, another district also organised a similar Detention Chamber on Chłodna Street and Chairman Czerniaków made a speech at its opening ceremony.
9 Tadeusz Bór-Komorowski, *Armia Podziemna* (London, 1952).
10 Jan Karski, 'Niespelniona misja', *Tygodnik Powszechny*, No. 11, Kraków, 15 March 1987.
11 Before taking poison, the Chairman left a suicide note addressed to the Council, which said: 'We have been told to have 10,000 Jews ready in the railway siding for tomorrow.'
12 These details were supplied by Dr Felicja Czerniaków who was called as a witness on 10 July 1948 by Judge Halina Weronka, a member of the Regional Commission for the Investigation of German Crimes in Warsaw (a photocopy of the evidence is published as supplement no.15 to Adam Czerniaków's diary, edited by Marian Fuks). In the same way – corroborating Dr Felicja Czerniaków's evidence – the day after the Chairman's death, Zygmunt Warman, who at that time was Council Secretary, described the circumstances of his death to several of his colleagues, including myself and the fact that the Chairman had left two letters on his desk, one to his wife and the other to the Members of the Council telling them of the demands made by the Einsatz Reinhard officials to provide 10,000 Jews the next day. In this context the content of the Chairman's letter to the Council given by Leon Tyszka in his book gives rise to serious reservations and doubts, particularly the words 'they demanded a transport of children for tomorrow'. There was no such demand and there was no such transport, and the deportation of children started only at the beginning of August 1942, whereas the Chairman passed on the order he had been given, namely 'to supply 10,000 Jews to the railway sidings the next day'.
13 The social activist Dr Henryk Szoskies was a member of the Jewish Council and left Poland at the beginning of 1940. The remaining part of Dr Felicja Czerniaków's letter to him as well as the circumstances connected with his leaving Poland and his friendship with Chairman Czerniaków are described in appendix 13 to Adam Czerniaków's diary. Now, after fifty years have elapsed since these tragic events, unfounded reproaches are no longer being voiced about Czerniaków's failure to call the people to take up active or even passive resistance, or that his suicide was an act of cowardice or that it occurred for private reasons. In an act of protest against the actions of the Nazi criminals, Chairman Czerniaków committed suicide

immediately after the representatives of the killers had left his office and so he consciously imparted a public meaning on his death. However, statements such as those of Henryk Bryskier (p. 100 of the *Pamiętniki z getta warszawskiego*), to the effect that 'The Chairman of the Jewish Council was definitely fully informed about the general situation in the order where it was stated how the authorities intended to carry out their programme' and that 'he understood perfectly well the meaning behind the word resettlement, its magnitude, its goals and its end', are so lacking in judgement and irresponsible, that they deserve nothing more than to be ignored.

14 Adolf Berman 'O losie dzieci żydowskich z zakladów Opiekuńczych w Getcie Warszawskim', *BŻIH* no. 28; October–December 1958.
15 Nachum Remba, Part of an essay about the Umschlagplatz in connection with the deportation of children and of Janusz Korczak published in Emanuel Ringelblum's *Kronika getta warszawskiego*.
16 Marek Rudnicki 'Ostatni droga Janusza Korczaka', *Tygodnik Powszechny*, Warsaw, No. 45, 6 November 1988. English version, POLIN, VII, pp. 219–223.
17 Ida Merzan 'Ostatnia droga Janusza Korczaka', *Folks-Sztyme*, No. 6, 8 February 1986.
18 Izrael Milejkowski, medical doctor, well-known social activist, Director of the Health Department of the Warsaw Ghetto Council.

# SISTER WANDA
## Anna Clarke

Her times demand answers which she takes over 40 years to give.

This story unfolds in July 1943, a few months after the final destruction of the Warsaw ghetto. A young girl lives in Warsaw on false papers not far from where the ghetto used to be. Her blue eyes and blond hair make it possible to move about the city – cautiously. There are questions about the destruction of her nation which her mind urges her to answer in one of several ways.

(1) Become so good at being somebody else that it becomes second nature and she might start telling herself as well as others that the destruction has nothing to do with her. Or loathe the pretence and live only for the day when it is no longer necessary.

(2) Decide that the Jewish nation was a second Sodom that was destroyed and that it deserved its fate. Hate the whole world for the perpetration of the deed or for having allowed it to happen.

(3) Blame herself for being alive – only the wicked stay alive. Or she can rejoice in being alive.

(4) Be filled with gratitude towards those who are helping her now or consider that it is the least they can do in the circumstance and that she herself would have done the same.

She does instead what another sensible girl, Scarlett, did. Promises herself to attend to these questions later, in due time, tomorrow. In forty years if necessary. Right now her hands are full with a script. With no elocution or movement lessons, make-up or prompter she is to memorize and play the part of heroine.

The steps which the hero has to go through: initiating, killing of dragons and coming home are of course the stuff of myth and tale. Some of these steps are also present in this story. It begins in a pit as deep as Joseph's well, it goes through miraculous rescue, it has a protecting angel in the form of a nun, continues through a forty year quest, a return to source and a coming home.

The nun, the title figure of this story and one who plays such an important role in it is like any of the legendary forces who step in and save the hero at a critical moment. Like birds who point the way, the pebbles shining in the night, or the woodcutter who saves the baby Oedipus or Miriam protecting the baby in the bulrushes. Just as well. Our heroine is singularly badly cast for the initiation. Neither her knowledge of romantic novels nor her naive beliefs are of use in the pit. Although no longer a babe herself she is as much in need of help as any babe in the woods.

So much for the mythical part of our story. But – like some and unlike other myths our story is true and verifiable in every detail. In particular the life of the nun, of Sister Wanda, is very well documented. The good nuns of the Immaculate Order in Poland have gathered a thick file on her courage, her resistance to barbarity and her practical skill in saving Jewish lives. It is precisely because the story is such a combination of the mythical and the factual that the story is told. So that it can be said again that truth is mythical and myth is true, today as ever.

The spirit of today's hero may be tried by modern means of suppression as it used to be imprisoned in a bottle or in the body of a frog – but the spirit is there. Today, as in fairy-tale times, the spirit of the hero prevails. It takes a long time. Forty years wandering in the desert were needed before the books were completed. Forty years it takes in this story before the spirit of self-knowledge and freedom speaks. Speaks of freedom to be who one is and of the freedom of giving gratitude to where it is due – only.

Yes, forty years is the span of time in which the present becomes the past. So are the events of World War Two becoming the past now and the spirit of detachment which is the prerequisite of truth is replacing the passions of the past. And this is another and final reason why this story is told – in an attempt to tell the truth, now that the fires have burned down slowly. Now for the pit.

By July 1943 news of the fate of Polish Jews had reached the world. A number of immigration papers were sent from abroad, mainly from the U.S. and South America, some from Palestine. By the time the papers came to Warsaw most of the addressees were dead. The papers were then offered to some of the ones who were still alive and in hiding. Those who had by various means obtained the papers came out of hiding and gathered in the Hotel Polski. My parents, whose own hiding places collapsed one after the other, heard of the Hotel and went in.

And in the Hotel Polski I saw my cousin Esther Syrkis, the romantic queen of my romantic youth. To my eyes she was the biblical Esther who obtained grace and favour in the eyes of the King. Later, much later, I thought of her again when reading about Lara carrying her pail in Pasternak's novel. Ester married later in life and emigrated to Palestine and her bitter fate caught her with a baby in wartime Poland. Even now, in the Hotel Polski in 1943 in a long flowery dress she queened it over her surroundings. She was here with her sisters Idunia and Mala, Mala's husband, and the three little daughters of the three sisters. They had exchange papers to go to Germany, and were getting ready to leave the next morning. With a pile of children's clothing getting rapidly smaller on her ironing board, she was telling me of Sister Wanda.

Sister Wanda had hidden her, her sisters and a sister-in-law of one of them. Found a job for Mala's husband as a gardener in one of the monastery's gardens. Most important of all, hid the three little girls. When the mothers came to claim them before coming to the Hotel, the children were 'full of lice', Esther took her eyes off the board to look at me – 'but alive and in one piece'. 'Don't write anything down, but here is her address. Go to her when in need and she will help you, too,' she was saying next morning, shortly before the whole group left in an orderly fashion. And to their death, as we now know. A few hours later the Gestapo Marias came and took away everyone still in the Hotel.

When the trucks came I was standing in the wide entrance gate of the Hotel. Two girls in a party of workers passing the gate on their way to register at a brick factory in the neighbourhood made room for me between them. The girls were quicker to take in what went on that I was. Outside the Hotel they let me go free, but not before one of them took Mother's wedding ring off my finger and money from my purse in reward for the escape.

My own meeting with Sister Wanda took place late in the fall of that same year when I needed a place to stay. From a dark street up a dark staircase and into a large dimly lit room where Sisters slept all across the floor. Soon I found a mattress, too. 'Why are you risking the lives of so many people because of me?' I asked Sister Wanda. 'For the love of the God we have in common', she answered.

Soon Sister Wanda had a job for me. A country estate had asked for a governess for a high-school boy. Sister Wanda had confidence in my ability to teach the required subjects except one. I was to teach the boy religion.

Five hundred years earlier, during the Inquisition, every nerve of the Jew strained in the struggle with the monk. Here now in 1943 was a nun in her cell patiently teaching me the arcana of her religion, the catechism, the prayers, the mass, to fool her parishioners. The miracle of the mass was the fact over which I stumbled over and over again, both the fact and the significance of the fact that the transformation of the bread and of the wine was happening in front of my eyes. My eyes could not see the prophet Elijah when, as a little girl, I was sent to open the door for him at Passover, and I was older now.

At the estate, my 14 year-old student showed little enthusiasm for study, secular or religious, thus leaving me plenty of time for the ponds, the woods and air of the countryside. Then on Sunday morning it was time for church.

Sister Wanda had warned me in Warsaw not to try to avoid going and I went. No one made any remarks about my behaviour either at church or later. But many eyebrows must have been raised. The way the cards were dealt, I never had a chance. In the fourth year of the war I certainly had no 'better', no 'Sunday' clothes. Neither Mother nor Father were synagogue goers and so I didn't have the inherited feeling for a suitable attire with what I had either. Never before except for a school excursion had I been inside a church, let alone during service in a little country church. I couldn't have known where to stand, to sit, to get up, make the sign of the cross or to kneel. The collection plate when it appeared must have found me completely unprepared – the fourth commandment flows deeply in Jewish blood.

The conversation at the dinner table after church was lively, cultivated and intelligent. Over fish from the pond we heard that one of the guests had worked before the war for Count Radziwiłł in the Count's huge feudal estates. There peasants had been found guilty and had been severely fined for a minor offence in the woods. Politely and mildly had our guest tried to intervene on their behalf, pointing out the meagreness of their earnings. 'Peasants are not to earn but to serve, and you, Sir, are a communist', whereupon 'I may be a communist but you, Count, are an idiot', was the exchange which landed them both in court for slander and defamation of character. The legal proceedings were interrupted by the outbreak of the war and then settled, perhaps forever, by the invasion of Stalin's army. This conversation became engraved in my memory forever, word by word, as we all sat there at the dinner table. It certainly was not because of any premonition of times to come, of how these communists, peasants, earnings, counts, will go down in history. Why, I had no premonition of what was to come in the most immediate future.

For of course I agreed to meet the guests again later that evening in the little drawing-room. And of course, I agreed that Sister Wanda was a remarkable person. Just how long had I known Sister Wanda, one of the guests wished to know, and was I in fact of the parish? Because, if so, perhaps we had friends in common. And, given the importance of influencing the young and impressionable mind of a boy, would I mind telling them the name of my school in Warsaw? One had friends in so many of the better schools, teachers and parents both. Not in mine, though, no, not in mine.

Next morning, it was still dark when her ladyship in her nightdress stood in my room. Partisans took goods and people during the night. There was turbulence in the village, they were sorry for the inconvenience, but it was for my own good. My ticket? Yes, absolutely, not to worry about the ticket. It will be taken care of and I was to go back to Warsaw the same day. 'Well, I should think that was the least that they could have done for you', snorted the young girl who was sent with me as an escort. 'What people'. Perhaps she was one of the peasants who were there to serve not to earn, or, not to give her the class consciousness she may never have had, perhaps she was just honest. Someone had to be honest for the world to continue. A few months later while I was in Germany working as a maid, the war ended. The pit was no more. Soon afterwards I married, and left Poland first for England and Germany then Canada.

For forty years the incident of the estate and the encounter with Sister Wanda germinated. Those forty years were the time of marriage, childbearing, emigration, teaching, making a home in a new country. There were also the years of inner shift from the cosmopolitan to the national. The process was long and perhaps needs a story in itself. In the fall of '88 I went to Poland, to hear the language and see the countryside again and also to find a trace of Sister Wanda who had helped me to survive. It took three weeks of search in Warsaw, a city which had been destroyed – and rebuilt street by street and house by house – to find a trace of so long ago. Finally, through luck and with the help of priests and nuns I found a nun who had known Sister Wanda personally. Sister Ena who is now a prioress herself, showed me a file of testimonies to Sister Wanda's activities.

After I had read through the file, Sister Ena took me for a walk and she talked. She told me that on one occasion when she was a novice under Sister Wanda she and all the other Sisters were called in. Things were getting very dangerous. The House was full of Jewish children and the Gestapo had already called Sister Wanda in more than once to question her. The Sisters were told of the situation. 'I was very young myself, only 16 and I was sorry for my life', Sister Ena confessed walking beside me. Once again I heard myself asking Sister Wanda why she was risking all those lives, and now I thought in panic, I wasn't asking a coy question at all. It was a very real question. Now here, after many years, am I expected to see, to recognize that she may have been wrong? That she may not have had the right to cheat parishioners, to teach me how to cheat, how to lie and blaspheme, that she should have asked and waited for everybody's consent before endangering their lives to save a life, a child, an old couple?

The panic didn't last long, I knew the answer. Asking permission is a luxury which is granted to some times and to some places and not to other times and other places. Wisdom is necessary to tell the difference between them, and Sister Wanda had the wisdom to act without permission in her time and in her place.

As soon as I was back in Ottawa I wrote the story down. And as I was writing I knew the story was incomplete. Incomplete, after so many years. But that was just it – why have I waited so many, many years. Out of gratitude and common decency I should have looked for and found Sister Wanda after the war or at least when she was still alive. Then why didn't I? Having gone to Poland, come back and living through it all again I think that I now know why. There were three reasons why I didn't go to look for Sister Wanda before.

First, the episode at the estate hurt my vanity – I failed a test, I didn't do my homework well enough, I let my tutor down. The star pupil of my class failed a test – imagine that. For a brief moment I was in Paradise and lost it through incompetence. Had I been cleverer or worked harder, I could have stayed in the company of the ladies and gentlemen of the estate, the embodiment of all the romantic heroes of my Polish childhood. For that childish vanity I ask forgiveness of the spirit of Sister Wanda

And yet, and yet. Why, really, didn't I try harder? It would have been easy, wouldn't it, to go to church a few times to see how it was done. To prepare a good cover story in anticipation of questions. Could it be that I wanted the impossible – I wanted the people at the estate to know who I was and like me just the same. Yes, I say now to the girl at the estate, that's it, isn't it? You were not incompetent or lazy, you the star pupil of your class. You just didn't understand it yet. Even in 1943 you still didn't understand that you couldn't be who you were and still be universally loved. And this brings me to the second reason why I waited so long before looking for Sister Wanda.

She said to me, as she did to others, that she was saving me for the love of the God which we had in common. Those were noble words and perceived as such by me and by others. This story is written in recognition and in gratitude for those words. But I was raised in a milieu of an intense interest in the affairs of this world, in the arts, in poetry, in politics. What I wanted to hear was the same as what I wanted to hear at the estate and didn't – that I should have been saved because of my right to live as a member of the same human race, and a loved member at that.

I was also a Polish citizen and a Polish Jew. Jewish people had lived in Poland for a thousand years, or for as long as Poland had existed as a state. During those years they fulfilled the obligation of *ora* and *labora*. In their taverns and in their shops they prayed as they worked. Along Polish roads, dusty in the summer and frozen in the winter, they walked with a heavy sack on their back to bring a few goods to the remotest village. As they walked they prayed. The very air of Poland was permeated with Jewish work and Jewish prayer. What I wanted to hear were words of recognition of my right to live as part of the country Sister Wanda and I had in common. Instead, I heard of the 'God we had in common'. Sister Wanda, wherever you may be now, I didn't feel then that you and I had a God in common. We had Poland in common, her language, literature, love of nature, style and elegance. That's what we had in common. The belief in God was what separated us for a thousand years. My God was the Jewish

God of the Old Testament and I wanted no other. Certainly, most certainly not in 1943. It was the inherited dread of loss of that God by conversion that made the learning of catechism so hard, and kneeling and crossing a danger. In my heart of heart I feared that each of these movements had magic. Of the two of us, the nun and the student, you were the liberal and I the fanatic. Forty years later I am glad. I'm glad that you were liberal and I'm glad that I was fanatic. We both took the right side at the time. And now that I've said this I'm satisfied that my story of Sister Wanda is completed.

# NOTES

# THE ACTIVITIES OF THE DEMOCRATIC SOCIETIES AND DEMOCRATIC PARTY IN DEFENDING JEWISH RIGHTS IN POLAND ON THE EVE OF HITLER'S INVASION

Aharon Weiss

This article is an attempt to set out and evaluate the actions of the Democratic Societies (KD) and the Democratic Party (SD) in defending the rights of the Jewish population between 1937 and 1939, against the background of the attitude of other Polish political parties to this issue. During this period, certain groups connected with OZON and the *Endecja* intensified their anti-semitic activities, in which racist elements adopted from Nazism were apparent. This process manifested itself in a number of areas: in the preparation of plans for a long-term 'solution to the Jewish problem'; in attempts to pass anti-Jewish laws in the *Sejm* and in the organisation of action against Jews in various aspects of economic and social life.

The Jews made great efforts to resist these attempts to undermine their position as citizens of the Polish Republic. They also found allies in the Polish democratic camp, especially within the ranks of the Democratic Societies and Democratic Party which were founded during this period, and did much to defend Jewish rights.

The Jews observed the activities of anti-semitic groups with some anxiety, particularly those in government circles who aimed at introducing theories and practices similar to those applied in Germany. Consequently Jewish society greatly valued the actions of individual Poles and political organisations who openly defended Jewish citizens and their rights. This was particularly so, because to defend Jewish rights was an unpopular policy. Those Polish democrats who did so became themselves the objects of indiscriminate attack from anti-semites of various persuasions.

In these years Poland underwent a serious crisis which was destroying the bases of democracy; totalitarian and fascist tendencies were also in evidence.[1] It was natural that in their struggle against them, Polish democratic forces, above all the Democratic Societies and the Democratic

Party, should also adopt a position towards the critical situation of the Jews.

The year 1937 marked a new phase in the deterioration of the situation of Polish Jews. The Piłsudski camp, the majority of which was in OZON, distanced itself considerably from its earlier position towards the Jews which had also been adopted by the BBWR (Non-Party Bloc for Co-operation with the Government) during the first *Sanacja* period. In his declaration of 21 February 1937, issued when OZON was formed, Adam Koc stated that 'it is necessary to approach with understanding the desire to preserve Polish culture and the natural attempt to achieve the economic independence of the Polish state'.[2] Whereas in May 1926 equal rights for all citizens of the Republic had been stressed, on this occasion Koc pointed out that the Jews were an alien element in the Polish state. The nomination of Jerzy Rutkowski, one of the *Falanga* leaders, as Koc's successor in the Union of Polish Youth (ZMP)[3] also contributed to encouraging and legalising extreme anti-semitic elements in Poland and their activities. Indeed, at the very first meeting of the ZMP, in Warsaw, Professor Mieczysław Michałowicz, the future leader of the Democratic Societies and Democratic Party, was severely criticized for 'supporting the Jews'.[4] Subsequently, attacks on members of the KD and SD were to become even fiercer.

The Democratic Societies were formed in 1937, a period when anti-semitic groups began a series of brutal actions against the Jews to enforce the introduction of the 'ghetto bench' in institutions of higher education. These restrictions, directed at Jewish students, were often accompanied by brawls organised by *Endecja* thugs which led to many Jewish students being injured – fatalities also occurred. These events, dangerous in themselves, also indicated the existence of a desire among certain social groups and government institutions for the introduction of 'Aryan clauses' in Poland.[5]

Jewish society made greater efforts to defend its rights. From 14–15 October 1937 a general strike was held by Jewish students in institutions of higher education.[6] In this struggle the Jews received quite wide support from Polish circles. Prominent representatives of the Polish intelligentsia protested against the 'ghetto benches'. These included Professors Tadeusz Kotarbiński, Zygmunt Szymanowski, Franciszek Vanuleta, Stefan Czarnowski, Stanisław Kułczyński and Kazimierz Bartel, to name but a few.[7] Many of these enlightened people were also members and sympathisers of the KD. The Democratic Committee leaders Professor Mieczysław Michałowicz and Marceli Handelsman, deserve special mention. They openly and uncompromisingly condemned 'ghetto-bench' politics and anti-semitic brawls at higher education institutions and on the streets of Polish towns. A coalition made up of various democratic youth groups stood up against these hooligans' activities. The contemporary Jewish press noted with satisfaction the common pronouncements made by the youth organization of the Polish Socialist Party (PPS), the Union of Independent Socialist Youth and the Youth Section of the Democratic Committees, protesting against discrimination against Jews and the undermining of democratic principles.[8]

The following statement appears in a declaration adopted with the establishment of the Democratic Committees: '... The increasing incidents of irresponsible terror, excesses and attacks by impudent sowers of violence and political or religious hatred which are inspired by enemy states but which are disguised as native nationalism, undermine the foundations of law and order ... True to the principles of Polish *raison d'état*, sanctified by the history of the republic, we challenge nationalism with the principles of equality of all citizens, condemning the linking of any internal solutions – social or economic – with the concept of race, nationality or faith.'[10]

Anti-semitic elements could not come to terms with the fact that there were groups in Poland ready to defend the Jews and to express solidarity with an oppressed minority. The members of the Democratic Committee and their leaders were attacked and attempts made to discredit them in Polish eyes. The following are a few examples of this: *Goniec* compared Professor Michałowicz [for protesting against the bench policy] with 'Siciński, hated by all Poles past and present (for the *liberum veto*).'[11] A pamphlet distributed in Warsaw's educational institutions (*Akademik Polski* – October, 1937) contains the following statement: 'The agent of the red Comintern, the flunkey of the Jewish mafia, Michałowicz, will be one of the first to be removed from higher education and from the whole of Polish life.'[12] *A.B.C.* declared 'The Michałowiczes, Kotarbinskis and Handelmans must be erased from Polish learning.'[13]

Jewish society reacted to these attacks on the leaders of the Democratic Committees in a number of ways. The following, for example, appeared in *Nowy Dziennik*:' ... The *Endecja* press is up in arms against Professor Michałowicz. It sees his opposition to the ghetto bench as a new *liberum veto*. But there are still honest people in Poland, who understand that the spokesmen of the *liberum veto* in Poland are not those who guard the constitution and refuse to be intimidated by terrorist gangs but those who dance in time to the music of terrorism and trample on all the laws of heaven and earth ...'[14]

The Kraków *Kurier Wieczorny* said the following about Professor Michałowicz:' ... Of course, various *Endecja* and fascist newspapers have let themselves voice brutal and aggressive remarks against a man with the courage to oppose reactionary, ignorant and barbaric ideas ... This *Endecja* fascist yelping cannot even rise as high as the boots of this man with whom the whole of Polish democracy feels solidarity and herewith sends him expressions of respect and recognition. May Poland build her future upon such men.'[15]

From 1937 to 1939 there was discussion in the Jewish press about how they should react to the anti-semitic fury at that time. Some maintained that the Jews were isolated in the struggle for their rights, but there were other views. Moshe Kleinbaum stated '... we are not isolated ...... Our alliance with the Polish democratic opposition depends on our having an interest in its victory.'[16]

In January 1938 there were changes in the leadership of OZON. Koc was replaced by General Stanisław Skwarczyński. Co-operation between the youth organisations of OZON and ONR (*Falanga*) was suspended.[17] The threat of Nazi German aggression against Poland was on the horizon.

The Jews also hoped that OZON would change its policy towards them, but these hopes were in vain. This was not only because no change for the better took place, but also because of increasing anti-Jewish acts. At the OZON conference from 19–21 May 1938 the Central Council accepted a 13-clause plan aimed at solving the 'Jewish question'.[18] The following are a few of its clauses:

2. Polish Jews impede the free development of political and social forces (in Poland).
3. The Jewish problem undermines peace and public order.
8. Special laws should be enacted to reduce the number of Jews in certain professions.
9. Jews must be removed from cultural life.
10 Jewish access to institutions of further education should be restricted.

The sense of the 11th clause was that Jewish assimilation should not be encouraged.

The policies expressed in this programme indicate a definite attempt to compete with the *Endecja* to influence anti-semitic elements. The politics of OZON and the activities of *Endecja* circles in these years led to attempts to introduce 'aryan clauses' in a number of areas of Polish social and economic life. Central, regional and local institutions were all affected. For example, by 9 May 1937 the Union of Polish Lawyers had accepted a resolution limiting the number of Jewish lawyers to the same percentage as the country's Jewish population. The *Sejm* approved a decree in this spirit on 8 May 1938.[19] The Union of Polish Doctors presented a demand on 29 May 1938 that Jews should not be admitted to the medical faculties of higher education establishments. Similar proposals for 'aryan clauses' were introduced by the Union of Engineers.[20] In 1939, in Wilno, the local branch of the Journalists' Union added a new clause to its statutes which meant that people with Jewish backgrounds could not be members of the union.[21] This kind of anti-semitic activity affecting the Jews' political and economic position met with an appropriate reaction from Polish democratic forces and, as has been mentioned, members of the Democratic Committee and Democratic Party played a leading role in this. Among the many events in support of the cause was the appearance of Wincenty Rzymowski at the Warsaw Lawyers' meeting, where a resolution to restore full citizen's rights to Jews was approved.[22]

The representatives of the KD played a substantial role in consolidating the forces of the left. The 1 May demonstrations of 1938 became an expression of solidarity for all the progressive movements in the fight against the abuse of democracy. In its statements the 'defensive' more than once emphasised the 'sins' of the KD which rested on their solidarity with the Jews.[23] The statement submitted to the Security Department of the Ministry of Internal Affairs concerning the demonstration of 1 May stressed '... the participation of the Jewish element in the ranks of the KD, especially of Jewish youth, recruited even from secondary schools, who gathered together with the students around the banner 'Down with the ghetto...'[24]

In declarations made by the leaders of the KD on the subject of the Polish situation in the context of the international arena and particularly with regard to Polish-German relations, the negative influence of events in Nazi Germany on Polish society was particularly noted. For example, Professor M. Michałowicz declared '... Witch trials, the tragedy of which we witness, are alien to us as a method. We shudder when faced with the spirit of the concentration camps, and the burning of books containing human thought...'[25]

Both the Jews and the Polish democratic forces did indeed have serious grounds for anxiety that extreme anti-semitic propaganda was filtering into the consciousness of Polish society from Germany, affecting even government circles. Thus at the Sejm meeting on 3 December 1938, the OZON leader, General Skwarczyński, demanded that the percentage of Jews engaged in the free professions should be limited. Further, yet more radical proposals were put forward by deputies Franciszek Stoch and Benedykt Kieńć. Their plans envisaged depriving Polish Jews of their citizenship according to the model of the Nuremberg Laws.[26]

The increase of *Endecja*-inspired violent actions throughout the country must thus be seen against this background. The latter, as well as other factors, was also significant for the formation of the Democratic Party which took place at this time. The Democratic Party continued the policies of the Democratic Committees towards the Jewish question. The following paragraph appears in a Democratic Party declaration about national minorities: '... The Jewish question, providing a springboard for anti-democratic forces, is above all a social and economic problem, and is increasingly more difficult to solve because of the flawed professional structure the Jewish populace has to work in, and the refusal of countries to take further immigrants. We condemn as barbaric any spreading of hatred and institutionalising pressure against Jews either by legal discrimination or forced emigration. In fighting persecution, which prevents assimilation, we demand a policy to change the occupational structure of the Jewish masses and to acquire territories for those Jews who wish to emigrate of their own free will.'[27]

It is necessary to make some observations at this stage about the Democratic Party programme and the Jewish question. Their programme does indeed differ greatly from the basic precepts of OZON which made impossible any chance of Jewish assimilation. The Democratic Party called for support for Jewish assimilation and had a liberal attitude towards voluntary Jewish emigration. However, the question needs asking whether the Democratic Party supported Jewish emigration because of its doubts about the possibility of solving the Jewish question for all Polish Jews within the Polish state. It is, I believe, essential to re-emphasise that the Democratic Party was one of the leading democratic parties in Poland defending the rights of Polish Jews. And indeed given the international situation at that time the chances of emigration were almost non-existent. Helena Romer-Ochenkowska, for example, saw the question of Jewish emigration from Poland this way: 'Three million people paying taxes, doing military service, contributing to the state treasury whether in money, enterprises or knowledge – it is not easy to abolish all that . . . three million people will not leave Poland that quickly, not even a million will escape, for where would they go?'[28]

A field of common struggle against reactionary and anti- semitic forces was the municipal elections begun at the end of 1938 and continued till half way through 1939. The electoral conflict was bitter and unremitting, and often accompanied by acts of violence on the part of government and *Endecja* elements. This led to increased co-operation between Jewish political activists and Polish democrats, so that we read, for example, in the electoral declaration of the Democratic Party in Łódź at the end of 1938: 'in voting for our candidates you will show those who admire tyranny and totalitarianism that Polish Democracy is a powerful force! We cannot allow the barbarity which triumphs in all its savagery in racist Germany to be victorious.'[29] The democratic forces including the Democratic Party, did indeed commit themselves to fighting racism and spoke out against the infringement of Jewish rights in the municipal elections. The election results showed notable gains for the democratic and left-wing parties in local government. The Polish authorities attempted to limit and reduce these gains, using administrative means, among others. In a few councils there was effective co-operation between Jewish councillors and progressive representatives.

Meanwhile, anti-semitic incidents continued and claimed new victims. In Lwów a Jewish student – Markus Lendesberg – was murdered by *Endecja* thugs early in 1939, 3 months before the outbreak of war.[30] Even the very real and close threat of Hitlerite aggression towards Poland did not curb the anti-semitic forces or their atrocities. On the contrary, at this very time they were encouraging malicious ideas and mistrust against the whole Jewish population.

Throughout this brief period, to the end of August 1939, the young Democratic Party continued to act, warning of the harm being done to the Jews and the consequences of anti-semitic action – namely the undermining of the Polish state and its defence forces during a time of increased danger from Germany. Stanisław Wieckowski adopted this approach to the problem: 'Today – when we must want all the minorities including the Jews to feel, like us, the gravity of the fatal hour, and be willing to stand steadfastly on the ramparts by our side, is this the time and place for racist propaganda? Is this a time for slogans of hatred or for harmful actions within the country when there are external threats of aggression?'[31]

In September 1939 German armies flooded into Poland. The realisation of the 'final solution' to the Jewish question in the years 1939–45 led to the almost complete annihilation of Polish Jews. The number of Polish victims during this tragic period was also huge. The question of help to Jews and the work of Democratic Party members in particular in saving Jews from death falls outside the scope of this essay.

## NOTES

1 Hanna & Tadeusz Jędruszczak, *Ostatnie lata Drugiej Rzeczy pospolitej, 1935–1939* (Warsaw, 1970), pp. 227, 239, 241.
2 W. Pobóg-Malinowski, *Najnowsza historia polityczna Polski, 1864–1945* (London, 1967), vol. 2, pp. 802–5.
3 Andrzej Micewski, *Z geografii politycznej II Rzeczypospolitej* (Warsaw, 1966), pp. 271–2.
4 *Nasz Przegląd*, 7 Nov. 1937.
5 *Warszawski Dziennik Narodowy*, 28 Nov. 1937.
6 *Nasz Przegląd*, 14–15. Oct. 1937.
7 Leon Chajn, *Materiały do historii Klubów Demokratycznych i Stronnictwa Demokratycznego w lata ch 1937–1939* (Warsaw, 1964), vol. 1, doc. 49, pp. 204–5 (referred to henceforth as Chajn – *Materiały*).
8 *Nasz Przegląd*, 7 Nov. 1937.
9 Chajn – *Materiały*, vol. 1, doc. 18, p. 164.
10 Chajn – *Materiały*, vol. 1, doc. 22, p. 170.
11 Chajn – *Materiały*, vol. 1, doc. 44, p. 201.
12 Chajn – *Materiały*, vol. 1, doc. 51, p. 207.
13 *Nowy Dziennik*, 5 Nov. 1937.
14 *Nowy Dziennik*, 22 Oct. 1937.
15 Chajn – *Materiały*, vol. 1, doc. 44, p. 201.
16 *Nasz Przegląd*, 26 Oct. 1937.
17 Hanna & Tadeusz Jedruszczak, op.cit., p. 245.
18 Resolutions of the Governing Council, OZON, 19–21 May 1938, Warsaw 1938.
19 Raphael Mahler, *Yehudey Polin beyn shtei milkhamot olam* (Tel-Aviv, 1968), pp. 165, 167.
20 Raphael Mahler, op.cit., p. 169.

21 *Warszawski Dziennik Narodowy*, 18 Nov. 1938.
22 Chajn – *Materiały*, vol. 1, doc. 113, pp. 262–3.
23 Chajn – *Materiały*, vol. 1, doc. 132, p. 277.
24 Chajn – *Materiały*, vol. 1, doc. 133, pp. 277–8.
25 Chajn – *Materiały*, vol. 1, doc. 139, p. 282.
26 Maria Turlejska, *Rok przed klęską* (Warsaw, 1960), p. 150.
27 Chajn – *Materiały*, vol. 1, doc. 357, p. 519.
28 *Nowy Dziennik*, 11 June 1939.
29 Chajn – *Materiały*, vol. 2, doc. 664, p. 342.
30 *Nowy Dziennik*, 11 June 1939.
31 Chajn – *Materiały*, vol. 1, doc. 370, p. 539.

# DOCUMENTS DEALING WITH THE HISTORY OF JEWS IN GALICIA IN LWÓW ARCHIVES

Dora Katzenelson

The manuscript documents on the history of the Jews in Galicia, which are kept in the department of manuscripts of the Lwów People's Library are only part of the vast legacy of the Jewish communities of this territory which are to be found in the archives of Lwów: in the historical and regional archives, in the Lwów University Library, in the Historical Museum, in the Museum of the History of Religion. However, even in the manuscript department, such materials are heterogeneous in subject, origin, type and language, scattered among various archival collections and found together with other historical material, so that research into them, their systematization and description, constitutes a very difficult task. The long ban on the study of Jewish themes, the shortage of qualified personnel, and especially the lack of an information base on bibliography and origin – all create additional difficulties in working with these documents.

In addition, our library receives hardly any information on what is being published around the world on Jewish themes; we have at our disposal only sources published before 1939: Bałaban, Behrson. Karo, and also Chashchalei, Lelewel and short classics, and incomplete runs of the periodicals *Chwila* and *Sygnaty*. The incompleteness of the informational base does not allow us to bring to light the extent of the manuscript material kept in our department.

Up to the present, the documents on the history of the Jews have been catalogued on a card-index, which should obviously be published as in the form of a catalogue-index. In this paper, I will try to give a general overview of what is to be found in the archives. The documents range from the seventeenth to the twentieth century and are very varied: Jewish manuscripts (codes and Torah scrolls); legal, economic, court and *kehilla* documents; material on the relations between different religions and on Judeo-Christian disputes; archive material on the origin and activity of

Jewish cultural and political figures; incomplete material, including pieces of information in annuals and chronicles.

In the department, we hold 63 Hebrew manuscripts, 53 (the collection of the libraries of the Jewish communities) have been described by Y. S. Honigsmann; 10 were discovered and described later: 9 in the collection O/N, 1 in the collection Ossoya. These Jewish manuscripts vary according to theme and genre: philosophical-theological tracts, poetry and prose selections of some authors; historical and genealogical works. The philosophical-theological tracts dating from the 17th to the 20th centuries reflect the Jewish culture of the region. We also have philosophical-astrological tracts from the 18th century. Some manuscripts were written for the education of children: 'The sacrifice of Isaac' by Sim Levin – head teacher in the Jewish school in Lwów (19th C.). There are also manuscripts on the Margulis's – a well-known family of rabbis (Brody, Rosdol), on Egudovich ( his father-in-law was a well-known rabbi in Prague) – and an unprinted book giving biographical facts about Jewish families in Lublin and elsewhere.

Among the collection of manuscripts from the libraries of the Jewish communities are kept two volumes of a catalogue of the Lwów *Kehilla* Library (beginning of the twentieth century). One of these catalogues contains an inventory of old Jewish literature, which was put together in 1940. Most of the books in this catalogue were lost in the years of the 'struggle against Cosmpolitanism' and only a small part have survived.

Besides legal manuscripts, the department has 30 Torah scrolls (XVII–XIX centuries); many of them have rich decoration with ivory incrustations or ornamental carving. Our department also holds various other materials. They include legal documents; instructions from the local authority, rulings of settlement, trading and other aspects of the relationship between Jewish communities and the cities and villages of the area, and also documents linked to the economic relations of the *kehillot* with the authorities: charters, receipts for rates and so on. These documents came to the department in different ways and are distributed in many collections, together with other subject matter. As a result they have only partially been collated and brought to light.

Rich information on trade and credit-finance contracts between Jews and Ukrainians, Poles and Armenians are contained in the legal books of the town and community courts of Lwów, Stanisławów, Zamość, and other towns in the region. There is also much material on the religious relations between Jews and Christians. Some documents deal with contacts and help for the Jews from the Christian communities. One describes a case where the Order of the Trinity took the Jews of Lwów to court in the 18th Century. Often, contacts between Jews and Christians are described in Christian documents of the different Christian communities. In the debt books of the Bank of Lwów we see Jews mentioned as permanent clients of the bank. There are 9 such books in the department, from the 17th-18th century. In addition, in the account book of the Benedictine monastery, burned down in 1648, appears evidence that Jews participated in its rebuilding.

We have documents showing the attempts to convert Jews to Christianity, including a philosophical-theological collection, outlining the subject matter and course of disputes which took place in Lwów in the middle of the 18th century; one part shows Jews adopting Catholicism. On the last page are the surnames of those who converted. (Obviously the followers of Jakub Frank). It is interesting that in one of the sections there are attacks on 'sectarians' insulting them and refering to them as Calvinists and Lutherans. In this same document, information is requested about the meetings of rabbis in the regions of Jaroslaw, Brody, Poznan and other towns (middle of 18th c.).

We also possess some anti-semitic materials. One of them is the tract of Jan Bucksdorf (18th Cent.), in which the Jews are criticized for their traditions, the alleged use of Christian blood, and their immoral behaviour. This is translated from the Latin. Rather interesting in this connection is the pamphlet 'O Żydach, Ormianach – z dołączenem hist-statystycznym na Podolu', 1851, author not known. Giving a brief history of the Jewish and Armenian communties, the author argues that the tragic history of both nations is a punishment for their immoral nature, for their inclination towards economic sharp practice and interest in money etc.. This strange pseudo-scientific work shows very clearly the inclination to persecute the Jewish and Armenian nations. In addition, it gives interesting information about the region around Podole, about its history, population and cultural development.

The next set of documents are those about the life and activities of well-known political and cultural figures of Jewish origin. A significant part of such people, influenced by the assimilationist current of the 19th century, made a large contribution to Polish culture. We have a lot of this type of material, but here we will mention only some of the most important. The documents include material on the following:

The rabbi and historian Yechezkiel Karo – his tracts and sermons and a genealogical study on the history of the family Horowitz written in Hebrew.

The ancient philosopher L. Rais – an architect from Lwów and also a historian and bibliographer. We have his articles and bibliographical material for a history of Lwow, some correspondence and biographical material written in Polish and Hebrew.

Material written by M. Goldstein, an art critic, collector and founder of the Museum of Jewish culture in Lwów (the first such museum in the region of Podolia); his biographical documents, collection of legal documents on the relations between Jews and Christians, on the attempts to convert Jews, and correspondence. The documents are written in Hebrew, Yiddish, Polish and German.

Y. Golenstadt, a colourful and singular personality, who was a founder of the Jewish Institute in Wilno in the 30's and was at the same time one of the closest followers of the School of Baudouin de Courtenay, very well versed in Russian, Polish and European literature. Later he moved to Warsaw. The life of this talented researcher ended in the Warsaw Ghetto, where he was one of the participants in the uprising. Amongst the material kept by the archive, there is a card-index for a biographical and bibliographical dictionary of writers of different nationalities; and also biographical material.

Philosophers of Jewish origin, like M. Epstein, a participant in the Polish uprising in 1863; H. Diamand, a leader of the PPS, the literary scholar and publisher, O. Ortwin, the Mickiewicz scholar and professor at the University of Lwów, Juliusz Kleiner. They all show the complex interrelation between Jewish, Polish and Ukrainian cultures at the end of the century – a process of assimilation and cultural exchange.

There is some very interesting material in *Sygnały*, a Jewish cultural, educational and political publication in the 20's and 30's in Lwow. The journal strove to achieve a broad outlook on the complex problems of the Jews in Poland. It provided space in its pages for Zionists, socialists and also for supporters of Jewish autonomy in Poland.

We also have material on F. Smolski, a well-known diplomat and politician, who was one of the initiators of the struggle for Jewish emancipation and the abolition of the ghetto in Lwow. As a professor in the University of Lwów, Smolski organised protests against the ghetto benches in the 30's.

There is, in addition, material from the archives of scholars who have written on Jewish topics. The Judeo-Christian relationship interested many Polish and Ukrainian theologians and philosophers, including Sobczanski and Terlecki, whose manuscripts are kept in the department. We also have material of Professor Górka who studied ancient Eastern Semitic languages, including Hebrew, as well as his essay 'Żydzi za Kazimierza Wielkiego'.

Information about the history of Jewish culture is also to be found in the collections of historians Golovoki, Kozlowski, Tiszkowski, Baracz and Menajder. Some aspects of Jewish culture were taught in the University of Lwów and we have materials on these courses.

Jewish themes are also to be found in Ukrainian and Polish literature and art. In our department, in the archive collection, is kept the manuscript of the score of the chorus 'Halevi' from the opera 'Zhigilka'. We also have the tales of the Polish writer, Alexander Ubisz, entitled *Reb Duvid*.

In the collection 'Ukrainian Comedy' is put together information on monuments by Jewish architects, including synagogues and cemeteries. This information is all the more valuable because at the present time most of these monuments do not exist.

To sum up, the documents kept in our department on Jewish history and culture are original, heterogeneous and reflect all aspects of the life of Jews in Galicia, their history and culture. This material should be systematized and put onto a card-index. Its preservation is vital and it should attract scholars from the whole of the Jewish world.

# REVIEW ARTICLES

## THE LITERARY AFTERLIFE OF POLISH JEWRY
### Zygmunt Bauman

In Poland, where once the largest Jewish community in Europe lived, Jewish gravestones slowly disintegrate for the lack of grieving descendants of the dead. The corpses beneath the gravestone have not been truly put to rest, however, for the haunted witnesses, now survivors.

From time to time, in a desperate yet vain attempt to exorcise the ghost of murdered neighbours, great hearts repent the guilt of the silent and indifferent ones. The Polish poet Jerzy Ficowski confesses that repentance will never be final in the haunted land:

> I would wish to be silent
> But keeping silence, I lie
>
> I would wish to walk
> But while walking, I trample

Nobel Prize Laureate Czesław Miłosz bemoans the guilt which, even if not earned, cannot be washed out:

> What will I tell Him, a New Testament Jew,
> Waiting two millennia for return of Jesus?
> My harrowed body will betray me
> And will count me among the helpers of death:
> The uncircumcised.[1]

The crimes could be individual and private; the guilt is collective and shared. The survivors are guilty, and their survival is their guilt. This is not a guilt which will be recognized in any human court of justice. But then moral conscience cannot be exonerated by human courts. Another Pole, Władysław Bartoszewski, said once that only those can say that they have done everything they could, who lost their lives.

No evidence of innocence will ever argue guilty conscience away. The Polish-Jewish scholar Emanuel Ringelblum, writing in hiding shortly before his deportation to the death camp in April 1943, left a balanced picture of Polish reactions to the rounding up and mass murder of their Jewish neighbours: 'The attitudes of the Poles to Jews were not uniform ... Polish fascism, embodied in an excrescent, bestial antisemitism, created conditions unfavourable to saving the Jews massively murdered by Germans, Ukrainian, Lithuanian and Latvian SS-men ... Taking into account special conditions in Poland, we must admit that the acts of Polish intelligentsia, workers or peasants who do hide the Jews are exceptionally noble, loyal to the spirit of tolerance which permeated Polish history'.[2] Every Jew who survived can recite a long list of Poles who helped him, often putting their own life at risk. And every Jew who survived will never forget those countless unknown enemies whose hatred or greed made an act of heroism out of the helper's human impulse: he won't forget the joyful or cold eyes that watched the last journey. On the other hand, all such counting, even if possible, would not help much. The stubborn fact cannot be wished away: a great nation which for eight hundred years shared the glory and the misery of Polish history was rounded up, transported to their death and murdered, and their death was prevented. This means guilt. One may try to argue the guilt away; rational arguments can be raised that the potential rescuers stood small chance of success, but a huge chance of adding their own lives to the millions that perished. But *rational* arguments cannot absolve a *moral* guilt.

'It is too late; this linen will never be washed clean' – wrote Polish writer Andrzej Kuśniewicz. And because it will never be washed clean, it is unlikely to be ever pulled out from the remote corner of the family wardrobe and aired in public. The suppressed memory of the massive murder poisons the consciousness of the nation who witnessed it; the fact that the nation of silent witnesses did not contribute actively to the perpetration of the crime does not make the matter much easier. And because the subconscious knows that the guilt is there and will hardly ever go away, the consciousness rebels and vehemently seeks excuses. If only the victim could be blamed ...

This seems to be the secret of the most spectacular of the Holocaust survivals: anti-semitism. It now lives, so to speak, without its traditional hunting ground: truly, out of its element. It has no new nourishment. No living experience to forage and to fatten on. As a matter of fact, this anti-semitism, like its original objects, is not alive: the hatred that outlived its objects is more like a dead, imperturbable rock. A solid rock, immovable and resistant to the sharpest of cutters. And the suppressed guilt is its foundation. Gravestones remained of the Polish Jews; stony, *fossilized* anti-semitism remained of the eight hundred years of the joint Polish-Jewish history.

How this joint history is retrospectively read out, depends on what one wants to find in it. From behind the fossilized hatred, most visible in that history, is a long record of mistrust of the Jews. In the interviews with the witnesses filmed thirty odd years after the 1946 Kielce pogrom, two persons remembered the hostel run by the Jewish Committee in which the homeless remnants of the once lively Jewish community were housed. According to one person, 'these people were sad and frightened, somehow out of place, not intending to stay; they did not fit the landscape at all'. The other person saw something else: 'They were well off, well fed, well provided for. They got food parcels and money from America'. The interviewees were asked to speak of the militiamen and thousands of ordinary residents of the town who pursued dozens of Jews through the streets and beat them to death; instead, some spoke of the injustices which the Jews were guilty of committing: 'they, the Jews, boasted: the streets belong to you, but the houses are ours ... No wonder people did not like them.'

Memory of the millions of men, women and children goaded to their death under German occupation was not the only guilt that needed to be suppressed. Isaac Deutscher pointed to the yet more sinister reasons for renewed post-war anti-semitism: 'The grave of the Jewish middle class became the cradle of a new gentile middle class in eastern Europe ... a *lumpenproletariat* which turned overnight into a *lumpenbourgeoisie*. The death certificates of the murdered Jews were their only valid trade licences ... The only way in which the new "middle class" can save not so much its newly acquired wealth but its nerves and a pretence of respectability is by smoking out the surviving Jew'. Empty houses, shops and workshops did not stay empty for long. when the few survivors among their past owners emerged from hiding or boarded westward trains from their Russian exile or refuge, they were met with eyes filled with fear and fear-fed hatred: lest they should claim their property, and on this occasion remind the new owners of the moments better left forgotten.

## THE HISTORIC ROOTS OF ANTI-SEMITISM

Deploying history to blame the victim was not a particularly difficult task, to be sure. The long Polish-Jewish cohabitation was a pliable stuff, fit to be moulded to suit many interpretations and to supply telling, cogent, convincing arguments for almost any thesis. The theses themselves changed over time. One that gradually became dominant in the Polish mind towards the beginning of the twentieth century was that the Jews were an alien hostile and poisonous body in the emerging Polish national organism, threatening the health and the very existence of a precarious Polish national identity.

This sentiment, however, could have hardly appeared before the 'Polish national identity' acquired its modern shape, i.e. was topped by an ideological mobilization and spawned cultural crusades and an effort to transform the chaotic leftovers of past history into a purposefully designed order. As Alina Cała points out, '[t]he idea of a single nation state, and the programmes associated with it of assimilating national and ethnic minorities, was foreign to pre-modern Polish thought. If a nineteenth-century peasant were ever asked if Jews should assimilate or emigrate, he would have been surprised and unable to respond. For him they were part of the unchangeable landscape as God had first created it. A demand to change the existing order would have seemed revolutionary to him' – that is, contrary to God's will, a prelude of apocalypse. 'The Jews with their side-curls and kaftans were part of life as created by God, testimony to the Passion of Christ, something threatening and strange, but necessary and unalterable'. It was only the modern Polish nationalism, with its programme of cultural homogeneity, with its struggle for a *Polish state* which was to become a *state of the Poles*, that delivered a decisive blow to the God-ordained order of things and set the world in a turmoil. The unclarity of the new situation and the sudden disappearance of the divine sanction was deeply upsetting. 'The frustrations caused by participation in these stormy changes were channelled in the direction of totalitarian utopias. One of them was anti-semitism . . . It is one of the paradoxes of history that anti-semitism strengthened the role of the Jew (or rather his myth) as a determinant of Polish national consciousness. Whole social groups discovered their national allegiance as an offshoot of the feeling of separateness from the Jews'.[3]

National identity offered an escape, and a shelter against that threatening ambivalence of which the Jews had become now the prime example (note that Russians or Germans, by far the more threatening enemy by any standard, played second fiddle to the Jews as a negative support of the budding Polish national identity; they were enemies all right – but too *unambiguously* 'other' and hostile for the purpose. Only the Jews were truly fit to exemplify in a clearly visible form the stakes of the national identity; that chaos against which national unity promised to defend).

The Jews were hardly ambivalent before modernization took off. Jewish ambivalence, destined to serve as focal point of nation-formative processes, was itself a product of these processes. A crucial part of the *kulturkampf* of the rising nation was the achievement of Polish cultural hegemony over the territory of the future nation-state, and thus the cultural conversion of ethnic minorities: this, first and foremost, meant the assimilation of Jews. And yet the assimilatory programme was (had to be) as ambiguous as the cultural map it aimed to homogenize; in its operation more ambivalence was generated than eliminated. The Jews who stuck to their traditional ways were singled out as a proof of the essential estrangement of Jews – all

Jews, any Jews – from the Poles and their national ambitions. The real ogres were, however, the Jews attracted by the indubitable splendours of Polish culture, those responding with good will and enthusiasm to the invitation to join. It was they who became the many exemplars of Kafka's *Odradeks* – mongrel creatures of unclassifiable identity, neither strangers nor *our own*, eluding all straightforward assignment and by the same token dicrediting in advance the order yet to be installed. The more successful their Polonization was, the more threatening was the resulting ambivalence. They dressed like Poles, behaved like Poles, spoke like Poles; lived like Poles, for all one knew, they could be easily *mistaken* for Poles. Hence their ambivalence called for constant vigilance. Vigilance against Jewish duplicity and slyness turned into the major weapon of the border-defence of the Polish nation.

Though the pool of assimilating Jews keen to embrace Polish culture never dried up, it had become clear well before the Polish nation-state was created that for the ever more conspicuously resented Jewish masses assimilation was not a realistic prospect. Already towards the end of the nineteenth century, alternative ways out of the ghetto began to be sought, debated and tried, and a most popular among them led to the distinctly modern forms of Jewish national identity: most influential among them were Jewish nationalism in the shape of several varieties of Zionism, and Jewish socialism in the shape of the *Bund* (with its programme of guarding and developing Jewish cultural uniqueness in the context of a humane, socialist Polish state tolerant to human differences). This political map survived through the twenty odd years of Polish independence.

During that period relations between the Polish state and its large Jewish minority were tense and fraught with mutual acrimony. The Jewish political élites attracted the suspicions of the Polish nationalists by siding with other national minorities of the multi-ethnic state in a shared resistance against the monopolistic aspirations of the ethnically Polish political élite (Jewish political leaders, in fact, had initiated a sort of 'united front' with the Ukrainians, Byelorussians and other non-Poles, hoping to force the government to observe the rights of minorities – and canvassed selected foreign powers to assist their efforts). On the other hand, however, the rising Polish nationalism and anti-semitic sentiments, aided and abetted by popular or official explanations of persisting economic depression, made it increasingly clear to the Jews that they were unwanted; their residence on the land where their ancestors had lived for centuries was now questioned. The last years of Polish independence were characterized by constantly discussed Nuremberg-style anti-Jewish legislation (never, to be sure, introduced in Poland), and the Polish foreign minister canvassing European governments to 'solve the Jewish problem' by providing outlets and resources for a massive Jewish emigration from Poland. The Jew most feted by the Polish government was Jabotinsky, the leader of the revisionist branch of Zionism, who promised cooperation in organizing the exodus of the Polish Jews.

No wonder that by the time the war broke, many a Pole was sufficiently primed to think, or at least not to object to his neighbours saying, that 'after the war we would have to erect Hitler a monument'. Jan Tomasz Gross suggested that if the Germans punished all assistance to the Jews in Poland much more severely than in any other occupied country, and if their threat proved effective in preventing massive resistance to the Holocaust, a large part of the explanation resides in the resentment felt for the Jews by a majority of Poles and the resulting isolation of the Jews. 'Brutal persecutions are easiest when aimed at small groups of people isolated from their own society ... The anti-semitism widespread during the occupation among Polish society was the reason for which the Germans so brutally and mercilessly murdered the Poles who did help the Jews – and the reason why the Poles find it so difficult to discuss the subject'.[4] The 'righteous among the Poles' often felt as isolated and abandoned by their own society as the hunted Jews they saved.

The Germans were not the only invaders of the Polish soil. The eastern lands of Poland, where most of the national minorities lived, were occupied in 1939 by the Soviet forces. For the Poles, there was no more difference between the two enemies than there was between the devil and the deep blue sea. For the Jews, the difference was one between life and death. The Jewish rejoicing at the sight of the invading Red Army was watched by their Polish neighbours with unspeakable horror. 'Very many Jews' – writes Aleksander Smolar in his exemplarily balanced account of the Polish-Jewish antagonisms – 'greeted the Red Army with enthusiasm, because they did not treat Poland as their Fatherland; they were pushed out of it, as the way to get rid of the Jews became the main topic of public debate ... The Jews, Communists and non-communists, educated and half-educated, as trustworthy people, entered the local administration and helped to organize Soviet power. Worse still, they assisted Soviet authorities in their chase of Polish army officers and members of the pre-war Polish administration'. This treachery was to be never forgotten nor forgiven by the Poles. As if in a textbook example of the self-fulfilling prophecy, the Jews did behave exactly as the Polish anti-semites kept saying they would and by saying it prompted them to do it ... And after the war the same situation repeated itself. The Jews, 'grateful to the USSR for saving their lives, socially isolated, culturally uprooted, aware of the resentment or hostility of their environment but dreaming of equality, fraternity, and of giving a good lesson to the 'forces of reaction', made excellent material for the new power. Not to mention the committed communists of the old guard, among whom the percentage of Jews was very high'[5].

Transformed by the assimilatory pressures into the frightening and hateful symbol of ambivalence and threat to national existence, the Jews (and *particularly* the assimilating Jews, the Jews eager to embrace Polish culture and Polish nationhood) were forcefully excluded from the membership of the Polish national community and faced with choices which could only add credibility to their estrangement and erect new obstacles to mutual understanding. Acceptance conditioned on assimilation proved to be a contradiction in terms. Assimilatory pressures contributed most heavily to the destruction of their own ostensible purpose. On both sides, the drama left a pungent after-taste which made the 'washing up of dirty linen' all the more difficult.

There are more than enough episodes and situations in Polish-Jewish history felt by both sides as something one would rather not discuss and preferably not remember. Suppressed and never faced in all their unpleasant truth, the memories fester and poison. Debates are inconclusive as they leave unsaid the very things which made them necessary in the first place. There is more than enough food for the Jews unhealed though one-sided aggravation against their erstwhile homeland, and for the bizarre phenomenon of Polish anti-semitism without Jews.

## LANGUAGE AS SHELTER

Of Julian Tuwim, one of the most influential and innovative Polish poets of the twentieth century, another Polish Jew and formidable literary theorist and critic, Artur Sandauer, wrote: 'Essentially, assimilation did not succeed; what has succeeded was the poetry, born of that failed assimilation and of unhappy love for Poland ... [A]s the other Poland refused to accept him, the Polish language remained his true homeland'.[6] The true homeland and the *only* homeland (as all true homelands are). Also, in no small a measure, an un-shared homeland, of a landscape little known and still less understood by those who happened to be born into the 'other Poland', closed for Tuwim, or those who, put off by huge locks, never knocked on the door and thus did not need to seek substitute shelters. In an unshared land, Tuwim's creative force could be let loose. The result was great poetry and a landscape which, though familiar, made many feel ill-at-ease. The landscape of Tuwim's homeland had been carved by assimilation: 'their look shapes us from inside, grafts itself upon us as a mistletoe, so that we can only see ourselves through their eyes'. An assimilating Jew absorbs, together with the culture of the society he enters, also its myths – 'including such myths as are hostile to him'. So did Tuwim in his poetic homeland the war was waged against the priggishness, yet the knight-errant was 'seen through the prigs' eyes'.[7]

Original and unique as poet and stylist, Tuwim was nevertheless a specimen of a type. He was an artist called upon to join a nation fighting for its place in a world filled with nations, and to help make flourish a culture which could make this place secure and honourable. He was also a Jew whose place '*in the nation*' was put in doubt when the place *of the nation* had been made secure by its statehood.

In the age when modern nations were born, the Poles were not only deprived of the political instruments of national self-constitution, but divided between the realms of three foreign dynasties. However hard the core, the peripheries of such a nation must have been diluted and the boundaries unclear. Polish nationalists had to fight off not just the political pretences of hostile and powerful states, but also the cultural claims of rival, strong or weak, but militant and ambitious nationalisms. Without a state of its own, Polish nationalism could rely only on the power of cultural proselytism. It needed as many allies as it could muster among the culture-creators and culture-distributors. No one asked too many questions about the birth certificates of the writers and the artists who treated the magnificence of Polish culture as their sacred cause. The cultural door of the nation-in-search-of-statehood stayed ajar and the newcomers were welcome (the door was to be slammed later, but not before real border-guards manned real political entries and exits). The nation needed cultural strength to compensate for the political weakness. Whatever the cause, the invitation seemed – and was – unconditional.

It did attract an uncounted number of Jews seeking escape from the ghetto. Polishness meant to them, like to all others within the orbit of Polish cultural influence, the chance to share in a rich, highly attractive culture – but it also meant the liberation from a caste-like (or, rather, outcast) condition. Since, however, the membership in Polish culture was in the case of refugees from the ghetto *acquired* and hence precarious – the Polishness of the Jews was easily distinguished by its exaltation: 'an exaggerated care for the excellence of language, pedantic observance of all customs considered distinctly Polish, a cult of Polish literature and art, often a truly fanatical nationalism and chauvinism'. The exaggeration followed (one is almost prompted to say: *logically*) the situation in which the examiners' attentions never relaxed, test-passing never stopped and there was no way of guessing whether the performance, however spectacular, would be accepted as satisfactory.[8] However understandable, the Jewish zeal was nevertheless destined to be sooner or later interpreted as a sign of inborn tactlessness, arrogance and pushiness.

And thus, paradoxically, the Polish excellence of the Jews carried the seeds of Polish *allo*-semitism: though split into anti- and philo-semitic camps, the Poles, in their majority agreed on the *otherness* of Jews. Whether because of their exceptional slyness or exceptional gifts, the '*the Jews were not quite like the Poles* and neither could nor should be treated as Poles'[9]. The less there was left of the once highly visible peculiarity of the Jews, which locked them in their caste-like existence without any need of ideological or scientific formula, the more the repulsion had to be theorised and made into the topic of public discourse and political initiative.

In the independent Polish state that came into existence after the First World War Polish nationalism lost (or, rather, discarded and disowned) its proselytizing zeal. The project of cultural conversion of non-Polish ethnic groups inhabiting the territory of the Polish state went on unabated, now assisted also by administrative manipulation and political coercion – but only in relation to the sections of larger national groupings, who could raise their own reunification claims against Polish territorial possessions. As the Jews could not possibly come forward with such a demand, their declarations for Polishness offered little political profit. For Polish nationalists, and particularly for the rising Polish national intelligentsia, the three million Jews resident inside the Polish state constituted a tangible threat to the Polish domination of cultural life: it was in the area of culture through which the Jews were once called to enter the Polish nation, that a sizable part of the Jewish minority most spectacularly excelled. The emergent modern culture of Poland was full of converted and non-converted Jews. Coming from urban centres and boasting the best education Poland could offer, they easily assumed the role of cultural umpires whom the native poets and writers, more often than not of rural if not peasant extraction, looked toward for guidance and accolade. Expectedly, the growth of their importance in Polish culture went hand in hand with the increase in the intensity and spread of Polish anti-semitism. Hence the 'unique phenomenon: the most beloved writers become, as persons the most hated'.[10] This incongruity profoundly affected both the Jews and their hosts. As the great part of Polish culture was now the product of persons 'tainted' with an alien and resented origin, culture and intellectualism as such became suspect; the nation did not trust its own artistic and literary culture, and such distrust offered a fertile soil for all sorts of anti-intellectual, obscurantist and retrograde movements for which the inter-war Poland gained infamous notoriety. For the Polish cultural creators of Jewish origin, on the other hand, this duality turned out to be an additional asset on top of the usual artistic and philosophic stimuli inherent in the contradictions of the assimilatory process.

To quote Sandauer again: '"to assimilate" means to "stay, defenceless, under the gaze of the others" and to accept without murmur the judgement canons and the aesthetic criteria of others. By so doing, the "assimilating individual" must also "consent to his own ugliness"'.[11] Jewishness was declared ugly, and so were all the so-called 'Jewish traits'. One could do something (at least in theory) to escape the ugliness of Jewish habits or manners of speaking – by self-drill. There was nothing one could do about one's looks – and this heinous gift of the genes tended to emerge unscathed from no matter how many bucketfuls of the baptismal water.

The Polish poet Antoni Słonimski, born Christian of an already Christian father, inherited from his ancestors – together with their passionate adoration of Polish culture – also a distinctly Jewish face; the first did not help him against the second. Like the others – the unconverted, those who openly flaunted their Jewish roots and those who tried to hide or deny them – Słonimski was unpalatable to the purists of Polish nationalism and thus disqualified by them as a Jew. The more racist Polish anti-semitism turned, the more the treatment accorded to Słonimski was to turn into a pattern.

All this left little room for self-deceit. Anti-semitism and above all the staunch refusal of cultural membership on non-cultural grounds, brought about a reaction against the parochiality that always lurks at the end of the nationalist itinerary. As cultural creators, the Jews of all shades of assimilation indeed stood out for their power to see through and beyond parochial constraints. This could not but antagonize the nationalists; this also could not but make of the cultural creators among Polish Jews the most dedicated and effective carriers of the modern experience and articulators of modern culture.

Treated as aliens by the Polish street, Polish-Jewish writers found their retreat and shelter in the Polish language. Here, they felt at home. As the linguistic home stood in the midst of a social desert, they lavished on it all their elsewhere unspent emotions. The language benefited, though not necessarily the benefactors. Most of the latter perished as Jews, only posthumously upgraded to the rank of the Poles – in recognition of their martyr death rather than their creative life. The few who did survive found in post-war Poland the all-too-familiar atmosphere of surveillance and vigilant censorship. Now, to be sure, they were not charged with the crime of Jewishness. The accusation was re-phrased and re-worded again and again, to suit the changing circumstances. Sometimes they were resented simply as the carriers of an unspecific 'alien spirit'. At other times as 'cosmopolitans', or 'Zionists', or 'Communists', or 'Russian helpers' (when it came to the account-settling with the Stalinist episode, the Jewish collaborators, as always, bore the brunt of a much louder breast-beating than anyone else; with much less effect, however, than in the case of anyone else). But always as aliens, or at any rate not-quite, not-fully Polish.

After the last survivors of the Holocaust ran away from the survivals of anti-semitism, no Jewish culture or Jewish institutions of any importance have been left on Polish soil. All the more remarkable is the towering presence of two blatantly and demonstratively Jewish, yet superbly Polish writers, supreme masters of Polish prose: Adolf Rudnicki and Julian Stryjkowski. Their language, originally a shelter, has turned into the temple of a nation-wide cult. Their books are sold out the day they are published. Readers love them, the critics lavish their praise on them. For whom do they write? Who reads them? What for?

## ADOLF RUDNICKI, OR POLES LIKE JEWS

Like so many other survivors, Rudnicki greeted the new socialist Poland with hope. In the mouth of the hero of one of his short stories written shortly after the war he put a bitter reproach addressed to a Jewish mother who complained about her son's refusal to leave the 'land of the graveyards': 'National, racial differences will find nothing to feed on – and for this reason, young people will not find them in themselves'. He deleted these words from a later version; instead, he wrote, wiser by a few years of dashed hopes and frustrated expectations:

> This new breed was to be made of gold – and yet it is not made of gold. In those 'first things' in spiritual matters, nature had the upper hand, and nature derides beautiful words. Nature did not allow itself to be evicted and made fools of those who imagined that she would surrender easily. The new breed was to be anti-chauvinistic, anti-racist, rational, internationalist. It was not.[12]

In view of such an experience, the question of self-identity becomes crucial, though ever less equivocal. At the beginning, the answer is ambivalent, as are the situations of Rudnicki's literary characters whose conversations only thinly disguise the author's own agonized soul-searching (often several characters could be burdened with them all – illogical, perhaps inane in their togetherness – they would not seem credible in one sane subject). One of such characters, speaking in the first person, bluntly declares: 'I always think of myself as a Pole: the rest is my, complicated business. If Poland thinks otherwise it is Her, complicated business.' And, it is the same character which later quarrels with another writer of Jewish origin:

> At all costs, you wanted to be like them. To squeeze yourself into their narrow stream, you overlooked the sea. To absorb the spirit of language, you learned how to be correct. It cannot be that you did not know what the effect would be of such pseudonimic authorship, of all these efforts to be more Polish than the Poles themselves. Listen to me! – I shouted. – You should have wrecked those sanctimonious frames with your difficult, painful, untidy contents; you should have cried of what aches you, cut out of your body the centuries-old, never fading pains; you should have pushed aside this pot full of *bigos* [a Polish popular dish] and thrust in front of them our bitter chalice. They would frown, but would reach for it in the end. You should have spoken of us, of us first of all, asked yourself all the time whose your contents are. Of their contents, you cannot tell much anyway!

One should have no pity for himself, live by speech, not silence. You would gain then as a writer, and perhaps we would all gain as human beings. The nearest and dearest would perhaps die differently. Not in the mud, not in the spittle, not in contempt.[14]

This should have been done for the sake of dying in dignity. But also for the sake of living in dignity. For the sake of the dead; but also for the sake of the living. From the pride of the survivors of the dead nation, the living may learn and gain. If they are ever to glean similarity in the life of the dead, they will find it only in the difference; it will never occur to them how *close* they are to each other as long as the *difference* is belied. Defiantly, aggressively, in full voice (and a resounding, captivating and emotionally shattering voice it is) Rudnicki states the *difference*. He also proclaims the *resistance* of difference. The difference as fate – and a mission. 'If you belong to the weak, choose the weaker still ... And never leave them, as you'll gain nothing by leaving, and as one day you will be thrown back among them anyway ... '[15]

The difference will stay because leaving the weak is hopeless and does not give strength. There is no welcome at the end of the escape route. The world you wish to escape into is jealously guarded. It is reserved to the strong, to the straight-backed, to those who detest the weak as they remind them of that weakness in themselves which they do not want to know about. In the end, you, the weak, cannot count on the strength of the strong. As a young Jew, running from the train heading to Treblinka, found out: 'When hiding in the cellar, he discovered the meaning of home ... Now, creeping along the woods, he understood the meaning of Homeland. These woods, these meadows looked foreign to him – yet more than anything else he dreaded men'.[16] When another young Polish Jew, this time in occupied Paris, found himself one day defended by the whole Metro against a Gestapo spy, he 'fell in love with France just like our peasant, who cannot stop being amazed that bread and wine can be daily food ...'.[17]

The secret of the weakness? Rudnicki offers his own addition to the *Aggadah*. The present-day Ahasverus, Rywan of Rywanów, (so his *aggadah* goes) in one of his many past avatars bore witness to God's original mistake: the man God made was weak, doomed to be tormented by doubts and contradictions, to suffer and forever vacillate. Rywan pointed out this God's error. In reply, 'amused by his style, God made the still incomprehensible decision: I condemn you to Seek the Way Out from the Error!'. Since then the Rywan of Rywanów seeks the way out from the error – for the sake of the poor human creature, itself an error of God's. But 'everyone is fed up with your suggestions and advice ... The world does not see the Error, you are for the world the Error, you alone ... They are not the error, you are ... This is why they hate you.' Rywan of Rywanów remembers the cock whose head father cut off on the Day of Atonement to earn God's forgiveness for the sins and miscalculation of his son. Rywan of Rywanów, the cock with a special talent to Seek the Way Out from the Error, cuts off once more his own head and sets out on one more of his countless journeys. 'If you need me, O Lord, the way I am . . . If you need me like this . . .'

> I was a brittle whole, unbelievably brittle, artificial. I think that it was from my fragility that all these thoughts about Knives have been born. There was not a single moment in which I did not feel that for someone like myself there was no room in Nature, that a mistake had been made, which would be rectified at any moment; and that would mean the end, of course. In my thoughts, I constantly saw a knife lifted above my head. A knife about to remove the mistake, repair the error. I waited for that knife, because I was the Error'.[18]

The error seeking the way out from error; seeking a way out from itself. An error on the run and without hope of arrival. For the error, the only guaranteed way out from error is death. An error cannot stop seeking repair; an error cannot stop seeking self-destruction. This is the way, perhaps, the Lord needs him; in this world full of errors, a *miscalculated* world.

'You have come to me, but I – I have emerged from the depths of the sea. And in me, like in the sea – is everything'. An error who since the day of Creation never ceased seeking the Way out of Error has something to say to all errors of the World. Those other miscreants are in all likelihood fed up by now with his search, his disaffection, his restlessness. They do not enjoy being seen as errors, being reminded of being errors. But in a moment of truth they know that they, too, are errors; flawed beings in need of repair, fragile and artificial. 'And then they come here to me'. For the wisdom, for the advice, for the despair they rejected and for which they hated and against which they raised their knives.

This seem to be Rudnicki's own solution to the mystery, the paradox of the astounding popularity his tragic, despairing, all-Jewish prose enjoys in the land without Jews. It is because the Jews were made into errors and forced to sample the fears and terrors of fragility, that all fragility and all mistakes of the world may recognize themselves in the Jews as in a mirror. Deeper and fuller than anyone else the Jews immersed themselves (or were they immersed?) in the perpetually flawed and under-defined human existence. Hence the hatred; but, also, hence the fascination.

A humpback 'first learned of his hump in connection with a sporting parade'. He was just making himself ready to take part, when he was pushed aside: go home, you have your breasts on the wrong side . . . Indeed,

> can you imagine a sportsman with a hump? Their perfection had only one devil; me. Their perfection made my hump heavier still. Their assault was aimed mainly at me, as I have long ago discovered. But I discovered more than anyone else in the world. My hump was their ridicule, it laid bare their weakness. Once, after a few drinks, I jumped to the front of a parade ... The spectators burst with laughter, while they, the sportsmen, marching behind me were suddenly good for nothing, unable to put together a single number ... My hump finished off their feast. I kept shouting: do not trust the fops! We are hunchbacks all, let us trust humps alone! I was astonished, how easily I reached then my purpose.[19]

Ridicule which hides the fear; laughter to mask the fact of being laughable; the adroitness of sportsmen on parade stigmatizes the hump, the humpback's existence calls the bluff of the sportsmen. The sportsmen wear their perfection with pride – and with horror. It is the truth that they try to numb in the hubbub of the parade, it is truth that they fear, and the truth that they cannot forgive. The splendour of the parade cannot be trusted; not by a hunchback, not by him, not by someone who tasted the bitterness, the gruesomeness of truth.

When the Warsaw ghetto burned, people in the street told each other: 'this fire is in the ghetto'. 'This sounded like "somewhere far away". They said: "it is in the ghetto" – and recovered their calm'. 'Detonations shook the earth, the streets, but not people'. These were the years of contempt. Smart and adroit German troops made the residents of Warsaw into hunchbacks – first some of them, the selected ones, the Jews, then a bit later the others. They made sure that the turns are properly taken, that the others had had their share of laugh before they were told of their own hump.

> This was a contempt felt by a lackey proud of using a WC, for an 'eastern' creature who uses only a wooden shack, by a lackey proud of shaving every day, for a creature who did not shave daily ... Since the war, I am in deadly fear of people too well dressed, too well washed, as this very fact cuts them off the rest, prompts them to look down at the slightly less well dressed. I always see them as they enter their huge offices early in the morning, sit in front of their big diagrams, the products of their cold, dry, orderly nights, containing designs for destruction of millions of lesser humans, like you and me ... I am in deadly fear of excessive order, even of the sportsmen, whose exaggerated smartness – it always seems to me – cannot lead to any good.

The experience of being at the receiving end of contempt was staged, but it was shared. We all know now, or at least we could know if we wished, that for everyone there is an order, a standard of smartness, a measure of dressing that could make him into a hunchback. Is not culture about making the humps grow? Is not contempt, that licence to snub and to despise and to kill, all culture is about? 'Culture is a narrow, rotten plank thrown over a pool teeming with crocodiles, who will get in the end what they want. True, one always needs a task; one time this could be culture another time an anti-culture – the pride is always the same – the pride, arrogance, conceit.[20]

What Rudnicki has in mind is an arrogant culture, a self-assertive culture, militant culture, an aggressive and intolerant culture. A culture sufficiently sure of itself to subordinate or kill. A culture that uses its splendours as a mask of oppression; sooner of later it may turn to be a bait set to attract the crocodile food. Promise of safe passage is loud yet unreliable. The threat of disaster grows in strength alongside the trust in the promise.

This is the wisdom the Jews learned sooner and more profoundly than their neighbours. They derived it first from the unhealed wound of rejected acculturation. Then, as if to remove the last trace of doubt, the truth of their wisdom was confirmed by the tragedy of the Holocaust – a tragedy which revealed the loneliness which centuries of shared life and suffering did not remove. This is the lesson hammered home by the work of Rudnicki – a legatee, warden and messager of that wisdom. It is perhaps because they feel that they need this wisdom or may well yet need it in the future, that young and not-so-young Poles grasp avidly each successive Rudnicki's story. Or, perhaps, they do it, at least for the time being, only because they wish to learn more about those strange, mysterious, incomprehensible people whom they only posthumously agreed to promote to the rank of their compatriots.

## JULIAN STRYJKOWSKI, OR THE DUTY TO REMEMBER

At the age of 85, Julian Stryjkowski has no time to waste. He writes avidly, greedily, obsessively. In a span of four years, he has recorded the stories of Moses, King David, Judah Maccabee – in his own words, 'the greatest prophet, the greatest king, and the greatest hero' in the tormented history of the Jews, these 'people with a hump on their backs – not the wings of freedom, like in fairy-tales, but rags of slavery'.[21]

On his own admission, this Jewish writer took, as a child, refuge in the Polish language. With that language he fell in love. The depth of feelings did not help the suitor, though. In the new Polish secondary school in the new independent Poland, the headmaster asked children to name their nationality. Little Aaron Stark, called himself a Jew. He explained his nationality, we imagine, in pure, precise and pleasing Polish. Yet he was expelled on the spot. 'The boy was thrown out from his Paradise'. The headmaster did not quite succeed, however. 'The child found his refuge. The Word accepted him. The Word and the child remained faithful to each other forever after'.[22] The Word offered a shelter to the homeless. It has also proved his exile.

Replying to the inquiry on the 'Meaning of Polishness', conducted by the Catholic literary journal *Znak*,[23] Stryjkowski wrote; 'When, as a Jewish child, who spoke Yiddish only, I heard a Polish word, I was dazzled'. The hero of the *Voices in Darkness*, woven out of childhood memories of the author – explains what being dazzled meant. His sister Miriam, a teacher in a Polish school, spoke Yiddish with her parents and the other brother, but she addressed her kid brother in Polish: 'Little Aaron smiled and nodded. Did he, or did he not understand? The words sounded beautiful. Those he heard most often the child linked with glittering objects: with mirror, glasses, hanging candlesticks'.[24] When Aaron was finally entered – not without a struggle – into a Polish primary school, his teacher of Polish was Berta Apfelgrün. 'One Jew teaches another Jew how to be a Pole'[25] – Aaron's uncle commented caustically, sadly – and truthfully.

The *shtetl* had its own dreams. Like all dreams, they were cut to the dreamer's measure. On a Saturday evening, in a rapidly darkening synagogue ('they lit the candles in the synagogue as late as they could; let Saturday last as long as possible amidst the Jews'), little Aaron listens to the quiet, low voice of the Rabbi. He does not understand the complexities, but he knows the Rabbi is telling the story of the Messiah. The Messiah rides into the town on a white horse. And after this glorious moment, no one needs to study in the *kheder* anymore, nor does his Mother need to freeze in her market stall. Bread grows on trees. 'Even on weekdays Jews don silk, braided coats and sing *zmires*, munching raisins and almonds. Saturdays never ends'.[26] When some time later Aaron overcomes his fear and peeps through a hole in the black fence surrounding the priest's orchard, he is stunned by the weightless, silent serenity and shining beauty of what he sees: 'Among the trees Saturday stopped and refused to go away'.[27] The *Sabbath*, this most Jewish measure of happiness and beauty, is on the other side of the invisible walls of the ghetto. It moves massively to that side once the walls, poorly guarded on the outside, are repaired and kept solid by those who stay inside them. The Messiah pitched his tents in the priest's orchard. Melodic sounds of Polish words, these holes in the black fence, allowed little Aaron to catch a glimpse of the eternal Saturday.

Julian Stryjkowski did not just look through the hole. Enchanted by what he saw and propelled by the Jewish messianic impatience, he flew over the black fence into the astounding beauty of the Polish language. He has become a venerated grandmaster of Polish prose. His novels capture the shine, the clarity, the unique emotional tension, the human warmth of the language in which he writes. The critics report the pleasure which grows and overwhelms them with every page of Stryjkowski's prose. Stryjkowski's language, they say, is *'pure like spring water'*.[28]

Stryjkowski came into Polish language to celebrate the Jewish *Sabbath*. The same force brought him into the ranks of the clandestine Polish Communist Party. The Messianic urge pointed clearly and unambiguously to the world of tolerance and forgiveness, of light and beauty, of holiness on earth, of the Sabbath seven days a week, which the Communists promised. Disenchantment came fast. At the same time, the news came that the nation who dreamt of perpetual *Sabbath* faced the greatest threat of its history.

Cast by war into remote places of the Soviet Central Asia, Stryjkowski began to write his first Jewish epic, *Głosy w ciemności* [Voices in darkness], (to be published only twelve years later) – and he has not stopped writing since. 'I erect gravestones for the nation who disappeared overnight; for the nation which took part in the creation of everything which came to be on this soil' – in these words he explained the meaning of his work to a Polish interviewer,[29] shortly after the inglorious, government-inspired, antisemitic campaign of 1968.

> My purpose is to perpetuate the memory of the Jewish nation who disappeared as if overnight from the Polish lands. To this day I cannot and will not come to terms with this fact. I want this nation, of which I come, to continue to live; at least in my work.[30]

Stryjkowski writes of the dead for the sake of the living. The memory of the nation who disappeared must live in the memory of the nation who survived. Let the selfsame Polish language, which lured the dead with its splendour and yet proved a cage for many, become their permanent and secure shelter now that they are no more. Let them enter through this language the enchanted land they once lived in without being a part of.

There were two sides to the way the Jews lived and to everything they did. Monotony of daily chores, the awesome regularity of the Holy Calendar, years and generations of re-reading the timeless Holy Scripture *da capo al fine* – and agitated search for hints, and clues, and signs of the imminent salvation. Fear of losing the shelter of tradition, in which the certainty of The Coming was ultimately vested – and gnawing feeling that Messiah's deepest significance was the removal of the obtacle of tradition in the way of man's direct communion with God. The wish to remain faithful to the traditional ways of the community, the horror of the effrontery and loneliness of self-reliance and autonomy – and the urge to gaze beyond the horizon that the tradition had drawn, closely guarded, and declared impassable.

In the *shtetl* of *Głosy w ciemnosci* and *Echo*, life went in circles with melancholic monotony. It was as cyclical as that of the peasant. Peasant time is kept in motion by the annual rhythm of field work attuned to the succession of the natural seasons. Jewish time was calibrated by the alternation of the Holy Calendar. As if to underline the cyclicality and completeness of the Holy order, each of the two novels confines its action to one year. In *Głosy w ciemności*, it is a year between Aaron's two successive birthdays. In *The Echo*, the year runs between the endings of his two successive schoolyears. The Holy and the secular merge. The rhythm of human life mirrors the timeless replay of the Holy cycle. This applies to the old and aging as much as to the young and growing. The second year differs from the first by being seen through the eyes which have grown one year older. Like the preceding year, it is measured by the passage from New Year to the Day of Atonement, to Sukkoth, to Chanukkah, to Purim, to Passover. And, of course, both years are punctuated by the weekly spots of beauty, tranquillity and serenity: the Sabbaths. Quotidianty draws its meaning from the waiting for the Holy Days.

In the course of both years, the community whose life rests on that timeless repetition fights for its survival. In the first year, the threat comes from Scharie. In the second, from Manes. Scharie is a rich property owner who robbed two impoverished sisters-in-law of their inheritance. Manes is a twelve-year-old boy who on the Day of Atonement publicly ate a ham sandwich. The community loses its fight against Scharie, and rejoices in the defeat. It gains a gruesome victory over Manes (the boy hangs himself to escape the curse), and bewails it.

Scharie is a pious, observant Jew. Uneasy about his own ignorance of the law, he lavishes respect on the community sages, orders and pays for the scrolls for a new synagogue, makes a point of being called to read from Torah on every Sabbath. Scharie upholds the tradition; he is its guardian, and he spares neither effort nor expense to protect it. He also forces his teenage son into an early marriage to escape a bad match – a girl whose child the son fathered but Scharie forbade to recognize. Scharie's life is a success story; formerly a manager of the communal bath, he turned overnight into one of the wealthiest men in town. As the miraculous turnabout coincided with the death of his mother-in-law, everyone knows – though but a few say it loudly – that his good fortune has been more than casually connected with the precious stones once in the dead woman's possession. Yet the robbed daughter's complaints are to no avail. The saintly Rabbi of Głogów refrains from pronouncing a verdict. He knows that the condemnation of Scharie would serve no useful purpose. Perjury, which Scharie was ready to commit, would be a disaster, the Rabbi must prevent him from committing it – at all cost. The Rabbi of Głogów knows that 'as long as there are people like Scharie, one must wage a war. Not with Scharie, but with oneself ... Scharie is 'a worm-eaten fruit' – one has to handle him cautiously, lest the worms should crawl out and infest the others. 'This is wisdom. The Jewish wisdom'.[31] To build dams around sin, not allow it to spill out; one sin makes the next easier. Let the worms remain inside, as long as the fruit's skin remains smooth and shiny. As long as that smoothness and shine adds to the glory to the community, its ways, its values ...

Manes is a youthful rebel, a kid brother of a boy who refused to stand up when commanded by a drunken *Hussar* – and for this disrespect was shot dead by the soldier. Communal opinion condemns the victim. He should have obeyed, given way; 'to give way, this is our two thousands-years-old wisdom. This is why we remain alive'.[32] Manes does not accept the verdict. He won't give way. There is no other drunken soldier around, though. The killed brother had to travel to far-off Hungary to find him. Manes can only throw a challenge to what is around, and around is the community. Manes eats his slice of ham on the Day of Atonement in front of hapless tailors in their Yom Kippur *talletim*. They beat him all right – but run for shelter, horrified, at the first sight of blood. The blow lands in a pile of cotton wool. The tailors would not make a hero out of Manes. They will now wait till his Bar Mitzvah, so that they can excommunicate him. Manes has broken the selfsame rules which Scharie professed to uphold, and did uphold with ostentation and panache. Manes' worms are all out, there is no way to stop them, they must be destroyed.

Modche Stark, little Aaron's older brother, who was with Manes' brother in Hungary when the original disaster happened, leaves the community for good. For Palestine. Aaron would go instead to a Polish school, where at the celebration of his first promotion he would recite the poem: 'Who are you? A little Pole. What is your sign? The White Eagle'.

The hump made of the rags of serfdom. How to shake it off? As a Jew sharing the land of Poles? As a Jew leaving behind the land of the Pole? Can one do it with the community? Outside the Community? Against the Community?

The *Przybysz z Narbony* (Visitor from Narbonne) Stryjkowski has dedicated to the fighters of the Warsaw Ghetto. In the Ghetto, the choices which the residents of Stryj spent two full years to ponder without getting wiser, were forced upon people in a flash. In a flash, it had become clear who was the enemy and who was the brother. Yet the choices were not clearer than before. Their condensation and their urgency made their complexity all the more protruding. And the conclusions – all the more difficult to reach.

Eli Ibn Gaiat arrived from his native Narbonne in a small Spanish town that was writhing in the clutches of the Inquisition. Young, confident and proud of his wealth, ancestry, and the public respect in which he had bathed since childhood, Eli was ill prepared for what he found. Furtive glances, whisper, half-finished sentences, stealthy gait, faces frozen into masks – all this was difficult enough to comprehend. Something else, however, was more bewildering yet. 'In Narbonne, everything was clear and simple. Evil was evil, good was good. When touched by suffering, however, evil and goodness mix up, swirl.' When told that, sometimes, evil ought to be covered up for the sake of good, Eli feels baffled and confused. 'So the world is like this? This gives me no peace ... The worst is the first crack in the thought. It is like a blemish on the surface of a fruit which inside is already rotten'.[33]

The cracks were, indeed, aplenty. In the span of a few days which divided Eli's arrival from his heroic and grotesque, redeeming yet purposeless death, goodness was soiled by evil, evil dressed as mercy, so that in the end one could not tell anymore where the frontier between them ran. Before he dies, Eli is confused. With his last breath, the meaning of his death escapes him.

The town lives in the sinister shadow of San Martin, the Inquisitor, the Assimilator Supreme: he swore to convert those who remain proudly and stubbornly Jewish, but also to unmask Marranos – the covert Jews hiding under their new garb of converted Christians. And San Martin *knows* that the converted Christians are – all of them, without exception – merely covert Jews. In the town, the air is filled with the acrid smell of burned bodies and the no the less poisonous, fearsome bewilderment of the living. Conversion, repulsive as it is, is but a temporary reprieve; or, rather, a trap. So is, in all probability, cooperation with the Inquisitor: no more than a stay of execution. Refusal to cooperate brings catastrophe closer, yet consent does not avert it. No attitude makes sense, and life without sense is unbearable. The sages of the *barrio*, the Jewish Quarter, strain in vain their wits, wisdom and formidable knowledge of the Holy Scripture to inject sense into the senseless. They seek the guidance of ethics, but moral injunctions spell suicide. They seek advice of reason, only to discover that the calculation of gains and losses is a trap set by the enemy; reason is a tool in the hands of those who set the rules of the game.

> Says the spokesman of appeasement – and *reason*:
> For one death, we will pay with sacrificing thousands. Let reason calm your just exasperation. For this, you need more strength than for swimming on the crest of a sweeping tide. A man who knows how to quell his fury in time, is worth more than two righteous ... If we wanted to repay every insult, we would run short of blood. We are a small nation, hurt and maimed for a thousand years. Let us not help the enemy to destroy us.

> Says the spokesman of resistance – and *moral dignity*:
> You won't appease the Inquisitor with the sacrifice of one man, like the goat thrown in the desert to Azazel. He will squeeze you out of life piece by piece, he will force you, like a worm, to crawl to an ignoble death ... I see horns of light on the head of the Youth from

Narbonne, and hear virtue in his voice . . . His deed may bring death, but this will be a life-giving death. The nation lives by the death of its heroes.[34]

'Your exploit was childish' – opines one sage of Eli's first, uncontrolled, public outburst of anger. Not childish, but mad – responds another. But 'let us respect our mad. It is they who make history'. 'I did not think of history' – admits Eli, confused.[35] Eli thought of clean hands. Is history made by people with clean hands? Or, rather, is a history made by those whose hands are dirty worth living? Can one live with unclean conscience? And what for?

The luminaries of the community soil their hands to keep the community alive. They put reason above morality; this is exactly what, they believe, their responsibility demands. Universally loved, gentle Doña Mariana turns informer; she denounces Eli for conspiring against the Inquisitor. The hands of the most venerable Rabbi don Balthasar Diaz de Tudela are blacker still. To save his son, hostage of the Inquisitor, and avert persecution of his flock, he betrays the names of neo-Christians who remained loyal to Jewish faith and thus condemns them to the pyre. Doña Mariana and Don Balthasar count the gains and the losses. Both believe that to lose a few is better than to condemn many. Both trust that they can ward off the destruction of many by helping to destroy the few. Both sacrifice the few yet save many. Or so they force themselves to believe. Or so they say.

Eli Ibn Gaiat would not have any of this. No amount of persecution can stop him. Perhaps being a visitor helps him to resist. Fewer bonds, fewer personal loyalties: easier to see the forest behind the trees, easier to overlook the trees behind the forest. Dagger in hand, Eli is ready for the arrival of San Martin the Inquisitor who threatened to desecrate the Grand Synagogue by his presence at the *Bar Mitzvah* of Don Balthasar's son. In the event, the Inquisitor does not turn up, as a token reward for Balthasar's treachery. Instead, Alonso arrives, dressed in the Inquisitor's cloak. Alonso once wrote leaflets calling the Jews of Seville to resist, and the authorities responded with death and fire. Now Alonso has gone mad. He wants to repent the sin of disobedience by donning the mantle of the victorious enemy and baptising his brethren to save them from the fate of Seville. Piercing the Inquisitor's cloak, Eli's dagger sinks into the body of a demented man. Heroism turns into a farce only to become a tragedy. In an immoral world, moral acts are denied not only effects, but dignity. In the end, they breed death. In the scuffle that follows the stabbing, Eli's skin is scratched with a poisoned weapon. Both Alonso and Eli die; the madman and his executor. The two failed heroes fall – not the enemy kept at a safe distance by the cowardly reason of Don Balthasar.

The ultimate perfidy of the oppressor: once the victim is coerced into a situation without good moral choice, once reason has been pitched against morality, one cannot any more tell cleanliness from dirt. Only madmen have the guts for heroism; heroes turn into madmen. Dignified death becomes as meaningless as the ignoble one, to which human worms crawl on their own, sane, will.

Another visitor, this time to the town of Stryj, the hometown of Aaron Stark, is Martin Heiber: a highly-educated, big-town lawyer, spreading the Zionist gospel among the baffled and incredulous residents of the *shtetl*. Like Eli, he feels humiliated by the confusion and indecision of the Ghetto – not very different from that of the *barrio*. Few listen to his appeals to courage and dignity; fewer still comprehend; no one agrees.

> We live in fast flowing, but shallow times. In such water only small fish can live. Our Jewish life is like a stagnant puddle. If a carp happens to be there, it must die. It will suffocate ... I searched, tussled like a fish on a sandy beach. I found nobody, nobody. Only minnows. On whom could I lean? On whom could I rest my faith? I wandered from town to town, looked people in the eyes. Emptiness everywhere. And I spoke of the Great Renewal![36]

What made the *shtetl* routine repulsive and unbearable to Heiber was the stench of serfdom and its spiritual sediment; complacency. The slavery which had been sucked in, digested, woven into bodies and souls of people who felt at home only in the ghetto. Consent to such life was indignity. Nonconformity was the only way to spiritual regeneration. A powerful idea was needed. Yet more than an idea, powerful men were needed. Such men as can stand up and say no. What they say 'no' to, was of lesser importance.

To Heiber, one such man was Herzl. Since Herzl's death, Heiber had looked for another one capable, like Herzl, of waking the sleeping giant of the nation out of his sleep. He found him, in Stryj, in the person of Aaron's father, Toivie the melamed.

Toivie was the most orthodox man in town – as staunchly and uncompromisingly religious as Heiber was secular and anticlerical. Toivie recogized but one authority: that of the Law. In the name of the Law, of the justice it commanded and the rules it ordained, Toivie was ready to fight any earthly power, however awesome. The Law was something never to be bent and never bargained with, whatever the stakes or benefits of compromise. In the name of the Law, Toivie – the only person in town – stood up to Scharie and demanded retribution for the robbed sisters-in-law and the girl abandoned with an illegitimate child. He paid sorely for his creed. Hounded and defamed by Scharie, deprived of his pupils, left alone by his friends, he was finally forced to leave the town and earn his living by teaching illiterate village children.

Surely I seem as foreign and distant to you as the West to the East – Heiber admits. The creeds which animated Herzl and Toivie had no meeting point. What united them, for Heiber, was the dogged determination with which they had been held, come what may. 'Since our leader Herzl died ... I sought in another Jew his strength, his confidence, his conviction of being in the right. In spite of everybody and all the defeats. You, one little man against the enormity of two thousand years, against the scoffer's jibes of "Utopia" ... '[37] Only such a self-confidence, such determination could give the people the ability to resist and to persist, against all odds and in defiance of all gains or losses. To pursue to the end, and at all costs. *What* to pursue, mattered little.

What the costs of such determination might be, Heiber did not know yet. The Century was still young and innocent, and so was Heiber's Zionism. He could get an inkling, though, of what was in store: he could learn it from the fate of Toivie the melamed, who step by step learned the costs of his tenacity. Toivie suffered, but so did everyone around him – and *because of him*. It took many victims to learn that no dedication, no lofty and novel purpose can outweigh the human suffering it caused. No crimes of Scharie could justify his, Toivie's, refusal to obey the last will of the dying saint, Rabbi of Głogów: to shake hands with his adversary. No loyalty to the Law could absolve him from the sin of letting his daughter die lonely in her exile, having first declared her dead. Indeed, *I was a God's policeman*, admits Toivie; and can there be a blasphemy worse than such conceit?

> If from piety of pieties, justice of justices, sin can be born like a bastard, where is that verge behind which the abyss opens? Or that infinity, God's attribute, one of the infinitely many of God's attributes? The infinite piety, the infinite justice. Can a man deck himself in such plumes? Do on earth what God does in Heaven? ... I felt contempt for the ignorant. I saw learning as the crown, knowledge as the highest dignity ... I, the judge, did God's job for Him; I was worse, I was only His judgment, while He is the judgment and the mercy ... '[38]

The path of Heiber has been so far innocent and clean, and nothing beclouds his admiration of straight backs and stiff necks. He lures Toivie to leave the ungrateful *shtetl* behind, to join him in his mission, to inspire Jews with his own proven readiness to fight to the end whatever the price. But Toivie knows already what Heiber is still to learn. 'My lie is mine and nobody else's. Your lie wants to devour thousands ... Nothing is more permanent than human frailty. Nothing is more certain than evil and misery ... You will surround the state, if you build it, with the fence of a new ghetto'.[39]

The story ends with Heiber and Toivie parting their ways. Toivie stays in the old ghetto to bewail and repent the wound which he knows his pride had inflicted. With his pride all in the future, all hope and no past, Heiber leaves the *shtetl*, and the story, to inflict new wounds of which he does not yet know.

It is not the enemy outside — seems to be Stryjkowski's message — who threatens Jewish survival, but Jewish false prophets. Kafka noted: '*Messiah may come only a day after his arrival*'. False are the prophets who announce his arrival a day before, as they themselves make that arrival impossible.

Old Tag, the hero of another Stryjkowski novel, *The Inn*, tells the following story which his grandfather heard allegedly from no lesser authority than the Holy Besht:

> There is a huge mountain, and a big stone on the top of that mountain, and pure water flows from beneath. There is a soul at the other end of the world. That thirsty soul longs all its life for this source with its clean water. But the soul will never reach this source and will never quench its thirst. That will happen only when Messiah comes. The soul must wait till he comes! Then, it will be all the same for everybody. In the meantime, the heart may burst.[40]

The source has not been reached yet. For all the suffering and its tragic end, the source seems not to be nearer now than it was all along. But the effort to reach it can and should be recorded. If only to know where it cannot be found. Both Toivie and Heiber failed to reach it. If they were lucky enough to return from their journeys, more misery was the only gain they would show for their labours; and they would have returned poorer of that moral purity which prompted them to start off on their expeditions. This, at least, is how Julian Stryjkowski remembers the reasons for which Aaron Stark hid in the shelter of the Polish Word.

Given its reasons, this was not just a hiding, and not merely a shelter. The refugees burdened the Word with all their unfulfilled hopes, promises received but not kept, and first and foremost with their dreams of the world of moral purity. They made the Word grow, expand, and rise to the seldom-visited moral heights. If it is true that assimilation arrived from outside as a painful pressure, it is true as well that it has been filled from inside by the ethical urge. It will be thus forever remembered as a folly, perhaps, but not a sin.

The refugees brought a gift to the hosts, and the gift will stay with the hosts even if the latter are slow to acknowledge its reception. It is Polish science, literature, poetry, art that gained most from the episode of assimilation. The bearers of gifts gained less. Half a century after their massive disappearance from the Polish soil (though not from Polish history), one of the Warsaw streets named after Hanka Sawicka, a Jewish girl who died as one of the leaders of the Polish anti-Nazi underground, may be renamed after Roman Dmowski, the founder of the biggest and most influential among the right-wing and anti-semitic camps in pre-war Poland – a man who used to complain that 'something bad is happening with our grass-root members. One can feel that the anti-Jewish attitudes in our ranks are weakening', and demand that 'anti-Jewish actions be intensified'.[41]

NOTES

1 Ficowski's and Miłosz's poems (in my translation) have been quoted after *Męczeństwo i Zagłada Żydow w Zapisach Literatury Polskiej* (Warsaw, 1988) pp. 401, 404.
2 Emmanuel Ringelbaum, *Stosunki Polsko-Żydowskie w czasie drugiej wojny światowej* [Polish-Jewish Relations during the Second World War] (Warsaw, 1988) pp. 176–7. In a thorough, insightful and carefully balanced analysis of the survival and transformation of 'Jewish memory' in contemporary Poland, Iwona Irwin-Zarecka admits the crucial role of the suppressed memory of Holocaust horrors: 'The problem here might be that Poles were such close witnesses that they automatically interpret any general questions about the Holocaust as a challenge' (*Neutralizing Memory: The Jew in Contemporary Poland*, New Brunswick, 1989, p. 166).
3 Isaac Deutscher, *The Non-Jewish Jew and Other Essays* (New York, 1968) pp. 88–9.
4 Alina Cała, 'The Question of the Assimilation of Jews in the Polish Kingdom (1864–1897): 'An Interpretative Essay', in: *POLIN* vol. I (Oxford, 1986) pp. 148–9.
5 Jan Tomasz Gross, 'Ten jest z ojczyzny mojej . . . ale go nie lubię' in: *Aneks*, no. 41–42 (1986), pp. 32–4.
6 Aleksander Smolar, 'Tabu i niewinność' in: ibid., pp. 97, 119.
7 Artur Saundauer, 'O sytuacji pisarza polskiego pochodzenia żydowskiego w XX wieku' in: *Pisma Zebrane*, vol.3 (Warsaw, 1985) pp. 467–8.
Of himself, Sandauer writes: 'Sandauer's life is a history of a Jew persecuted for his origin. As a writer, however, he is someone very (perhaps excessively?) Polish on account of his language. His purism betrays a neophyte'. One can discern a self-portrait in Sandauer's fictional hero 'Mieczyslaw' (an ultra-Polish Christian name) 'Rosenzweig' – 'a hero built of two halves hating each other'. Cast between the equally unprepossessing alternatives (a non-authentic and bleached identity, or self-hating and demonizing personality), Sandauer admits to being suspended in a state of 'unstable balance', in which he 'sees any choice as naivety' (comp. ibid., pp. 526–9). At no stage of the checkered political history of post-war Poland does Sandauer quite fit the prevailing mood. Always an outsider, a 'de-bunker' by nature, a pedantic, pungent, sullen and quarrelsome critic, Sandauer succeeded in antagonizing all the otherwise warring camps of the Polish literary world in more or less equal measure.
8 Artur Sandauer, 'O człowieku który był diabłem' in: *Pisma Zebrane*, vol. 1, pp. 103, 107.
9 Aleksander Hertz, *Żydzi w kulturze polskiej* (Warsaw, 1988) pp. 164–6. Hertz remembers a letter received from his friend, decorated with the highest Polish distinction awarded for supreme military gallantry: 'I had to be courageous. If I had faltered, it would be said that the Jew was a coward'.
10 A striking example of the allo-semitic view can be found in the Diaries of Witold Gombrowicz, hardly an anti-semite: 'When I hear from those people that the Jewish nation is like other nations, I feel like listening to Michelangelo insisting that he does not differ from the others'. 'Those who received the right to superiority have

no right to equality'. 'The history of that nation is a secret provocation, similar to the biography of all great men – a provocation of fate, inviting of disasters that can help fulfill the mission of the chosen nation'. (*Dziennik 1953–1956*, Paris, 1957, p. 121).

11 Artur Sandauer, 'O sytuacji pisarza ... ', p. 460.
12 Ibid., p. 468. Of the inter-war life of the Jews assimilated into the Polish culture, Efraim Kaganowski, a Jewish writer from Warsaw, left a few shuddering, perceptive sketches: 'Cafe Ziemiańska, where the avant-garde of the Polish-Jewish congregate, writers, poets, artists come here – a curious family, that on every opportunity complains of the "Jewish gathering". They are not yet sure of their Polishness and suddenly notice that they are surrounded only by other Jews. This is why they feel here so well, at home'. 'It is hopeless in the narrow Jewish streets. But it is also gloomy in the affluent Jewish flats. And only late at night in a large Jewish bourgeois restaurant ... can you meet creatures from another world, whom you have never seen so far in any Jewish place. They come with an expression of people who are lost in their way or of tourists in search of the exotic. One journalist whispers: "Do you see that man over there, with that woman? Do you know, who are they? They found themselves for the first time in Jewish surroundings ... " After a while I saw that famous assimilator dancing with his companion among the Jewish crowd. But this Jewish night-life does not intoxicate. On their way back home the night guests do not feel drunk. The Jewish eyes are fearful and vigilant. These men want to be crushed in the crowd so that they can stop feeling how lonely they are' (*Warszawskie Opowiadania*, Warsaw, 1958, pp. 174–5).
13 Comp. Adolf Rudnicki, *Żywe i martwe morze* (Warsaw, 1957); 'Regina, Regina Borkowska' in: *Wspólne Zdjęcie* (Warsaw, 1967); *Kupiec Łódzki* (Warsaw, 1963) pp. 10–11.
14 *Żywe i martwe morze*, pp. 68, 74.
15 Adolf Rudnicki, *Sto Jeden*, vol.III (Kraków, 1988) pp. 129–30.
16 *Żywe i martwe morze*, p. 663.
17 *Sto Jeden*, vol. III, p. 96.
18 Ibid., pp. 136–7, 16.
19 Ibid., pp. 110, 46–7. The *hump* is a well established trope in the Polish-Jewish literature. Perhaps the most famous example of its use is Julian Tuwim's of a hunchback imagining his suicide: he would buy a most beautiful necktie and hang himself with it. To no avail, though: 'No one will say "what a wondrous necktie"/ Everybody'll comment "what an awful hump" ... '
20 *Sto Jeden*, vol. II, pp. 18–9, 107, 136.
21 *Głosy w ciemności* (Warsaw, 1957) p. 194.
22 'Azyl', *Znak* no. 390–1 (1987), p. 188.
23 'Azyl', p. 188.
24 *Głosy w ciemności*, p. 266.
25 *Echo*, p. 269.
26 *Głosy w ciemności*, p. 32.
27 Ibid., p. 141.
28 'Ojczyzna pamięci Juliana Stryjkowskiego', *Miesięcznik Literacki* no. 8 (1988), p. 67.
29 Interview with Zbigniew Taranienko, *Literatura* no. 35 (1972), p. 3.
30 Interview with J. Niecikowskim, *Współczesność* no. 22 (1971), p. 3.
31 *Głosy w ciemności*, p. 281–3.
32 *Echo*, p. 48.
33 *Przybysz z Narbony* (Warsaw, 1978), p. 279.
34 Ibid., p. 297–300.
35 Ibid., p. 181.

36 *Głosy w ciemności*, p. 399.
37 *Echo*, p. 309.
38 Ibid., p. 136.
39 Ibid., p. 320–1.
40 *Austeria* (Warsaw, 1966), p. 89.
41 Comp. Slawomir Majman, 'Long Live Vandee', in *Warsaw Voice*, July 16 1989, p. 6.

# JEWISH THEMES IN 'THE BEAUTIFUL MRS SEIDENMANN' BY ANDRZEJ SZCZYPIORSKI

Laura Quercioli

Slawek Funk used to repeat continually: 'I am Polish, not Jewish. My great-great-grandfather was baptized in 1848 in the Church of Saint Marcin. There are famous Polish personalities among my ancestors and their relations: a Vice-President of Toruń, a Senator of the Republic, a member of the Legions of Piłsudski, a Rector of a university, a lawyer who defended Lwów and a soldier who fought in the war of '20. All my friends and acquaintances are Polish. I do not know any Jews. Half my class at the Gymnasium emigrated to the West and I stayed here.

Nevertheless I am also Jewish, since other people think so.

'The first time I went to the barber's on the Rynek, as a child, someone asked me: "Hey, little one, are you going to the *tsaddik* of Ger?"

'And on many subsequent occasions, for example at Zośka's reception when Tomek was drunk and shook hands with me and explained to me that he was not anti-semitic.

Or not long ago, Piotr, who had undergone a religious conversion, came to see me to tell me that he loved me because I belonged to the people of Christ. Or when I was at school, when after drinking *alpaga* we got into a fight with some boys from Nadbrzeze. I got cold feet and Bodek said: "Jews are always Jews."

'So, why should I not consider myself Jewish,' continues Slawek, 'since other people think I am? But I cannot accept it, because I feel myself to be only Polish. In any case, my great grandfather was baptized in 1848 in the Church of St. Marcin. There were famous Polish personalities among my ancestors: a Vice-president, a Senator of the republic, a legionnaire....'

This is Slawek's dearest wish, to find a way of proving once and for all that he is Polish; an unrealisable fantasy. But lo and behold the right moment comes. It does not matter whether it happened in a dream, in the delirium of a fever or when he was awake. It was real.

The police had rounded up several dozen men. Slawek was among them. Now they took him to the wall of execution. When they arrived they were told that the Poles would be killed and the Jews would be allowed to go free.

'What are you?', the commander of the soldiers asked of each.

'I am Polish', Slawek Funk replied.

The others said they were Jews. The soldiers allowed them to leave and they hurried away.

The firing squad was lined up, the order was given and the shots rang out. The captain came up to the corpse and observed it thoughtfully.

'What a stupid Jew', he said.[1]

This story of Jerzy Trammer is a good introduction to the subject of Jewish-Polish relations, a thorny and painful topic, which has been compared to a minefield where every word, even the most innocent, can start a conflagration. Each of the 'opponents', the 'two saddest peoples in the world', as they were described by the poet Antoni Słonimski, himself Jewish and Polish, has suffered too much and lost too much and can only confront with raw nerves the subject of their reciprocal misunderstandings. Too many suspicions and too many silences separate them. Among the many obstacles there are even some of personality. As Andrzej Szczypiorski, the writer with whom I shall chiefly deal in this article, wrote:

> Jews and Poles resemble each other precisely in this. They are both characterised by hyper-sensitivity and a tendency to interpret every stupid remark as made against themselves, going about, looking for latent evil intentions everywhere. As if all this had any importance in the daily lives of Jews and Poles. . . . [2]

A first concrete barrier in the way of reciprocal understanding is provided by the language and by the mental furniture itself. The historian Krystyna Kersten wrote in a recent article:

> Here words, definitions and even simple statements cease to be useful instruments for describing reality. The conspiracy of silence that surrounds this problem has deeply embittered it, and was broken only a few years ago. I am not thinking so much of official silence as of the means of dealing with the Jewish problem in interpersonal relationships, even between people most intimate with each other. In fact, it has always been easier to avoid such a prickly subject.[3]

Kersten is surely right in underlining the burden of this incapacity in speaking about anything which has any relevance to Judaism; it is a phenomenon which is common among Jews too. Incidentally, it should be remembered that the word for Jew itself, *Żyd* in Polish always has, at least a share of derision and contempt. On the other hand, it is also true that the silence imposed by the regime at least until the 1980's has had a profoundly deplorable effect. Szczypiorski, in the article quoted above, talks about the stereotype of the anti-semitic Pole and argues that it was the Polish press itself and the changing attitudes of the regime which have contributed to its dissemination in the West:

> It is impossible for people accustomed to freedom of thought and speech to imagine a world which is subject to the harsh discipline of state censorship, which decides even whether the most innocent footnote is to be printed. There, the state enjoys an exclusive monopoly of information and is in charge of the mass media and edits, by means of its censors, every word from beginning to end, every paper, every radio or television programme and even every tiny piece of printed paper, including visiting cards, soap wrappers and the labels on the bottles of mineral water. In these countries, one can never even dream of clarity in public opinion.[4]

Yet, it cannot be said that after the war and with the advent of 'actually existing socialism', the Jewish question was excised from literature (though, as Miłosz says, most poetry about the annihilation of Polish Jewry is to be considered good only because it is well-meaning in its intentions).[5]

Henryk Grynberg, the Polish-Jewish essayist and writer, has even claimed that

> Polish literature has more effectively dealt with the subject of the Holocaust than the literatures of the super-powers, that is, than Russian and American literature, or than ambitious literatures such as those of Czechoslovakia and Yugoslavia, or that of the old masters, the English, the French and the Italians. Polish literature in this field can vie with Jewish literature, but its results are not yet adequate; indeed one requires much more of it because it has been an eye witness, because it found itself at the epicentre of the greatest crime in history.
>
> The Polish writer does not achieve his end, he does not accomplish his mission if he does not take account of his enormous theme, if he does not take up a position and express a view on this event.[6]

Many writers have listened to Grynberg's call and, of course, the value and the perspective of their works differs extremely. Moreover, the Jewish topic has always been, more than others, a subject liable to every kind of political manipulation.

Far from losing its emotional significance in a *Judenrein* Poland (the story of the Carmelite nuns in Auschwitz bears witness to this), the Jewish question has become increasingly an obligatory point of reference for every reflection upon this country, on its past, its destiny, its 'soul'. As a matter of fact, especially in the last decade, the Jewish topic has become more and more a vital subject for the Polish intellectual. The discovery of the role played by the Jews in Polish history and reflection on it, an understanding of the real relationship between the two peoples, have become essential to the current process of historical and cultural renewal. As Rafael Scharf argued years ago in this journal, the Jews appear to Poles in search of self-knowledge, as a witness who must be listened to carefully and who must, of course, be questioned.[7]

But going behind the superficial fascination of the topic, it remains to be seen whether what could appear now to be a positive image of the Jew in the newest literature will prove so in the longer run; if this argument is not being used for the construction of a moving patriotic hagiography or to prove theses already established in advance.

Unfortunately, we can already detect the instrumental use of Jewish themes and stereotypes in one of the most successful Polish novels of recent years, Szczypiorski's *The Beautiful Mrs. Seidenmann*, in which a series of prejudices and preconceptions in the approach to the Jewish question are mingled with a doubtful general vision of history and with an irritating tendency to wishful thinking. Szczypiorski, generally a fascinating and esteemed writer, seems here to have lost his grip in a rhetorical journey which has carried him off the road.

The novel's Polish title, *Początek* (Beginning), is to be understood as referring to the beginning of the new Poland or in other words, of the new world, that which rose from the ashes of Oświęcim – Auschwitz. It is divided into 21 chapters and almost as many characters appear in them (I counted 18). The narrator presents them first in the middle of the war in 1943, the year of the insurrection of the Warsaw ghetto, Warsaw being the city in which the action takes place.

Szczypiorski shows us the past, the future and the moment of death of many of his characters. Their different destinies develop accoarding to a noticeably schematised and rigid plan: we see for instance how Paweł Kryński, the central character, perhaps partly the enbodiment of the author, being a freedom fighter during the occupation, a friend of Jews, an insurgent in Warsaw in 1944, becomes – as he must – a member of Solidarity and is imprisoned in 1981; or how the good and upright Judge Romnicki, the incarnation of the spirit of pre-war Poland, a chivalrous and loyal person, not to mention his necessary years of imprisonment under Stalinism, dies, uncorrupted, in 1956

in a small provincial town, in the house of distant relations who had taken him in when he was released from prison. *In this country there are always people who will care for those who have been wronged* (p. 64, my italics).⁸

The dreadful informer Lolo becomes the manager of a factory in socialist Poland and is, moreover, the only negative Polish character in the entire novel, abounding as it does with martyrs and heroes.

Jewish characters are altogether six: Irma Seidenmann; Henio Fichtelbaum, a school friend of Pawełek Kryński; his father, the lawyer Fichtelbaum and his younger sister Joasia; Artur Hirszfeld, a Jew saved and baptised by a nun, a man who is to become an important ministerial servant and a ferocious anti-semite; and Bronek Blutman, traitor and informer.

Mrs Seidenmann, the eponymous heroine of the novel:

> was a light blonde with blue eyes, a straight, shapely nose, and a delicate, somewhat ironically-contoured mouth. She was a very beautiful woman, thirty-six years old, with a sizeable fortune in jewellery and gold dollar coins (p. 19).

and moreover a

> beautiful and intelligent woman so preoccupied with the problems of X-rays and the riddles of radiology that she seemed not to notice the hell in which they all lived ( ... ). Now and then she reproached herself for hearing with a certain indifference the news from the other side of the wall (p. 19).

When arrested by the Nazis

> She did not feel in the least that she would die because she was a Jew, for she did not feel herself to be Jewish (p. 24).

Blutman, the Jewish informer, has actually denounced her and taken her to the Gestapo. She is saved by Polish friends and acquaintances, but, as we see from subsequent events, her rescue proves to be of no great help to Poland: she becomes, in fact, a high-ranking employee of the Ministry of Education (which means, at least in those latitudes, the servant of a regime imposing rigid thought-control). The Ministry is situated – Szczypiorski's irony and fate – in the same building on Szucha Street which was the Gestapo headquarters during the occupation.

One of the favourite themes of a certain type of Polish propaganda is the Jewish participation in the governmental apparatus during the years of Stalinism. (On its strength of numbers there are, obviously, no data, but perhaps it is unnecessary to argue the point: suffice it to say that until 1968 there were in Poland no more than roughly 25,000 Jews, amongst 30 million Poles . . . ). In fact the so-called Jewish sins during the era of Stalinism are intended to provide at least a partial justification for the anti-semitic excesses of the 1960s, simultaneously liberating the Poles from the collective sense of guilt for all the wrongs committed in this century against their semitic fellow-citizens.[9]

Indeed, as Henryk Grynberg has so convincingly described, for Polish rulers and ruled alike, it has proved highly useful to investigate which Jewish names turned into Polish among the cadres of the political police, among the 'red bourgeoisie', among the writers of the regime. In the same way it has been advantageous to forget the same names, even more if turned into Polish, of those who took part in the underground movement against the Nazis, who fought in the Warsaw Uprising and in the army of Anders, of those who were imprisoned and tortured by the Stalinist militia. It is convenient to cite, as Szczypiorski does in the article 'Poles and Jews', the high percentage of communists among Jews before the war as a 'paradoxical' explanation for Polish anti-semitism, cheerfully forgetting that, even if so many Jews were communists, at least as many were right-wing and traditional and religious, and provoked the anger of their 'Aryan' countrymen no less.

Meanwhile, in the novel, Irma Seidenmann is compelled to emigrate by the anti-semitic campaign of 1968. Let us listen to Szczypiorski's reflections on this historical moment:

> If the same people [the Jews] that yesterday had held influential positions within the Party and within the police, today declare in the Western world that the Poles are nothing but bloodthirsty anti-semites – they should remember that they have been the victims of their own methods, ideology and political group. It was not the Poles, but the very political establishment created by them with their own hands years before – which reminded them in 1968 of their Jewish origins, which condemned Zionism, which finally forced them out of the country ( . . . ).[10]

One could understand, from the fragment quoted above, that the whole Polish political establishment was formed by Jews, by Jews affected by a lust for self-destruction. In the light of these statements, Irma Seidenman's behaviour in Paris becomes less surprising. Indeed, the events of 1968 affect her much more deeply than the years of Nazi occupation, because what happened to her then seems to have sealed the fate she set for herself 'with her own hands'. This could be an explanation of the striking occurrence that, in all the numerous pages dedicated to her self-consciousness, it never, not even once, occurs to her to recall with gratitude the heroism and courage of all those who put their lives in danger to save her from the Nazi prison. Because even in the distance of her Parisian exile, thinking about Poland, Irma

> didn't remember Stuckler, Müller, Mr. Filipek, Pawełek. She didn't remember Dr. Adam Korda [Stuckler is a Nazi officer; the others are her benefactors – ], but only those men in her office ( . . . ) and also the bloated, swollen, ill-disposed faces of those who spoke with her later; the hands of customs officials on her baggage, papers, books and notebooks (p. 103)

The writer perhaps forgives her, adding in the same page

> People have a right to be unfair when God afflicts them with misfortune

even if to us it could seem that all Irma's misfortunes were prepared by men, and not by God.

To bring more clearly to light the writer's position it is useful to return to the previously cited article of 1979:

> In 1968 there had to leave Poland even people who had exercised an unbridled power in the Party, in the police force and in the bureaucracy of the State for more than 20 years. Certainly not all of them were equally to blame and not all of them acted against the vital interests of the country. They took with them, however, into the world not only the necessary bitterness of exile but also the burden of the wrongs, if not crimes, that they had committed ( . . . ). Among the exiles of 1968, the majority was composed of people for whom, since I am Polish, until the end of my days I shall ask for mercy, even though personally I do not feel guilty of what the representatives of state bureaucracy of the Party have done in my country ( . . . ). However, among these exiles there are also people with whom, as a human being, I shall not shake hands, because they have done too much harm to other human beings. The fact that they were victims of the customs of their own political and moral environment may arouse compassion, but not respect.[11]

Szczypiorski tries to sit on both sides of the fence, and it is no surprise that he does not completely succeed. He asks forgiveness for the Jews who were compelled to seek exile in 1968, but his main anxiety remains to plead not guilty of the crimes committed by the political machinery of his own country. He admits that the majority of the exiles were completely innocent, but in this novel of his, which is supposed to be also an essay on Polish history and Jewish-Polish relations, or which at least has been interpreted as such, he chooses the character of an exiled Jewish woman who is guilty, doubly guilty (Irma Seidenman even knows very well that she is unfair to her homeland, but dismisses the feeling with a shrugging of the shoulders). Meanwhile Szczypiorski consoles himself with the certainty that

> One can say without exaggeration that the history of Poland, and perhaps not only of Poland, has not known such a popular and spontaneous movement in defence of the Jews.[12]

as that which developed in Poland in 1968 [!].

Reading the novel, we can feel perhaps compassion for Irma Seidenman, because she is 'lost in foreign lands, rather comical, like most old and solitary women' [sic] (pp. 186–7); but not respect.

Blutman is a completely wicked character: an informer of the Gestapo – it is not easy to imagine something worse. He, a Jew, is the one who betrays the Jewess Seidenman, while others, Poles and even Germans, will come to her rescue. A more complex and interesting character is that of Artur Hirszfeld, alias Władysław Gruszecki.

When we meet him for the first time he is

> seven-year-old Arturek, a boy with a good appearance but with a bad look in his eye, that betrayed the deeply embedded proclivities of his cursed race (p. 52).

He obstinately refuses to take up the new 'Aryan' identity given to him by Sister Weronika, to help him escape the persecutions. He seems thus, notwithstanding the enigmatic 'bad look in his eyes', one of those destined, like Joasia whom we shall mention below, to return to Judaism and not wish to deny his own uncomfortable roots; he seems to be a personality proud of its own truth and its own originality. He becomes instead a

> not very tall, nearsighted man. His name was Władysław Gruszecki (...) one of those people who do not know moderation (p. 53)

destined to 'surpass his mentor in Catholic zeal' (p. 53) and to have 'an anti-German and anti-semitic complex' and to make himself a pillar of an 'aggressive and intolerant' religion (p. 55). In 1968 he is not dismissed from his post as an important servant of the Ministry of Agriculture (the reasons for it are not reported) and

> he expressed his joy over the fact that Poland was finally ridding herself of Jews. 'We must be a nation of a single, common, native blood!' he said (p. 55–6).

When, many years later, he meets Pawełek, who has come out of an internment camp, Hirszfeld-Gruszecki obviously does not understand him; on the contrary he reproves him for having followed romantic chimeras and 'the tone of his voice was almost accusing' (p. 155). Notwithstanding his unbridled Polishness, Gruszecki, as is shown during his encounter with Pawełek, does not understand and does not know the real spirit of Poland, its real destiny. The cynical rationalism of this desperate man is foreign to the spirit of the nation (maybe it's all a question of blood and race, after all?). His patriotism is totalitarian and misunderstood; his love for the home country makes him opt for

> friendship with the Soviet Union, for he regarded friendship with the Russian nation as the foundation of a better future for his beloved country (p. 54).

Like Irma, and more than her, Gruszecki is author and accomplice of Stalinist sins; he is, moreover, one of those who carry the guilt for the crimes against the Jews in '68, and for all other misdeeds which tortured Poland in the following years.

For him too we can feel compassion, but not respect; he too is allowed a partial 'extenuating circumstance', because he 'must have suffered terribly' (p. 55). But is this enough?

We can, however, feel respect for the lawyer Jerzy Fichtelbaum (even if he too is a communist sympathiser). He is an assimilated Jew with 'the look of a shepherd from the land of Canaan in his eyes' (p. 75), who dies with dignity in the Warsaw ghetto, in two very moving pages. Henio Fichtelbaum, his son, the best school-friend of Pawełek Kryński, also dies; Henio even decides to return to the ghetto to die with his people, like Ernie Levy in *The Last of the Just* by Schwarz-Bart; our Henio is also a 'capricious, handsome, dark' boy (p. 13), with 'capricious, lightly curled lips, dark, thick hair above his brow' (p. 148–9). Henio flees from the ghetto in 1940 and, although so dark-skinned, wanders round Warsaw and its environs for two years without being denounced or blackmailed or anything of the kind. But let us not impose limits on the possible. However, at least one point in the story of Henio has definitely disquieting accents. Lo and behold, this 'capricious Jewish teenager with red, voluptuous lips' (p. 149)

> made a mistake because he had become self-confident, and since he was only eighteen success had gone to his head. He went to the pastry shop on Marszałkowska street, forgetting about his look. Later, he justified his lack of caution by telling himself that never before had he studied his face from the perspective of racial characteristics, and what's more, no one had ever called his attention to Jewish features as something worthy of observation (p. 27–8).

Alas! Has Poland ever been a country where it was possible to be unconcerned about one's own 'racial characteristics', or where 'Jewish features' could be unnoticed? (is there indeed any such country?) Least of all could it be so in the years preceding the Second World War. At page 159, writing of 'holy Polishness, drunken, whoring, venal' Szczypiorski recalled that this was also an anti-semitic country, 'its mouth stuffed with claptrap, anti-semitic, anti-German, anti-Russian, anti-human', the place where one could meet 'the foxy snouts of *szmalcowniks* (blackmailers), the boorish ones of March 1968'. It is really a pity that he proceeded to forget this for the remainder of the book. What was Poland in the years just before the war, a Poland in which the Jewish lineaments of Henio Fichtelbaum were supposed to be unobserved? In Rafael Scharf's words:

> Is it undue sensitivity which makes us remember the 'Endecja' (National Democractic Party), the 'Chadecja' (Christian Democratic Party), the ONR (National Radical Party) – political parties whose main programme was a more or less brutal battle against their Jewish fellow citizens? Was it a figment of our imagination that there was an officially approved boycott, discrimination in all areas of state service, daily incitement in the press, the programmatic and primitive anti-Judaism of the Church, the sporadic pogroms?[13]

As Marek Edelman recalled, nationalistic Poles used to beat up all the Jews who were trying to cross the trendy Nowy Świat, main street in Warsaw. How does Szczypiorski imagine this and similar events possible, without a constant, methodical and hysterical observation of somatic features, of physical appearance? But the writer insists:

> If before the war he had distinguished himself in school in anything, it had been for his love of science, not the shape of his nose and lips (p. 28).

We have already seen how our author considers the Jews who, having forgotten or denied their Jewishness, had tried to assimilate within their surrounding environment. In a revealing page Szczypiorski gives us his comprehensive judgment on the historical and ethical debate over the annihilation of European Jewry, over the Jewish identity shaped by the *Shoah*, and generally over contemporary Judaism.

> People who years later came to live on top of Henryczek Fichtelbaum's bones did not often think of him, and if they did, it was with a certain pride and vanity that here they were, the greatest martyrs under the sun. They were doubly mistaken. First of all, because martyrdom is not like nobility that one can inherit, as one can a coat

of arms, or an estate. Those who lived on top of the bones of Henryczek Fichtelbaum were not martyrs in the least; at most, they were profiting from someone else's martyrdom, which is always stupid and dishonourable. Second, they did not notice that the world had gone forward, leaving far behind the events of the war with Adolf Hitler (p. 33).

At this point, it would surely be naive to expect that Szczypiorski would spare us that most topical and burning subject, the conflict between Israelis and Palestinians. In the novel, the problem is exemplified by the figure of Joasia Fichtelbaum, Henio's younger sister.

Joasia is a little child when saved by Polish friends of her father, namely by the Judge Romnicki and, like Hirszfeld, by Sister Weronika. Joasia, however, differently from Hirszfeld, decides to return to Judaism, takes the name Mirian Wewer and goes to live in Israel. In the last chapter, in giving the baby to the nun who intends to baptise her, the noble Judge Romnicki makes a long peroration, otherwise beautiful and moving, in defence of Judaism (and is it not alarming that it should be a Pole who takes up the defence of Jewish values, while the anti-semitic slogans are left for the Jews?)

> She will be a Jewish woman, one day a Jewish woman will awaken in her and she will shake the foreign dust from herself, to return to where she came from. And her womb will be fertile, and she will bring forth new Maccabees into the world. Because God will not forsake His own people! ( . . . ) One day Judith will awaken in her, will draw the sword, and will cut off the head of Holofernes (p. 197).

The comment of the author is

> And just as he said, a Jewish woman did awaken in Joasia, but not like the one he had foreseen. Perhaps the Judge did not fully understand God's designs, or perhaps it was for a trivial reason (p. 197).

What is this trivial reason? Maybe Miriam simply lacks intelligence and culture. Although she has studied up to her twenties, for instance, she is not even able to recognise any analogy between the 'imperious stance' of the Israeli soldiers and that of soldiers of other times and countries: 'she wasn't educated enough' (p. 199).

But perhaps we shouldn't blame the Polish schools: there seems to be something in Miriam, which in a rather strange way distorts all her emotional world. In fact her eyes

> were full of tears and her heart full of pride, gratitude and ardent faith (p. 198)

only when she

> for the first time saw a powerful man with one kick smashing a Palestinian door

then

> leading into the blinding desert sun the bewildered fedayeen, their woman and children.

This is the reason for her pride and joy. Of course, she doesn't even for a moment think with compassion of the 'frightened and helpless fedayeen' nor about anything else. What we still learn about her is that she has a brief moment of uncertainty, but soon forgets about it; that she has a foolish, deaf, Israeli husband twice her age; and that she lives (could there be any doubt?) in a 'kibbutz on the West Bank' (p. 154). Therefore the good Judge Romnicki was mistaken! He should have imagined that in today's world the Jews have no other chances than to become tools of Stalinism, or accomplices of Israeli imperialism. This, unfortunately, seems to be the moral of Szczypiorski's sermon.

In this novel, which claims to be a choral fresco of Polish society from the post-war years until the present day, and to illustrate such an important passage in European history, in this novel which has won prizes and which has been a best seller in many countries, and whose author is president of the Polish-Israeli Association, who are the Jewish characters who, denuded of their superficial pathos, could represent authentic and positive values? Alas, there are only those of Henio and his father, the passive Jews, the Jews who have accepted their doom: only the Jews who died.

At this point it may be necessary to add that Szczypiorski's vision of the world, as expressed in *The Beautiful Mrs. Seidenman*, is rather extravagant and confused not only as regards Jews, not only as regards Poland's place in Europe ('outpost of the free world, squeezed in between tyrannies', 'A narrow bond of hope'), Russia ('Prussian pride, cruelty, bestiality, contempt, arrogance', p. 130), but that it is contradictory and misleading even about Polish opposition of the 1980s, as in the long fragment in which the writer maintains that only the people who have experienced all the most cruel and gruesome forms of detention and punishment of this century (Auschwitz and Kolyma included) can claim to be 'truly free men', and be able to 'speak calmly about the world and about human dignity' (p. 128). The practical and theoretical implications of these statements are at least frightening, but, strangely enough, to my knowledge only Leszek Szaruga[14] has noticed it. Maybe this is due to the efficacy of the moral blackmail imposed by Szczypiorski on his reader, or to the skilfulness of his eloquence.

It should be recalled, moreover, that the novel continues to receive literary prizes and honours, like the recent Nelly Sachs prize, given by the German city of Dortmund to those 'who maintain spiritual tolerance among peoples'.[15]

*The Beautiful Mrs. Seidenman* is a lost opportunity, and it is questionable whether Polish-Jewish relations, tangled as they have always been, can be ameliorated by it.

The severe judgment inspired in Joshua Rothenberg by the doings of Artur Sandauer is apt to describe the 'case' of Szczypiorski:

> (Poland) which has produced both a celebrated school of mathematical logic and an excellent theatre of the absurd continues to excel in its contradictions and incongruities.[16]

## NOTES

1 Jerzy Trammer, 'Świr' *Res Publica*, no. 2, 1987.
2 Andrzej Szczypiorski, 'Polacy i Żydzi – podsumawanie diskusji', *Kultura* (Paris), no. 11, 1979.
3 Krystyna Kersten, 'Rok 1968: motyw żydowski', *Res Publica*, no. 5, 1988.
4 Szczypiorski, 'Polacy i Żydzi' *Kultura*, Paris, no. 5, 1979.
5 Czesław Miłosz, *Świadectwo poezji* (Warsaw, 1987).
6 Henryk Grynberg, 'Holocaust w literaturze polskiej', in *Prawda nieartystyczna* (Berlin, 1984).
7 Rafael Scharf, 'In Anger and Sorrow: Towards Polish-Jewish Dialogue', *Polin: A Journal of Polish-Jewish Studies*, Vol. I, (Oxford), 1986.
8 All quotations are taken from *The Beautiful Mrs Seidenman* (Great Britain, 1990). Translated by Klara Glowczewska, 204 pp.
9 Henryk Grynberg, 'Życie jako desyntegracja', in: *Prawda nieartystyczna*.
10 Szczypiorski, 'Polacy i Żydzi'. On this point see also Szymon Laks, *Szargam Świętości* (London, 1980).
11 Szczypiorski, ibid.
12 Szczypiorski, ibid.
13 Scharf, ibid.
14 Leszek Szaruga, 'Co nam mówi Andrzej Szczypiorski?', *Puls*, no. 3, 1987.
15 It has been said that this, like other German prizes won by this novel, was due to the very fact that in reality here the best of all characters portrayed is that of a German, Müller.
16 Joshue Rothenberg, 'Contradictions and Incongruities', *Soviet-Jewish Affairs*, no. 1, 1984.

# ABOUT THE 'JEWS-IN-POLAND' EXHIBITION IN KRAKÓW JUNE–OCTOBER 1989

Aleksander Zyga

The 'Jews – in Poland' exhibition, held in the main building of the National Museum in Kraków from June to October, was visited by large crowds of Poles and foreigners, mainly Polish Jews not only from Israel, but from Europe and other parts of the world. It constituted an event unprecedented in the history of Polish exhibitions and one which surpasses anything hitherto attempted in this sphere.[1] The Kraków exhibition was striking for its sheer flair, scale and variety. A very large number of works of art on Jewish subjects were brought together, not only from other Polish museums, but also from private collections and foreign museums. In the past, some paintings on this subject had been brought out of hiding from museums and could be viewed at exhibitions dedicated to the work of individual artists in various salons and fine arts societies both in Poland and abroad in the form of lithographs, copperplate and woodcut reproductions, and through the use of more modern reproduction techniques. These works also appeared as printed illustrations in Polish and foreign pictorial magazines and art periodicals. They could sometimes be seen in catalogues and albums or read about in reports and reviews of exhibitions, and occasionally in histories of Polish art and books about Jewish painters of world renown.

This kind of selective artistic production by both Polish and Jewish artists from its beginnings almost to the present, testifies not only to the presence of Jews in the Polish lands, but also to their participation in the history of Polish art and culture. It also constitutes a record of the centuries-old Diaspora, which has now receded into the past.

Above all, one is struck by the scale and extent of the Kraków exhibition in view of the fact that in the past there was scarcely any interest in this subject in the history of Polish art, and it had been largely limited to illustrations of literary texts and historical works about Jews and a few references and allusions in art criticism. As a result, the organisers of the

Kraków exhibition have had to grope in the dark, apparently carrying out a kind of investigation of museums, for the history of Polish painting offered them no serious study on this subject. Indeed, it appears that almost the only guideline they were able to follow was the essay written by Antoni Mazanowski at the end of the 19th century. This treatise, unique in the history of our art criticism, is a discussion outlining the more important paintings by Polish-Jewish artists in the last quarter of the 19th century.[2] A few other discussions and articles about Jewish paintings mentioned by Mazanowski and by other Polish and Jewish artists were also available, mainly found in picture books illustrated with plates of paintings by Jews all over the world, and in Jewish periodicals published in Poland and abroad. However, these are not part of the still incomplete bibliography of Polish art, as valuable critical evaluations and discussions which form part of the history of Polish art criticism often (and how often!) have not been included in it. Those evaluations and discussions dealing in the main with the history of Jewish artists which have appeared in Jewish publications are not only in Polish, but also in Yiddish and Hebrew.[3] So nearly all that is generally known about the role of Polish Jews in painting, art and art theory, and their part in the history of Polish art, and above all about their contribution to and participation in Jewish painting world-wide, can only be found in foreign studies. Not easily accessible to the Polish reader, these include: Jozef Sandel's book *Jewish Motifs in Polish Art*, written in Yiddish, which deals with paintings by Polish artists as well as those by Jewish painters;[4] and Cecil Roth's book of plates in English, in which the author, while also covering the work of Polish artists, assigns Polish painters with a Jewish background to the not-too-precisely-defined realm of 'Jewish art',[5] as some of his predecessors indeed had done.[6] There are also a number of publications which are not available in Polish libraries, including books of reproductions of paintings and sketches – some by Polish Jews.[7] A book on Jewish motifs in Polish painting compiled by Halina Nelken, which has been promised for several years now, appeared in 1991, published by I. B. Tauris in London.

Information on how the material in the Krakow exhibition was selected is provided in the Introduction to the *Catalogue for the Exhibition 'Jews – in Poland'; June-August 1989*. The exhibition did not include all Polish paintings and sculpture on Jewish themes. The exhibition organisers aimed 'to gather together artistic evidence which would, in the widest possible sense, represent that life' (p.5), though in view of the exhibition's title, works by foreign artists depicting Jewish life in Poland had to be considered. Accounts of various art exhibitions, referring to paintings and sketches on Jewish themes, most of which have probably already gone astray (they can no longer be found either in Polish or foreign collections, public or private) bear this out.

*The Catalogue* informs us that the Krakow exhibition was organised by a team which included Danuta Dec, Krystyna Moczulska, Janusz Walek, under the direction of the 'author of the scenario' Marek Rostworowski, a well-known Kraków art historian, and the patronage of the then Minister of Art and Culture, Aleksander Krawczuk. *The Catalogue* elaborates on the purpose of this exhibition, at the same time explaining its title, organisation and documentation. In the preface to the main part of *The Catalogue*, Tadeusz Chruścicki, direction of the National Museum in Krakow, writes that the Krakow exhibition is 'like a chronicle in painting . . ., intended to contribute to increasing knowledge of and evoking Jewish history in Poland' (p.5). Marek Rostworowski's extensive 'Introduction', which follows the preface, is exploratory and constitutes the first extended discussion on the subject in the history of Polish art criticism. It explains why the title was chosen and discusses its composition and categorisation into five parts: i) 'In Poland'; ii) 'In the face of God'; iii) 'Amongst the Poles and as Poles'; iv) 'Endlösung' (the Final Solution); and v) 'Generations'. Historical criteria were applied, as can be gathered from the scheme and disposition of the exhibits. The essays which follow the Introduction – 'Jews in Poland from the Middle Ages to the end of the 18th century' by Maurycy Horn, and 'Polish Jews in the 19th and 20th Centuries', by Jerzy Tomaszewski – provide the reader and the viewer with material on the socio-political situation and on Jews' living conditions in the Polish lands and on how Poles and Jews co-existed. The last and principal part of *The Catalogue* contains documentation, arranging the painters and sculptors in alphabetical order, and referring to the various exhibits in the different parts of the exhibition, giving the artists' dates of birth and death, their location in the exhibition and the owners of the exhibits. (This information is also given for the Jewish 'heroes'.) This documentation, which includes 1,455 exhibits (in fact, there were even more at the exhibition, as *The Catalogue* was sent to the printer a year before the exhibition opened) is rounded off by indices of artists and lists of (87) black-and-white and (six) colour illustrations reproduced in the final section of *The Catalogue*.

The title of the Kraków exhibition recalls Cyprian Norwid's well-known poem 'Polish Jews' (1861), in a somewhat different form with a 'holding of the breath' – as the author of the Introduction puts it – between the two words, in order to avoid a stereotypical title such as 'Jews in Art' or 'in Polish painting'. At the same time, taking the title of the exhibition from Polish poetry suggests certain convergences and analogies with Jewish themes in Polish poetry, something that is borne out in the Kraków exhibition with fragments of classical poetry about Jews by both Polish and Jewish poets. These include a poetic fragment about Jankiel from *Pan Tadeusz*, Mieczysław Romanowski's *Rabbi*, Jan Kasprowicz's *Ajzensztok's Szai*, Julian Tuwim's, *We, Polish Jews*, a folk song about Berek Joselewicz, and excerpts from translations of Jewish poetry from Yiddish and Hebrew.

The title of this vast, almost panoramic, exhibition is so broad that it creates the impression that the exhibition is geographically and thematically limitless, except for the historical boundaries of Jewish co-existence with the native population from the time of their arrival in Poland. Geographically, the artistic exhibits encompass the major concentrations of Jewish settlement in Poland, and therefore, apart from the Prussian sector (where the Jews assimilated fastest with the Germans), concentrations with a long history and a permanently unresolved 'Jewish problem'. These include Warsaw, Wilno, Kraków, Kazimierz, Lwów, Brody, along with small Galician towns, not always identified, and also towns in the Kingdom of Poland, established at the Vienna Congress of 1815. Exceptions to this rule include exhibits with a 'neutral', 'universal' character, frequently not defined geographically, appearing as archetypes and depicting professions practised by Jews with references to scenes of religious ritual from their daily life and customs. Thus an exhibition title such as 'Jews – in Poland' did not bar entry to paintings about Polish Jews by foreign artists or to paintings by Polish Jews about 'foreign' Jews, though the latter were not represented at the Kraków exhibition. The spectator is quite simply stunned by the monumental scale of this exhibition – by the number of exhibits as well as their variety. Even a careful perusal of *The Catalogue* cannot assist the disorientated visitor, as the arrangement of the exhibits on historical criteria in no way helps the viewer to identify them (nor do they have any corresponding numbers). That means the visitor has to find them by following an alphabetical list in *The Catalogue*. Because certain paintings by particular artists were dispersed among different sections of the exhibition, it was sometimes difficult to 'assign' some of the works to specific sections of it. The resulting divisions do not allow one to grasp their artistic individuality, particularly the differences which distinguish 'the artistic-ideological language' in the works of the Polish painters from that of Jewish ones. But this, after all, was not the purpose of the Krakow exhibition.

The exhibition consists of both large and small oil paintings, portraits, works of graphic art, reproductions and (less frequently) photographs of notable works of art, and even picture postcards of the work of distinguished artists – from the early 19th century to the mid-20th century, in the earlier period, by Polish artists, later, also by foreign ones, and, from the mid-19th century, by Jewish artists as well. The oil paintings and smaller canvasses have been displayed along the walls of the particular exhibition rooms, allowing the visitor to view them from a better perspective; the smaller ones have been arranged in glass showcases (graphics), which is conducive to more intimate contact. However, there is inevitably a certain thematic association or even a partial historical convergence between the canvasses on the walls and the smaller ones, and even between the miniatures.

'As if in counterpoint' – as Marek Rostworowski writes in his Introduction – 'there is in the Kraków exhibition a landscape by Monika Krajewska, photographed long after the Holocaust, entitled *Time of Stories* (1984), of ruins with sacramental objects lying strewn about, and above which hang enlarged book-plates of black-and-white images of ruined synagogues and abandoned cemeteries' (p. 12).

These remains of the Jewish presence in Polish lands – of a seven-branched candlestick alongside scattered tombstones from Jewish cemeteries with large plates of ruins showing Jewish synagogues overgrown with grass, weeds and even small trees, suggest to viewers, particularly older ones, be they Polish or Jewish, that this kind of archaeology, already permanently receded into the past, constitutes a kind of topographic legend authenticated by a fragment from Cyprian Norwid's *A dorio ad phrygium*. For a middle-aged or younger viewer, it may even suggest a myth, as evoked by the following fragment of a poem by Aaron Zeitlin:

> That which is today, which only just,
> Is now in the past
> [ . . . ]
>
> It is a long while since this happened,
> It is a long while since this came to pass
> In a once deep and gloomy
> valley.
>
> It was a long time ago
> in some land,
> a very long time ago,
> once upon a time in Poland

Indeed, the paintings included in the first three parts of the exhibition, which reflect everyday domestic and religious Jewish life and customs in the Polish lands, and which chiefly date back to the middle and later 19th century through to the Second World War, rise to the rank of legendary and even mythical works of art. Thus, in the first two parts of the exhibition, the paintings, studies and sketches are predominantly by Jewish artists who, as the best judges of their milieu and its rituals and customs, had nevertheless been kept hidden from Christian Polish eyes or were rendered obscure or simply ignored by Polish artists for so long. The latter, as they were looking in from the outside, if they ever bothered to approach Jewish subjects for their artistic creation at all, tended to characterise figures from that milieu as 'aliens'. Examples can be seen in the following paintings: Julian Karczewski's *Jewish Funeral in Wilno* (1892), Tadeusz Popiel's *The Torah Holyday*, *The Purim Feast* in Wacław Koniuszko's Kazimierz paintings, and Stanisław Grocholski's (1858–1932)

*Praying Jews* (1892). Certain 'Jewish' paintings depicting the Jewish milieu do so much more effectively and, from the artistic point of view, are undoubtedly much more successful and accurate than analogous literary works, even those considered to be in the first ranks of Polish literature. Consequently, the section entitled 'In Poland' includes paintings, chiefly by Jewish painters, which show secular rituals of Jewish daily life, 'landscapes' and the principle Jewish professions in centres such as Wilno, Kazimierz on the Vistula and the Kraków suburb of that name, and include ghetto architecture, genre painting scenes of weddings and funerals, Sabbath and annual celebrations and children studying in *hederim* and *Yeshivot*. Polish painting in this field is represented by works of the following artists (if one limits the list to the most prominent individuals) in roughly chronological order: Franciszek Smuglewicz, Wincenty Smokowski, Julian Karczewski, Stanislaw Czajkowski, Aleksander Turk and Tadeusz Tondos. But among the Jewish painters, a whole artistic pantheon from Artur Markowicz to Leon Lewkowicz can be listed. The paintings found in this part of the exhibition are complemented by showcases full of lithographs and sketches of Jewish types and images of famous rabbis, reformers and Jewish Hasidic leaders from all over the Polish lands, headed by the *Tsaddik* of Kozienice. Among the more important paintings from the first part of the Kraków exhibition, one notices the absence of any Jewish canvasses by the Danzig painter Wilhelm Stryjkowski – not even a photograph or a woodcut. His work on Jewish subjects was shown in exhibitions in Kraków, Lwów and Berlin, and reproduced in 19th century magazines in Poland and abroad. These works include *Danzig Jews in the Synagogue*, *In the Jewish Cemetery* and *Tashlich*. Other drawings that are missing include Andrzej Grabowski's *A Jewish Wedding* and Jewish drawings by his brother Wojciech. It does not appear to be the case that the absence of Stryjkowski's paintings from the exhibition was because the artist did not speak Polish, as the Krakow exhibition claims not to have barred entry to works by foreign painters – and works by Italian painters connected with the royal court of Stanislaw August Poniatowski found their way into the exhibition, but more about that later.

When discussing works by Jewish artists in the first three parts of the exhibition (the last of these will later be considered in greater detail), it is hard not to mention Maurycy Gottlieb (1856–1879), a pupil of Jan Matejko, and 'the first great Jewish artist' from the artistic 'Drohobycz Basin' whose creative individuality showed great promise but who died very young. An enormous photograph of the painting *Jews with a Torah*, which is in the Tel Aviv museum, hangs by the entrance of the section 'In the Face of God'. The inner emotional dilemma visible in his paintings, resulting from his complex ethnic and religious circumstances, immediately becomes apparent in the often unfinished sketches, studies and portraits of this talented 'Israelite', as he was described by contemporary Polish art critics and reviewers of early exhibitions of his works who thus tried to indicate his tendency to assimilate himself with Polishness and to annex his individuality to the realm of the history of Polish art. Gottlieb was aware of this: 'I am a Pole and a Jew and I would like to work for the sake of one and the other, God willing.' Characteristically, while attending an exhibition of 'one of our most genuine artists, a painter like Michalowski (and, had he not died young, we would probably say – as great as Michalowski)', Jan Lechon stated that Gottlieb 'wanted to be Polish, and was Polish, but he has never been recognised as such. His *Self Portrait Wearing an Ancient Polish Noble's Robe* symbolises his tragic fate'.[8] At the same time, Maurycy Gottlieb's paintings form, as it were, a counterpart to the inner emotional dilemma experienced by first generation Polish poets with a Jewish background, such as Henryk Marzbach (1836–1903) and Aleksander Kraushar (1843–1931). In the Introduction to *The Catalogue* of the exhibition, Marek Rostworowski emphasises the importance of Maurycy Gottlieb's artistic work in the scheme of Jewish themes in Polish painting: 'On the one hand there is the view from inside, revealing his own nation's countenance, unknown to the Polish nation (*Day of Atonement* and the portraits), and on the other, there is Gottlieb's personal, modern, orthodox approach to the sacred traditions' (p.19). It is therefore not at all surprising that the paintings of this Jewish artist prompted critics, on the one hand, to acknowledge him as the first true Polish painter of Jewish extraction, and on the other, to consider his work as a part of world-wide Jewish artistic output.

Later Jewish artists managed to avoid Maurycy Gottlieb's dramatic dilemma, as by then the majority of them clearly identified themselves with Jewishness, despite assimilationist tendencies in their paintings, because Jews had always been aware of their national identity. Works in the Krakow exhibition which best illustrate this sense of identity include representatives of a later generation of Jewish artists, such as Samuel Hirszenberg's (1864–1908) *Talmud School* (1887) and some small sketches, Maurycy Trebacz's (1864–1940) and Artur Markowicz's canvasses, as well as the eulogisers of the 'human' and architectural landscape of the Kazimierz Ghetto in Krakow.

Even a cursory glance at the selection of paintings about Jews in Polish painting at the Krakow exhibition, whose principal objective was to give a comprehensive picture of Jewish life in painting, clearly suggests discrepancies in both the choice of subject, 'scenes' and 'moment' in Jewish life being recorded and in their treatment. In canvasses by Jewish artists, one finds almost exclusively an isolated Jewish environment showing Jewish ritual religious ceremonies, portraits and images which are all limited to Jewish personages and their professions, all depicted from the inside, and most of them set about a background of synagogues, Jewish cemeteries, *hederim*, *yeshivot*, Jewish ghetto districts and architecture. In short, in addition to immortalising their existence, these paintings and sketches reach deep into the Jewish psyche, in the portraits and images of famous and noted rabbis and religious leaders, and so on. A tendency to avoid a purely homogeneous treatment of Jewish 'figures' can be detected in some paintings and sketches by Artur Markowicz, who attempts to show the poverty of everyday Jewish life, an aspect normally avoided and unobserved in the works of other Jewish artists, and particularly in paintings by Poles. By recording the insulation and isolation of the ghetto from the rest of the inhabitants in this way, these Jewish painters are reaching out for their own national and denominational traditions. In their content and expression, their paintings clearly contrast with 'Jewish' paintings and sketches by Polish artists, who present that life as a manifestation of the Diaspora, that is to say, as a Polish topographic and human landscape. Indeed, the situation was not much different as far as literary works were concerned. The first literary attempts of Jewish writers entering or trying to 'break into' Polish literature, mostly in Yiddish, whether poetry or prose, were also limited exclusively to descriptions and depictions of 'native' ethnic-denominational milieus. In this respect, there are unmistakable analogies with paintings with Zionist themes by Jewish artists at the end of the 19th and the beginning of the 20th centuries. One can safely come to such a conclusion, after reading Eugenia Prokopówna's recently defended doctoral dissertation on the subject of Polish-Jewish literature in the inter-war period.

The difference discussed above is most strikingly apparent in the third part of the exhibition 'Jews – in Poland', entitled 'Amongst the Poles and as Poles', regardless of the subject and how Jewish themes are depicted and whether they are contemporary or historical in nature. Some of the paintings by Jewish artists on Zionist themes included in this section actually appear distinctly to contradict the second clause of this title.

This section of the exhibition can surely be considered the most controversial, from the point of view of the selecting of exhibits, their arrangement and the significance of the paintings, studies, artistic works and sketches included. Being the most thematically far-reaching and broadest in its ability to reflect the life of the Diaspora, it becomes a veritable 'chronicle' of Jewish life within the Polish domain. Before discussing the contribution of Polish painters included in this section, it must be mentioned that in Poland, the initial ventures into painting on Jewish themes were made by anonymous and frequently unknown Polish and foreign artists. This was because Jews were forbidden, under the threat of excommunication, to practise iconography, for fear that they might fall under the spell of idolatry. Therefore the only Jewish painters who dared to reach out into the closely-guarded milieu which was totally inaccessible to 'outsiders', were those who had broken all close bonds with orthodoxy and caste. The real discoverers of Jewish themes in Poland were foreigners, painters living at King Stanisław Poniatowski's court headed by Jan Piotr Norblin. It was precisely these foreign painters who became fascinated and attracted by the exotic clothes, language and customs of contemporary Polish Jews, which the natives had not taken much notice of.

Near the entrance to the third section of the Kraków exhibition one is met by a large canvas by Piotr Michalowski entitled *Jews* (*circa* 1845), a fragment of which appears on the cover of *The Catalogue*. It shows strongly individualised 'figures' of Polish Jews. On page 19, *The Catalogue* describes the canvas: 'Jewish faces deep in thought [. . .] marked by strange beauty and by their hard lot, which is reflected in various psychological states projected by the artist in the serious facial expressions seen in five of the men, the waning glances of the old, as well as the mildly ironical ones of the young.' The first known signs of Polish-Jewish presence in our painting are characterised by hostile stereotypes, dating back to the 15th–16th centuries, such as an *The Last Judgment*, a Carpathian icon from Poland near Chyrow, representing an imaginary scene of ritual murder, dated to the 15th century by an anonymous 16th century artist; and a 17th century painting, *The Dance of Death*, in the church of the Bernardines in Krakow. The anti-Jewish sentiments of these paintings concur with the general anti-semitic ideology of literary 'representations' in old Polish literature.

The introduction of Jewish themes into painting, which was first seen in the depiction of Jewish types and figures in the context of the Diaspora, was undoubtedly encouraged by the widely publicised struggle for reform and equal rights for Jews in the 1790s, particularly associated with the debates in the Four-year Sejm, and the discussions at that time about the rights of bourgeois status to which the Jews were assigned. From then on, although very sporadically at first, the Jew became an integral part of the Polish landscape in all pictures reflecting important events, records and historical moments. Examples of this can be seen in the paintings of Michał Stachowicz (1762–1825) such as *A Celebration to Commemorate the Founding of the Kościuszko Mound on the St. Bronisława Mountain in Kraków on 16 October 1820* (circa 1822), or *Prince Józef Poniatowski's Entry into Cracow* (1821?) as well as other paintings and sketches by the same artist, depicting genre scenes with Jews. The great master Jan Matejko also succeeded in immortalising Jewish participation in earlier Polish historical events. Some fragments of his works represented in the Kraków exhibition bear witness to this: *The Polish Commonwealth Welcoming Jews* (1889); *Prussian Homage*, which includes a figure representing Michael Ezofowicz accepting a knighthood (1882); a compositional sketch for the painting *The Banishment of Jews from Kraków in 1494* (1892); and *The Constitution of 3 May 1791* (1891).

At the time, the biblical motif of *Maccabees* (1830–1842), a painting by Wojciech Kornely Stattler (1800–1878) actually had a patriotic function, because it emphasised an implicit parallel between the history of the Polish and Jewish nations – something which appeared elsewhere, particularly in *emigré* and domestic journalistic writing. The fact that Stattler's painting was not included in the exhibition in Odessa as well as the opinions about it held by both Mickiewicz and Słowacki, indicate that the painting was indeed read in this way. The publication of the poem *Maccabees*[9] by a Galician writer in the fifth issue of *Tygodnik Polski*, in 1848, in Lwów produced similar results.

While following up Polish patriotic elements in Jewish themes and their resonance in Polish painting in relation to Jewish contributions to Polish poetry and prose, one cannot pass over in silence the recurrent 'imaginative visions' in paintings and drawings of Jankiel, the 'honest Jew' from Mickiewicz's *Pan Tadeusz*. These began in 1859 with Wojciech Gerson's woodcut for the first edition of the poem included in the poet's collected works, and were continued, *inter alia*, by illustrations by Elviro Andriolli and Juliusz Kossak and, among Jewish artists, Maurycy Trebacz's paintings such as *Jankiel's Concert* from *Pan Tadeusz*. On the subject of 'Jewish' illustrations for works with Jewish themes with a patriotic resonance and a comic bent, it is a pity that not a single artistic testimony to the attitude of Polish Jews to Napoleon was shown at the exhibition 'Jews – In Poland', such as the amusing woodcut by Franciszek Kostrzewski, based on the light-hearted folk legend *Napoleon and the Quarrelsome Jews* by August Wilkoński in the first volume of the 1873 edition of Wilkoński's collected humorous stories (could this be because of the satirical eloquence of the drawing?).

A legend about King Casimir the Great's love affair with the Jewish woman Esther has had a favourite place among historical and Diaspora painting in Poland. It was first used by Wojciech Gerson in his *Esther and Casimir the Great* (1870) (not shown at this exhibition); he was also the creator of *Welcoming the Jews/Wandering Jews Asking Casimir the Great for Asylum in Poland* (1874), which was often reproduced in 19th century illustrated magazines. It was also used by Francizzek Zmurko (1858–1910) in his *Casimir the Great and Esther* (1811). Polish-Jewish reconciliation in Warsaw, in 1861, found particular expression in large canvasses by eyewitnesses, spectators and participants alike, such as *Funeral of Five Dead Victims in Warsaw in 1861* (entitled in the Introduction *Funeral of Victims of Repression in 1861* – p. 21) by Aleksander Lesser, the first completely assimilated Polish painter of Jewish extraction, who devoted his artistic talent to Polish historical painting, and *Funeral of Five Dead Victims of a Demonstration in Warsaw in 1861* (1865) by Henryk Pillati, who also created the painting *The Death of Berk Joselewicz in Kock* (1861). In the display cases, these paintings are complemented by colour lithographs of the same Joselewicz, created by Juliusz Kossak during the days of Polish-Jewish fraternisation, as well as copies and reproductions of his work with a quotation from a folk-song about this Jewish hero, as well as lithographs produced in Maksymilian Fajans' lithographic studio of Joselewicz and Jewish leaders at that time with Rabbis Ber Beisels, Markus Jastrow and Izaak Kramsztyk. Other works connected with this period, along with Artur Grottger's *Warsaw Jews* from his cycle *Warsaw II* (1861), include a canvas entitled *Temptation* (1894) by Wojciech Weiss (1875–1950), showing a Jew in a state of indecision whether or not to hand over to the Russians a cargo of weapons belonging to the revolutionaries, and a somewhat earlier painting, *The Wounded Insurgent* (1881) by Stanisław Witkiewicz (not included in the *Catalogue*), in which, again cautiously, from a distance, a Jew is watching an insurgent's funeral; finally, Władysław Rawicz's (1832–1863) portrait of the chief administrator of the Podlaski province who was executed by the Russians. The exhibition also included paintings and sketches on Jewish martyrdom after the defeat of the 1863 insurrection, showing the exile to Siberia of Jewish participants. The works of such exiles are among the many that belong to this category, for example those by the Jewish painter Aleksander Sochaczewski (1843–1922), such as *Aleksander Sochaczewski and Mikolaj Czernyszewski* – a sketch for the painting *A Farewell to Europe* (1890–1894) – and other sketches for this cycle, and *On the Way to Penal Servitude, the Author in Irons in the Centre* (1895–1897), and also *To Return to the Native Land* – Jacek Malczewski's (1854–1929) portrait of Dr Jozef Tislowitz who was deported to Siberia.

The patriotic leitmotif in this part of the exhibition is completed by pencil drawings and painted scenes from the lives of legionaries and portraits of them from the First World War by Leopold Gottlieb (1879–1934).

The remaining problem, indicated in the title of this part of the exhibition, 'Jews as Poles', is connected with patriotic Jewish involvement in the struggle for independence, in solidarity with the Polish nation, and this was central to the assimilationist programme, primarily in the work of Jewish artists. Although this problem was easily discussed by Polish journalism and literature, in the 'plastic' language of painting, it was less easy to achieve and less evident.[10]

An attempt to fill the gaps in the historical detail of the co-existence of the two national groups, with an assimilationist intent, was made, albeit much later on, by Artur Szyk (1894–1951) in his painting, *The Jew Michal Landy Picks up the Cross which has Fallen from the Hands of Karol Nowakowski Killed in the Demonstration of 12 April 1861 in Warsaw* and others, and in the selection of miniatures of the *Charter of Kalisz* (1927–1928) presented at the Kraków exhibition. Just as throughout the works of Polish artists depicting the patriotism of Jews and their support for Polish struggles for independence, and in paintings on Jewish themes in general, Jewishness seems to be perceived through a Polish prism, so, for example, in Artur Szyk's works, it is Polishness seen from the point of view of Jews, those Jews dubbed 'Israelites' by all assimilators and advocates of assimilation, which is singled out. In 1933, Marian Morelowski wrote about that Jewish artist: 'In his work, he represents Polishness as seen through the eyes of an Israelite, and apprehended quite differently from how it would have been seen by an Aryan artist, a Pole. However, it would be a big mistake to criticise this point of view. On the contrary, it is precisely here, in my opinion, that a more interesting and apposite aspect comes to light – the fact that the artist was able to give expression to his sincere psychological and ethnic values in a frank manner. These peculiarities seem more appropriate in the presence of this great love for Poland, the common motherland. Szyk has been able to show us Polishness as seen and refracted in an Israelite psyche and it is this which is much more engaging than an attempt to evade one's own character would have been. If he had not chosen such an option, he would inevitably have produced only banal creations.'[11]

A tendency that contrasted with the trend underlining the Polishness of Jews in the annals of Polish national history began to appear, in Jewish works of art depicting pogroms in the Polish territories, which were the result of the growing signs of anti-semitism, particularly in the Polish Kingdom and in Russia. The creators of these works were largely Jewish artist 'victims', although somewhat earlier on, Jan Stanislawski (1860–1904) had made a point of dealing with this subject in his small sketch entitled *Jewish Pogrom on 26 December 1881 in Sewerynow in Warsaw*. Another painting with a similar message, *After the Pogrom* by Artur Markowicz, was hung (no one knows why) at the beginning of the present exhibition, to provide a final link with the former Polish artistic testimony to anti-semitism. This part of the exhibition certainly lacked, if not paintings, at least photographs representing the works of Maurycy Minkowski (1882–1930), the creator of such canvasses as *A Synagogue and the Day of Atonement*, *Farewell to the Sabbath*, *After the Pogrom* and *Waiting for a Train in Siedlce*.[12] Not only were these canvasses or reproductions absent from the Kraków exhibition, there was no sign of any works or images by Samuel Hirszenberg, mentioned above, who was the creator of such works as *Yeshiva*, and *Holiday in the Ghetto*, and some historical canvasses like *Fugitives*, *The Black Banner*, symbolising the age-old fate of the Jews as wanderers.[13]

The trends embodied in both contemporary and historical painting representing different attitudes of Jews towards Poles, and vice versa, during crucial moments of the struggle for independence, as well as the reaction to the first harbingers of the growth of anti-semitic tendencies are shown, in the central part of the Kraków exhibition, by an immensely rich variety of paintings and graphics hung along the walls or placed in the showcases. These pictures testify to the extreme diversity of that Diaspora; there are many genre paintings, scenes and studies with Jewish figures, invariably with a Polish landscape as background, Jewish types and

countless portraits of notable Jewish personalities. These are testimony to
the advanced level of culture among the Jews as well as the desire of
successful Jewish individuals to immortalise themselves in paintings. In
addition, in Polish literature, there are book illustrations showing Jewish
figures and fragments of lithographic prints with Jewish figures and types.
This most heterogeneous mirror of Polish–Jewish co-existence with its
richness and diversity appears to complete the image of Jews in Polish
literature of the 19th century. The third part of the exhibition, in contrast
to the first part, with which it is thematically linked, contains pictures,
studies, sketches and drawings by Polish artists whose subjects include
Jewish settlements and communities as well as ghettos, and which also
depict a variety of professions practised by this people. The special way in
which Polish artists treated them is always visible, a manner devoid, in
contra-distinction to the attitude in literature, of historical, satirical or
grotesque elements, which tended to dominate nearly all the main
illustrated magazines printed in the Polish Kingdom, as well as less
important works of 19th century literature, such as *Tygodnik Ilustrowany*
and *Kłosy*, along with reproductions of 'serious' paintings on Jewish
themes. In the Introduction to *The Catalogue*, Marek Roskworowski hints
at the conventions ruling this sphere: 'The celebrated Jewish humour is
nowhere to be seen in the silent images of domestic life, in which, if
anything, Norwid's "serious nation" is presented to us. Of course, humour
does sometimes break through to the surface in pictures of festivals,
particularly Purim, the Jewish carnival, and of weddings. However, Jewish
humour seems to be better appreciated by Poles than by Jews themselves,
which becomes apparent in the third part of the exhibition.' (p. 15) The
depiction of Jewish drollery and humour, and especially humour relating
to Jewish community life, which are rarely found in the works of the
Kraków exhibition, is determined by the attitude to Jews of Polish artists
and is, with very few exceptions, absent from the exhibition. It is likely that
this is as a result of the somewhat partial selection of the exhibits, although
one cannot ignore the importance of the aesthetic principle prevailing here
and also in Polish literature since the mid-19th century, which did not
allow any serious treatment of Jewish subject matter but relegated it to a
lower, second-rate, unaesthetic and even plainly unattractive sphere,
suitable only for satirical and grotesque treatment. Jews were only
permitted to provide the subject matter for lower literary and artistic
genres such as satire, comedy and fairy-tales, and in art, only caricature
which has been denied the status of art. For example, according to the
anonymous art critic discussing Wincenty Smokowski's *Making Haste for
Sabbath* in the *Gazeta Warszawska* in 1845, even though caricature 'is a
difficult exercise, it will nevertheless always remain the lowest branch of
art, although it requires more practice and preliminary study'.[14] Moreover,
this view also converged with the nearly obligatory view in Polish literary

criticism, particularly its conservative faction, that the Jewish theme in literature was really only suitable for comedy and burlesque, or for pamphlets and satire. Michal Grabowski, the conservative critic in the Petersburg group who welcomed Julian Klaczko with open arms when the latter began to write in Polish after having given up Hebrew, seeing this phenomenon as a sign of the author's fusion with Polish society and of the prospect of his work being absorbed into Polish culture, went on to rebuke Aleksander Groza for introducing a Jewish hero on an equal footing with the Cossacks in his poem *Sub-prefect Kaniowski*. He even found it impossible to forgive Mickiewicz himself for the Jewish motif in *Pan Tadeusz*: 'To describe in the poem the hideous architecture, reminiscent of Jerusalem, of the two Jewish inns facing each other, amounts to nothing more than an imitation of the banging of a cannon by a collision of consonants. Clearly, both one and the other were prompted by an unpoetical frame of mind.'[15]

If this problem did not really exist for Jewish painters, who by recreating 'their own types' were reaching to their own traditional roots, and could not, after all, (except for converts), ridicule and caricature their own co-religionists, it did take on greater significance when non-Jewish painters put brush and pencil to canvas. The problem became apparent as a result of their attitude to 'the aliens', to the Jewish question and to the people and it almost always depended on the ideology expressed in the corresponding treatment of Jews in their works. If the aesthetic theory mentioned above, which still lingered among conservative critics and aestheticians during the rise of naturalism was a factor, for example in the work of Henryk Struve, the relative absence of stereotypical and comic figures of Jewish innkeepers, especially when portrayed with a Jewish inn as background – figures very much abused, hackneyed and prevalent in Polish imaginative literature and graphic drawings, wearing sidelocks and gesturing, for example in the exhibited paintings of Wincenty Smokowski and in some sketches and lithographs by Jan Feliks Piwarski, has actually proved beneficial for the 'Jews – in Poland' exhibition.

Certainly the creator of the Kraków exhibition ruled out paintings, sketches, drawings and caricatures of this type, so as to avoid any monotony, uniformity or trivialisation of Jewish themes and figures, in the way they had usually been portrayed in second, if not third-rate Polish literature and art – whereas in first-rate literary works and painting, Jews were generally given serious treatment. In this respect, the organiser of the 'Jews – in Poland' exhibition was guided by his own strong views of the way the Jewish problem was treated by Polish painters.

For example, the multi-faceted character of the Diaspora, demonstrated by the exhibits, contrasts with the depiction in painting of Jews as secluded and their confinement to religious rituals and ceremonies – a result of their being seen as 'aliens', and one which condoned them being shown as ridiculous. Just as every Polish nobleman had to have his proverbial Jewish *factotum* without whom he could not get along, so the role the Jews played in Polish village life and in the life of the bourgeoisie and of other national minorities in Poland was equally important. The paintings depicting journeys, market-days, fairs and weddings, inn scenes, and the countless studies and drawings of Jewish types and trades, especially of the work of craftsmen bear witness to this fact. From the oil canvasses and Indian ink drawings of Franciszek Smuglewicz (1745–1811) and Wincenty Smokowski's *Jewish Wedding* (after 1858), *Sabbath Procession/Travelling Jews* (1842), continuing through the paintings of Franciszek Kostrzewski (1826–1911), one must above all mention the earliest known paintings in this field and, displayed in this part of the Kraków exhibition, those by Antoni Piotrowski (1853–1924), Aleksander Gryglewski (1870), Tadeusz Rybkowski (1838–1926), and Stanislaw Grocholski (who was discussed earlier), not to mention a whole litany of lesser artists. In the field of graphics, the artist who surpassed everyone else in the sheer number of his drawings and paintings was Jan Feliks Piwarski, with selected lithographs from his *Zincographic Album with Drawings* (1841) and *A Warsaw Picture Stall* (1851–1858), including authentic depictions of archetypal Warsaw Jews, thus immortalised. These are accompanied by little-known drawings by the poet Cyprian Norwid, next to the only drawing by Jozef Ignacy Kraszewski, but with the total absence of any sculpture by Teofil Lenartowicz, all of whom, in addition to Bruno Szulc, whose drawings are to be found in display cases in the next exhibition hall, represent the work of the Jewish 'hermaphrodites', i.e. writers-artists.

In the field of book illustration, as with the etchings in Leon Hollaenderski's book *Israelites en Pologne* (missing from *The Catalogue*), it is Elviro Andriolli who towers above all others, with work including illustrations to Eliza Orzeszkowa's *Meir Ezofowicz* (1879), which had already been published in the first edition of this novel in the periodical *Klosy*. In order to show this type of work in its entirety and variety, one would like to see at least a cursory representation of the humorous drawings of Franciszek Kostrzewski in August Wilkoński's *Ramotki* (Humoresques great and small, 1872) which have already been mentioned, and the Jewish illustrations by Juliusz Kossak. When discussing 'Jewish' illustrations, one becomes aware of the absence of two classics of this type, of Jewish origin, at the exhibition. It may well be the case that the reason they were excluded (in addition to the selection process) was their greater popularity abroad than at home. One case in point involves the famous German modernist illustrator of Jewish books, Ephraim Lilien (1874–1925) who also came from the 'Drohobycz Basin', and who is not even acknowledged in the *Polish Biographical Dictionary*, something that is all the stranger since he considered himself to be Polish, even though others saw him as a 'foreigner'.[16] The other illustrator, Edward Loevy (1857–1910), one of three artist brothers, came from the Nalewki district of Warsaw and was a favourite of Franco-Jewish publishers.[17]

Even a cursory inspection of the Jewish repertoire of Polish artists in this part of the exhibition shows that not a single one of the leading 19th century Polish painters avoided the Jewish subject. The same was true for the representatives of the younger generation of Polish artists, regardless of the direction, school or artistic style they followed. Among modernist painters following different directions and belonging to different schools, we may find names such as Stanislaw Debicki (1866–1924), Julian Fałat, Jacek Malczewski, Jozef Pańkowski, Władysław Podkowiński, Leon Wyczołkowski (Stańczyk), Boleslaw Cybis and Tytus Czyżewski, all of them creators of numerous scenes, pictures and portraits of Jewish life, and each represented by at least one sketch at the exhibition. As is the case in the rest of the exhibition, the sketches by Polish artists, became intermingled with works by Jewish artists.

Along with these modernist and secessionist canvasses, sketches and studies containing Jewish figures, one must mention the paintings of the 'Young Poland' group – idealisers of the peasantry – including Wincenty Wodzinowski's (1866–1940) *In Tune with the Countryside* (1889), Wlodzimierz Tetmajer's *Love-making in the Inn* (1894), bearing witness to the fact that it was almost impossible for any rural 'enterprise' to take place without Jewish participation. This is again shown by Stanislaw Wyspiański's *Wedding* (1901), which is linked with Karol Frycz's lithographic image of *Rachel from S. Wyspiański's 'Wedding'*, which is a picture of Helena Sulima, the legendary performer of the role of Pepka Singer in this 'Young Poland' national drama, and the only evidence at the Kraków exhibition of the creation of Jewish characters on the Polish stage. But there was certainly no shortage of such performers of Jewish 'types' either in plays by Polish authors or in translations, even if one only mentions the creations of Helena Modrzejewska, Wincenty Rapacki, Jozef Kotarbiński, Kazimierz Kamiński and Franciszek Fiszer. Only two small drawings from Wyspiański's Jewish sketches appear at the exhibition – *The Interior of a Synagogue from the Year 1746 in Nowy Sącz* and *A Young Jew* – even though it is well known that others are tucked away in private collections, including drawings of Jews in Rymanow, on postcards sent from that health resort.

As has already been mentioned, the section under discussion in some respects complements the pictures of the life of Polish Jews against the background of their own settlements and ghettos, and is a testimony of their day-to-day co-existence with Poles in the mainstream of life. At the same time, both the paintings and the graphic prints have been arranged in such a way that their genre and artistic character have been ignored. This has been done as if they were historical records in a fashion, according to the painting styles, schools and trends which allow them to show the advance of Jewish artists into Polish art and, simultaneously, the advance of the Jewish bourgeoisie and intelligentsia to accessibility to positions of social, political and artistic status and with it the possibility of participating in Polish public and cultural life. This process is illustrated with portraits of Jewish scientists (Abraham Stern), philanthropists (Mathias Rosen), bankers and financiers (*inter alia*, Leopold Kronenberg, the Epsteins), not to mention the artists themselves. According to the Introduction to *The Catalogue*, portraits and images of many Jewish booksellers and publishers who played a very important role in the development of the Polish book trade, especially in the Polish Kingdom and in Galicia, have been left out of the exhibition. In this part of the exhibition, doubtless due to the Diaspora theme, its title and background, it is the works of Polish artists which predominate.

However, the preponderance of exhibits and of occasional drawings becomes clear in the fourth part of the exhibition entitled 'The Final Solution', which is the closing section of this intended artistic chronicle of co-existence between Poles and Jews. It includes paintings and sketches on Jewish martyrdom in Poland during the German occupation and Second World War, at the same time seeming to close the age-old Diaspora story with the tragic finale of extermination. It is symbolised by the following well-chosen quotation from the translated fragment of Itzhak Katznelson's (1886–1944) *Song about the Murdered Jewish Nation* (1944) which is visible above the exhibits in this section: 'This too was a story – sometime long ago begun by the Pentateuch, it continued to this day . . . a very sad story – who would think of calling it beautiful.' It is this sad story in painting about the *gehenna* of the Polish Jews which completes this part of the Kraków exhibition, that contains fewer displays than any of the other sections. Among the testimonies in painting and drawings of this martyrdom, tragedy and extermination, are scenes from ghettos, executions and murders, most of them actually created at a later date, as the years of war and occupation were the least conducive to 'the process of immortalising' Jewish 'fortunes' through art. There is also a large selection of sketches depicting the martyrdom of Jews in Wysokie Litewskie by Jozef Charyton (1910–1975), who witnessed it both in that town and in Kamieniec. Marek Oberlander, Wojciech Linke, and the late Jonasz Stern (1904–1980) have works included, to name but the most important artists.

The last section of the exhibition, 'Generations', stands somewhat apart from the chronicle of the long history of the Diaspora in Polish art arranged round specific issues. Its portraits of Jewish personalities (including artists) and its portraits by Jewish painters are arranged chronologically, whenever technically feasible. The result is a mosaic-like gallery of the most diverse characters from the two national groups that are, however, excessively intermingled. It starts with portraits and portrait sketches by the 18th century Jewish portrait painter Krzysztof Radziwillowicz and goes nearly to the present day; examples include Leon Lewkowicz's portrait sketches, and heads of Jewish boys and portraits of Jewish poets and artists like Bolesław Leśmian, Julian Tuwim and Antoni Słonimski. In this not-too-successfully organised mosaic-gallery, where portraits of sometimes mutually remote schools, trends and styles are juxtaposed, and where only a real connoisseur of art history can find his way round, as the exhibits are not numbered (making it impossible to locate portraits which are included in *The Catalogue*) – one is nevertheless able to observe a cultural change among the Jews between the end of the 19th century and the outbreak of the Second World War: the progress of their civilisation, their cultural, social and artistic life. For – as we read in the Introduction to *The Catalogue* – a number of the Jewish artists were considered to be innovators and belonged to avant-garde trends and styles. It is quite impossible to select a list of portraits of the famous personalities and the names of their creators from the throng of the mosaically-arranged works; it is, quite simply, necessary to see them.

In these digressions and discussions about the 'Jews – in Poland' exhibition, we have largely omitted the question of the artistic value of the paintings on show. Generally speaking, no great masterpieces except for some canvasses by Polish artists like Aleksander Gierymski, Wodzinowski or Wlodzimierz Tetmajer are to be found here. It is not possible to conclude that the absence of more representative works of art in this sphere has been caused by the scarcity of items included in *The Catalogue* as compared with the actual repertoire of the exhibition. The few paintings and drawings which are now abroad, or lost, or which have been destroyed, could very easily have been replaced by photographic images of woodcuts or simply photographs which are to be found in catalogues or illustrated magazines both at home and abroad.

Illustrators' artistic contributions to 19th century Polish magazines – genres such as the stereotype, the comical and the satirical caricature – were also completely left out of this exhibition. The same applies to amateur folk 'paintings' and to carved Jewish images, which have recently even become the subject of art history research.[18] But it is a well-known fact that, as was the case with Polish folklore about Jews, it was the Church and the aristocratic and conservative circles controlling so-called popular literature for the masses, which determined this form of expression. The graphic reproductions found in the showcases of the 'Jews – in Poland' exhibition, which generally originate from 19th century Polish illustrated magazines of the 19th century, do not have any printers' imprints (giving date of origin and source). This oversight could easily have been avoided, following the pattern of the excellent documentation accompanying the remaining exhibits, by simply looking them up in Ludwik Grajewski's *Bibliography of Illustrations in Polish Periodicals of the 19th and Early 20th Centuries*. The same goes for the lack of dates for some painters, for example the dates of birth and death of Andrzej Mniszech, which are available in *The Polish Biographical Dictionary*.

The serious treatment given to Jewish subjects by the artists in the exhibited paintings and sketches is confirmed by the original subscripts and titles which are found beneath them. In general, the name 'Jew' seems to predominate, signifying a member of a caste, a separate religious denomination, a nationality and a tribe and even a race, all at the same time. In contra-distinction to Polish literature, where this name has a contemptuous (sometimes 'neutral') connotation – even Mickiewicz was obliged to give the Jew Jankiel the epithet 'honest' – in painting, this name is taken seriously, 'objectively'. This was appropriate to the content and expression of the work (despite the portrayal of 'aliens'), particularly in the paintings and sketches by Jewish artists, as it tended to be an expression of their ethnic identity. In early writing by Jews in Polish, in order to avoid the sensitive, contemptuous and emotionally-charged expression 'Jew', euphemisms such as 'Israelite', 'A Pole practising the Mosaic faith', 'Jew-Pole' were often used interchangeably, and nearly all the artists of the exhibited works, regardless of national origin and religious affiliation, clearly indicate in their titles that the subject and content of their works is '*Jewish*' life. This is particularly true of the titles of paintings and sketches by Jewish artists, which resolutely testifies to the existence of a national Jewish consciousness, even without any official declaration about Zionist affiliation. The rare instances where terms like 'Israelite', both as noun and adjective, are found in the titles of the exhibits, it is only in their French versions, i.e. in the subscripts to the Jewish illustration of Leon Hollaenderski's book *Israélites en Pologne* (1846, not in *The Catalogue*), *Les Israélites polonaises en costume de la Garde Nationale 1830–1831*, or in German ones, i.e. *Marsch der Israelitischen National Garde Warschau* (1848), which, for unknown reasons, was translated in the subscript as *March of the Old Testament Believers of the National Guard* rather than simply *March of the Israelites of the National Guard*, a name which was in wide use among Jewish assimilators and Polish supporters of assimilation. It appears that the old Polish name for a Jew, 'Old Testament Believer', originated as late as the end of the 18th century. The only work at the Kraków exhibition with this word in its title is a copy by Walenty Ciechomski of Aleksander Gierymski's painting *At the Cemetery of the Old Testament Believers*. The term 'Old Testament Believer' was rather an official title, which was used as much by Jews themselves as by government departments to denote their religious affiliation.

It must be asked whether the 'Jews – in Poland' exhibition can be considered to be a 'chronicle' of Jewish life in Poland, as the organisers' intention was described both in the Preface and the Introduction, where its mission as a 'mirror' of the Diaspora was particularly emphasised. This is not quite the case. That this exhibition is something of a historical record is, in actual fact, most strikingly visible in its third and fifth parts, chiefly in the chronology of styles and artistic trends. The exhibition is a 'mirror', but replete with problems, or rather each of its parts comprises such a mirror in its own right; however, this mirror is shattered, and the broken pieces have not always been put together with great success. But such is the fate of exhibitions which are so difficult to assemble; one wishes to include in them as far as possible, all associated issues but they do not necessarily lend themselves to doing this in a clear and consequential manner.

However, this 'mirror-like chronicle' does contain an enormous amount of rich material suitable for a large variety of research, giving scope for various analogies connected with Jewish themes in Polish literature and art and on the subject of the characteristics of work by Jewish artists, and their affiliation to Polish and Jewish art, and so on.

One cannot help but admire the immense amount of work which must have one into both the preliminary research and the bringing together and organising, for the first time ever in the history of museum exhibitions, of such an enormous number of such widely dispersed paintings and smaller works on Jewish themes – but most of all, the exemplary documentation including the artists' dates of birth and death and the sources of the exhibits which have been provided. This is the first exhibition of its kind mounted on such a large scale, the first important step in the field of identification and cataloguing of Polish art about Jews, which have hitherto attracted little interest from historians of Polish art, both in Poland and abroad. This exhibition constitutes the first, important step on the road to achieving a comprehensive artistic picture of the Diaspora.

## NOTES

1 *Kultura ocalona* (Rescued culture) in the National Museum in Warsaw in 1983 and *Wystawa dzieł artystów żydowskich 1918–39* (An exhibition of the works of Jewish artists 1918–1939), Artistic Exhibitions Agency in Olsztyn, 1988. '*Jews – in Poland' Exhibition, June–August 1989*, see *inter alia*, p. 5 of T. Chruścicki's *Foreword to the Catalogue*.
2 A. M[azanowski], 'Jews in recent Polish painting' (*Echo Muzyczne, Teatralne i Artystyczne*), 1885, no. 90, pp. 244–245.
3 *Polska bibliografica sztuki 1801–1944*, vol. 1. *Malarstwo polskie*, Part 1 . . . Edited by Janina Wiercinska and Maria Liczbinska, Wroclaw – Warsaw 1975.
4 Warsaw, Idisz-Ruch Publishers 1956.
5 *Jewish Art. An Illustrated History*. Edited by Cecil Roth, London 1961. See St. Frenkiel, 'Jewish art', *Wiadomości*, London, 1962, no. 21, p. 9.
6 See K. Kraus, 'On the Occasion of the Zionist Congress', *Pravda*, 1902, no. 14, p. 162.
7 See, *inter alia*, Peter Mazer's *Jüdischer Alltag, Jüdische Feste*, reprinted 1988 (First edition, 1981).
8 J. Lechon, *Dziennik, III*. Published by the Polish Cultural Foundation, London 1973, pp. 678–679.

9 See, *inter alia*, Cz. Klak, 'Literacka młodóśc Jana Zachariaszewicza' in *Z tradycji kulturalnych Rzeszowa i Rzeszowszczyzny*, (Rzeszow 1966), pp. 180–182.
10 See op. cit., A. M[azanowski].
11 M. Morelowski, *Iluminator Artur Szyk a problem rasowo-etniczny w sztuce*, Wilno, 1933, pp. 22–23.
12 See, 'Nasi artysci. Maurycy Minkowski', *Świat* 1911, no. 34, p. 6, and *Polski Słownik Biograficzny*, v.XXI, p. 305.
13 See Z. Sarnecki, 'Wystawa krajowa w Krakowie', *Gazeta Lwowska*, 1887, no. 215, p. 3; and 'Z żalobnej karty', Samuel Hirszenberg, *Świat* 1908, no. 39, p. 12, and Clarus [A. Nowaczynski], 'Niezwykla kariera krakowskiego dyrektora w Szkole Stztuk Pięknych w Palestynie', Ibid., 1907, no. 29, p. 16 and Stoslaw [Choloniewski], 'Samuel Hirszenberg' Ibid., no. 8, pp. 4–15.
14 [Anonymous] 'Wystawa Sztuk Pięknych, 'Gazeta Warszawska', 1945, no. 193, p. 3.
15 *Korespondencja literacka* M . . . G. (Michala Grabowskiego), Wilno 1942, part I, p. 75.
16 Dr. Jozef Flach, 'Nasi malaze. E. M. Lilien', *Życie i Sztuka* (a supplement to *Kraj* published in Petersburg) 1910, no. 46, p. 538; J. Kozlowski, 'Lilien – Artysta polski i swiatowy', *Slavia Orientalis*, 1988, no. 4, pp. 583–597.
17 *Polski Słownik Biograficzny*, v. XVIII, pp. 514–515.
18 O. Mulkiewicz Goldberg, 'Obcy w obrzędach wesela', *Polska Sztuka Ludowa*, 1978, v. 22, no. 2 and 'The Motif of the Book in Polish and Jewish Folk Milieu' in *Studies on Polish Jewry. Paul Glikson Memorial Volume*, edited by Ezra Mendelsohn and Chone Shmeruk, Jerusalem 1987, pp. 39–49.

# CONTRIBUTORS

**Zygmunt Bauman** is Emeritus Professor of the University of Leeds. He taught previously at Warsaw and Tel-Aviv Universities. His recent publications include: *Modernity and the Holocaust* (1989), awarded the Amalfi European Prize for Social Science and *Modernity and Ambivalence* (1991).

**Czeslaw Brzoza** is an Associate Professor (*doktor habilitowany*) at the Institute of History, Jagiellonian University, Kraków. He specialises in modern Polish history, putting special stress on the inter-war period. His publications include *Polityczna prasa krakowska w latach 1918–1939* (The political press in Krakow, 1918–1939, Kraków, 1991), *Bij bolszewika. Rok 1920 w przekazie historycznym i literackim* (Beat the Bolshevik. The 1920 war in historical and literary tradition, Kraków, 1990), *Proces 12* (The trial of the twelve, published underground in Warsaw in 1984) and *Reforma rolna w województwie krakowskim 1945–1948* (Agrarian reform in the Kraków province, 1945–1948, Wroclaw, 1988).

**Anna Clarke** was born in Poland and spent her childhood in Warsaw and Łódź. The end of the war found her in Schleswig-Holstein, where she became an interpreter-translator for the British Military Government and met her future husband. She married in London, returned to Germany with the Allied Control Commission and emigrated to Canada in 1954. She has taught Russian history at Carleton University and International Relations and Western Civilisation at Algonquin College. She has broadcast frequently for the CBC.

**Joanna Rostropowicz Clark** graduated from the Departments of Polish Philology and Philosophy at Warsaw University. She received her Ph.D. for a dissertation on comparative literature at the University of Pennsylvania in 1991. She has published literary criticism in *The Nation* and *The*

*Polish Review* and is at present teaching a course on 'The Jewish Experience in Eastern Europe' at Rutgers University.

**Adam Gałkowski** is a historian attached to the Institute of History at the Polish Academy of Sciences and from 1991 has been attached to the Polish Scholarly Centre in Paris. He has written many articles and reviews dealing with Polish history in the nineteenth century. He is co-author and co-editor of the biographical dictionary *Uczestnicy ruchów wolnościowych w Królestwie Polskim 1832–1855* (Participants in movements for freedom in the Kingdom of Poland 1832–1855, Wrocław, 1990) as well as several volumes of documents (1831–1865).

**Ryszard Marek Groński** is a playwright and film-writer, the author of a documentary history of Polish cabaret and of works for adults and children. He writes a weekly column in *Polityka*. He was born in Łańcut in 1939 and by education is a historian. He is a member of the Association of Polish Writers.

**Dora Katzenelson** was born in Białystok in 1921. She spent the war in the USSR. In the 1960s, she worked as a teacher in Chita, Eastern Siberia, where she conducted research into the deportees from Poland in the nineteenth century to the Nerchinst Penal Colony. For the past 25 years she has worked in Drohobycz, West Ukraine. Since her retirement, she has been studying Polish and Jewish materials in the Lwów archives.

**Mark Kiel** is rabbi of Congregation B'nai Israel in Emerson, New Jersey and Visiting Assistant Professor of Jewish History at the Jewish Theological Seminary. His dissertation dealt with the study of Jewish folklore and nationalism in Russia.

**Ariel Kochavi** is lecturer in History at the University of Haifa. He is the author of several articles on British foreign policy, displaced persons and war criminals. His book *Displaced Persons and International Politics* (in Hebrew) will be published shortly.

**Jerzy Lewinski** was born in Turek in 1911. He went to school in Łódź and studied law at Warsaw University. He was an officer in the Polish army and fought in the resistance in Warsaw. After the war, he was a prosecutor in Polish war crimes trials and subsequently legal counsel to the Polish film industry.

**Zenon Hubert Nowak** is Professor of History at the Mikolaj Kopernik University in Toruń. He is principally interested in the history of Central and Eastern Europe in the late Middle Ages and in the history and culture of Jews in the towns of Prussia.

**Laura Quercioli** is an Italian scholar and works in Rome with Jewish organisations. She has held research scholarships in Poland and at the Oxford Institute for Polish-Jewish Studies and has published several articles about Polish-Jewish literature in post-war Poland.

**Ritchie Robertson** is a University Lecturer in German at Oxford University and a Fellow of St John's College. He has published *Kafka: Judaism, Politics and Literature* (Oxford: Clarendon Press, 1985; German translation published by Ketzler, 1988) and *Heine* in the 'Jewish Thinkers' series (London: Peter Halban; New York: Grove Press, 1988), and has translated E. T. A. Hoffmann's *The Golden Pot and Other Tales* (Oxford University Press: World's Classics, 1992) and Heine's *Selected Prose* (Penguin Classics). He is co-editor, with Professor Edward Timms, of the yearbook *Austrian Studies*.

**Marek Rudnicki** is a graphic artist and painter. He was born in Warsaw in 1927 and moved to Paris in 1957. For many years, he has painted portraits of prominent individuals for *Le Monde*. These are shortly to be the subject of a one-man exhibition at the *Bibliothèque Nationale*.

**Szymon Rudnicki** is Professor of History at Warsaw University and pro-dean of the Historical Faculty. He is a member of the Anglo-Polish Historical Commission and of the Scholarly Council of the Jewish Historical Institute in Warsaw. He is, above all, interested in the politics of the right and fascism, Polish-Jewish relations and large landowners. Among his books are *Działatność polityczna polskich konserwartstów 1918– 1926* (The political activity of Polish conservatives 1918–1926, Wroclaw, 1981) and *Obóz Narodowo-Radykalny. Geneza i dzialalność* (The National Radical Camp. Its evolution and development, Warsaw, 1985).

**Shaul Stampfer** is Lecturer in the Department of Jewish History at the Hebrew University, Jerusalem. He is the author of *Shalosh yeshivot litaiyot* (Three Lithunian Yeshivas, Jerusalem, 1982) and has written widely on demographic topics.

**Aharon Weiss** is Senior Lecturer in the Department of Jewish History, Haifa University, Editor of *Yad Vashem Studies*, co-editor and co-author of the *Encyclopaedia of Jewish Communities* and author of studies on the Holocaust in East Europe and on the Jewish-Polish and Jewish-Ukrainian relations during World War II.

**Tomasz Wiśniewski** was born in 1958 and spent nine months in prison for political offences in 1982–3. He graduated in Polish philology from Warsaw University and is at present working on *Kurjer Poranny* in Bialystok. He has written widely on Jewish topics.

**Józef Wróbel** is a lecturer in the Institute of Polish Philology at the Jagiellonian University in Kraków. His principal interest in Polish literature in the twentieth century, above all Polish-Jewish writers. He is the author of *Tematy zydowskie w prozie polskiej 1939–1987* (Jewish themes in Polish prose 1939–1987, Kraków, 1991). At present, he is working on a monograph on Adolf Rudnicki.

**Aleksander Zyga** is a graduate of Polish philology at the Jagiellonian University, Kraków. Unable to pursue a scholarly career because of his political opinions, he became a freelance writer. He is the author of *Krakowskie czasopisma literackie drugiej polowy XIX wieku* (Kraków literary journals in the second half of the nineteenth century) as well as many articles on folkloric and regional themes. He has edited collections of letters and has written reviews on Jewish themes in Polish literature.

www.ingramcontent.com/pod-product-compliance
Ingram Content Group UK Ltd.
Pitfield, Milton Keynes, MK11 3LW, UK
UKHW021317180426
11947UKWH00015B/1276